Persuasion & Influence

FOR

DUMMIES®

Persuasion & Influence

FOR

DUMMIES®

by Elizabeth Kuhnke

A John Wiley and Sons, Ltd, Publication

Persuasion & Influence For Dummies®

Published by
John Wiley & Sons, Ltd
The Atrium
Southern Gate
Chichester
West Sussex
PO19 8SQ
England
www.wiley.com

Copyright © 2012 John Wiley & Sons, Ltd, Chichester,

Published by John Wiley & Sons, Ltd, Chichester, We

WILEY

MIX
Paper from
responsible sources
FSC® C013056

About the Author

Elizabeth Kuhnke is an international conference speaker, best-selling author and qualified coach who aims to provide her clients with the skills and knowledge to live the lives they envision, and make the changes they desire. Her clients and colleagues call her 'Diamond Polisher' because of her ability to smooth, sharpen and shape talented individuals, enabling them to reveal their true brilliance. Her three-pronged approach to client development is based on demonstrating respect, establishing rapport, and producing results. She believes that dogged determination combined with a healthy dose of fun are vital for success.

For over twenty years, Elizabeth has nourished a steady client stream of FTSE 100 companies, professional services and charities, providing one-to-one and group coaching in key areas relating to interpersonal communication including personal impact, confidence and influencing skills. Elizabeth's combination of advanced degrees, a career in the performing arts, expertise in administering psychometric instruments and a passion for personal best are some of the reasons clients turn to her for support.

She's been compared to an Olympic athlete, who never gives up. She has been equated to a pit bull because she never lets go. And she has been likened to a radiator, because she generates warmth. She is often quoted in the media addressing issues concerning confidence, persuasion and influence, voice, body language and public speaking skills.

Persuasion & Influence For Dummies is her second book for Wiley. She is currently working on the second edition of *Body Language For Dummies*. Contact Elizabeth through her website at www.kuhnkecommunication.com.

Author's Acknowledgments

When I set out to write this book my intention was to learn, have fun and make a meaningful contribution to your life. I never anticipated the combination of pleasure and pain this undertaking would bring. I thank my family, especially my husband Karl, for his unconditional love, copious cups of tea, walking Henry in the rain and keeping the home fires burning during long days and lonely nights. To my children, Max and Kristina, your constant love, support and cheering me on feed my passion and nurture my soul. To the Diamond Lights – Tom, Katie, Evie and Charlotte – thank you for growing the business and protecting my interests during my absence. To Haidar, Helen, Resli, Annie, Kate, Judy, Wanda and many other amazing coaches who specialise in persuasion and influence, thank you for your time, generosity and for sharing your experiences with me. To my friends, big hugs and many thanks for your encouragement, giving me the space to write and checking in to make sure I was still around. To my clients and colleagues, I value your belief in my abilities and the endless opportunities you offer me to learn and practise persuasion and influence with you. To you, the reader, I thank you for buying this book and hope it serves as a positive influence in your life. Finally, my most sincere thanks to this book's fabulous editorial team, led by Simon Bell and Brian Kramer, who persuaded me I could do this and persisted when lesser mortals would have thrown in the towel. You all encompass the belief that 'Not brute force but only persuasion and faith are the kings of this world.'

Publisher's Acknowledgments

We're proud of this book; please send us your comments at http://dummies.custhelp.com. For other comments, please contact our Customer Care Department within the U.S. at 877-762-2974, outside the U.S. at 317-572-3993, or fax 317-572-4002.

Some of the people who helped bring this book to market include the following:

Acquisitions, Editorial, and Vertical Websites

Project Editor: Simon Bell

Commissioning Editor: Claire Ruston

Assistant Editor: Ben Kemble

Development Editor: Brian Kramer

Copy Editor: Kate O'Leary

Proofreaders: Mary White, Kim Vernon

Production Manager: Daniel Mersey

Publisher: David Palmer

Cover Photos: © Jeffrey Coolidge

Cartoons: Rich Tennant
(www.the5thwave.com)

Composition Services

Project Coordinator: Kristie Rees

Layout and Graphics: Lavonne Roberts, Corrie Socolovitch

Proofreader: Rebecca Denoncour

Indexer: Ty Koontz

Publishing and Editorial for Consumer Dummies

    Kathleen Nebenhaus, Vice President and Executive Publisher

    Kristin Ferguson-Wagstaffe, Product Development Director

    Ensley Eikenburg, Associate Publisher, Travel

    Kelly Regan, Editorial Director, Travel

Publishing for Technology Dummies

    Andy Cummings, Vice President and Publisher

Composition Services

    Debbie Stailey, Director of Composition Services

Contents at a Glance

Table of Contents

Introduction

*H*ow would you like to change people's beliefs and behaviours so they say 'Yes!' to your requests, proposals and propositions? How would you like to convince and motivate others in an ethical way to do as you'd like them to do? How would you like to win the admiration, trust and confidence of other people, in order that they follow your lead while thinking the idea was theirs all along? If you want to accomplish any or all of the above, read on.

Getting people to say 'Yes' to your requests is the focus of this book. In the chapters that follow, you discover the triggers that gain people's acceptance and win their buy-in to your ideas, suggestions and recommendations. You find out how to engage with others so they trust you and believe in your credibility. And you uncover ways of thinking, speaking and behaving that ensure that others perceive you as honest, reliable, sincere and likeable.

Persuasion and influence are poles apart from manipulation, although people who don't understand these words' subtle differences often use the terms interchangeably. In a nutshell, *manipulation* is about using any means necessary to get people to do what you want them to do in order to fulfil your needs or desires, regardless of whether what you want is in the other people's best interests. Persuasion and influence are about guiding people to make decisions based on reliable information and a sound relationship with you, in order for them to do what's best for them. (I explore the important distinctions a bit more in Chapter 1.)

Savvy persuaders and influencers demonstrate respect for the people they want to persuade. Through word choice as well as non-verbal behaviour, persuaders and influencers seek to understand where the other person is coming from. They ask non-judgemental questions and actively listen. They feel what others are feeling, understand what they're saying and motivate them to take specific courses of action. The most successful persuaders and influencers know what they want and how to convince others in ways that serve everyone's needs and interests.

By following the suggestions and recommendations in this book, you can become an effective persuader and influencer. This doesn't happen over-night, because developing your persuasive and influencing skills, like all skills, takes patience, practice and desire. That said, if you want to become a better persuader and influencer – and are willing to practise the techniques set out in this book – then nothing and no one can get in your way.

So, if I've persuaded and influenced you enough to read on, please do so. This book is your guide to becoming a skilled persuader and influencer.

About This Book

In this book I investigate the power of persuasion and influence and how by demonstrating trustworthiness, credibility and expertise you can win over the hearts and minds of your target audience, be they staff, colleagues and customers, or friends, family and partners. I explain how to convince your listeners by appealing to their needs and desires, as well as by the way you use your voice and body language. You discover how to listen actively, to understand not only what the speakers say and feel but also what they don't express in their words. You find out how to capture your listener's attention and how to adapt your style to meet the preferences of others whose decisions you want to influence.

The point of this book is for you to take on board and develop the skills and mindset required to persuade and influence others, and to become aware of the techniques when someone's applying these techniques to you. Finally, this book is designed to help you get what you want by gearing your proposals in an ethical way that meets the best interests of your audience as well as your own desires.

Conventions Used in This Book

I'm pleased to say that you'll find no jargon in this book. When I introduce a new term, I *italicise* it and then define what it means. Web and email addresses are in monofont, and the action part of numbered steps and the key concepts in a list are in **bold**. To be fair to all readers, I alternate using male and female pronouns by odd and even chapters.

Foolish Assumptions

While I know the pitfalls of making assumptions, I'm prepared to assume that you:

✔ Are interested in persuasion and influence and know a little bit about the subject

✔ Want to improve your ability to persuade and influence others

> ✔ Are willing to reflect on your current approach and respond to the suggestions offered in this book
>
> ✔ Want the best for yourself and for others

How This Book Is Organised

One of the great things about *For Dummies* books is that you can dip in and out of them at will. The books are written in modular form, therefore you don't need to start at the beginning to understand what comes at the end – and if you choose to read the last chapter first, you don't give away the plot. If you're looking for something in particular and aren't in the mood to read through the whole book to find it, flip to the index or the table of contents, which are designed to help you locate what you want quickly and easily. If you're just keen to get started, open the book wherever you want. There's plenty for you to gain no matter which page you turn to.

Part I: Preparing to Persuade and Influence

In this part, I share a dynamic plan that puts you in prime position for persuading and influencing others. You discover all the essentials, including how to establish a connection with your listeners, put together your case, reveal your credibility and display your expertise.

Part II: Developing Your Persuasive and Influencing Skills

In order to persuade and influence, you need to discover or develop some core skills. I demonstrate how to listen better to your target audience in order to understand what matters to them. I then offer advice for capturing your audience's attention and adapting your approach to meet different people's decision-making styles. You also discover how to put yourself across in a convincing manner, no matter how similar or different your listener is compared with you.

Part III: Picking the Right Approach

In this part, I explore different ways of persuading and influencing others depending on what matters to them and what floats their boats. You discover how to identify what drives people to make the decisions they do, as well as how to adapt your approach depending on what people want and need. I show you how to get others to do what you want them to do based on their relationship with you, and I give you ideas on how you can persuade people to follow your suggestions through the examples you set.

Part IV: Putting Persuasion and Influencing Skills into Practice

With these chapters, you gain a feel for the power of your body and voice as powerful instruments for persuading and influencing others. You discover how a purr can be more powerful than a bark, and how the way you lean towards or bend away from people can entice them to come on board with you.

Part V: The Part of Tens

If you want a quick and concise overview of how to persuade and influence your clients, colleagues, boss, staff and others – whether in writing or through the spoken word – turn to these chapters. You find ways to turn technology into your friendly persuader, indispensible tools to include in your persuasive toolkit, and the ten core persuasion skills you need to hone.

Icons Used in This Book

To focus your attention and highlight points of particular relevance, consider the following icons.

This icon highlights stories of friends, relatives, colleagues, clients and acquaintances whose experiences of persuading and influencing I think may be useful for you. There are occasions where I have altered names and details to protect the privacy of the contributors.

While you don't need to read the information here to enhance your persuading and influencing skills, you may find the facts and data fascinating.

If you remember nothing else from what you've read in the chapter, this icon highlights an important point to store away for future use.

To help prevent personal or professional harm, pay attention to this icon.

This icon provides an idea that can save you time or prevent frustration.

If you want to practise what you're reading, this icon gives you a simple technique to try on your own.

Where to Go from Here

While all the material offered in this book is designed to help you become a world-class persuader and influencer, not all of what I have to say may be relevant or pertinent to your specific needs or interests at this time. You're safe in reading what you want, when you want. The facts are solid, the data substantiated and the information confirmed. Furthermore, you don't have to worry about the information being time-sensitive. Although many of my examples and anecdotes come from current coaching work or things I observe in the news or media, the core principles of persuading and influencing others do not have a sell-by date.

If you're interested in preparing to persuade and influence, begin with Part I. If you want to develop your non-verbal behaviours, flip to Part IV. If you want to grab your listener's attention, turn to Chapter 8. Or if you want to begin putting together a compelling case, thumb your way to Chapter 4. Everything is here for the taking.

I hope that you benefit from what's inside these pages. I also want you to enjoy yourself while you navigate this book, discovering how to become the persuasive and influential person you can be. Here's your chance to make a difference in your life – and in the lives of others.

Part I

Preparing to Persuade and Influence

In this part . . .

This part gives you the basic toolkit for becoming a successful persuader. Here you can find out the essentials about establishing connections with your audience which can then develop into robust relationships. I show you how to make your case with credibility and integrity, and you can also find out how to establish your credentials as an trusted expert in your field.

Chapter 1

Laying the Groundwork for Persuasion and Influence

In This Chapter

▶ Understanding influence and persuasion

▶ Being clear about what you want to achieve

▶ Taking on successful behaviours and attitudes

▶ Turning to others for inspiration

*R*egardless of how intuitive, experienced, powerful or educated you are, if you can't build relationships with other people, if you can't establish your credibility and demonstrate your trustworthiness, if you can't convince others through your words and actions to follow your suggestions, you stand little chance of making a difference in your career or your life.

The relationship you have with yourself as well as your relationships with others serve as the foundation of all your life's endeavours. Unless you are confined to a vacuum, the majority of your time is spent engaging with other people. You must work with other people in order to do anything and everything – including achieving satisfying, inspiring successes.

The days of 'command and control' leadership in the workplace and beyond are over. From my experiences with both personal and professional relationships, 'connect and collaborate' is the new and improved mantra. In most relationships, including those in the professions and industries, the twenty-first century brings a more educated workforce, flatter management structures and an emphasis on teamwork over individual accomplishment. All of which means that people can no longer play the 'because I said so' card in order to get others to change their behaviours and beliefs. In short, persuasion and influence has replaced force and coercion.

In this chapter you discover the mindset, characteristics and attributes of successful persuaders and influencers. You find ways of building effective behaviours into your own repertoire in order to persuade and influence others' choices, and you explore the value of working with others for mutual benefit.

Defining Persuasion and Influence

Many people use the verbs *to persuade* and *to influence* interchangeably, and while the terms are similar, subtle differences also exist. The following sections tease out the differences between persuasion and influence and then find their commonalities and interlinked qualities.

Distinguishing between the two

Both persuasion and influence involve deliberate changes in attitudes and behaviour – but *how* the change happens differs. When you deliberately try to change another person's behaviour through your own words and actions, you're practising persuasion. If you can change another person's thoughts, feelings and behaviour based on your character, you're practising influence.

Influence is about having a vision of the best outcome and motivating people to turn that vision into a reality. Some leaders, for example, can bring about change simply through the power of their personalities, without having to put into words what they want you to do. Over the course of time they have built up an arsenal of trust and credibility. By contrast, persuasion is a way of presenting a case that sways others' opinions and makes them believe certain information.

Both influence and persuasion share the same objective of creating change in someone else's behaviour or attitude. Persuasion requires that you communicate what you want, whereas influence works silently through example. When you sway someone's opinion by presenting your case convincingly, you're consciously practising persuasion. When people change their attitudes, feelings and behaviours based on your personality, you're practising influence.

You can boil the definitions down to this: *influence* is a catch-all term based on a person's character that defines a deliberate effort to direct or change someone's attitudes, feelings or behaviour through example. *Persuasion* is about communicating through both your verbal and non-verbal channels in a way that purposely changes someone's attitudes and behaviour.

Some say that persuasion is about winning hearts and minds, while others say that's the job of influence. Others say that persuasion can spur people to take action without the persuader gaining their sincere buy-in, while influence, in which you take the time to develop rapport (see Chapter 2), is a prerequisite to getting someone to make a particular decision. I say that, without trust at the core of whatever approach you take, you struggle to either persuade or influence anyone over a long period of time. The following sections 'Utilising the power of persuasion' and 'Employing the impact of influence' explore the strengths of both approaches in detail.

For this book, which primarily looks at persuasion and influence within business contexts, I'm working from a definition of persuasion as being a way of convincing others to take action without the persuader necessarily having garnered their sincere buy-in. By contrast, when you influence a person, I believe you do so more through your reputation than your actions; you've invested the time to demonstrate respect, build trust and establish rapport. However, I also use the two words interchangeably with the understanding you can use both appropriately in order to produce positive results.

Contrasting with manipulation

The difference between persuasion and influence and their distant cousin manipulation has to do with purpose and intention.

According to the Merriam–Webster dictionary, *manipulation* has several meanings, two of which I find particularly interesting for the purposes of this book. Manipulation involves:

- ✔ Controlling or playing upon by artful, unfair or insidious means – especially to one's own advantage.
- ✔ Changing by artful or unfair means so as to serve one's purpose.

In the wrong hands, persuasion resembles manipulation. While you can gain short-term compliance through manipulation, you don't gain trust and credibility, both of which serve you much better in the long run.

The ethical persuader and influencer works from a position of fairness, honesty and mutual benefit.

Ethics is a sub-set of philosophy that explores questions around moral conflicts, such as good/bad, right/wrong and virtue/vice. I cover some ethical concerns related to persuasion and influence in Chapter 5. For an entire book on the topic, pick up *Ethics For Dummies* by Christopher Panza and Adam Potthast (Wiley).

Utilising the power of persuasion

In life you're either persuading someone or someone's persuading you. The key to persuasion is knowing what motivates a person and then gearing your approach towards that.

Persuasive techniques include:

- ✔ Being clear about what you want
- ✔ Respecting the other person
- ✔ Appealing to his values
- ✔ Stating your proposal to meet his needs
- ✔ Listening for feelings as well as content
- ✔ Demonstrating empathy
- ✔ Matching your tone of voice and body language to his
- ✔ Going for win–win outcomes

Notice that I didn't include relying on proven and reliable data in the preceding list. Of course you need accurate facts and figures, but the way you present them is more critical. Data is open to interpretation, and until you establish yourself as a person of influence you must be doubly prepared to present your case persuasively in order to influence your listener's attitudes and behaviour.

When time is of the essence – or your relationship with your audience doesn't involve much trust – turn to your persuasive powers. (When I talk about low levels of trust, I'm not referring to negative emotions or dishonesty. Building deep trust takes time, and you may not always have all the time you need; see Chapter 5.)

Understanding patterns of motivation

The two major motivations in life centre around the desire to gain something and the fear of loss.

- ✔ **If someone is motivated by the desire for gain,** he wants more of what he values in life – for example, respect, wealth, health and happiness. As a persuader, you need to find out what he wants and show him how he can gain more of what he values by adopting your proposal.

- ✔ **If someone is motivated by a fear of losing,** he wants to hold on to what he already has – such as health, financial stability, a relationship or an achievement. You can persuade him to consider your proposition to prevent that loss from happening.

Both patterns of motivation are often at play in one situation, for the same person. For example, when I was worried that my son and I would miss a connecting flight, I wanted to gain by speaking at a prestigious conference and widening my circle of influence. I also feared I would lose by inconveniencing the organisers if I turned up late or not at all. By appealing to both my desire to gain something and prevent loss, Max had no trouble convincing me to do as he said.

The fear of loss is frequently stronger than the desire for gain, which is why people often fear change. Change represents risk and uncertainty. Fear of potential loss can feel threatening. When you know what people fear losing, you can position your proposal in a way that protects what they value. Demonstrating how your proposal avoids any loss for them persuades them to act in a way that helps you achieve your goals.

Persuading ethically

Be discriminating in your use of persuasion, or someone may accuse you of selling refrigerators to Eskimos, taking coals to Newcastle, or selling combs to bald people. While these groups may buy from you once, the chances of them buying from you again are pretty slim after they realise you sold them something they didn't need.

To avoid being perceived as a manipulator, practise ethical behaviour. I devote a large section of Chapter 5 to the overlap of ethical behaviour and persuasion.

Applying persuasive techniques with integrity and a sincere intention to seek a positive outcome for others is a powerful tool for change. When you take the time to get to know the person you're persuading, when you invest your time and interest in building rapport, and when you prove yourself as credible and trustworthy, persuasive techniques such as *framing* – the way you view a person, place or experience and the meaning you give it – mirroring and matching, and timing are appropriate tools to use. (Flip to the index to find out more about these techniques, as I refer to them frequently throughout the book.)

Employing the impact of influence

While most people hunger to be influential – whether with friends and family, or colleagues and clients – they're hard-pressed to define what they mean by *influence* or *influential*. They know it's good and has a reputation for being positive and powerful. They also know that it's not about impressive-sounding titles, big salaries, or getting what you want when you want it by using the right words at the right time. It's not something that's given to you on a plate or that you can purchase online. Instead, influence is an earned commodity. The nitty-gritty of influence is *trust* and *time*. To become influential you have to:

- ✔ **Be patient.** Influence is built over time, whether you're a parent, a friend or the CEO of an international corporation.

- ✔ **Build trust.** Be reliable, dependable, consistent and honest when dealing with people.

- ✔ **Listen to people.** Take an interest in their personal and professional lives to demonstrate that you care about them.

- ✔ **Praise people's efforts.** When you acknowledge the achievements of others, they feel safe around you and believe you're looking out for their best interests, and when you require them to perform, they will.

If you ask me what's at the core of influence, I have to say trust. My mother, an influential woman in her own right, instilled in my sister and me the belief that trust is the foundation upon which all else stands. Trust is at the core of influence, and while trust is attainable, developing a truly trusting relationship and becoming influential takes time and patience.

I know of no magic formula or big secret to establishing trusting relationships, but I do know that you build trust by:

- ✔ Being honest, loyal and respectful.

- ✔ Getting to know people, being curious about them and seeking to support them.

- ✔ Listening to and acting on what people tell you in ways that are beneficial to all. (See Chapter 7 for more on the power of listening.)

- ✔ Recognising people's accomplishments and making them feel good about themselves.

The more trust you can establish, the more influence you gain. Practised persuasive techniques aren't necessary when you're working for the good of someone else who trusts you. You've already established an influential relationship with them, because they trust you, and when they trust you, they perform for you.

Influence is an earned privilege. Like putting money in the bank, you garner the trust of the people you want to influence before you start drawing on it. Without trust, there's no influence.

Influence is built on a powerful combination of trust and credibility that has stood the test of time. By consistently behaving in a way that's true to your values, you build trust. By consistently proving that you know what you're talking about, you build credibility. The steps to becoming influential are simple and ethical:

✔ Be true to your values

✔ Behave in a consistent manner

✔ Be constant in what you say and do

The best leaders rely on their ability to influence others as a means of producing productive outcomes. After taking the time to build a trusting relationship with another person, you can make a quick phone call and set the ball rolling for what you need or want quickly. You've already invested in establishing trust and credibility.

Combining persuading and influencing

In order to be successful – whether in your career, at home with family and friends, with people who provide you with a service, or anyone whose decisions and behaviours you want to shape – you need strong skills for persuading and influencing, often utilising both simultaneously. For example, having built a positive reputation over time based on your consistency, reliability, honesty and trustworthiness, you may then include a specific persuasive technique – such as reciprocity, scarcity, likeability or social proof – to move someone from point A to point B. In other words, you influence someone's decisions through your personality, and convince him to do what you want through your persuasive techniques. You can read more about the persuasive techniques I mention here in Chapter 10.

You can safely assume that the top persuaders and influencers possess a high quotient of emotional intelligence, which can be simply defined as an ability to bring out the best in yourself and others. Later in this section you can read more about this form of intelligence, in the sidebar titled . . . Emotional intelligence!

The appropriate combination of persuasion and influence resembles the mix of experience, tools and skills you need to build a house. Influence is the foundation you establish through solid relationships that you nourish and cultivate over time. A solid foundation is the result of your intentions and behaviours that build trust, establish credibility and add value to your relationships. Persuasion is a specific tool you use as required in order to achieve the best result. Persuasion is also a skill that includes talent and technique (that you apply with charisma) in an effort to get things done there and then.

When you persuade and influence people into changing their attitudes or altering their behaviours, you're empowering them to make their own choices, rather than forcing yours onto them. Not everyone's going to want to change, even if adjusting attitudes or actions is in their best interests. In addition, most people baulk at the idea of someone forcing his opinion onto them. If you struggle to get someone to change his behaviour – getting your son to clean his room, a neighbour to trim his trees or a colleague to finish projects on schedule, the following strategies may help overcome his resistance, and encourage him to consider your suggestions and come up with a solution he owns:

✔ **Appeal to his beliefs and values.** More than being resistant to change, people are resistant to being changed. If someone thinks that your idea threatens his core values, he may become defensive and not listen to you. If you believe that what someone's doing is not in his best interests, point out how the behaviour is at odds with his beliefs and values.

✔ **Point out the consequences of his behaviour.** People only change their behaviour when they believe the risks of standing still are greater than the risks of changing direction. Show him what he stands to lose if he keeps doing what he's doing.

✔ **Ask relevant questions.** It's easier for people to accept and believe an idea if they feel they've discovered it themselves rather than if you imposed yours on them. Ask the other person what he thinks would be the best course of action or if he thinks that a suggestion you offer may work.

✔ **Be prepared for resistance.** Not everyone's going to think that your way is the best way. If someone disagrees with you, listen to what he has to say and try to see the situation from his point of view. That way, you can find out his objections and come up with ways of addressing them.

✔ **Understand what motivates him.** Emotion is the greatest human motivator, whether it's positive – love, appreciation, aspiration – or negative – guilt, fear, anxiety. The most effective way of getting people to change is to appeal to their motivators rather than your personal desires and beliefs.

✔ **Let go of your emotional attachment to your ideas.** What works for you doesn't necessarily work for others. Keep your mind open for counter-arguments and feedback to your suggestions. A person may very well come up with his own solution by arguing against yours.

Persuasion and influence are both a science and an art that rely on the specific approach you take and on emotion. You must delicately balance how much you persuade a person based on various principles, such as the law of reciprocity ('You scratch my back, I scratch yours') or scarcity ('Only three spots are left!'), or any of the other motivating forces I cover in Chapter 10. In addition to the persuasive approach you choose to take, you have to keep in mind that whatever decision a person makes is based on an emotional response. You can find out how emotion and persuasion fit together in Chapter 3.

Emotional intelligence

The subject of *emotional intelligence* (or EI) continues to raise questions about its basis, methods and reliability. In simple terms, *EI* is your ability to recognise, evaluate and manage your own emotions as well as the emotions of others. Although EI may be enjoying popularity at the moment, it's been around for a while:

✔ In the mid 1800s, Charles Darwin explored emotional expression in survival and adaptation.

✔ In the early 1920s, the American psychologist EL Thorndike coined the term *social intelligence* to describe how people understand and manage others.

✔ In his classic book *Frames of Mind: The Theory of Multiple Intelligences* (Basic Books), first published in 1983 and now in its third edition, Harvard University professor Howard Gardner posits the existence of several types of intelligence, including *interpersonal intelligence,* which he defines as the ability to understand other people's intentions, motivations and desires, as well as *intrapersonal intelligence,* which is the ability to understand yourself, including your own fears, feelings and motivations.

✔ In his book *Emotional Intelligence: Why it can matter more than IQ* (Bantam, 1996), Daniel Goleman states that four components comprise emotional intelligence: self-awareness, self-management, social awareness and relationship management.

While numerous names and descriptions are ascribed to the concept of emotional intelligence, there's a shared belief that traditional definitions of intelligence are no longer adequate in understanding and explaining performance outcomes. For an overview of EI, turn to a copy of *Emotional Intelligence For Dummies* by Steven J Stein (Wiley).

Figuring Out Your Desired Outcomes

Knowing what you do want gives you something to aim for. As my godson Joshua told me one day, 'It's a lot easier to land your prey when you know what you're aiming for.'

Simply put: successful influencers and persuaders know what they're aiming for. They know what they want and how to achieve their desired outcomes. They're willing to invest in what they want and are patient in their pursuit. They consider the benefits of what they want, the impact their propositions have on others, and what it takes to get people to buy in to their proposal.

The following sections explore the process of setting goals that satisfy you and motivate others – all in an effort to produce great things together.

Getting clearer about what you want

Do your friends and family, boss and colleagues a favour and figure out what you want. Equally importantly, do yourself a favour and figure it out for yourself. When you know what you need and want, convincing others to accept your ideas is easier.

Knowing what you want may not always be easy to figure out. Fortunately, several established tools can help you clarify and then reach your goals, including one that I find particularly useful: creating SMART goals. Read more about creating goals that are Specific, Measurable, Achievable, Realistic and Time-bound in Chapter 12.

If you struggle to clarify what you want to achieve, you may want to work on crafting some SMART goals with a coach or someone you respect who can listen to you and ask thought-provoking questions.

Respecting others

As my daughter recently said when introducing me at an event, 'Anyone who knows my mother knows her strict adherence to the Rule of Three. Being true to type, tonight she's sharing with you her three Rs. When you treat others with respect and establish rapport, you can produce outstanding results.'

People are more willing to listen to your suggestions if you demonstrate your interest in them and respect them. When people feel you care about them, they're prepared to go the extra mile for you. You don't have to like the other person, nor do you have to be similar to them. You just have to respect them for the person they are if you want to produce positive outcomes. Great successes result when people work together in respectful relationships where everyone embraces differences as part of being human.

Treating people with respect is about understanding their needs and concerns and acting in ways that honour them. You must take them as they come, without judging them. As I was taught as a child in Sunday school, 'Judge not, lest ye be judged' (Matthew 7:1). For more about treating people with respect and building rapport, flip to Chapter 2.

Working together to achieve your goals

Working together to achieve goals is a lot easier than striving to do everything on your own. One person simply cannot envision, design and deliver a great proposal without some input from others. A company's chief financial officer can't turn in his end-of-year financial reports without working with the company's controller, accountant and administrators. A salesperson can't sell without a product or service. Nor can a world-class athlete achieve greatness without his support team firmly in place. Prove to me that people don't need the support of others in achieving their goals, and I'll personally send you a signed copy of this book!

Working together to achieve an outcome that meets people's values, needs and concerns requires input from many sources. Everyone who is affected by decisions needs to feel that he has been part of the decision-making process. If a choice is imposed on individuals who don't have the opportunity to have their say, they're less likely to buy in and then follow through than if they had some input themselves.

Getting input from everyone whose life is affected by a proposal is not always possible. When that's the case, individuals must rely on others – such as agents, advocates or assistants – to speak on their behalf and make sure that all issues that affect the individual are considered. For example, advocates for people with learning disabilities and mental health problems can speak on behalf of their clients to:

- Express their views and wishes
- Secure their rights
- Represent their interests
- Access information and services
- Explore options and choices

Embracing the Attributes of an Effective Persuader and Influencer

Effective persuaders and influencers know what they want, and they're not afraid to go for it. They're action-orientated go-getters who make things happen. While they have a clear vision of what they want (see the preceding section), they're also patient and understand that Rome wasn't built in a day.

The following sections reveal six of the core attributes that I encourage in my coaching clients who want to become better persuaders and influencers. In addition, I encourage my children to adopt these traits, because persuasion and influence are as important in day-to-day living as they are at the office.

Laying the Groundwork for Persuading and Influencing

Persuading and influencing don't occur naturally. The process requires thought, action and practice. Really good persuaders and negotiators plan their approach, having considered the character, issues, needs and concerns of the person they're persuading. See *Negotiating For Dummies* by Michael C Donaldson (Wiley) for more about this specific type of persuasion. In addition, specific characteristics, traits and mindsets are required if you're to be a top-notch persuader and influencer. In this section I share with you those qualities I believe are necessary if you're to be the best persuader, influencer or negotiator you possibly can be.

Showing that you're trustworthy

Do what you say you're going to do and behave in a consistent way. When people know what they can expect of you, they trust you to live up to – or even surpass – their expectations based on what you did in the past. Your circle of influence widens and your persuasive powers increase.

When people see you living your values, they feel safe around you. They know you're being true to who you are and know what they can expect from you.

You can demonstrate your trustworthiness in the way you treat people, in the way you approach your work, and in the way you run your life, particularly in the way you:

- Act in accordance with your values
- Treat people with respect
- Behave with honesty
- Demonstrate integrity
- Follow through on promises
- Aim for mutual benefit

When you show that others can count on you to do what's required to get the job done, you demonstrate that you're true to your word.

Throughout this book you read about the importance of trustworthiness during the process of persuading and influencing others. Perhaps of all the characteristics, trustworthiness is the most important because it makes the foundation that other attributes rise from.

Demonstrating confidence

Like a magnet, people who are comfortable with and connected to themselves draw you towards them. You just want to be around someone who demonstrates clear thinking, an open attitude, a balanced perspective and a willingness to stand up for what he believes in. By being connected to yourself – in your core, in your heart and in your head – you radiate a rock-solid foundation that others can trust. The ideal is neither apologetic nor aggressive; you simply radiate confidence in your ability to handle what comes your way. You can go with the flow yet, when the time comes, make decisive decisions. Under pressure, you demonstrate strength and resolve. If you don't have the answers yourself, you know where to go to find them. Read more about demonstrating this type of confidence in Chapter 6.

Behaving ethically

The film *Wall Street* (1987), with Michael Douglas staring as Gordon Gekko, became famous for introducing the world to the phrase 'Greed is good.' These words became a sounding cry throughout the business, while organisations and governments seemed to jettison ethics as the financial rewards increased. An unprecedented money meltdown was necessary to reveal what happens when behaviour strays to the wrong side of ethical.

Whilst seeking a definitive definition of the word ethical, I kept running into the word *honesty*. Other words and phrases such as *responsible, fair* and *a sincere concern for the good of others* also cropped up. If you're honest in your dealings with people, if you behave in a responsible fashion and demonstrate a sincere desire to work for the benefit of others, I'm prepared to say that you're behaving in an ethical way.

When I was a child, my parents taught me to be honest, responsible and to seek good for all. Pretty basic and effective, in my eyes – but now these principles are being taught at university and through online courses. For more about ethical behaviour, go to Chapter 5.

Having a positive and balanced mental attitude

Persuasive and influential people don't waste their time on negative thoughts or ill wishes for others. They seek harmony and want to see everyone come out a winner. They don't hold grudges or speak negatively about others, and they're true to their beliefs. They enter the persuasive process with positive intentions, knowing that going for a win–win outcome is the best way to demonstrate trustworthiness. The best persuaders and influencers seek the best for all.

Give some thought to the theory that behind every negative action is a positive intention. This concept comes from neuro-linguistic programming, which you can read more about in *Neuro-Linguistic Programming For Dummies* by Romilla Ready and Kate Burton. If a particular action seems harsh for the circumstances, look behind the behaviour to discover possible reasons for it. Emotions such as jealousy, fear and anxiety are frequently at the heart of mean and unpleasant behaviour, rather than people just being mean for the fun of it.

Being goal- and action-orientated

Not ones for sitting around waiting for Lady Luck to come to them, persuaders and influencers go for the goal, letting nothing get in their way.

Goals and objectives are tools to help you develop your persuasive and influential personage. When asked about going for your goals, the American actor Richard Chamberlain said, 'If you want something badly enough, and are willing to do whatever it takes to achieve it, then nothing, no one can stand in your way.' To that, I add that whatever you do, make sure it's ethical and sits comfortably with your values (see Chapter 2).

 If you find yourself feeling lethargic whenever you head for your goal, check whether it's a goal you're actually committed to. Unless you really want what you're going for, you're not going to be too excited about doing what's required to get there. See Chapter 12 for more on goal setting.

Focusing on win–win outcomes

The poster people for persuasion and influence are generous and like to see each individual come out a winner. Aiming to achieve outcomes that work for the good of everyone draws people to you. If the people you want to persuade understand that your recommendations contain something good for them, they're much more willing to hop on board with your proposal.

Your persuasion and influence to-do list

Following is a list of behaviours for you to adopt that help you become a person of influence and persuasion. Rather than tackling them all at once, pick one or two to begin with, focusing on them for a week or so until you've embedded the action into your behaviour. You might also text yourself an occasional reminder, enlist a friend's support, or even tape your list to your bathroom mirror so you can look at it every morning and night as you brush your teeth.

✔ **Show up on time.** While some people use the waiting game as a power play, I say that unless you're the bride (who's allowed to keep people waiting for a few minutes), show up on time, prepared and ready to go.

✔ **Dress the part.** Like actors at work, look the part you're playing. Determine what attire is appropriate for the image you want to portray and dress accordingly. See Chapter 10 for more dress and grooming ideas that don't bust your clothing budget.

✔ **Treat others with respect.** When you show that you value others, their opinion of you rises, increasing your level of influence and your ability to persuade.

✔ **Demonstrate a genuine interest in people and projects.** People like feeling special, valued and appreciated. If you show your interest in them, they feel good about you. And when people feel good about you, they're prepared to do what you ask of them.

✔ **Aim to lessen the other's load.** If you can help someone, do. The person remembers you with positive feelings long after the action. As my niece Jenny says, 'People may not remember what you said or what you did, but they always remember how you made them feel.'

✔ **Be generous in your words and actions.** Speak well of people and behave with kindness. Acting with negativity tarnishes your reputation. People figure that if you're saying something bad about one person now, nothing can stop you from speaking negatively about them in the future. Avoid judging and gossiping. Negativity comes back to bite you when you least expect it.

✔ **Think about your words and actions.** Determine which behaviours can get you to your goals and which are likely to keep you from achieving them.

✔ **Envision the end point.** Include as much practical detail as you can in order to energise you and keep you going. When the going gets tough, when you meet setbacks and resistance, having a clear vision of what you're aiming for helps keep you on track.

✔ **Make sure your arguments and point of view meet the other person's needs.** People are willing to go along with you as long as they feel responsible for their actions, and not because you manipulated, coerced or bullied them.

Aim for mutually positive outcomes. Like a magnet, success draws people to it. To achieve win–win requires letting go of personal agendas and seeking success for all. You must listen actively (see Chapter 7) to what others say so you can understand their issues and seek commonality.

When someone's working for his own agenda, the person tends to talk more and listen less. Pay attention to your personal balance of talking and listening during conversations when you want to change someone's beliefs or behaviours.

Gaining Inspiration from Others

Look to your role models. If you don't have any, find some.

 Keep your eyes and ears open and seek role models wherever you can find them. Pay attention to the people around you. Note how they treat others, and adopt their behaviours as yours, as long as their behaviours sit comfortably with your values. Where your role models come from doesn't matter. What matters is *how* they behave.

When you seek role models, be specific in what you need and want. Quiz yourself on the benefits you're seeking so you can be clear about the areas within yourself that you want to enhance. When you allow yourself to acknowledge that you can benefit from others' experience and expertise, you give yourself the opportunity to enhance your level of influence by seeking out the best of the best.

Observe people whenever you can. What do you notice? How are they behaving? What are their voices like? What effect do their voices have on you? How do they look? Describe their gestures and how you interpret them. How would you describe their attitudes based on what you observe? What about them appeals to you? By answering these questions, you give yourself models of verbal and non-verbal behaviour you can emulate – or not – depending on what you want to reveal about yourself to others.

Look for people whom you respect and admire, and bring them into your world. Pay attention to how they behave, and emulate those behaviours. You can have a number of role models in life – and they don't even have to know they're your role models. For example, when I worked in New York, I lived down the street from a 24-hour convenience store. Maria, the hardworking woman who owned the shop, always greeted me with a smile on her face and a cheery 'Hello, miss' whatever the time of day or night. Her friendly attitude and hospitable behaviour made me feel welcomed and appreciated. She still serves as a role model to me for the type of attitude that I aim to incorporate into both my work and social life. It's okay to see a person as a role model for a specific trait or cluster of traits. Not everyone necessarily incorporates all the traits you admire, and some may even have a few you find objectionable.

When considering your role models, look to people outside your immediate sphere of influence. If you admire someone's behaviour and want to gain by learning from the other person, ask. Tell him who you are, what you want from him, and your reasons for wanting him to be your role model. And be sure to tell him what you're willing to do for him in return. While it's always helpful to communicate with someone face to face – observing the other person's reactions tells you more than just the words he says – emailing and calling him on the phone are acceptable alternatives. Just be sure to let him know he doesn't have to do anything additional or different, and that all you want is to observe him and possibly ask a few questions along the way.

The good news about becoming a tip-top persuader and influencer is that you can develop your skills as long as you're willing to open yourself to the process and then practise the necessary attitudes and behaviours.

Always begin your path towards any goal – including working with role models – by listening. Paying attention to the way a person speaks, including his voice quality – tone, pace, pitch and volume – as well as the words he chooses indicate his thoughts, beliefs and feelings. In addition, listen for what he doesn't say, because that gives you further information you can benefit from knowing. As my daughter reminds me, 'You've got two ears, two eyes and one mouth. Use them in that order to learn from others.'

Successful persuaders and influencers are great listeners. They let others tell their stories without interrupting or judging, while allowing all the time that others need to speak. They listen for what others say, as well as for their unvoiced issues. They respond with interest and care. Jump to Chapter 7 for more.

Chapter 2

Finding Common Ground with Your Audience

*H*ow often do you take the time to consider what matters to you and what motivates and drives you to achieve your goals? Likewise, how often do you take the time to consider what matters to others, including your clients and colleagues, as well as your partner and your family and friends. What motivates and drives each unique person you encounter to strive for her goals? If you're anything like most of the people I know at work and in life outside the office, the answer to all these questions is, 'Not often enough.'

Getting caught up in day-to-day tasks and obligations can easily lead you to forget to take the time to think about yourself. Furthermore, you need to see the people around you as individuals – not just as means to an end. If you want to persuade people, you need to know what matters to you, what matters to them and how you can put the two together.

An ancient Chinese proverb states that if you don't know yourself or your enemy, you always lose the battle. It goes on to say that if you do know yourself and your enemy, you always win. While 'enemy' may be too harsh a word in the context of getting to know the audience you want to persuade or influence, the principle still applies. The more you know about yourself and the people you want to persuade, the better your chances of convincing them that your way is the way to go.

In this chapter I take you through the process of self-reflection, understanding others and building relationships – all with the goal of helping you to better reach mutually satisfying outcomes.

Considering Yourself

Understanding and knowing yourself means various things to different people. Self-knowledge includes knowing:

- ✔ What you want in your life
- ✔ What your strengths and weaknesses are
- ✔ What motivates you and brings you peace
- ✔ What you want to change about yourself or about your life
- ✔ What you have achieved so far
- ✔ How you prefer to relate to others
- ✔ What your most important values and beliefs are
- ✔ How you view yourself

The best leaders have a high degree of self-awareness. They take the time to know themselves, including what matters to them, what motivates them and what holds them back. On 9/11 and the days that followed, Rudolph Giuliani, the former mayor of New York City, dealt with unimaginable demands including encouraging the workers at the disaster site and consoling the bereaved. In addition, he was fighting his own private battle with prostate cancer. In his book, *Leadership* (Miramax Books), Giuliani says that in spite of sharing the grief of those who looked to him for hope, he couldn't let his emotions override his duty to serve the people who elected him. Oprah Winfrey is self-aware enough to recognise that by revealing her personal story, taking risks and getting attention she can influence others and make big things happen, whether it's building a school for girls in South Africa or creating one of America's most successful and longest running television programmes. She also knew that after 25 years of hosting her show it was time to call it a day to focus on new ventures. Both Winfrey and Giuliani know the value of self-awareness when it comes to making the right choices at the right time.

My American Journey by General Colin Powell (Ballantine Books) and *Leadership Lessons from West Point* by Jim Collins and Major Doug Crandall (Jossey Bass) are filled with insightful and inspirational anecdotes highlighting the value of self-awareness. For a funny, profound and enlightening tale of self-awareness pick up a copy Elizabeth Gilbert's book, *Eat, Pray, Love* (Bloomsbury) or see the film.

The following sections cover a bevy of tools and techniques that can help you dig deeper into yourself – and, in the process, hopefully discover new, powerful truths.

Looking in the mirror

Much of your awareness of your thinking, reactions and behaviours is subconscious. While you may notice that you're in a good, bad or mediocre mood, unless you're already well-versed in self-awareness, chances are slim that you know the root cause of your attitude and feelings – and, even more importantly, what to do about them.

By taking the time and making the effort to know yourself, you're able to observe and reflect on how your thoughts, words and reactions impact on you as well as on others. When you grasp the effect of your behaviour, you're able to do something about it, including doing more or less of something, or making alternative choices.

The more you grasp what is true for you – your values, attitudes and points of view – the more you're able to grasp the impact of your thoughts, words and behaviours on others. Truth can be tricky to define. While there are objective truths – the sun rises in the East and sets in the West; you need nourishment to survive – there are subjective truths that come from your personal beliefs and experiences. What's true for you may not be true for your neighbour. That's okay as long as you and she respect one another's right have your own personal truths and take them into account when you're negotiating property lines, noise pollution or the best day to hold the village picnic.

Listen to your inner voice to get in touch with yourself. What you say (and don't say) during your internal dialogues helps you understand what your body, mind and soul are experiencing and communicating. When you combine listening to yourself with self-reflection – taking the time to figure out who you are and what makes you tick – your self-awareness increases, enabling you to make more judicious decisions than if you were shooting in the dark. Investing time in self-reflection, recognising your core values – those things that are most important to you – helps you clarify what you want to be, do and have in your life, including how you want to feel and behave. Self-reflection allows you to identify your traits and monitor your interactions with others. Self-reflection isn't easy, and you may find out things about yourself that you don't like. Stick with it. The more time you spend digging deep while considering who you are, the more you understand yourself. The more you understand yourself, the more you can direct and control your behaviour and create positive, productive relationships.

Numerous instruments and tools can help you find out more about yourself. The Internet abounds with an array of tests, tools and tips to guide you on your journey to self-discovery. These include:

- ✔ Personality questionnaires to help uncover your personality type and current mindset
- ✔ Aptitude and ability tests designed to assess your logical reasoning or thinking performance

The fear factor

Cultivating self-awareness can be scary; you never know what you may uncover. Try dealing with the uncertainty like this: you may have done numerous scary things in your life so far – going on a blind date, making a formal presentation, asking your boss for a pay rise, being interviewed for a job you really want, bungee jumping. With these and other high-stakes endeavours, the scariest part is thinking about them. After you're committed to the action, you have little time for fear.

No matter how scary, if you want to make changes in your life or in the lives of others, you need to know who you are and what you stand for before you can take action. The more you understand yourself, the more you're able to live your values and reach your goals. In addition, when you discover who you are, you're able to give more of yourself to others, benefitting your relationships while contributing to your self-esteem and confidence. The more you know about yourself, the better able you are to find common ground with others.

✔ Feedback appraisals to help employees recognise their strengths and weaknesses and become more effective

While you can utilise these tests and evaluations on your own, you gain the greatest benefit when you work with a qualified administrator, coach or counsellor who understands the implications and can explain the findings in a positive, productive way. Whoever interprets the information is there to help you recognise your behaviours and how others may view you. You must trust the person you choose to work with because of the personal nature of the findings, so interview several professionals before making your final decision. If you decide to go down the route of working with a professional to learn more about yourself, expect to pay her for her expertise.

In the workplace, it is common for the human resources and learning and development departments to administer tests and surveys to measure skills and effectiveness. If you want to find out more about yourself and haven't been offered an assessment, ask for one.

To help you gain an understanding of who you are, write ten honest endings to the phrase 'I am . . .' by filling in the blank with a phrase that sums up your current view of yourself and shows how your behaviour supports this view. If you want, you may replace the word 'am' with 'feel'. For example, you might say, 'I am positive and outgoing, and demonstrate this by the way I take on challenges and show interest in other people' or 'I feel anxious about what's coming next in my life and show this in my hesitancy to begin projects and my reticence to engage with others.' Although you don't have to, you may want to share your responses with a trusted friend or colleague who will listen without judging or refuting what you say. While you may feel comfortable doing this exercise with your partner, you may want to pick someone more neutral to avoid any possible conflict or argument about what you reveal.

Making the case for self-awareness

All this talk of spending time with yourself may sound selfish, but it's not. If you don't look after yourself and come to know who you are, no one else will bother either.

People who lack self-understanding, including understanding the reasons why they think, feel and behave in the ways they do, are doomed to a *Groundhog Day* way of life. Over and over again, they make the same mistakes, creating the same results.

When you harness your self-awareness – and in the process get out of a seemingly unending loop of disappointments – you also:

- ✔ **Enhance your decision-making process.** No longer confined to subjective reasoning – in which you view issues based strictly on your personal beliefs, ideals and opinions – you can stand outside of yourself and look at situations from an objective point of view. The benefit of considering people, events and issues objectively is that your decisions are uninfluenced by your personal opinions, emotions or prejudices. You make your decisions based on real facts not conjecture. When you detach yourself personally from the issues and consider them from the other person's viewpoint, you gain a wider perspective that leads to fairer decisions. Fair decisions tend to be rooted in ethical behaviour, which you can read about in Chapter 5.

- ✔ **Get better results within your relationships.** Other people – including your friends, family, colleagues and staff – appreciate your willingness to share the real you, which enhances your interactions. Knowing who you are frees your energy, so you're more open to understanding others.

- ✔ **Communicate more effectively.** By cutting to the core of the subject under discussion, you're able to share information with openness, honesty and integrity. (Flip to Chapter 5 to find out more about integrity and persuasion.) You're also more open to understanding your listeners' concerns, allowing you to better tailor your message to address their needs. You can find out more about tailoring your message in Chapter 12.

> ✓ **Increase your prospects for career progression.** Demonstrating self-knowledge requires maturity and a willingness to dig deep to get to the important stuff. In addition to discovering what makes you good at what you do, you may discover what holds you back from achieving your goals. By identifying negative beliefs that drive destructive behaviour, you can change your approach to one that brings you prosperity, peace and happiness, both in your working life and in your life with friends, family and acquaintances. The more you know about yourself, the more likely your life is to flourish, both at home and in the office.

Instead of thinking of this process of self-discovery as navel-gazing, actively embrace the opportunity to go deeper into truly understanding yourself. The worst that can happen is that you become a more effective leader and, as a result, your business success increases. For those of you who don't work outside the home for pay, self-awareness can lead to personal contentment and productive relationships in your daily interactions with others.

Looking through the Johari Window

In 1955, the American psychologists Joseph Luft and Harry Ingham developed a simple and useful model to demonstrate and enhance self-awareness and mutual understanding between individuals and groups. They named their model Johari, a blend of their first names.

It continues to be relevant and valuable for personal and group development, including for improving communication and developing relationships, because of its emphasis on behaviour, empathy and cooperation. For more information about the power of empathy when influencing others, see Chapter 3.

If you think of a four-square grid, like a window with four panes, you can visualise the concept of the Johari Window. The horizontal axis represents the individual, including what she knows and doesn't know about herself. The vertical axis represents others and what they know and don't know about the individual.

Over the years, users of the Johari Window have adapted its terminology, particularly when describing the four regions. You may come across different names for the four quadrants shown in Figure 2-1, but the meaning of each region is similar to what I describe in the following sections.

The process of self-disclosure and seeking feedback can be filled with landmines. Be aware of your own limits and sensitivities. The extent and depth that you want to go into in understanding yourself must always be your own choice and not foisted upon you by someone whose intentions may be good but whose ability is lacking, or someone who doesn't have your best interests at heart, because you may discover traits, feelings and characteristics you're unable to cope with on your own. If you find that you're in over your head, seek advice from a trusted advisor, colleague or professional who has experience in providing feedback. And if you want to bow out of a situation or conversation graciously, say something along the lines of, 'Thank you for your interest and concern. I'd like to take away what you pointed out and think about it in my own time.'

	Known to self	Not known to self
Known to others	**OPEN AREA** Behavior, attitude, feelings, knowledge skills etc.	**BLIND AREA** Ignorance about oneself, issues in which one is deluded etc.
Not Known to others	**HIDDEN AREA** Information, feelings, fears, hidden agendas, secrets etc.	**UNKNOWN AREA** Feelings, behaviours, capabilities, aptitudes etc.

Figure 2-1:
The Johari Window helps develop self-awareness.

Quadrant 1: Open area

In this space you find information about you that both you and others know. Examples can include your eye colour, your knowledge level, and your feelings and emotions.

The more open you can be with others about who you are, the more effective and productive both you and the people you work, play and live with can become. When your Quadrant 1 is brimming with information, and good communication and cooperation occur, you are much less likely to experience distraction, mistrust, conflict or misunderstanding.

If you know someone well, this area is probably fairly large and well-developed. If you don't know her well, the space is probably smaller and filled with fewer details. Don't be hard on yourself about the size of a Quadrant 1; if it's small, you probably just haven't had time to get to know one another.

In order to expand your Quadrant 1 you need to:

✔ Explore your blind spot (see the following section), which expands the quadrant horizontally. Solicit feedback and actively listen to it. See Chapter 7 for more on active listening, and Chapter 5 for more on feedback.

✔ Disclose information about yourself, which expands this area vertically. Answer questions posed to you by others or offer relevant information on your own.

Quadrant 2: Blind spot

This space encompasses information that others know about, but that you don't know yourself.

For example, you may have annoying habits – like interrupting, judging or criticising – that you don't realise. You may be blind to the fact that you consistently push your own agenda and fail to consider how your words and actions affect other people and their feelings.

You can decrease the size of this area and increase your open area by soliciting feedback from others and taking on board what they say. You want to reduce the size of your blind spot as much as you can because this is neither an effective nor a productive place to hang out.

When you're in your blind spot, you're ignorant about yourself and are possibly deluded about particular issues. Others may purposely withhold information from you, either because they don't want to hurt your feelings or they want to sabotage your career. By keeping you in the dark – restricting access to data and decisions or conveying incomplete, inaccurate or exaggerated information – someone can contribute to your lack of knowledge about what's going on with you, your career or your relationships. Whether you're blind at work or in personal relationships, being unaware of what's going on is a hard place in which to create productive relationships.

Phillipa was happy in her marriage and thought it was strong. She and her husband, Stewart, are financially well off, share common interests, have four healthy children, two homes and an active social life. When one of her friends intimated that Stewart was having a long-term affair with a mutual acquaintance, Phillipa was devastated. Furious with her friend for destroying her picture of reality by planting doubt in her mind, she confronted Stewart and the other woman. They both admitted the affair, saying that it was just physical, they had no intention of breaking up their marriages, and they thought that what she didn't know wouldn't hurt her. Phillipa's marriage is in tatters, her friendship with the person who told her about the affair is strained, and Phillipa's belief in the sanctity of marriage has been severely tested.

Quadrant 3: Hidden area

In this area you know things about yourself, but you keep them hidden from others. Information you keep here may include fears, feelings, hidden agendas, secrets, sensitivities – anything you know about yourself that you choose not to reveal.

Keeping certain personal and private information under wraps is natural and even appropriate as long as the information has no bearing on the health, safety or productivity of others. However, if the information you're keeping hidden can benefit others and enhance relationships, then I encourage you to disclose and expose it – in an appropriate amount and way, of course. Too much information is of little use to anyone and can feel like a self-serving information dump with little or no benefit for the listener.

The less you hide about yourself, the more chance you have of finding common ground with others, developing rapport (see the 'Building Rapport' section later in this chapter) and creating understanding, cooperation and trust. In addition, as you reveal yourself to others, you reduce the potential for misunderstanding, poor communication and conflict, all of which undermine the possibility of building rapport and finding common ground.

The amount you choose to share about yourself must always be at your own discretion. Pace your disclosure and reveal only as much as you're comfortable sharing. In addition, consider the other person and how much she can handle at the time. For example, if you tell someone something really personal about yourself – like details of a recent indiscretion – too early in your relationship, you could put the other person off you forever.

While you may feel comfortable disclosing personal information about yourself, others may be less keen or able. When it comes to finding out about others, don't push someone to reveal herself until she's ready. You may appear nosy instead of simply interested.

Quadrant 4: Unknown area

In this quadrant, no one knows anything about you – not others, not you yourself. The issues tucked inside here take a variety of forms, including:

- ✔ Underestimated or untried abilities, as a result of lack of opportunity or trust
- ✔ Unrealised natural abilities or aptitudes
- ✔ Unknown fears or aversions
- ✔ Unknown illnesses
- ✔ Repressed or subconscious feelings

This information can be deep down inside you or right up at the surface influencing your actions and behaviour. People who lack experience or struggle to believe in themselves tend to have fairly large Quadrant 4s.

If your Quadrant 4 is larger than you'd like, you can reduce it by making a conscious effort. Go on a journey of self-discovery through soliciting feedback from others, trying out new behaviours or working with a coach or a counsellor. If you do decide to seek the support of others, make sure they're credible and experienced if they are providing support. Make sure you trust the person to be sensitive and discreet, because you may uncover issues that leave you feeling vulnerable. Whatever you do, don't beat yourself up if something previously unknown and unanticipated suddenly appears. Getting to know yourself is a journey and, like all journeys, some parts are fun and easy, while other parts are more challenging. It's how you manage the journey that shows who you really are.

Identifying your values

In the simplest terms, what you value is what's important to you. *Values* drive your behaviour, and they can stop you in your tracks. Your values affect your choices, regardless of whether you're conscious of your standards or not. From your selection of friends, to the jobs you take, to the purchases you make, your values drive your decisions.

Your values motivate you to behave in one way while prohibiting you from behaving in another. For example, if, while working late, you find a folder at reception with your boss's name on it, marked 'private and confidential', you may be sorely tempted to look through it. But if you value honesty, trustworthiness and integrity, these principles will probably keep you from taking a quick peek or having a good long read-through, no matter how tempting the contents may be.

Regardless of the role you're playing in your working life – boss, client, colleague or subordinate – or in your private life – partner, parent, friend or customer – your core values remain the same. Some values change across different contexts, but your *core values* stay with you no matter what. For example, when you get your first job, you may value money and status. Once you have a family, you may value work–life balance more than the balance in your bank account.

Values determine your priorities and serve as a measure for how well your life is turning out. When the choices you make match your values, life is usually pretty good. When your choices don't align with your values, that's when things go wrong. Outside influences such as your culture, family and life experiences establish these essential foundational principles at different stages in your life, determining what matters to you.

Examples of core values include:

- ✔ Service to others
- ✔ Self-control
- ✔ Dependability
- ✔ Tolerance
- ✔ Order
- ✔ Curiosity
- ✔ Accountability
- ✔ Being the best
- ✔ Happiness
- ✔ Love

In addition to core values, you have *secondary values* that are important to you in some contexts but are less important in others. For example, you may value feeling loved in your life away from the office, while at work you value achievement; in fact, you may not even consider love in the context of work. Then you find someone to share your life with, and possibly have a family. While one of your core values is love and you're working 70-hour weeks, you may find that career achievements take second place to family as internal stress and conflicts rise.

When you define your values you discover what really matters to you, and by understanding your values and priorities you can determine how best to live your life.

When you live by your values, you feel at peace. You're confident, constructive and in control. When you compromise your values, you feel uncomfortable and uncertain – as if you're living a lie. Knowing what matters to you and living by those values makes living with yourself easier and provides a platform for further understanding who you are.

Understanding who you are and what makes you tick can provide direction in your life. Use the following activity to discover your core values:

1. **Read over the entire list of values that appears in Table 2-1.**

   This is merely my partial list of values. You may have other values that I don't list in the table, so feel free to include any words that are appropriate to you in the blank spaces in the table.

Table 2-1   My Current Values

Abundance	Dynamism	Impact	Open-mindedness	Relaxation	Teamwork
Approachability	Empathy	Impartiality	Optimism	Reliability	Temperance
Achievement	Encouragement	Independence	Order	Religion	Thankfulness
Accountability	Enjoyment	Ingenuity	Organisation	Resilience	Thrift
Attractiveness	Enthusiasm	Inquisitiveness	Originality	Resolve	Tidiness
Authority	Energy	Insightfulness	Outrageousness	Resourcefulness	Tradition
Balance	Experience	Integrity	Passion	Respect	Trust
Belonging	Expertise	Intelligence	Peace	Reverence	Truth
Bravery	Exuberance	Intuition	Perceptiveness	Restraint	Understanding
Brilliance	Fairness	Inventiveness	Perfection	Richness	Unflappability
			Perseverance		
Boldness	Fame	Investing	Persuasiveness	Rigour	Unity
Calmness	Fearlessness	Joy	Philanthropy	Sacrifice	Usefulness
Compassion	Ferocity	Judiciousness	Playfulness	Sagacity	Valour
Connection	Fidelity	Justice	Pleasure	Sanguinity	Variety
Consistency	Financial independence	Keenness	Poise	Security	Vitality
Credibility	Firmness	Kindness	Power	Self-control	Vision
Curiosity	Flexibility	Knowledge	Practicality	Selflessness	Warmth
Confidence	Forgiveness	Leadership	Pragmatism	Self-reliance	Wealth
Control	Freedom	Learning	Precision	Sensitivity	Willingness

Commitment	Friendship	Liberty	Preparedness	Service	Winning
Competitiveness	Frankness	Listening	Presence	Shrewdness	Win–Win
Congruency	Fun	Logic	Privacy	Silence	Wisdom
Courage	Gallantry	Love	Proactivity	Skilfulness	Wittiness
Completion	Generosity	Loyalty	Professionalism	Simplicity	Wonder
Courtesy	Gratitude	Making a difference	Prosperity	Sincerity	Worth
Decisiveness	Green issues	Mastery	Prudence	Solitude	Youthfulness
Dependability	Growth	Maturity	Punctuality	Speed	Zest
Depth	Guidance	Mellowness	Reality	Spontaneity	
Determination	Happiness	Meticulousness	Reason	Stability	
Diligence	Harmony	Modesty	Reasonableness	Strength	
Dignity	Helpfulness	Motivation	Recognition	Structure	
Discretion	Honesty	Neatness	Recreation	Success	
Discovery	Humility	Nerve	Refinement	Support	
Drive	Imagination	Obedience	Reflection	Sympathy	

2. **Identify which values are most important to you in your life right now.**

Choose the values that jump out and feel absolutely integral to who you are. Circle these values or highlight them with a marker.

At this point, choose as many words as you want. You're looking for values that are important to you here and now that can serve as a common point for understanding yourself.

3. **Review your selected values and group together the ones that are similar.**

For example, you may group enthusiasm and exuberance together as one larger concept.

4. **Indicate with an A the values that are absolutely fundamental to your life, and with a B the ones that are nice to have.**

5. **Look over your A-category values and choose your top five most important values – the ones that you simply can't live without.**

If you're struggling to figure out your top five values, pretend that you're on a lifeboat that's sprung a leak and taking on water fast. Because of the weight of your values, you can only take five with you unless you want to go under!

Working down to your top values may take some time and effort. Don't worry if you feel conflicted as you weigh the relative importance of two values. You're getting deeper into your heart and mind now.

6. **Reaffirm your values.** Make sure your values fit with your life and your vision for yourself. Ask yourself the following questions to help you confirm your choices:

   • Do these values make me feel good about myself?

   • Am I proud of my top five values?

   • Do I feel comfortable and proud to tell my values to people I respect and admire?

   • Do these values represent issues and causes I'd support, even if my choices aren't popular and put me in the minority?

7. **Write your five selected values on a separate sheet of paper and list your reasons for choosing each.**

For example, fun is one of my values, both inside and outside the office. Everything I do needs to include an element of fun, or I have little reason to invest my energy in doing it. Another value of mine is making a difference, because I feel I'm privileged in my life and want to give back to others.

8. **Share your results.** Whether you choose to write your values on a sheet of paper and tack it to your refrigerator, bathroom mirror or workspace, carry them with you in your wallet, or share them with someone you trust, make your values public. Work through your values on your own and then share them with someone you trust.

Personally, I've found this type of activity useful to go through individually and then share with a partner/spouse or a good friend. Discussing your results and listening to another person's can solidify your choices as well as open your eyes to where another person is coming from.

Noting your beliefs

Beliefs are the foundation of all you say and do. They impact on your values and attitudes and are reflected in your behaviour.

Beliefs aren't true in the sense that you can scientifically prove them. However, they are what you believe to be true for you. Even more importantly, beliefs direct behaviour, as Figure 2-2 shows. Some beliefs are empowering, while others limit your possibilities.

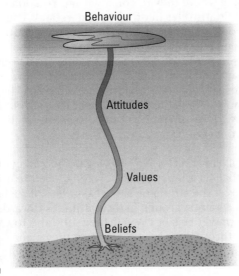

Figure 2-2: Beliefs are the foundation of a person's behaviour.

Behaviour

Attitudes

Values

Beliefs

When people's values or beliefs are diametrically opposed to yours, you may struggle to connect. In order to persuade others, you don't have to share their beliefs. But you do need to acknowledge their beliefs are core to who they are and they have the right to believe what they do – just as you do.

Spotting your attitudes

If you were to sum yourself up in a word or two, which would you choose? Optimistic? Pessimistic? Open-minded? Tight as a turtle? Being aware of your attitudes, moods and points of view goes a long way in understanding yourself and finding common ground with others.

If both you and the person you want to get to know are open-minded optimists, you're going to have a relatively easy – and perhaps even uplifting – time finding common ground. The same goes if you are both pessimists and worriers. While pessimism may be a dreary place to hang out, knowing that you share common attitudes can still feel comforting.

Ralph Waldo Emerson said, 'To different minds, the same world is a hell, and a heaven.' When you're seeking to establish common ground with people whose attitudes are different from yours, keep listening and show you're interested in understanding where they're coming from. You don't have to agree with or even like their attitudes in order to understand. The more you show other people that you value their right to hold their own attitudes, the more they're going to open up to you, giving you information that will serve you when the time comes to persuade them to see things from your point of view. Who knows, you may even be able to change their attitudes, depending on how well you listen, absorb and reflect back what you hear! The point isn't about who's right and who's wrong, the point is about figuring out how people's attitudes make sense to them. You don't have to share similar attitudes to everything to make a connection.

Fred is a right-wing Republican and Len is a left-wing Democrat. In terms of political preferences and beliefs, their attitudes couldn't be more different. During their discussions over the strengths and weaknesses of social and fiscal policies, they found common ground in their attitudes towards family and the right to make informed decisions. While their attitudes towards many issues are different, through conscientious effort they managed to find common ground upon which they've been able to build a friendship.

Your attitudes are based on a combination of beliefs, values and life experiences. Your attitudes are your established way of responding to people and situations. In other words, your attitudes drive your behaviour.

Although values and beliefs are tightly interwoven – both share the idea of individual choice and are used to guide your actions and behaviour as well as forming your attitudes – you can distinguish distinct differences between the two concepts. *Beliefs* are personal convictions people hold to be true without actual proof or evidence, such as all people being (or not being) created equal. Beliefs are assumptions people make about the world and grow from what people see, hear, experience and think about. *Values* are concepts that people consider pure and inviolate; they are standards people turn to when defining what is moral, right and desirable, and serve as broad guidelines for behaviour.

Your body and mind – including your body language and your word choices – have a major impact on your attitude. See for yourself:

- ✔ Stand up and slump into your hips. Let your head drop and your chest cave in. Say to yourself, 'Life's so tough. I'm a useless parent. I'll never be able to finish this project. I'm no good at anything.' How do you feel? Chances are your attitude's tanking and heading for the basement.

- ✔ Stand up and let your shoulder blades melt down your back. Open your chest and lift up from your waist as if you were filled with helium. Hold your head with your chin horizontal to the floor, feeling as if it's floating on a clear, still lake. Connect with the floor beneath your feet – as if you had a tap root driving deep into the ground, making you strong yet resilient. Say to yourself, 'Life's full of challenges waiting for me to meet them. I am calm, capable and confident. I can succeed in whatever comes my way.' Now check out your attitude. Feeling better?

Bottom line? Whatever you tell yourself is true for you, is true for you. As Henry Ford said, 'Whether you think you can or think you can't, you're right.'

You reflect your personal truth in the way you hold your body, in the way you breathe and in the way you speak.

Choosing your attitudes

You always have a choice as to what attitudes you adopt – in fact, I can't think of a single circumstance in which you don't.

While I'm ashamed to admit this, I have experienced times when I, the eternal cock-eyed optimist, have said that someone or something *made* me feel angry, upset, worthless, insignificant or stupid. I know that other people and things do not make me feel a specific way, but still I fall into this trap when I'm tired, lacking in confidence or feeling out of control. It's always my choice to respond as I do, and the same is true for you. No one makes you carry a particular attitude. The choice is yours.

No one's telling you what attitude you should have, and if people are, they don't have that right. If you feel angry about something that happened, that's your choice. If you feel good about something someone said or did, that's your choice, too.

Because you do have a choice about what attitudes you take, I suggest that you're better off reacting in a constructive rather than a negative way. That way you can think and act positively – and live a long and healthy life.

In order to neutralise negative attitudes and develop more positive attitudes:

- ✔ **Surround yourself with people and messages that convey positive attitudes.** You're more at ease when you're in a positive frame of mind.

  When I get stressed out at work, I look at my pinboard filled with motivational quotes I've gathered that help spur me on. One of my favourites is by Dale Carnegie and says that you never see an unhappy horse or a bird with the blues, because they're not trying to impress other horses and birds. Another comes from my late mother, who used to say, 'I know that if I can laugh at it, I can live with it.'

- ✔ **Focus on the present.** You can't change what happened in the past, nor can you live your life in the future. All you can really affect is what's happening right now. Observe your thoughts, feelings and everything around you here, now, in this present moment. Let go of any judgment about what you're feeling, thinking and sensing. Just be aware of what's happening. For more about the benefits of living in the present, read *Mindfulness For Dummies* by Shamash Alidina, and *Cognitive Behavioural Therapy For Dummies* by Rhena Branch and Rob Willson (Wiley).

- ✔ **Look forward to a positive future.** Set yourself goals for what you really, truly want and direct your energies towards achieving them. As Buddha said, 'What we think, we become.' Create positive images for yourself, filled with motivational sensations including sounds, smells, feelings and colours. Feed your mind with positive messages and good stories to help you realise your goal, letting all your senses take part in fashioning the future you want for yourself. Make your vision of your future as clear and specific as you can and then take the necessary actions towards making your future become your reality.

- ✔ **Focus on the solution.** Spending time fretting about a problem ties up your energy. Stop rehashing what went wrong and start thinking and talking about ideal solutions. While problems are negative, solutions are positive. For example, if you're facing a task that you don't know how to do, instead of focusing on all the mistakes you might make, break the task down into manageable steps and take action. Once you begin thinking and planning in terms of solutions, you become positive and constructive.

✔ **Look for the good and let go of the bad.** You could start by taking a sheet of paper and dividing it into two columns. For a few days, jot down all the negative thoughts that come into your head in one of the columns, and in the other rewrite each thought in a positive way. For example, 'I'll never get this project finished by the end of the week' could become 'I'll get most of the project finished by the end of the week.' Tasks become a lot easier when you approach them with a positive attitude.

✔ **Look for the valuable lesson.** Gain insight and learning from your experiences that you can apply in future events. While valuable lessons are aren't always fun or easy in the short term, when you look at them with a long-term view, whatever bumps and bruises you encounter along the way take on a whole new meaning. Whatever lessons you learn, integrate them into your goals and plans for the future.

✔ **Think like successful people think.** Successful people know that a positive mental attitude is their gateway to success. If you surround yourself with positivity, live in the present, plan for the future, focus on solutions, concentrate on the good, and apply valuable lessons, you will receive the rewards that come with a positive mental attitude.

If going for a positive mental attitude currently feels like a step too far, just aim to neutralise your negative attitudes. Doing this is just as good a goal as going for gold. By getting rid of the toxic relentless negativity in your life, you may find you actually deserve happiness and feel-good feelings.

Recognising your drivers

Your alarm rings. You open your eyes. You need to begin your day. But what specifically moves you to get up and out of bed each morning?

Motivation relates to an internal process that propels people to do what they do. Webster's Dictionary defines motivation as 'the psychological feature that arouses and organism to action' and 'the reason for action'. Robert Dilts, one of the most creative trainers and authors in the world of neuro-linguistic programming, cites needs and desires as internal motivators, and incentives, rewards and reinforcement as external motivators. Sigmund Freud postulates that motivation is 'the pleasure principle', in which people seek pleasure and avoid pain, while Aristotle proposes that motivation is, in part, the result of an 'appetite' that gets a person pursuing a desired outcome. In its simplest terms, I see motivation as 'a call to action' that gets a person moving from point A to point B.

Some people want to get away from where they are. Others want to go someplace else. And then there are those who are happy to stay put. Depending on what drives you to do the things you do, you find yourself being pushed, pulled or simply stuck in the middle.

Figuring out what drives you to do the things you do helps you understand yourself. When you're open to understanding yourself, you're likely to be open to understanding others. Recognising your drivers helps you figure out what leads you to your goals, which can include finding common ground with others or influencing their beliefs and behaviours. See Chapters 1 and 12 for more on goals.

As I say earlier in this section, concepts and theories about motivation abound. Some say that people are driven by their interest in or enjoyment of a task itself, and that these drivers exist within you – like being motivated by a sense of achievement. Others say that motivation comes from external factors like tangible rewards or the threat of punishment. Still other theories say that people are pushed away from behaving in particular ways while others are attracted to, or pulled towards, their goals.

I say that people are motivated by different drivers at different points in their lives, depending on what they need at the time. When you make the effort to notice your own – and others' – needs, desires and concerns, you can pick the best driver for the job. If you want to gain further insight into motivational theories, you can start with *Neuro-Linguistic Programming For Dummies* by Romilla Ready and Kate Burton, and *Cognitive Behavioural Therapy For Dummies* by Rhena Branch and Rob Willson (Wiley).

To get to know what drives you, begin by exploring motivational theories. While there are countless websites devoted to the subject of motivation, I particularly like www.businessballs.com, where you can explore the theories of numerous highly respected social psychologists in one place, including Abraham Maslow, whose Hierarchy of Needs I look at later in this chapter. Search the Internet for inspirational and motivational quotes. Finally, spend some time reflecting on what you enjoy and what you're good at. Earlier in this chapter I explore the value of self-reflection and how you can benefit by getting to know who you are. As Mark Twain said, 'Twenty years from now you will be more disappointed by the things that you didn't do than by the ones you did do. So throw off the bowlines. Sail away from the safe harbour. Catch the trade winds in your sails. Explore. Dream. Discover.'

Understanding Others

Knowing what ring other people's bells, float their boats and get them out of bed in the morning is invaluable when you want to influence their outlooks and behaviours. Appreciating their values, recognising their attitudes and being familiar with their fears, follies and fantasies helps you move them from A to B.

Connect with people, not problems

The next time you encounter a problem with another person at work or elsewhere in your life, stop. Mentally stand back and evaluate things. Think about what needs to happen in order to correct the situation. If at all possible, meet with the other person involved in the situations, one to one. Discuss what's going on. Point out where you're seeing a problem and ask whether the other person sees it too. Ask the person to help make an action plan for getting things back on track. Your meeting doesn't have to take hours; just a few minutes of active listening (see Chapter 7) can work wonders. Acknowledge the other person's point of view and avoid being judgmental by focussing on behaviour and not opinions. Emphasize the facts and what you've observed in the other person's behaviour rather than relying on your – or others' – opinions and interpretations of what the other person's behaviour meant. Use 'I- messages' to minimize conflict. For example, you could say, 'I felt disappointed when . . .' rather than 'You disappointed me when . . .' Use 'bridging phrases'- such as 'Thanks for taking the time to meet with me' or 'I've been wanting to speak with you about . . .' before jumping into the core issues. Focus on future goals and how to achieve them. The best future goals are those that all interested parties want and are willing to commit to accomplishing.

By engaging with the other person, the two of you can deal with the problem directly. You can avoid a lot of negative emotion because together you're coming up with a plan.

You're educated and experienced enough to know that everyone views the world differently based on individual values, beliefs and past events. Even though you may share similar attitudes and experiences, your unique point of view (see the preceding section) means that your interpretation of events and impressions of people are going to differ from others'. Indeed, personal perspectives are like fingerprints: no two are the same.

Yet in spite of knowing that no two people are alike and that people are entitled to their own opinions, don't be surprised if you occasionally forget and communicate via your own perspective, leaving the listener wondering what you're talking about. If the person you're speaking with looks at you quizzically, stop and ask whether you're making sense to her. Pay special attention to her body language, which tells you more than the words she says. You can read about body language in Chapter 13.

When you know how someone views her life experiences, you're more able to find common ground with her than if you spend your time wondering, judging or surmising. Of course, understanding another person and her perspective takes time. But in the end, the results you can produce are well worth your effort.

When you're seeking to understand someone, open your mind and remove all prejudices, biases and judgments. Listen actively to what the other person says, with the intention of understanding her regardless of the specific role you play in a relationship (see Chapter 7). By understanding other people, you have the key to finding common ground. And when you have common ground, you're in a position to persuade them to accept your point of view.

Listening carefully and asking questions that show you're genuinely interested in learning about the other person pays dividends. The more you're able to establish rapport and build a relationship, the more able you are to persuade and influence that person. I give you some ways of establishing and working with rapport in the 'Building Rapport' section later in this chapter. If you want to know even more about rapport and relationship building, read *Neuro-Linguistic Programming For Dummies* by Romilla Ready and Kate Burton. Or pick up their *Neuro-Linguistic Programming Workbook For Dummies,* which features a host of exercises to help you improve your rapport-building skills.

Identifying their values

If you want to identify someone's values, stop, look and listen – and then take the appropriate actions.

Use the words and phrases listed in Table 2-1 to help identify other people's values as well as your own. Identify the items in the table that connect with how another person speaks and behaves, and use them to create a base from which to identify what matters to her.

Watching them

You can observe someone's behaviour in order to identify her values. For example:

- ✔ If she does what she says she's going to do, if she turns up for meetings on time, if she uses words like 'commitment', 'promise' and 'reliable', you can work out that trustworthiness and dependability are two of her values.

- ✔ If she uses phrases like 'going with the flow' and 'following her feelings', dresses in a casual way and has a collection of amusing objects in her office, you may be right in predicting that she values fun and creativity.

Before making any judgments or evaluations, always verify what you observe. Confirm your understanding by asking a few non-judgmental questions and gathering further corroborating evidence, or you may find yourself making incorrect assumptions and landing in awkward situations.

Pay attention to what people talk about as well as their word choices and the way they use their voices (see Chapter 14 for more on the impact of tone and word choice). Watching carefully and listening attentively without judging helps you identify what matters to them.

Asking quality questions

Whenever possible, ask people questions about themselves, their work and what matters to them. I realise this recommendation sounds simple, but for some reason many people don't make the most of this straightforward technique. When you're in a conversation, really listen to what the other person's saying. Pick up on a point with a statement like, 'That's really interesting. Tell me more about that.' Or show that you've been paying attention and are interested in what she's saying by responding with, 'So, do I understand you to mean that . . .?' This questioning technique demonstrates that you care about the person and what she's saying. For more about effective listening techniques turn to Chapter 7.

In order to move from the mundane 'How are you?' to the more meaningful 'Who are you?' you must practise the art of effective questioning. *Open-ended questions* – questions that begin with what, how, who, where and when – are much more effective than basic yes/no questions for eliciting detailed information and leading you to further conversation.

Begin the questioning process by asking a question of yourself: if you could wave a magic wand and find out everything you want to know about this other person, what would you want to know? Your answer can lead you to formulating effective, specific questions to ask the other person.

Spotting their attitudes

Like yawning, laughing and crying, attitudes are infectious. Before someone opens her mouth, you can tell by the way she positions her body what her attitude is. Is she slumped in her chair, her chin hanging on her chest and a blank look in her eyes? Is so, chances are something's gone wrong. Conversely, if she's bouncing in her seat, with twinkling eyes and a big grin across her face, you're probably right in guessing that something really good is going on.

By observing body language, noticing the words people use and listening to their tone of voice, you can tell tons about others' feelings, moods and emotions – all of which go into making up their attitudes. For detailed information about the power of body language for understanding people's attitudes, turn to Chapter 13 or my book *Body Language For Dummies* (Wiley).

Scaling Maslow's pyramid

In his 1943 paper *A Theory of Human Motivation,* Abraham Maslow presented his theory of motivation as a hierarchy of needs, with the most fundamental needs – physiological and safety – positioned at the base of a pyramid, and higher-level needs, including self-esteem and self-actualisation (which can broadly be translated as 'reaching your full potential') in ever-higher layers. While a number of theorists and researchers have argued convincingly against Maslow's proposition – with some in recent years placing 'parenting' at a higher level than self-actualisation, causing all sorts of psychological fury, especially from single adults – the model continues to be one of the most valid, relevant and highly quoted theories in the realm of human motivation.

Maslow states that before you can satisfy a higher need, you have to satisfy the ones beneath. His premise is that you're not going to concern yourself about being loved and belonging to a group of friends until you've sorted out your basic needs for health and safety, including where your next meal's coming from and putting a roof over your head. Only after you've satisfied the basics do you consider moving up the pyramid where you're able to fulfil needs including love, belonging and self-esteem.

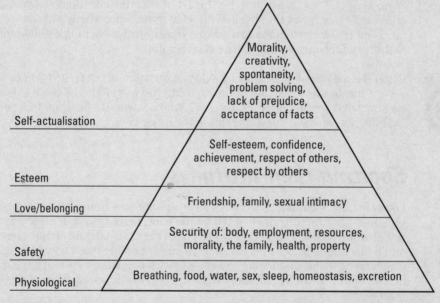

Self-actualisation — Morality, creativity, spontaneity, problem solving, lack of prejudice, acceptance of facts

Esteem — Self-esteem, confidence, achievement, respect of others, respect by others

Love/belonging — Friendship, family, sexual intimacy

Safety — Security of: body, employment, resources, morality, the family, health, property

Physiological — Breathing, food, water, sex, sleep, homeostasis, excretion

Maslow refers to the four bottom levels of the pyramid as *deficiency needs.* At the base of the pyramid are basic physiological needs, including food, water and sleep. Once you've met those needs, you move onto safety needs, including health, property and means of supporting yourself (and your family if you have one). After you're satisfied you've taken care of that level of need, you step up the pyramid as you seek a sense of belonging and acceptance, whether by large social groups – such as clubs, professional organisations or religious groups – and/or small social connections, including close friends and family. The highest of the four 'deficiency needs' is esteem, where you gratify your need to be respected, accepted and valued. If any of these basic needs are not met, you feel nervous and on edge, and you won't feel any desire to move up the pyramid until they are satisfied. For example, in times of war, famine and other calamities in which your lower-level needs are swept away, you stop concerning yourself about your self-esteem and head to the bottom of the pyramid where you seek safety.

The model is more subtle and sophisticated than it first appears, and you need to avoid being overly rigid when interpreting and applying the theory. While people generally move up and down the hierarchy depending on what's happening in their lives, most people's set of drivers (see the 'Recognising your drivers' and 'Recognising their drivers' sections) are comprised of elements of all the levels.

What happens to people tells you a little about them. How they react to what befalls them tells you much more – particularly what their attitudes are. Once you've spotted someone's attitude, reflect back what you observe by mirroring and matching the behaviour. Once you've established common ground through the way you're moving your body and speaking in synch with the person, stay in tune by pacing her. After she's comfortable with the way you're interacting, you can then lead her to where you want her to go. For more about mirroring, matching, pacing and leading, go to Chapters 13 and 14.

Recognising their drivers

When you can recognise what drives other people to do what they do, you're well on your way to finding common ground with them. As I note in the 'Recognising your drivers' section, earlier in this chapter, various things motivate people, including recognition, achievement, fear of reprisals, pride, the ability to learn, freedom to do challenging work by themselves, security, power, self-actualisation, meaning, significance and self-esteem.

When you're finding common ground with others, pay attention to what excites them. Listen to the way they speak and move. If their eyes are bright and wide open, their bodies are leaning forwards and they're speaking quickly in higher tones than usual, you can be pretty sure what they're talking about is revving their engines. Encourage them to talk about their aspirations, their likes and dislikes, their families, friends and interests. The more you can find out about what spurs people into action, the better positioned you are to influence their decisions and persuade them to go along with yours.

Ask people questions about their goals and aspirations to help you discover what drives them to take action. Some thought-provoking questions to find out about others in a friendly way include, 'If your life was a novel, what would the title be and how would it end?' 'Which actor would you like to have play the story of your life?' 'If you could live your life over again what would you do differently?' 'If you could be anything you wanted to be, what would that be?' In addition to asking others questions about themselves, be prepared to answer questions about yourself to build rapport. You can find out more about how to build rapport later in this chapter.

Building Rapport

Rapport is about making a two-way connection between people. It is the foundation for any relationship. When it comes to building rapport, size doesn't matter. You can develop rapport on a one-to-one basis or with a group of thousands. Great leaders understand the value of rapport in persuading people to adopt their suggestions and in directing their behaviours.

- ✔ The word itself comes from the French verb *rapporter,* which means 'to return or bring back'.

- ✔ Without rapport, you have little chance of successful communication – and without successful communication, you have no chance of persuading the other person.

- ✔ In neuro-linguistic programming terms, rapport in its highest form is a state of affinity with yourself as well as between you and another person. When you're in a state of rapport, you're able to create feelings of trust and understanding.

- ✔ When you're in rapport with another person, both parties share a sense of trust, harmony and understanding. You're on the same wavelength mentally and emotionally, joining another person where she is rather than forcing her to go where you want her to be.

- ✔ When you demonstrate that you accept another person's point of view, where she's coming from and how she communicates, the way is clear for you to influence her.

Of course, you want to take other people to some place other than where they are, if where they are isn't where you want them to be. But rather than shoving, pushing and pressing them into submission, you can build on your rapport to gently pace and then lead them to your new frontier, as I discuss in the later 'Pacing and leading' section.

Follow these principles to establish rapport:

- ✔ **Seek connection.** Get to know the other person. Take a genuine interest in her. Find out who she is and where she comes from. Uncover what she enjoys doing at work and at play. The more you know about someone – including background, attitudes and values – the more points you have for finding where you connect. See Chapter 3 for more on how to connect with another person at an emotional level.

✔ **Reflect back what you observe.** Notice how she breathes and match your pattern to hers. Pick up on the key words and favourite phrases she uses in her conversation and subtly build these into your own. Pay attention to the way she likes to handle information. Is she a detail person or does she talk about the big picture? When you speak, replicate her patterns in yours. Adopt a similar stance to hers in your gestures, expressions and postures.

✔ **Give her the benefit of the doubt.** Believe that whatever she intends to convey is for the good, even if her words and actions may not always seem to support this belief. By treating her as if her heart was in the right place, you're more likely to establish rapport than if you don't.

✔ **Treat the other person's resources with respect.** Time, energy, favourite people and money are important to people.

✔ **Stay in the flow.** Rapport is a process not a state. You may fall in and out of rapport several times during the course of a conversation or meeting. Indeed, you may want to break rapport at certain times such as when you have a task to complete, need to speak with someone else, or just want to end the conversation. But like switching on and off a light, you can reconnect whenever you need or want to.

There may be times when you want to break rapport, such as when you need to bring a conversation to a close. At those times, instead of matching your behaviour to the other person's, create a mismatch by subtly reversing the nonverbal behaviours that led to achieving rapport. You can do this by breaking eye contact, slowly turning your body away from the other person, moving your body. If you're still having difficulty breaking rapport, tell the other person you're sorry but you have to end the conversation. That's bound to do the trick!

When you're building rapport with someone, you're creating similarities between yourself and the other person. A simple mantra you can recite to yourself as you develop and utilise your rapport skill is 'Build similarities, diminish differences.'

Mirroring and matching

When two people are in rapport with one another, it's as if they're dancing, moving as one. You don't even need to hear what they're saying to know that they're in unison, with their energy flowing elegantly from one to the other and back again. When people are in this state of rapport, they're mirroring and matching one another's behaviour and attitude.

When you mirror and match someone, you become highly tuned into thoughts, feelings and how the other person experiences the world. You may feel as if you're listening with every fibre of your body. When you're in rapport with another person, simple mirroring happens naturally. If you find that you're struggling to build rapport, you can deliberately mirror and match someone until the rapport becomes natural. Chapter 14 covers everything you need to begin matching vocal tones, breathing rates, energy levels and body movements and postures.

Pick someone you want to build rapport with. As the two of you converse, notice how the other person's breathing rate and speech patterns reflect each other. For example, if she's speaking quickly, her breathing rate is likely to be quick as well. After a minute or two of observation, begin to subtly match the way the other person speaks and breathes. (You never want to seem as if you're disrespectfully mimicking the other person.)

Practise mirroring the behaviours of people you see while watching television. Not only can you practise in the privacy of your own home, but the other person never knows what you're trying to do! Chat shows and interviews are ideal programmes for this exercise.

When it comes to building rapport, you want to match the way someone speaks as well as the words she says. For more about speaking in a way that your listener can relate to, turn to Chapter 10.

Pacing and leading

When you're finding common ground with other people and building relationships, get into their rhythms by pacing them first – with the goal of eventually persuading them to accept your point of view.

Pacing is when you listen attentively to another person with the intention of understanding what's going on for her. You really listen. You acknowledge someone for who and where that person is, right now.

Think of pacing as running alongside a train that you want to be on. If you tried to jump straight onto the train from a standing position, you'd most likely get whacked by the moving carriages and never stand a chance of catching the train. Another choice is to run alongside the moving train until you're moving at the same speed, and then jump on. (Please do not attempt this example, because the consequences can be most unfortunate!)

When you're pacing, you're demonstrating patience, flexibility and respect. You're picking up and matching other people's behaviours and vocabulary (see the preceding 'Mirroring and matching' section), while actively listening for the values, moods and attitudes that lie behind the data and details they're telling you.

Pacing to lead is a gradual process and requires patience. While pacing is great for establishing rapport, if all you did was pace someone, you both might be breathing in the same rhythm, matching one another's speaking patterns and moving in harmony, but nothing much beyond that would happen. If you want to change someone's point of view – if you want to lead her to new ways of seeing things or behaving – you have to slowly change what you're doing to get the other person to follow.

You can think of pacing and leading like the martial art aikido. When a person attacks you, rather than returning the attack with a similar force, you incorporate your attacker's energy into yours and move in synch with her energy. Then you can take the lead. While the concept of attacking may be counterintuitive to building rapport, the image of going with the energy flow and turning it around to take the lead is an elegant explanation of pacing and leading.

St Francis of Assisi spoke of seeking to understand before being understood. When you want to persuade someone to see your point of view, seek to understand how she sees her world first before taking her into yours. In other words, pace then lead.

I recently attended a conference where I experienced a clear example of pacing and leading. The programme organiser came onto the stage and said, 'It's Tuesday morning, 8 a.m. You're all here because you accepted the invitation to come, and you may be wondering what's going to happen over the next two days. We're all here for the same reason: to connect with our colleagues, learn about our goals for the coming year, and celebrate our successes. I know you want to meet – if not exceed – your targets, and I know you're interested in finding out how we're going to do that.' If you look at what the organiser said, you can see how she paced the group by meeting their reality: it was Tuesday morning, 8 a.m., and they were all there for the same reasons. Once she had paced the group, she then began leading them by indicating where she wanted them to go: 'you may be wondering what's going to happen . . .' and 'I know you want to . . .' By pacing first she built rapport, which then enabled her to lead her listeners to a new point of view.

When you're *leading,* you go from pacing the other person to guiding her to see a different point of view.

No one wants to be led to a new way of thinking until she has first been paced – listened to and acknowledged. If you want to be a persuasive persuader or an influential influencer, pace the other person's reality – how she currently views the world – before leading her to your point of view.

If you want to experience pacing and leading, start off with a friend or trusted colleague. Begin by making verifiably true statements about where you currently are. For instance, you could say, 'So, here we are. It's Monday morning, 8 a.m. – the start of another week. The birds are chirping, the sun is shining and the kettle's boiling.' Continue until you have made at least ten statements. She may make confirming noises like 'Um hum,' or 'Yes, that's right.' Note your friend's body language and reflect it back in yours. Approximate her breathing and speaking patterns as well as her body language. When you're ready to lead, slightly shift your body position and make a subtle change in your voice and breathing patterns. Say something like, 'I know you want to make a difference in how we work together and are wondering how you can do that.' By making this slight alteration in your pattern, having first established rapport through pacing, your friend should be ready to move along with you. If you observe resistance, go back to pacing her, reflecting what you observe in her behaviour and words. You might say something like, 'I thought I heard a little hesitation in your voice. Am I right?' If she agrees, let her take the lead in the conversation, matching and pacing her until rapport has been re-established, and then try leading her again.

Chapter 3

Establishing an Emotional Connection

*Y*ears of scientific research reveals that emotion rather than rational thought propels consumer behaviour. Emotions similarly guide you to establish connections with people and things. Your feelings drive you to act on your decisions, and then your intellect kicks in to justify your behaviour. As I note frequently: People buy on emotion and justify with fact.

Pure logic, dogged persistence and personal enthusiasm are not guaranteed persuaders. While adopting a top-down authoritative approach – where privilege and power are conferred on those in senior positions – may work in the armed forces and bureaucratic organisations, you can have more success in a commercial environment – as well as in any environment where you need to persuade others – if you make an emotional connection with the people you want to win over by demonstrating that you care about them as individuals and not just as a means to an end.

Establishing an emotional connection requires getting to know the individuals you want to influence. By knowing what excites them, what offends them and what entices them to take action, you're more able to persuade them to do what you want than if you hadn't taken the time to connect.

In this chapter I show you ways of making emotional connections with the people you want to persuade and influence. In addition, you discover how to effectively balance the needs of the head and the heart. By treating people like responsible adults and respecting their feelings, you gain their trust as well as their commitment to you.

Demonstrating Your Emotional Commitment

Although you may shy away from the E-word, without emotional commitment you never connect with your colleagues, customers and constituents – let alone your family, friends and other significant people. No matter what industry, profession, religious group or political party you belong to, when you reveal your emotional commitment, others are more likely to come on board than if you hold back on your own commitment. If you're not willing to put yourself on the line, you can't expect anyone else to put themselves out there.

You create emotional connections and show your emotional commitment when you

✔ Engage with your heart, mind and soul

✔ Invest your emotions in a relationship

✔ Share your feelings with another person while seeking to understand his feelings

Revealing too much emotion is just as disturbing as displaying too little. On the one hand, you're engulfing the other person with an overwhelming abundance of feeling – on the other hand, you're starving them of all sensation. When you've the ideal blend of emotion and intellect, you feel wise, evolved, balanced and in control.

The following sections explore ways to effectively get in touch with others' feelings while making the most of your own.

Conveying empathy

When you're establishing an emotional connection, you need to demonstrate a bit of *empathy*. When you empathise, you recognise and share the feelings that others are experiencing and you anticipate their reactions. You take your lead from the emotions on display, engage with your heart and invest yourself in your relationships. For more about building relationships, see Chapter 2. For more on empathy as a tool for active listening, flip to Chapter 7.

When you engage at an empathetic level, you're able to pick up on the emotions behind the words someone speaks, as well as the feelings someone displays through non-verbal behaviour. Chapter 13 talks more about body language when conveying and deciphering feelings, while Chapter 14 examines the power of your voice beyond the words you say.

After you know how others are feeling and can respond in ways that make them feel valued and understood (see the next section 'Engaging with other people's feelings'), you're in with a chance when the time comes to persuade them to adopt your point of view.

The word *empathy* is derived from the Greek word *empatheia*, meaning physical affection and passion. At the end of the 19th century, the German philosophers Theodor Lipps, Hermann Lotze, and Robert Vischer adapted the term, creating the German word *Einfuhlung*, meaning 'feeling into', which was eventually translated in 1909 by British psychologist Edward B. Titchener into the English term.

The word 'sympathy' is often incorrectly substituted for the word 'empathy'. While both terms describe acts of feeling, empathy is feeling *with* the person, and sympathy is feeling *for* the person. When you feel empathetic, you can put yourself in someone else's place, gain a sense of what he's experiencing and attempt to understand his reactions. When you feel sympathetic, you may feel for the other person, but you don't necessarily relate to what he's experiencing.

Showing too much empathy – or empathising with lots of people, often and intensely – can wear you out. If you've limited time to listen to someone, tell them upfront. Your time is valuable and you don't have to give it away if you don't want to. Don't try to fix someone's problem. Be there to listen and ask questions and let the other person come up with his own solutions (See Chapter 7 for tips on listening).

Engaging with other people's feelings

Emotional intelligence is a person's belief in their ability to recognise, calculate and control their own, and others', emotions. If you doubt that emotions impact on your choices, look at the people, objects and experiences in your life. You choose who you do business and are friends with, which contracts you sign and even how you decorate your home and office largely based on how you *feel* about the people, subjects and places you're interacting with. For example, my husband's office is filled with pictures and models of sailboats not just because they're attractive, but because they remind him of the challenges and good times he shared with his father when they sailed in the cold and windy Baltic Sea.

Engage with someone at an emotional level and you can feel the levels of rapport rise (See Chapter 13). By caring for and understanding other people, you confirm their sense of themselves and make them feel they've something of value to offer. You also significantly raise the likelihood that they're going to join your league of champions and do whatever they can for you. For more detailed information about emotional intelligence and its impact on persuasion, see *Emotional Intelligence For Dummies* by Steven J. Stein (Wiley).

The power of emotional connections

When Liz, the Head of Learning and Development for a global telecoms company, met Anne, an executive coach who was starting up in business, the two immediately liked one another. Liz soon hired Anne to coach an executive who was struggling with public speaking and presentations. Anne quickly helped the executive improve his skills, impressing Liz in the process. Liz took Anne out to lunch and offered her two insights. 'Firstly, you've got to get published,' she began. 'It doesn't matter whether it's a pop book or an academic journal, you've got to be published so the people you're working with can reference you. Secondly, you've got to charge more. If you don't raise your prices substantially, the big players won't take you seriously.' Anne was amazed at Liz's generosity and kindness. When she asked why Liz was being so helpful, Liz replied, 'Because I like you and want to see you do well.' Since that time, Anne's career has skyrocketed. She coaches throughout Liz's organisation, is quoted in the business press and has had several articles published. Her first book is a bestseller and she's currently writing her second. Anne always credits Liz for her support and never fails to provide continuous outstanding service to the company based on their relationship.

For inspiration on how to connect with someone at an emotional level, think of courtroom lawyers. These keen observers of human behaviour and psychology know that in order to win juries to their sides, they have to engage with both their own feelings – and their listeners' feelings. They have to demonstrate intellectual and emotional belief in what they're advocating through both their words and their actions. And they must do so without appearing phony and manipulative. The moment courtroom lawyers come off as fakes or frauds, they lose their credibility.

Your credibility is equally important when you're looking to make an emotional connection. If someone doubts your honesty and trustworthiness, you can kiss your chances of persuading him to accept your point of view goodbye. For more about the importance of credibility when seeking to influence others, see Chapter 5.

Establishing an emotional connection requires that you've a clear and correct sense of how other people feel. Your proposition has to make sense to them as well as appeal to their interests. In addition, you may have to adjust your tone or approach to find a common ground for creating rapport. For detailed information on the part rapport plays in the process of establishing an emotional connection, turn to Chapter 2.

While connecting with your own emotions and the emotions of others may sound a heavy order, you can practise the following techniques to connect emotionally with your listeners:

- ✔ **Look others in the eyes when you're speaking to them or when they're speaking to you.** The eyes are the mirrors to the soul and reflect their owner's emotions and feelings. You can tell whether people are interested in connecting with you by the way they catch – or don't catch – your eye. Avoid staring though, because doing so can make you look creepy and make the other person feel uncomfortable! If someone refuses to connect with you visually, offer something you both can look at together, such as a picture, a graph or an object that's relevant to what you're talking about. If he still refuses to look at you, just keep talking and ask him questions to engage him in the discussion. For more about eye contact, turn to Chapter 13 or have a look at *Neuro-linguistic Programming For Dummies* by Romilla Ready and Kate Burton (Wiley).

- ✔ **Match your postures and movements to your message.** When you want to connect emotionally with another person, ask yourself: What does the way I'm standing, sitting and moving say about me and my emotions. Slouched and slumped doesn't convince people that you're interested in them (or in much of anything, really). Sit tall and demonstrate your alertness by focusing all your attention on the other person – and watch your ability to connect improve.

- ✔ **Make your gestures and facial expressions clear and appropriate to your message.** Avoid an overabundance of motion and intense looks, which can become distracting and dilute your message. On the flipside, too few gestures and expressions leave your audience wondering how much you care about what you're saying. If you're uncertain about your gestures and expressions, practise in front of your bathroom mirror to see what you look like. In addition, observe the gestures and expressions of other people and add them to your toolkit.

- ✔ **Speak in terms your listeners can understand.** Avoid jargon and expressions that can cause confusion. While you may know what you're talking about, you can't count on your listeners understanding unless you communicate using words and phrases they comprehend. See Chapter 8 for more tips on holding people's attention.

- ✔ **Pay attention to your appearance.** What messages do you potentially transmit through the state and style of your clothes, hair, teeth and nails? What do you smell like? People take in meaning through all their working senses and make judgements about people based on what they look, sound, smell and even feel and taste like.

- ✔ **Vary your voice.** Using the same pitch or speaking at the same speed is dull and monotonous. Putting purpose and intensity into your voice convinces your listener that you're emotionally connected to yourself, your message and your listener.

✔ **Add humour.** One of the quickest ways to establish emotional connections is through laughter. As long as your humour is audience appropriate, use it to swiftly establish connections.

✔ **Ask for feedback.** Getting your listeners to participate in dialogue makes them feel that they and their opinions are valued. When you make someone feel valued, they want to connect with you. Statements like, 'I'd like you to tell me how well I'm addressing you . . .' or 'I'd appreciate feedback on how I'm . . .' show that you welcome their input and make them feel appreciated.

✔ **Enjoy the process.** Connecting with other people at an emotional level takes you into a territory where sharing feelings is a fun and productive place to be.

See Chapter 13 for practical advice on how to practise and successfully implement many of the preceding recommendations into your presentation style.

Balancing head and heart

All feeling and no intellect can make a person tiresome – as can the opposite. While I encourage you to establish emotional connections with other people as a part of the persuasion and influence process, I also advise you to add a bit of logic, rationality and objectivity to the mix.

While all people have feelings that are primal to who they are, tidal waves of emotion can destroy your chances of forming relationships with others, as much as dull, dry, intellect can deaden the desire to connect. The key is to strike a healthy, useful balance between expressing what's going on in both your heart and your head.

If your experiences are anything like mine, you've been in situations where another person's passions bubbled over like a giant cauldron of feelings that left you staggering in its wake. Although the other person shared a great deal of emotion, you were unable to connect with any of it.

Conversely, you may have found yourself in situations where the other person was so detached from his emotions that you wondered whether any feelings existed inside the suit in front of you. Try as you may to tease out a hint of personality or feeling, you gave up on the prospect of connecting.

In Chapter 13 you can find ways of establishing rapport with other people. By meeting someone where he is, whether his emotions are high or low, you can engage with him, establish his trust and then take him to a place that suits your style better.

Ethos, pathos and logos

The Greek philosopher Aristotle lived and worked in and around Athens about 300 years before the birth of Christ. A student of Plato and teacher to Alexander the Great, Aristotle influenced philosophy, theology and most other 'ologies'.

He notably summarised the job of a persuader as moving people from where they are to where you want them to be. In order to shift resistant or disinterested listeners, you have to get them to understand your views and believe in what you're saying. Aristotle said that it doesn't matter whether you're funny, provocative or articulate, as long as your audience comes on board. In terms of your approach, do what works best depending on the situation. In addition, you can combine methods; for example adding a bit of humour to a serious, logical, fact-driven argument. The point to remember is that your goal is to persuade people to your point of view and that the task may require different methods.

Aristotle also proposed that moving people to where you want them to be involves the three modes of persuasion: ethos, pathos and logos:

- ✔ **Ethos. You've got to be credible.** If you're not believed, you're not going to be followed.

- ✔ **Pathos. You've got to have heart.** If you're lacking in empathy (see the earlier section 'Conveying empathy'), you don't stand a chance of connecting at an emotional level.

- ✔ **Logos. You've got to tell a good story with logical appeal, one that engages and entices your listener.** Combine anecdotes, quotations and metaphors with emotion and credibility to create your own powerfully persuasive potions.

Respecting Others' Feelings

Feelings and emotions are tied to values, attitudes and beliefs. And values, attitudes and beliefs impact on the choices people make. To argue with or judge people's feelings is counterproductive at all times, especially when you want to persuade the person to see your point of view, accept your proposals or agree to your suggestions. In Chapter 2 you can find out how to identify other people's values and spot their attitudes.

Respect is fundamental to establishing an emotional connection. To paraphrase the great African-American baseball player Jackie Robinson, 'I don't care whether you like me or not as long as you respect me as a human being.'

If you think that someone's feelings are silly, stupid or un-supportable, think again. People's feelings come from their own experiences, not from yours. Based on your skills and knowledge, you may struggle to understand how others can feel the way they do. But you must also realise that they may struggle to understand how *you* can harbour your attitudes and opinions.

Accept that people have the right to feel as they do – even if their feelings are different from yours. Of course, accepting other people's rights to their feelings is sometimes much easier to say than to do. In a world where blame is rife and judgement is ubiquitous, people often divide into opposing camps of who's right and who's wrong. While seeing beyond your own perceptions of truth may be difficult, you must work to realise and accept that everyone's truth is true for him.

Letting it out – without judgement

If you want to establish an emotional connection with other people, begin by encouraging them to express their feelings. Grant others the right to say how they feel without judging them in the process.

If you judge others' feelings, you're likely to alienate them and cut off any chance of establishing an emotional connection. Telling someone that he's wrong for feeling the way he does, or that he shouldn't feel a particular way or that his feelings are stupid are signs that you're criticising him and his feelings. Even if you really don't think that you actually are belittling someone, listen to what he tells you and defer to his point of view. If he's feeling judged, you need to change the way you're speaking and behaving if you want to improve the situation.

Respecting someone's feelings means treating others with consideration and allowing them the right to express themselves without interruption. It means leaving your judgement at the door.

When you respect someone's feelings, you make the other person feel valued. You open the door to a relationship filled with trust and goodwill. In Chapter 7, I give you techniques for making other people feel valued and how to respond to their feelings.

Letting others put their points across

Rid the world of conversational bullies, and the world will be a better place. You've seen it happen countless times and may have experienced the treatment yourself: just as you're about to make your point, your nemesis comes barging into the conversation, usurping your place in the dialogue and relegating you to the edge of the debate.

A distressing lack of respect

In Jane Austen's book *Emma,* the character of Mr Woodhouse, Emma's father, struggles to accept that other people can feel differently from himself. Because of his attitude, family and friends frequently find themselves having to kowtow to his wishes, often at great inconvenience to themselves.

The distress caused by lack of respect for other people's feelings is a theme that runs throughout the novel. As Austen highlights, showing respect for others' feelings is considerate, and while social etiquette requires polite consideration, a major difference exists between polite consideration and sincere courtesy. The former is a social necessity for keeping up appearances and not a guaranteed sign of respect. Sincere courtesy, on the other hand, demonstrates genuine kindness and empathy.

As opposed to Mr Woodhouse, Emma's confidante Mr Knightley is consistent in his displays of consideration and respectfulness. Able to see things from other people's perspectives, he adapts his behaviour according to what he observes, treating people with respect. Throughout the book, Austen demonstrates the negative repercussions of failing to respect other people's feelings, which by the end of the novel her heroine, Emma, comes to understand.

In spite of your good intentions and desire to understand someone's point of view, you can get carried away with your own thoughts and ideas. Or you may be so excited by what you hear that you interrupt without meaning to. At this point, you're no longer finding anything out. You can't discover anything when you're speaking, and in order to establish an emotional connection, you have to find out about the other person.

In addition, when you interrupt someone, they're going to think twice before sharing their thoughts with you again. Interrupting and failing to let other people put their points across inhibits communication and reduces your chances of establishing a productive relationship.

Avoid falling into the interruption trap by following these simple strategies:

- ✔ **Remain silent.** You can't interrupt if you're not talking. You may have to make a conscious effort to refrain from speaking while another person converses. However, making the effort and allowing others to finish their thoughts pays dividends in the end.

- ✔ **Close your mouth.** When you open your mouth while someone else is speaking, you signal that you've something to say and indicate that you're done with listening. If you struggle to keep your mouth shut, imagine a drop of glue has been placed on your lips. When your mouth is closed, you can't interrupt.

✔ **Open your mind.** If you're forming opinions while the other person speaks, you're not listening. Let go of your instinct to come in with a 'Yes, but' and simply hear them out. Save your comments until you've taken in everything the other person is saying.

✔ **Take notes.** One of the reasons people interrupt is because they think faster than others speak. Ideas naturally sprout into your head while someone's holding forth. In order to combat the urge to interject your thoughts while someone else is speaking, keep brief notes of your thoughts so that when the time comes for you to speak, you still have the points you want to make.

✔ **Change your goal.** A conversation is made up of talking and listening. Make listening your goal for the conversation rather than talking and watch your urge to interrupt fade.

✔ **Focus on the other person.** If you approach the conversation with the thought of making yourself look good or getting your point across first, you may as well give up on establishing an emotional connection. Seek to understand the other person first and watch their desire to connect with you heighten. When you focus more on someone other than yourself, you interrupt less.

✔ **Don't justify your interruptions.** You may want to jump in during a conversation to show you support the other person, perhaps by providing critical information, emphasising his point or demonstrating your enthusiasm. Don't. The most helpful behaviour you can adopt is to let the other person speak.

✔ **Show signs of agreement.** Head nods and non-verbal sounds (like 'mmm, uh huh') lets the speaker know you're paying attention without interrupting their flow. You can gain more pointers about how to show these signs in Chapter 7.

While I'm all for letting others have the floor and present their views, you need to be strategic about how you do so. If you have points you want to make, be sure that you do. Saying something along the lines of, 'I've heard what you've said and would like to comment', 'I'd like to build on your ideas' or 'What you're saying ties nicely into my point about . . .' acknowledges the other person's agenda and lets you address yours, too.

Suppressing your emotions

Tamping down your own emotions gives others the space to express their feelings without being judged, interrupted or out emoted – all of which helps you build rapport and trust.

I'm not suggesting that you shut down your feelings or withdraw your emotional connection. In fact, research shows that turning off or taking away emotion is often disastrous for relationships and leads to tension and agitation. Instead, I suggest that you put your feelings on the back burner while other people are speaking and allow them the opportunity to express theirs so they feel heard and acknowledged. When you get your turn to speak, make sure that you let others know how you feel about the subject so you don't become a martyr to your own emotions. For more information about the positive impact of listening to others, see Chapter 7.

Whether someone's overjoyed, annoyed or just at the end of their tether, an appropriate response is to engage with the person's mood. Don't try to change it or turn it into your own. Simply allow others the chance to express their feelings and hold yours at bay. You show respect and consideration by allowing others to express their feelings without getting in their way. Any other response is selfish and plain insensitive.

Chris's boss Kevin invited him to his office to voice concerns about the latest sales initiative, which Chris was having trouble getting his team to subscribe to. Every time Chris started addressing his unease about the programme, Kevin interrupted, saying things like, 'I know how you feel', 'When this happened to me', 'It's not as bad as you think' and 'You've got to make this work regardless of how you feel about the decision'. At no point did Kevin ask to hear more about Chris's feelings or acknowledge that he understood why Chris was feeling as he was. Chris felt that his emotions were secondary to Kevin's and that Kevin had paid no attention to anything he was saying. Chris left Kevin's office feeling defensive, disrespected and uncommitted.

People mostly communicate their emotions through voice and body language. When you let your emotions rule you, whether at work, in public or during family discussions, you can lose your cool and behave in ways that do you more harm than good. In order to keep this from happening when your emotions are about to burst forth, concentrate on speaking in your regular tone of voice and give rational arguments. Never say anything insulting or sarcastic. Breathe deeply from your abdomen and if you're tempted to burst forth with a stream of expletives, silently count to ten. (For more about breathing techniques, turn to Chapter 14.)

Showing That You Care

If you want to persuade someone to accept or adopt your position, you need to show that you care about the other person. If you don't, you offer no incentive for others to follow you. When you care about people, your thoughts and behaviours are in their best interest. By considering their position, you demonstrate your awareness and concern for them and their issues. Showing that you care is one way of establishing rapport and rapport is the way to a person's heart.

In order to care about someone, you have to know:

- ✔ What are his interests, issues and concerns?
- ✔ What motivates, inspires and keeps him up at night?
- ✔ What are his goals and ambitions?
- ✔ What is his greatest triumph and his biggest regret?
- ✔ What is his greatest strength and his greatest weaknesses?

Without crossing boundaries, find out as much as you can about the people whose buy-in you seek. The more you understand what makes someone tick, the more you're able to engage. While you definitely don't want to come across as a stalker, you do want to know what matters to someone.

When Romey was looking for volunteers to support the local church, she asked the parishioners how they felt about the current state of the church, what changes they wanted to see, what traditions they wanted to keep, what they wanted to leave as their legacy and other questions that gave her insights into their beliefs and commitment. By getting to know the local congregation, she was able to approach those whom she believed would be the best volunteers for raising the church's profile in the community.

When people feel they matter to you, they're more willing to open themselves to you than if they feel their presence, thoughts and contributions are of no consequence. For more about recognising and identifying what motivates and matters to individuals, see Chapter 9.

Clarifying issues

In any relationship, what matters to one person may not matter to another and issues inevitably arise. A similar dynamic occurs in groups – one person or sub-group may feel one way, while the rest feel another. The sooner you clarify these differences, the better. If you leave issues to fester, they soon become rancid, poisoning the emotional connections you aimed to establish.

One size fits all

If you don't know others well or haven't had time to discover more about them, you can still show them that you care. I consider the following universal principles applicable to all genders races, and creeds:

✔ Treat people as individuals and respect their dignity.

✔ Treat everyone equally, kindly and considerately.

✔ Act as an advocate for an individual's rights.

✔ Respect people's right to confidentiality.

✔ Keep people informed.

✔ Listen and respond to people's concerns and preferences.

✔ Recognise and respect people's contributions.

✔ Support people in performing at their best.

✔ Communicate in a respectful and helpful way.

Verbal and non-verbal signals are clues to possible issues. The tone in people's voices, their rates of speech and the expressions on their faces reveal feelings and emotions below the surface. Watching and listening for tell-tale signs give you a head start in understanding and clarifying unresolved issues. For example:

✔ A low, slow voice indicates that not much energy is pushing or pulling a person's engine.

✔ Lowered eyes and a scowling expression tell you someone's probably not well pleased.

✔ Hands waving in the air and a voice pitched at a glass-breaking decibel mean someone's pretty excited about something.

When people speak, they're providing you with information, including what they're thinking and how they're feeling. By paying attention to a person's tone of voice, pace of delivery and body language, you've valuable data that you can use to clarify issues. Flip to Chapters 13 and 14 for more on gathering this data.

If you genuinely want to clarify issues, you have to understand them first. Getting to know what the issues are takes time, care and genuine interest. Consider these approaches to working out what's on people's minds:

- ✔ Clear your mind of all distractions and give your full attention to the other person.

- ✔ Make an effort to meet face-to-face with the people you want to persuade. If that's not possible, because of the nature of international business, schedule conference or Skype calls on a regular basis. Make sure that you consider time zones and see to it that everyone's schedules are respected. If someone always has to take a call at 4 a.m., he's not going to be happy or emotionally engaged.

- ✔ Ask others about their opinions, concerns and perspectives. Then listen to their responses to your questions.

- ✔ Share your own views with them and illuminate the plus points of your position.

If your mind wanders onto other matters, or if you react with moral judgements and start planning how you're going to respond, stop and refocus on the speaker. If you've lost the course of the conversation, you don't need to apologise or explain yourself. Simply ask the other person if he can repeat what he said, showing that you want to understand his concerns and issues.

During this process, take time to summarise or paraphrase what someone else says and ask for confirmation that you understand correctly. Doing so verifies that you grasp the outstanding issues. In order to understand someone's point, you have to listen for the feelings behind the spoken words as well as the message itself. See Chapter 7 for tips on effective listening.

Demonstrating your interest in another person makes them feel worthwhile and appreciated. If they feel that their issues matter to you, they're much more likely to engage and build rapport with you.

Striving for mutual benefit

After both sides share their views, invite discussion and debate – and then seek shared solutions. Revising your ideas in concert with others' needs and concerns reflects your desire to reach mutually beneficial solutions. Not for one moment must you think that if you compromise or revise your opinions and ideas you're being weak or are in the losing position during a tough discussion. Instead, you're showing strength when you recognise that changing conditions require different approaches than those you originally thought would work. As you prepare to become a master persuader, focus on clear goals and behave as though everyone can come out a winner. Someone who's in it for himself is quickly spotted as a self-server, which doesn't go down well when you're not the person being served.

Connecting in a far-flung world

In today's digital world, virtual teams with their members scattered across the globe are a normal part of international business. Clarifying issues plus building rapport and emotional connections are difficult when people come from different cultures and time zones. Issues around trust, conflict, responsibilities for tasks, culture and communication are common. To build and nourish trust, team members must understand the cultures they're dealing with and how to communicate clearly and effectively. Managers must take active steps to find commonality among team members and create opportunities where differences exist. Blended approaches to communication, including email, phone calls and visits to different sites help build relationships and maintain the team members' emotional connection with one another. Research shows that, in teams with a high level of trust, power shifts from one member to another during the life cycle of the project they're working on depending on the stage and its requirements. Power originates from knowledge and the most powerful individual on the team is the one with the most relevant information at any one time. Coercive power is seldom used and emphasis is placed on collaboration. When managers share power with the team members, trust levels and emotional connections increase because everyone feels like an equal partner rallying around a common goal.

Include positive language to encourage cooperation and interaction, increasing the likelihood that you can all reach your goals. Use expressions like 'win-win, cooperation, benefit, gain, encouragement, trust, team effort, equality, flexible and enthusiastic'. The more positive the language, the more chance you stand of reaching a mutually satisfying conclusion.

People are willing to make sacrifices if they believe you genuinely care about their views and are ready to modify your position in response to their needs and concerns. But be prepared to compromise and adjust your viewpoint as well, if necessary.

Others perceive you as trustworthy and flexible when you come into a relationship with an open mind and a willingness to incorporate others' suggestions. Over time, you may become known as someone who listens and works in the best interests of others, which in turn makes others more trusting and flexible in their attitudes toward you.

You can't engage people and gain their commitment without highlighting the shared advantages of your proposal (see the nearby sidebar 'Burger buy-in' for a compelling case). Sometimes clear benefits exist and you can easily point them out. However, when mutual benefits aren't obvious or meaningful, you have to adjust your position to make the proposition appeal to their needs and concerns. Always go into the discussion knowing what the other person wants and always be prepared to compromise to reach a mutually satisfying outcome.

ANECDOTE

Burger buy-in

Monica is an account executive for an advertising agency. Her client, a fast-food chain, was introducing a new promotional campaign in which a burger, chips and soft drink were packaged together at a low price.

At corporate headquarters, the proposal made sense. Research showed that customers perceived the chain's products as being higher priced than its competitors', and the company wanted to adjust this view. However, because the franchisees' sales were strong, they were concerned about the short-term impact this decision would have on profit margins.

Rather than presenting headquarters' perspective as a way of convincing the franchisees, Monica showed the various restaurant owners how the new approach benefited them by increasing the profits in each of their stores. To back up her assertion, she referred to examples where the campaign was already being successfully piloted, quoting statistics, examples and percentages of increased sales and improved customer perceptions.

Closing her presentation, Monica quoted from a letter written by the company's founder. The letter appealed to listeners' emotions as it extolled company values and highlighted the importance of the franchisees to the company's success. In addition, the letter emphasised the company's position as the leader in the low-priced food industry. The franchisees lived and breathed the company's core values and beliefs, and hearing them repeated confirmed in their minds the organisation's concern for their welfare and the magnitude of its winning formula. In addition to giving Monica a standing ovation, the franchisees voted to support the new pricing plan.

The best persuaders connect with the people whose buy-in they need by speaking with them, studying the issues that matter to them and listening to their problems and concerns with an open mind. Without a solid understanding of your audience, you don't stand a chance of engaging with them and gaining their commitment.

TRY THIS

Study the issues that matter to the people you want to persuade. Test your ideas with trusted confidantes and ask questions of the people whose buy-in you want as a means of collecting essential data. Taking a thoughtful and inquisitive approach leads you to the best way of appealing to your listener.

Chapter 4

Putting Together a Compelling Case

*W*hen you want to persuade others, your proposition has to make sense to them. No matter how compelling your proposal is to you, if it fails to ignite your audience with passion – or at least a modicum of interest – your efforts to bring others on board are wasted.

People are only interested in how your request applies to them. Sad, but true. So, when you want to persuade others, you need to understand them and then position your proposal in a way that's compelling to them. Find out about their beliefs, values and motivators (see Chapter 2). Turn to others who know them to uncover the issues they're facing. The more you know about your audience's desires, needs and concerns, the better you're able to prepare and present a convincing argument.

In this chapter, I show you how to make sense to other people by appealing to their values and assuaging their doubts. In addition, you find ways of vibrantly presenting your proposal, proposition – indeed your story – with a passion that enthuses your listener and whips up support.

Making Sense to Others

While you may find this truth difficult to live with, persuasion requires time and effort. The best persuaders take the time to find out more about the people they want to influence – and come to mutually satisfying shared solutions (see the 'Illuminating advantages and shared benefits' section, later in this chapter).

The days of command-and-control leadership where authority is held at the top of the establishment and people are expected to do what they're told without question are long gone. Except in traditional hierarchical professions such as the law and medicine, instant communication and globalisation have eroded the customary pecking order. In most workplaces and organisations today, people and ideas flow around, and decisions are made closer to where their impact is directly felt. As a persuader, you need to keep your eyes and ears open to understand what's needed on the ground as well as what is proposed at headquarters. Today's business environment is filled with workers from diverse backgrounds, generations, nationalities and upbringings – all collaborating in cross-functional teams of equals. One outcome is that people no longer simply ask what they should do; they want to know the reasons why. This situation is where the process of persuasion comes into play.

The same principles apply wherever you need to figure out other people and present your suggestions in ways that enlist their action. Rather than imposing your ideas on others, whether they're family members, individuals you volunteer with or friends with whom you socialise, be prepared to answer their questions, then listen and respond to what they say. When your suggestions make sense to them, they're usually willing to follow your lead.

While persuasion does entail moving people from where they are to where you want them to be, the process is more complex than simply cajoling or demanding. In order to stand a chance of getting people to come on board with you, you must

- ✔ Find common ground with the people you want to influence (see Chapter 2)
- ✔ Connect at an emotional level (see Chapter 3)
- ✔ Present proposals that are plausible (see Chapter 5)
- ✔ Provide vivid evidence for your proposal (which I discuss later in the 'Providing proof' section)

The following sections explore ways of uncovering what motivates people – touching upon their values and providing them with proof – in order to convince them of your position's merits.

Appealing to their values

More than 2,300 years ago, the Greek philosopher Aristotle pointed out that demonstrating a shared set of values with people you want to persuade wins you more points than basing your arguments on logic alone. Sharing similar values leads to trust and understanding – and with those two components in place, you stand a better chance of persuading someone than if your value systems are in opposition.

When others believe that you relate to and care about what's important to them, they're going to respond more positively to your suggestions than if they think that you're only out for yourself. This principle holds true no matter whom you're interacting with, whether it's people at work, family members or a group of volunteers.

Appreciating a variety of values

People hold values in different categories, and the more values you share with them, the more likely they are to trust and relate to you. The following categories of values overlap and while it's not necessary to categorise the types of values you hold, recognising them adds to your self-awareness as well as the awareness of what is significant for other people.

- ✔ **Personal values** encompass your beliefs based on your experiences and circumstances, and can change over time. Prioritised in order of importance to you, they include concepts such as loyalty, responsibility, honesty, trustworthiness and integrity.

- ✔ **Social values** address the rights of the wider society in which you live. They may include justice, freedom, liberty, equality and national pride.

- ✔ **Political values** are based on the best way to govern a larger group – be it a country or an organisation. Subjects such as welfare, democracy and civic duty fall into this category. History, experience, family, friends and people whose beliefs you agree with or admire can influence your political values.

- ✔ **Economic values** involve finances and include beliefs around taxation, private and public ownership of property and the concept of supply and demand.

- ✔ **Religious values** are spiritual in nature and include how you treat others, how you behave and forms of prayer and worship.

- ✔ **Instrumental values** regulate how you establish and achieve your goals, ensuring that you attain your desired outcomes in socially acceptable ways. Having evolved over time, groups and individuals rely on instrumental values to create successful societies – instrumental values include courage, truthfulness and civility.

- ✔ **End-state values** are what you seek, rather than the journey you take to get there. End-state values can include happiness, renewal and prosperity.

Uncovering values

Getting to know others takes time, and in today's world of constant and instant communication, time is a precious, protected commodity. While instinct can take you a long way in understanding people, getting your information direct from the horse's mouth is more reliable than a haphazard hypothesis.

When you want to find out what people value, ask them. Sounds simple enough, yet all too often people feel uncomfortable asking personal questions. While you can always make assumptions, understand that if you do so, you may make a wrong guess. Better to ask and know for sure than operate on erroneous beliefs. You can initiate a conversation indirectly focusing on values by discussing ideas about what is right and wrong, good and bad, important and not so important. This way, you can find out what the other person values and then target these values.

You can easily find out much more about someone else's values by asking three simple questions:

> ✔ Question 1: What's important to you?
>
> ✔ Question 2: What is important to you about that? (You can also ask, How do you know when you've achieved what's important to you?)
>
> ✔ Question 3: What else is important to you?

Say you want to know what's important to a potential client when she's selecting a supplier. Perhaps she gives you a detailed answer loaded with insights into what she truly values. Good for you! However, if her response to the first question is simple and direct – for example, she says 'service' or 'cost' or 'a proven track record' – you can find out more by asking her to elaborate. You may ask her how she knows when she's received excellent service or what it is about service that is important to her. Her response to this second question helps you understand her values in more detail. And if you want to gain further information, ask her a third question – what else is important to her when selecting a supplier? If you still want more detail, you can return to Question 2.

After you gather the necessary information, you still need to decide how to make the best use of it. For example, if a client tells you excellent service or value for money is important to her, you can provide testimonials from satisfied clients. This approach works equally as well in a non-work environment. Suppose someone tells you that honesty is high on her list of values, you can share examples of where you've demonstrated honesty in your life. By responding to the other person's highest value and proving that you're up to the job, your chance of persuading the other person to follow your lead greatly increases.

Aligning with group values

Organisations, both in the profit and the not-for-profit sectors, frequently hold value systems that all members of the group adhere to. The purpose of having group values to is provide a useful structure for identifying principles that can serve as the standards for group behaviour and decision-making.

Jumping on the bandwagon

With the steady stream of innovative products, it's not unusual to hear about crowds of people standing in line at 4 a.m. to get the latest Apple iPad, concert tickets or other 'must-have' items while the rest of the world waits and wonders. These early adopters provide product insight and are key to influencing customer choices. They're critical to launching new products and tend to have the following characteristics:

✔ **'Venturesomeness'**: Early adopters are daring. They both want and are willing to try things that are new and different.

✔ **Social integration**: Early adopters have a wide range of contact with others who are interested in the same items and frequently interact with these contacts.

✔ **Cosmopolitan**: With a broad point of view, early adopters tend to seek out what's beyond their immediate neighbourhood or community.

✔ **Social mobility**: Early adopters tend to set their sights upwards on the social scale.

✔ **Privilege**: Frequently, early adopters are in a financial position where they can afford to try something new.

If you or your organisation produce truly ground-breaking products or services, target early adopters through social networks, blogging, mobile apps, digital magazines, YouTube or any other user-generated content sites. Traditional forms of media, like print and television, are also viable target areas, although their costs may be prohibitive. Twitter, where celebrities, experts and friends mingle is a great place to promote your products and engage your followers at no cost to you.

Group values can consist of three main value categories:

✔ **Core values:** These stipulate the attitude and character of the organisation and are usually found in the organisation's credo or code of conduct.

✔ **Protected values:** Found mostly in sectors that are concerned with health, the environment and safety, these values are protected by rules and standards.

✔ **Created values:** These created values are the ones that all stakeholders expect in return for their contributions to the organisation and are frequently found in the sections on objectives.

In order for group values to be effective, each individual within the group must adopt the beliefs outlined in the values statement. In the corporate world, getting people to do so is particularly challenging because organisational goals and values are frequently in conflict, especially when organisations are facing financial difficulty.

Sceptics tend to see group values as little more than a strategy to 'rally the troops'. The best group values are based on a fundamental philosophy of what is best for people both within and outside the organisation and that provide a sense of purpose for the individuals beyond making money.

The more the merrier

In 1969, social researchers Stanley Milgram, Leonard Bickman and Lawrence Berkowitz designed a simple study to explore the power of social proof. They had an individual stand at a busy street corner in Manhattan and told him to look up at a particular spot on a tall building and keep his focus there. The researchers then recorded how many people stopped and looked up or gave a fleeting glance as they walked by. The researchers ran the experiment several times, increasing the number of people who originally stood on the corner looking upwards.

Findings showed that when just one person was gazing upwards, only 20 per cent of people passing joined the other person or gave a cursory upwards glance. However, when five people gathered together and looked at the spot, 80 per cent of the passers-by joined the group or looked up with interest themselves. Thus, the more people who participate in an activity, the more inclined others are to join in.

Providing proof

When you provide proof, you create a short cut for people to make decisions. Although p*roof* and *evidence,* which I cover later in this chapter, are often used interchangeably, the difference is that *proof* removes all doubt that something is true whereas *evidence* suggests that something may be true.

Words and images as proof

Modern technology has changed the way businesses provide proof to their customers:

- ✔ Testimonials, surveys and expert opinions are readily available to substantiate claims and provide proof of a product's popularity, effectiveness and reliability.

- ✔ Company websites are ubiquitous and provide customers and consumers with testimonials, substantiation, and verification of their products and services – all forms of modern-day proof.

- ✔ Social networking through sites like Twitter, Facebook, YouTube and LinkedIn enables businesses to build proof in the form of customer trust, loyalty and respect by forming personal relationships with end users.

See the 'Catch the buzz' sidebar for additional changes in providing proof to customers and consumers.

Market research shows that roughly 14 per cent of people are willing to adopt new products and technologies even when they believe that they're lacking complete information. These people are referred to as 'early adopters' within specific areas –for example, technology, products, fashion, art and politics – and tend to rely on their own intuition and vision when making a choice. The remaining 86 per cent require further proof before buying into a new product or idea.

People and behaviours as proof

When pressed for time or in an ambiguous situation, groups and individuals turn to other people to determine how they should behave, especially when these people are similar to them. The assumption is that, if everyone else you relate to agrees that a course of action is the right way to go, then it must be so. For example, the collective responses of many individuals based on the initial responses of skilled and brave first responders saved countless lives as people fled the twin towers without questioning the reasons in the aftermath of the 9/11 terrorist attacks on the World Trade Center.

Human beings are social animals, and social animals like to belong to groups. *Social proof* is an observable fact that occurs when people in a group rely on the group's response to an event to determine how to behave. While you may find occasional dissenters, research shows that because people value the sense of belonging, they usually find an idea, product or trend more appealing when other people do, too. If the group behaves in a certain way, they must know what they're doing, right? For more on social proof, see 'The more the merrier' sidebar later in this chapter and Chapter 10.

Even if someone doesn't originally subscribe to your proposition, if the majority of the people in the group do, more likely than not the outliers will change their thinking to go along with the rest of the crowd. For example, other people's actions and opinions serve as one type of proof that particular ways of thinking and behaving are in their best interests.

Elaine works as a cocktail waitress in a popular city bar. At the start of her shift, she puts a few pounds into her tip jar to indicate that previous patrons have left her gratuities as a way of expressing their appreciation for her service. By putting a pound or two in her jar, she hopes that customers may feel that they're doing the right thing by tipping because others have done so, too.

People look to the behaviour of others as a way of validating their own behaviour. According to research, 90 to 95 per cent of the population engages in social behaviour that complies to the norm. People look to the majority to serve as proof that the choice the larger population makes is the correct way to proceed.

In addition to social proof determining something as alluring or tempting, social proof can lead to determining that certain things are unappealing – or even wrong or immoral.

Catch the buzz

In addition to traditional forms of advertising, word-of-mouth marketing – or *buzz marketing* because the news spreads rapidly through one-to-one conversations online and in the real world – has become a popular way for companies to provide proof to potential purchasers.

The people who spread buzz marketing information aren't celebrities (the spokespeople who traditionally provide proof of products' worthiness). Rather, these 'buzz-bees' tend to be people who influence what's cool, such as DJs, party planners and celebrity stylists as well as writers and bloggers who work outside traditional media and publishing channels. These individuals are not as hampered by corporate rules, so they can share what they like and don't like, which gives the appearance that their recommendations are more authentic than paid for advertising. Then, their readers decide whether they want to follow the taste-makers' choices or not. Companies provide buzz-bees with products, such as cars, smart phones or access to private clubs, in order to prove that the product is the product of choice. For buzzing to work, you have to believe that the people you're listening to are discriminating, or that they know what they're talking about. Procter & Gamble was one of the pioneers of the buzzing approach when it recruited hundreds of thousands of 'in the know' teenagers to coax their friends to try Procter & Gamble's teen-tailored products. American Idol, Miller Lite, Ben & Jerry ice cream, French's Potato Sticks, Herbal Essences Organic shampoo, General Motor's Hummer and OverweightDate.com all have benefitted from buzz marketing. While buzz marketing may seem the cool way to go, beware. Although it was estimated to be a $150 million industry in 2005, according to the most recent financial reports I can find – and that was only in the United States – the downsides of buzz marketing can land you in hot water because of provocative practices that may even be illegal, according to Jonah Bloom, the executive editor of *Advertising Age*. Be aware of the following major issues if you want to incorporate buzz marketing into your persuasive efforts:

- ✔ Taste-makers change rapidly and often. If you're going to engage in buzz marketing, you've got to be ever-watchful of the media landscape. Be flexible and super-responsive.

- ✔ What expectations do you have? Are you looking for an endorsement from someone – or is just having them use your product enough?

- ✔ Disclosure. Do people need to know that the product/service was given to the taste-maker for free – but everyone else will need to buy it? I say yes, but my family tells me that I'm stuffy and old media! I prefer to think of myself as having integrity. For more about how integrity influences persuasion, have a look at Chapter 5.

Advertisers and marketers understand the principle of providing social proof to lend credibility to their products. When an advertiser tells you that its product is the 'fastest growing' or 'largest selling' one of its type on the market, the company is not saying that the product is better than others. The company's really saying that scores of other people think that it is better, and back up their thinking by purchasing the product, which is proof enough.

Build your reputation as an expert in your field by tweeting, blogging and appearing on YouTube. Speak at events, publish articles, get to know the producers at your local radio stations and offer to speak on your subject and make contact with journalists who write about your subject. Producers and journalists are always looking for expert sources. The fact that others find you interesting, amusing or a source of valuable information can serve as proof that you've something worthwhile to offer. For more tips on how to build your reputation, turn to Chapter 5.

Some people argue that tweeting, blogging and YouTube are inappropriate for certain sectors and products, such as health insurance or engineering regulations. I believe that as social media becomes more and more a part of business life, you must incorporate them into your PR and marketing strategy, taking advantage of the opportunities the medium offers. If you want to find out more about the benefits of successfully using social media for promoting yourself, your products or your services, pick up copies of other Dummies books such as *YouTube For Dummies* by Doug Sahlin and Chris Botello (Wiley), *Twitter Marketing For Dummies* by Kyle Lacy (Wiley) and *Blogging For Dummies* by Susannah Gardner and Shane Birley (Wiley).

Testing Your Ideas with Trusted Confidants

In addition to finding out as much as possible about your audience (see Chapters 2 and 3), you must investigate and envision your audiences' situation, including their needs, issues and concerns, from every angle before you open discussions. Turning to people you trust to provide you with reliable information and unbiased points of view helps you put together proposals that appeal to your target audience and not just to your own agenda.

Seek assistance as you work your way through your ideas. Seek out people whose judgment, experience and opinions you trust, both at work and outside the office environment. The more you gather reliable input, the more compellingly you can present your case. A trusted colleague, confidant or advisor can be a powerful reality check before you plunge into a major pitch. In particular, the insights of others can be useful, especially when identifying the best way to invest limited resources, finding holes in your supporting evidence and brainstorming alternative choices.

Brainstorming is a helpful technique for stimulating thinking in a flexible and creative way when you're looking for ideas and solutions. Make sure that you apply the following rules when you engage in a brainstorming session:

> ✔ **Generate as many ideas as you can.** The more ideas you generate, the more chance you have of producing an effective solution.
>
> ✔ **Withhold criticism.** Focus on extending and adding to ideas. Suspend all judgment until later in the process when you need to decide on the best solution.
>
> ✔ **Encourage unusual ideas.** Look at the situation from a new perspective and let go of any assumptions you may have. The creative ideas you and others come up with may lead to the best solutions.
>
> ✔ **Combine and improve ideas.** Several ideas merged into one may make for a better single idea.

Turn to your family, friends, colleagues and anyone you trust and who supports you and wants to see you do well in your life. Whoever you turn to, make sure that they're on your side and aren't gossips, disloyal or indiscrete.

Evaluating the evidence

While you may believe that the information you present is enough to sway anyone to your point of view, substantiating your points with well-researched and well-selected evidence strengthens your argument. In fact, if you push a proposal without substantiation and supporting details, your chances of making a compelling case are slim.

Provide as much and as varied evidence as you can in order to make your case convincing, including:

> ✔ **Facts and statistics:** Measurable information, such as hard data and numerical proof, demonstrates that something is true all or most of the time. Be sure to define any essential, technical or easily confused terms early on in your presentation. Although facts and statistics are less debatable than other forms of evidence, they're usually a challenge to make fresh, interesting and compelling. With this truth in mind, always choose the facts and statistics you present carefully. Go for just one great number or percentage in order to support your story quickly and effectively.
>
> Cite your sources when necessary to support your case and focus on facts that aren't commonly known.
>
> ✔ **Anecdotes and examples:** Personal stories from individuals who can support your position provide an emotional quality to your evidence that appeals to your listeners' beliefs and values. Anecdotes must be believable and relatable – even if they summarise exceptional results. For example, as great as your product or service may be, you're probably not Edison inventing the light bulb although you may be the next Steve Jobs, Mark Zuckerberg or Oprah Winfrey.

> ✔ **Expert opinions:** Bringing in the big guns to support your proposal lends credibility to your position.
>
> Avoid biased opinions, which audiences can quickly spot and ultimately undermine your cause.
>
> ✔ **Analogies:** When you compare two similar points, you can then demonstrate that, if something is true for A, it is also true for B. Of course, you must establish that A and B are enough alike in order for this tactic to work.

When you're evaluating your evidence, know what you want to achieve, analyse your audience and research your topic. Try out your evidence with your trusted confidants to see what works and what doesn't. Audiences are different and you want to keep each one interested – without raising unwarranted concerns or extensive debate into the nature of your evidence.

Pondering perspectives

When you're putting together a compelling case, make sure that you consider the impact your proposal will have on the people you're persuading before you make the actual presentation. Engage the individuals in conversation and listen to their views. Take on board their points of view and incorporate them into your proposal. The more you're perceived as caring about their positions, the more willing they may be when considering yours.

Key questions you can ask include:

> ✔ What are the issues you're currently facing?
>
> ✔ What do you believe are the strengths and weaknesses of . . . ?
>
> ✔ What is currently working well?
>
> ✔ Where can improvements be made?
>
> ✔ How would you like things to be a 6 months to a year from now?
>
> ✔ What do you need in order to make that happen?
>
> ✔ What may get in the way of that happening?

Canvass key individuals who have their ears to the ground and who know the mood and expectations of the people you want to persuade. Keeping an open mind and including all perspectives in your proposal suggests that you're willing and able to consider a subject from multiple viewpoints. Someone who demonstrates openness and a willingness to compromise stands a better chance of presenting a compelling case than someone who's blinkered in her thinking.

Divide your audience into three clusters: those who are likely to agree with your proposition, those who may agree with it and those who definitely will not agree with it. Find as many reasons for each position as you can in order to broaden your view and give you a variety of perspectives to work from. After that, you can begin crafting your responses and counter-arguments (see the following section).

Planning and polishing your arguments

When you're putting together your proposal, you have to know exactly what you want from your listener. Being clear in your own mind about your desired outcomes enables you to present your arguments in a way that serves both you and others.

If your proposal doesn't satisfy other people's needs, don't expect them to leap onto your bandwagon to satisfy yours. If your proposal makes a world of sense to you but your audience doesn't want to comply, they may still do so because they have to – but without much grace, willingness or enthusiasm.

In order to get others to join you, consider how your request benefits them. Ask yourself what you can do to encourage them to do what you want.

For example, if you're in charge of your local community fundraiser, you can offer to host all meetings at your home and provide free refreshments in return for individuals to agree to taking responsibility for the different requirements like publicity, raffle prizes and finding a suitable location.

When you're putting together your argument, you need to consider how you're going to develop it, shape it and present it. In order to do so:

- ✔ **Find out as much as you can about your audience and your subject.** The more knowledge you have, the more able you're to substantiate your position.

  The more you know about what's important to your audience – including their needs, concerns and points of view – the better you're able to position your arguments in ways that makes sense to them. For more information about understanding your audience, see Chapter 11.

- ✔ **Shape your argument based on your audience's position.** Decide what part of your content is relevant and useful for your purposes.

- ✔ **Organise your content and choose your tone before you make your presentation.** See the sidebar 'Two approaches to powerful presentations' for successful formats.

As you put together and then present a compelling case, do all following:

✔ **Treat your listeners as intelligent and reasonable people.** State your position clearly and simply. Blinding your listener with fancy phrases, technical jargon and complicated reasoning is unlikely to further your cause.

Perhaps even more importantly, avoid using argumentative and abusive language when presenting your case. When you present your position, treat your listeners with respect in order to create rapport. (See Chapter 2.) Words and phrases that can undermine your proposals and credibility include any that cast blame or come off as confrontational or disrespectful, such as 'that's not my job', 'I don't know', 'that's not what you said' or 'if it hadn't been for you . . .' In addition, avoid any overused words and phrases that sound worn out and unoriginal, such as *opportunity of a lifetime, blue sky thinking* or *vis a vis.*

✔ **Focus on the kinds of evidence your audience is likely to find persuasive.** Appeal to their values (see Chapter 2) or adjust your approach to match their decision-making style (Chapter 9) to provide evidence that attracts your listeners' attention.

Suppose you're a proponent of flexible working practices and want to convince someone whose viewpoint is that all employees can work from the office at specified times to meet their workload. When putting together your argument, highlight those cases where employees have been able to meet their requirements while working in less traditional ways.

✔ **Pay attention to timing.** When you or your audience are tired, hungry or in a hurry, you're less likely to make a persuasive proposition. Whenever possible, schedule your presentation for a slot when both sides have the time and energy to address the subject.

✔ **Tell your listeners why they must address your suggestion now.** Let them know what will happen if they don't resolve the situation sooner rather than later. Even if you don't have a particularly compelling explanation for the timeliness of your request, find one. Why put off until tomorrow what can be done today? If time is an issue for the people you want to persuade and it's not that much of an issue for you, you can present your proposal by saying something like, 'I can give you a little more time if you can give me . . .'. This approach is similar to reciprocity that I look at in Chapter 10.

✔ **Start strong; finish stronger.** When presenting your argument, present your second-strongest point first and then save your strongest for last, leaving it ringing in your audience's memory.

✔ **Be direct and specific in telling people what you'd like them to do.** By making your points clearly, you leave no doubt in their minds of what you want to have happen. Whether they agree with you or not, at least they know what you expect.

Two approaches to powerful presentations

Over the centuries, persuaders have successfully presented information in notable ways. No need for you to reinvent the wheel when crafting a compelling proposal; just look to the examples of others.

The American psychologist Carl Rogers (1902–1987) believed that, in order to persuade another person, you need to listen to her, understand her and find a common ground. Specifically, Rogers recommended that you

- ✔ Introduce the problem and demonstrate your understanding of the other person's position.

- ✔ State the contexts in which your opponent's position may be valid.

- ✔ State your position and the contexts in which it's valid.

- ✔ Show how the other person's position can benefit from adopting elements of your proposal. If you can show that the two positions complement one another, and supply what the other one lacks, you're in an even better position to win them over.

Rogers's approach is especially useful when the topic is emotionally charged because it downplays emotion and highlights rationality.

Nearly 2,000 years before Rogers, the Roman Statesman and attorney Cicero (106–43 BCE) said 'If you wish to persuade me, you must think my thoughts, feel my feelings and speak my words.' His approach to *classical argument* is based on the belief that you can get people to change their minds by applying the following formula:

- ✔ **Introduction:** You set the scene for changing minds, suggesting that something important is about to happen. You can tell a story that illustrates your point or highlights the need to resolve a problem.

- ✔ **Narration:** You provide background information to help your opponent, – as Cicero defined the person you aim to persuade – understand the issue. This section can include research and references to others' opinions on the subject.

- ✔ **Partition:** You list the points that you aim to prove. You can also highlight the areas that you and the other side agree and disagree on.

- ✔ **Confirmation:** You present the proof of your case and the main points of contention. You can include evidence, examples and quotations from reliable sources. Each point is addressed through *deductive reasoning*, in which you argue from accepted fact to its implication, or *inductive reasoning*, in which you argue your points by using examples.

- ✔ **Refutation:** You take the other person's position and show why her points aren't valid. Of course, you should address the most likely counterarguments and do so respectfully, fairly and accurately.

- ✔ **Conclusion:** You sum up your points, appealing to your listeners' emotions and helping them understand the significance of your proposal. You encourage them to change their attitudes, rousing them to take a specific course of action. Cicero's classical argument approach is most appropriate when you want to demonstrate your knowledge about the specifics of your subject as well as where you found your information and is particularly useful for anyone arguing a case in court.

Creating an Attractive Position

Having figured out the points you're going to address, you need to present your position in terms that inspire and resonate with your listener. The more attractive your position, the more compelling your case.

Language that is vibrant, appealing and tangible is infinitely more persuasive than words and phrases that are dull, dry and dreary.

To create an attractive position, find out as much about your audience as you can, tailor your approach to meet their needs and be willing to compromise. Be prepared to give and take in order to produce a shared, sustainable solution. See Chapter 5 for tips on compromising.

Showing that you're credible, willing to learn and open to new ideas demonstrates that you're prepared to come up with a solution that satisfies everyone.

Illuminating advantages and shared benefits

Sometimes the shared benefits that may result from a proposal are clear, in which case creating an attractive position is relatively easy. When the mutual advantages are less obvious, you have to sharpen your antennae and collect further information. You may also need to alter your initial proposal or incorporate compromises.

While some people resist compromising and see it as a sign of weakness, the smart persuaders know that compromising demonstrates that you value the other person. Rather than risking the loss of a possible long-term relationship by forcing your approach onto others, seek to find solutions that benefit each of you. Burning bridges is a dangerous game to play with anyone you work with. You never know when your paths may cross in the future or who she knows who may be beneficial to you. The advantages of compromising are that it's a natural style for most people and it's a fair way of making a decision.

Without asking questions, listening to answers and assimilating what you understand to be true for the other person, you're going to struggle to figure out the shared benefits inherent in your proposal. (Chapter 7 highlights the importance of listening in the persuasion process.)

As you put together your proposition, closely study the issues that matter to your audience. Engage the individuals you plan to speak to in conversations and observe them in meetings to collect essential data. Refer to your trusted confidants (see the section 'Testing your ideas with trusted confidants' earlier in this chapter). The more you know about what worries the decision-makers and keeps them awake at night, the more you can position your proposal to soothe their anxieties.

George is responsible for process engineering at a manufacturing company that supplies parts to the aviation industry. He was excited about his new design for the work flow for routine maintenance, which significantly shortened the turnaround time for servicing. Before presenting his proposal to the company's managing director, he spoke with Alex, a colleague in the company who knows the MD well and is aware of his business concerns. Alex informed George that the MD was more concerned about profitability than speed and explained that the most important point to highlight was how the new system could increase the company's profits in the short term by lowering the operating costs.

At first George was flummoxed as he had planned to focus on efficiency and was planning on requesting additional funding to make the process work. However, after finding out about the MD's concerns, George revisited his proposal and made considerable changes to his position in order to make it more appealing to the MD. By adapting his approach, including changing the design so it no longer required further investment, George was able to drive down costs. He then meticulously documented both the cost savings and increases in profitability that the company would achieve and presented his new plan to the MD. Having responded to Alex's feedback, George presented a proposal that addressed the MD's concerns and won the go-ahead for the project.

Making the benefits tangible with vivid language

Words can hypnotise and entrance – or bore a person senseless. When you're putting together a compelling case, make sure that your words fall into the first category.

While facts and figures are likely a necessary part of your proposal (see the 'Evaluating the evidence' section earlier in this chapter), they don't establish emotional connections. Present your evidence in a way that captures and contains your listener's attention by including examples, stories, metaphors and analogies to give life and soul to your position.

As I say in Chapter 3, people buy on emotion and justify with fact. Personal stories and anecdotes are engaging and make your points come alive. From the orators of ancient Mesopotamia to the great persuaders of today, people use vivid and compelling language to emphasise what's important, stimulate emotion, increase understanding and spur others to action. (See the sidebar 'Oratory and the political stage' for more.)

Dull language conveys a lack of original thought and is a lazy way of speaking. If you want to grab your listeners' attention, avoid phrases like, 'This year's profits were up by 50 per cent'; see how they react when you say, 'Our profits soared 50 per cent over last year's results.'

Lively language enthrals your listener and makes what you're saying easy to understand while adding interest, originality and vibrancy to your message. Focussing on active, descriptive and specific verbs propels your thoughts along and is a good place to start when you want to energise your language and boost your listeners' attention. Avoid jargon, like *right-sizing* and *strategising* as such phrases can quickly become stale and annoying.

Studies show that reports that rely solely on market research, financial projections and other forms of hard data are perceived as not entirely informative or comprehensible. Because numbers are abstract, they fail to be meaningful or memorable to most audience members. By contrast, stories and vivid language capture your audience's attention and enable people to relate to the points you're making, especially when these stories and language tie into the subject you're discussing.

Oratory and the political stage

Ted Sorensen, the late John F. Kennedy's speech writer, described words as being the tools that the President of the United States uses to run the country and garner the support of the world.

The popularity of oratory in politics has ebbed and flowed over the centuries. In the early 18th century, political speeches were read rather than presented, and the public perceived politicians as untrustworthy if they appeared hungry for power. As a result, oratory was seen as an undesirable attribute. By the late 18th century, that view changed and oratory became a desirable skill for politicians – sometimes with disastrous consequences.

✔ William Henry Harrison (1773–1841), the ninth president of the United States, was portrayed by his opponents as a frontier fighter and hard-drinking man, encamped in a simple log cabin. In fact, he was a member of the Virginia aristocracy and a student of history and the classics.

Following his election, he was determined to rehabilitate his reputation, using his inaugural address as his platform. In spite of his rhetorical flourishes, he failed to consider the axiom 'less is more' and spoke for three hours on a freezing cold day in March 1841. Less than a month later, Harrison, who had caught a cold the day of his inauguration, died of pneumonia.

✔ On the other hand, Abraham Lincoln's Gettysburg address (1863) is one of the greatest speeches ever delivered. Limited to a mere 278 words, Lincoln's speech captured the hearts and minds of his audience.

✔ Former President Bill Clinton says that he tries to make his speeches like a piece of jazz music, in which he's got the words and rhythm in place and grants himself the chance to ad-lib in the middle. As Clinton says, the impact of your words isn't just about their beauty but also whether they change the way people both think and feel.

The following rhetorical devises can unleash the great power of words. Consider adding a few – three or four – to your next presentation to add power and passion:

- **Anaphora:** You repeat the same word or phrase at the beginning of each sentence in order to build emotion. Churchill's war-time speech in which he repeated the phrase 'We shall . . .' utilised anaphora. In your own speech, you can say something along the lines of

   'We shall work in harmony. We shall seek a mutually satisfying solution. We shall never give up until we reach our goal.'

- **Epistrophe:** You repeat the same word or phrase at the end of a sentence in order to make an emphatic point. Barack Obama's speech at the 2004 Democratic National Convention emphasised the inclusive quality of the United States of America by stressing the word 'America' at the end of his phrases. For example, in your speech you can stress the word 'confidence':

   'You can conquer your fears when you act with confidence. You can thwart your foes when you act with confidence. You can achieve your goals when you act with confidence.'

- **Parallelism:** You repeat the same syntax, such as verb–adverb–noun, which adds balance, rhythm and clarity to the thought. For example:

   'By failing to agree to this proposal, I believe that we'll lose our competitive edge, reduce our healthy net profits and risk our loyal customer relationships.'

- **Antithesis:** You join together two contrasting or opposing ideas to create a relationship between them, enriching the debate. For example:

   'Rather than focusing on the cost, let's focus on the value. Rather than focusing on the risk, let's focus on the reward. Rather than focusing on the problems, let's focus on the opportunities.'

   You may notice that in this example, I also include anaphora to build emotion.

- **Climax:** You lay out ideas to increase their power, emphasise their importance and build emotion. This approach combines profundity, emotion and vibrancy. Martin Luther King Jr.'s 'I Have a Dream' speech in which he repeats this famous phrase is an example of a climactic approach, in which the last thing the listener hears is what they remember.

   For example, when you build your case for a new project, you can say,

   'Implementation of this project is vital, not just for the success of the team, my personal success or the CEO's success. It's vital to the success of our company's shareholders.'

✔ **Anticlimax:** You bring something that's emotionally charged down to a moderate level. For example:

'What's your concern? Losing your investment? Feeling insecure? Making a choice?'

✔ **Inoculation:** You anticipate and answer objections before they arise to allow your case to move forward without being challenged. You bring up your listener's concern and offer a counterargument, quashing the concern before it's stated. For example:

'Some of you may be concerned about a drop in productivity from changing desk locations, so what we've done is given IT and Facilities management overtime to have everything put into place over the weekend, ready for Monday morning.'

✔ **Transitions:** You help organise the listener's thinking, saying what's been said and leading onto what follows. For example:

'Up to this point, we've been talking about . . .

Now, I'd like to open the discussion to address . . .'

✔ **Hypophora:** You ask a question that may be on your listener's mind or that's beyond your audience's current knowledge level, and then answer it. This technique maintains your listener's curiosity and interest. For example:

'You may ask 'what does this have to do with our quarterly budget. Well, the answer is . . .'

More than talk

Margaret works with young offenders who've been incarcerated for crimes ranging from theft to drug dealing to assault with a deadly weapon. An upper-middle-class white woman, Margaret – from outward appearances – seems to have nothing in common with the boys she mentors.

With each new group, she tells the boys stories from her life to build an emotional connection and rapport. Like many of the lads she works with, Margaret comes from a single-parent family and has had to help support her siblings. She also tells them that when she was an actress working on television, she lived what some may see as a glamorous

lifestyle – meeting A-listers, attending award ceremonies and travelling to exotic locations. 'Then,' she says, 'I met cocaine.' From here, she outlines in graphic detail her downward spiral until she took hold of her actions and turned her life around.

By telling her stories in vivid detail, she establishes credibility, trust and an emotional connection with her audience. She makes them more willing to engage, connect and be persuaded to reconsider their options for their lives after serving their sentences. As a result of the compelling way that she opens up and tells her stories, Margaret is consistently ranked in the top three most influential people in the prisoners' lives.

Chapter 5

Establishing Your Credibility

● ●

In This Chapter

▶ Proving your prowess

▶ Building on your personal connections

▶ Demonstrating your trustworthiness

▶ Sharing and soliciting opinions

● ●

*E*stablishing your credibility is the cornerstone of persuasion. When you present an audience with a new idea, for instance, their first response is to determine whether you're credible. What you're suggesting may be risky for them in terms of time and resources, and they may be reluctant to take on board what you're asking of them.

Nobel-Prize-winning peace activist and Burmese opposition politician Aung San Suu Kyi, former CNN journalist Christiane Amanpour and former South African President Nelson Mandela are credible individuals. They live their values by displaying trustworthiness and consistency. They are accountable for their actions and they can be depended on to follow through on their beliefs.

Credible people are trustworthy. You can count on them doing what they say they're going to do. You can believe what they tell you. Credible people do their homework and come to the table prepared, informed and with open minds. You can trust them to listen, act in the best interest of others and share credit for good ideas. Are you credible?

Integrity, consistency and the ability to resist radical mood swings are fundamental to establishing your credibility. If you lack sufficient credibility, you stand little chance of influencing people's behaviour or persuading them to take on board your suggestions. The good news is that credibility is a quality you can develop and nurture.

In this chapter you discover the components that constitute a credible person. I also show you how, with desire and practice, you can develop your credible characteristics, increasing your ability to persuade and influence others.

Developing Robust Relationships

Many managers, mothers, friends and lovers overestimate their credibility. They don't understand that credibility derives from two factors: the level of expertise others perceive in them and the relationships they establish.

✔ At the heart of robust relationships is integrity. Respect, reliability and an ability to communicate with openness, honesty and trust fit into the mix, too. You know when your relationship is robust because you support – and are supported by – one another, and you listen without judging. Disagreements are resolved with respect, support and by treating individuals as equals. If you find yourself in a relationship where criticism, contempt, defensiveness and a refusal to cooperate are commonplace, your relationship's in big trouble.

✔ When you hold a track record of sound judgment, or show that you know your stuff about your topic, products or proposals, you're bound to receive high ratings for the expertise factor. (See Chapter 6 for more information about the persuasive value of expertise.)

✔ When you consistently prove that you're a good listener, that you remember the best interests of others, and that you're generous in sharing credit for new ideas, your relationships flourish.

You build robust relationships by listening, offering supportive and constructive feedback (when solicited, of course), and working in the best interests of others. Demonstrating an interest in others, without becoming intrusive or just plain nosy, shows people you care about them, creating a considerate and open environment, ripe for you to apply your influencing skills.

In the following sections I explore ways of building robust relationships. If you take an interest in others, they feel valued and worthy. When you demonstrate trustworthiness, people are willing to follow your lead. Helping and supporting others shows that you care about them, and they in turn will want to help you. When you act in an honest, reliable and steadfast manner, people know they're in safe hands and trust that you can be counted on to consistently behave with integrity.

Taking an interest in others

Robust relationships develop when you're genuinely interested in the other person. Show sincere curiosity and concern for others, and they respond willingly to your suggestions. People are prepared to help you if you take an interest in them.

People aren't stupid. They know when your curiosity is authentic and when it's strictly for your own personal gain. Feign interest and they're likely to reject your interest in a second. Pretend to care when you couldn't care less, and the conversation comes to an end. Even worse, they may show you the door.

Proving to someone that you're interested in them requires giving them your full and complete attention. Find out about their interests, aspirations, views and concerns. Doing so builds bonds. Think about what their needs, concerns and motivators may be. To avoid guessing and making incorrect assumptions and to show that you're genuinely interested in what's important to them, ask people the following:

✔ What do they require to do their jobs well?

✔ What's getting in their way?

✔ What inspires, drives and motivates them to come to work every day?

The more you know about other people, the more effectively you can create rapport (see Chapter 2). And the stronger the rapport you establish, the greater the mutually satisfying results you can produce.

When you take an interest in others, you build their confidence and self-esteem. You make them feel important, valued and worthwhile. Let someone know that they matter and watch them respond positively to your opinions, thoughts and recommendations.

The following highlight some of the most effective ways you can show your interest in others:

✔ **Look them in the eyes.** Whether you're meeting them for the first time or have a regular on-going relationship, look other people in the eyes when you speak with them. Looking people in the eyes with your eyes opened and focused on theirs makes you come across as friendly and sincere. Notice how other people use their eyes when they're being friendly and sincere. If you're unsure as to how you come across, practise in front of a mirror or with a friend until you feel comfortable with looking people in the eye. You can read more about the power of eye contact in Chapter 13.

Even if you only have a few seconds to engage, use that time to make the other person feel like he's the most important person in the room. If you're engaging with a group, do everything you can to share a few seconds of visual connection with each person individually. Have your eyes ready and open to catch other people's eyes as they're talking. When you lock eyes with someone who's been talking and scanning the room, you can make him feel like you've been listening to him the whole time.

✔ **Call them by name.** Using a person's name in all forms of communication makes him feel acknowledged as an individual. When you remember someone's name, you pay the person a subtle compliment, indicating that he made an impression on you. If you struggle to remember important details like names, titles and more, pick up a copy of *Improving Your Memory For Dummies* by John B. Arden (Wiley).

✔ **Pay attention.** Respond to what others tell you by paraphrasing back what you hear and reacting empathetically. Avoid responding in parrot-like fashion. Doing so is insulting and shows that you're not really engaged. Instead, actively listen for both what the person says and the underlying feelings you observe. Read more about the value of active listening in Chapter 7.

✔ **Provide encouragement.** Encourage others and watch their spirits lift, their self-confidence rise and their efforts soar (see Chapter 12). Encouragement stimulates cooperation and contribution, and forms bonds, understanding and acceptance. See the 'Trusting others – and being trustworthy' and 'Helping others' sections, later in this chapter, for more.

Encouragement and praise are different. The consensus among teaching professionals is that children should be encouraged rather than praised, because praise can lead to competitiveness while encouragement leads to further success. I understand what the educators are saying, and still believe that praising someone boosts morale.

✔ **Offer words of praise.** A genuine compliment can make a person's day. Incorporate admiring comments and flattering remarks, or simply say something nice about someone else to help build self-esteem.

✔ **Maintain contact in the old-fashioned way.** If you're anything like me, your inbox is heaving with unanswered emails waiting for a response. So choose to connect via a quick phone call, a card or (gasp!) a letter sent through the post. Even if all you're saying is 'Hi. I'm thinking of you,' the effort shows that you care.

More often than not, people make contact these days because they want something from other people. Be different. Break from the pack. When you get in touch the old-fashioned way just because someone's on your mind, you let the person know you care about him as a person and not as a potential source of information, customers, clients or whatever.

✔ **Ask questions.** Asking questions shows that you're interested. Whether you're asking about a colleague's plans for the weekend or inquiring after family, showing that you're curious about what's important to others encourages them to share what's important to them with you. Asking simple, non-threatening questions about the other person, like 'What are your plans for the holidays?' 'What line of work are you in?' or

'Where are you from?' is a way to get the ball rolling if you don't know the other person. If you know the person moderately well, you can ask about his interests, and as you get to know people better, you can ask more searching and interesting questions such as 'If you could live your life over, what would you like to do?' It is said that small minds talk about people, moderate minds talk about events and great minds talk about ideas.

✔ **Acknowledge people.** When you acknowledge others, you're letting them know you value them and think they're important. Paying attention to others, even if only for a moment, contributes to their sense of self-worth. You rise in their esteem. Whether you say a friendly hello in the hallway, seek out someone's company at a large gathering or recognise another person's efforts in a public forum, you show that you're someone who cares about and takes an interest in others.

✔ **Demonstrate respect.** In order to earn respect, you've got to show respect. To me, *respect* means remembering people's names, showing consideration for their time and space, valuing them as individuals. Gossiping, acting inconsistently and behaving in a false manner are all disrespectful. These tactics don't earn you any brownie points – and ultimately strain relationships. For more about treating people with respect, flip to Chapters 1 and 3.

✔ **Remember special events in people's lives.** Birthdays, anniversaries and holidays are times to let people know you're interested enough in them to take time to acknowledge milestones in their lives. My sister gave me a perpetual calendar with the birthdates and anniversaries of family members, to which I've added friends, colleagues and clients. I keep the calendar by my desk, where I can see a month at a time, giving me no excuse for missing those important dates. Buy cards whenever you get the chance and keep them in your desk with a book of stamps. You can also record important dates on your computer to remind you when an event is coming up. Online greeting cards make sending messages simple and fun.

Trusting others – and being trustworthy

When people trust you, they're receptive to your suggestions. They open up to you, and you can guide them to where you want them to go. The basic ground rules apply whether you're building trust in a one-to-one relationship or with a group. As long as you demonstrate that you're credible, reliable and that you keep to your word, while displaying confidence and knowledge, you can establish trusting relationships with swarms of people as well as individuals.

Being trustworthy is about your behaviour not your personality. Failing to follow through on commitments, promises and obligations fails to win you friends and influence people. Unless you want to establish your credibility as a person who can only be trusted to fail to follow through, always do what you say you'll do. See the 'Following through on promises' section, later in this chapter, for more.

Factors that contribute to your trustworthiness include:

✔ How long someone has known you

✔ Your reputation as a person of your word

✔ Past experiences people have had with you

✔ What others say about you

✔ Any ulterior motives you may harbour

In order for you to establish your credibility, you have to demonstrate your trustworthiness. Don't be surprised if people try to test you on that point. If someone doesn't know you, they may be suspicious of you and what you want from them. The other person may try to test you to discover any prejudices or biases you hold and seek to reveal any ulterior motives you may be hiding.

Respond to these trustworthiness tests by behaving in a consistent manner. When people see you acting in ways that they're used to, you confirm their existing attitudes and beliefs about you. Their doubts will soon fade. If someone's testing or confronting you, rather than urging him to trust you – or even worse, asking why he doesn't – skip the verbal debates and focus on your behaviour. Actions really do speak louder than words.

Helping others

Helping others shows that you're a good person. Building a relationship based on trust, and demonstrating a desire to assist people, enhances your reputation and establishes your credibility as someone who puts the well-being of others high on your agenda. Lending a hand can take various forms, including offering information, providing introductions, cooking someone a meal, helping out with homework or doing anything that makes someone's life easier.

The first step in helping other people is to listen to what they tell you. Rather than giving advice, ask questions. Seek to understand what their concerns are before diving head first into providing solutions and offering answers. Coming up with recommendations is pointless unless you know what people need. In Chapter 7, I share tips and techniques for effective questioning as part of listening.

Exceeding expectations and providing extra value enhances your reputation as a helpful person. See Chapter 12 for more on expectations. For example, if you agree to meet someone for lunch, call the restaurant and book a table. If the restaurant doesn't take reservations and it's a popular place where it's hard to get a table, arrive early so that when the other person shows up you're already seated and he doesn't have to stand in line. If you're making a presentation, anticipate questions in advance, so when they come, you're prepared to answer them. Even if no one asks a question you thought they might, you can include it in your presentation by saying something like, 'People often ask me . . .' By having provided unexpected and relevant information, you impress your listeners by surpassing their expectations.

The feel-good factor of making a positive impact on another person's life is a tonic. Even if you're having a hideous day, by helping out another person you can head to bed knowing you made a constructive contribution to someone else's life.

At least once a week, help someone however best you can. Whether you're lending a hand at the office or assisting family and friends, you can find plenty of ways to bring benefit to others. Some ways you can make a positive contribution to other people's lives include:

- Contributing to an online forum
- Commenting on a blog
- Sending out a positive tweet
- Forwarding useful information to people on your contact list
- Driving someone to an appointment
- Collecting a friend's child from school
- Preparing a tasty meal, setting the table and cleaning up afterwards

What goes around comes around. When you help others, they're likely to help you in return.

Behaving honestly, steadily and reliably

For you to establish your credibility, you've got to be honest, steady and reliable. Whether you're selling an actual product, your research related to a product or even just an idea, if people can't trust you to be steady, honest and reliable, you have little chance of establishing your credibility. Away from an office environment it's equally important that you behave in a steady, honest and reliable way. You wouldn't want someone lacking in any of these three qualities to look after your aged parents or ill child, nor would you encourage someone lacking in these attributes to housesit while you're on vacation.

While the three characteristics overlap and are frequently used interchange-ably, subtle differences exist:

- **Steady.** A steady person is sensible and able to make rational decisions.

- **Honest.** Someone who is honest embodies integrity, truthfulness and straightforwardness.

- **Reliable.** You can count on a reliable person to do what he says he's going to do. Consistent, dependable, responsible and trustworthy are synonyms for this characteristic.

People who demonstrate honesty, steadfastness and reliability seek to under-stand through active listening (see Chapter 7) and working in the best inter-ests of others. They have an advantage when going into any situation that requires persuasion because, through their past performances, they prove that others can trust them.

To prove that you're reliable, do what you say you're going to do. If you want to verify that you're an honest person, be straightforward, up front and tell the truth. And if you want to confirm your steadfastness, behave in a stable, sensible and consistent manner.

According to Shakespeare, honesty is the best policy, and I'm not about to argue with the Bard. That said, in the minds of many, honesty and integrity are for others, not for them. In other words, what's good for the goose may not be so good for the gander.

In a survey conducted by Starwood Hotels and Resorts, 82 per cent of CEOs admitted to cheating at golf. The same percentage said they loathe people who cheat. It sounds to me like there's a mismatch here. While people demand honesty from others, they're willing to be flexible with the truth when it suits them. You only have to look at the examples of corporate greed and dishonesty from the last few years to see that, for some, honesty and integrity aren't a top priority. That said, many organisations include in their hiring practices and codes of conduct honesty, integrity and reliability as part of their core values.

Confucius based his principles of honesty on treating people how you want them to treat you. Harmony is fundamental to Confucian philosophy and a recognition that eventually everyone will be at the mercy of others. Therefore, you put yourself in the context of your whole life and future generations, choosing to do or say nothing that would tarnish your family's reputation for honesty.

Because most Westerners struggle to understand these deep notions of hon-esty, the Chinese and Japanese often refer to those who don't understand the Confucian notions of honesty as barbarians, or people who don't share a recognised culture.

If you want to apply Confucian practices of honesty in your own life – seeking harmony and mutual consensus – aim to behave with dignity, self-respect and an understanding of all people.

Different cultures and social systems have different view of what's honest. Before going into a negotiation or engaging in any relationship that goes beyond surface-level interactions with someone from a culture different to yours, take the time to find out more about the other person's customs, beliefs, values and behaviours. In addition to speaking with people who have lived and worked in different cultures, you can find a lot of information about cultural differences on the Internet. There is also a host of information about different cultures and social systems in *Cross-cultural Selling For Dummies* by Michael Soon Lee and Ralph R Roberts (Wiley) as well as in my book *Body Language For Dummies* (Wiley).

When preparing to persuade, make an honest assessment of where you stand in terms of your credibility and expertise. (In Chapter 6, I address the inter-relationship between expertise and credibility.) Ask yourself the following questions in order to determine how well you're doing:

✔ How might others perceive my knowledge about what I'm proposing? How well do I know the products, the strategies or the reasons behind what I'm proposing?

✔ How good is my track record in the area I'm seeking to persuade someone to consider? Do people know about and respect what I've done in this area in the past?

✔ How does each person I want to persuade view me? Do people see me as honest, reliable and supportive?

✔ Do the people I want to persuade perceive me as being emotionally, politically and intellectually in synch with them?

✔ Who do I trust enough to give me an honest evaluation on my answers to the preceding questions?

Honesty, which I write about in this section, and integrity, which I explore in the following section, are at the foundation of robust relationships. Both honesty and integrity imply trust, and without trust relationships don't stand a chance of succeeding.

Reflecting Your Integrity

My clients frequently speak of integrity and how important it is to them in establishing and maintaining relationships. When I ask them to define the term, they tend to stumble and stutter as they search for definitions that make sense and provide frameworks they can live by as well. They often use words and phrases like 'soundness', 'stability', 'sincerity', 'honesty', 'incorruptibility' and 'showing good sense'. My favourite definition to date is, 'Integrity is doing the right thing, even when nobody's watching.'

Integrity is undoubtedly a virtue. Philosophers define integrity in a number of different ways, sometimes leaving me scratching my head and wondering what they're talking about. The meaning of the word depends on the context in which you're applying it. For example, an ecosystem, a database and a work of art can all display integrity.

To keep things simple and practical, I'm talking about integrity as a person's or organisation's general character. In this section, I focus on integrity as the relationship you have with yourself, and acting with fairness and honesty while considering the implications of what you're doing and the effect it may have.

Integrity is about doing what is right rather than what is convenient. Whether at work, home or play, when you act like the good person you appear to be, you're acting with integrity. When you act with integrity, you stand up for what you believe in and do what you say you're going to do. You can be counted on to keep your promises and consider what's best for everyone rather than what suits your own personal goals.

Dr William Menninger, the US psychiatrist and co-founder of the Menninger Foundation in Topeka, Kansas, considered integrity to be one of the six essential elements that are the key to success, the others being sincerity, humility, courtesy, wisdom and charity.

Behaving ethically

Ethical behaviour is at the heart of integrity. Without ethical behaviour at the core of business, an organisation risks its reputation, credibility and long-term performance. The same is true for your behaviour in the world outside the office walls. Respecting the dignity and rights of other people while behaving with honesty, responsibility and fairness is as important in your private life as in your public dealings with others.

Ethical behaviour includes acting honestly, fairly and impartially. When you behave in an ethical manner, you respect the dignity, diversity and rights of groups and individuals. Someone who is truly ethical behaves in a responsible way, treating people fairly and with honesty, even when doing so is inconvenient or difficult.

Ethical behaviour is about doing the right thing. When a company acts in ways its stakeholders consider to be fair and honest, it takes into account the *impact* of its decisions – who does the decision affect or harm? – as well as the *fairness* of its decisions – will everyone affected consider the decision to be fair?

Some business leaders believe that ethical behaviour increases costs and reduces profits, thus justifying expense-cutting choices such as hiring child labour at low wages in developing countries. Turning a blind eye to the fairness factor, they see paying below-minimum wages as simply another way of lowering costs. On the other hand, some businesses, such as the Fairtrade Foundation (`www.fairtrade.org.uk`), have established an ethical brand through a belief that consumers are willing to pay more for products from companies that respect the environment and offer acceptable wages. As a result, these companies see their sales increasing, offsetting their higher costs.

Businesses can assess their approach and commitment to integrity by asking:

✔ What approach does the company take to instil ethical behaviour when considering its short- and long-term strategic and operational goals?

✔ How does the company define behaving with integrity, how will it be achieved, and what does success look like in terms of profitability and other measures?

✔ How do the company's values, code of behaviour and support systems fortify and promote integrity throughout the organisation?

Business practices that meet the requirements of the law but are considered unfair by stakeholders – including the public – can lead to bad publicity. For example, while restaurants paying minimum wage and keeping a portion of staff tips to boost profits are not breaking the law, they run the risk of losing goodwill.

Identifying and evaluating factors that affect an organisation's integrity, and recommending and implementing strategies to protect the business are part of a leader's job. You need to have an appropriate framework in place if you're sincere about promoting integrity in the workplace, as Figure 5-1 shows. Begin by setting standards that promote high levels of integrity. Then communicate the expectations of integrity and ethical behaviour to ensure that the standards, values and processes are clearly understood. In addition, endorse and practise a strong culture of integrity. Thirdly, ensure that any cases of failure to adhere to the rules of conduct are reported and investigated, protecting whistleblowers from victimisation and discrimination. Manage any breaches of standards, and guarantee that everyone is treated fairly. Finally, monitor the effectiveness of the integrity framework to assure that it's working as it's meant to.

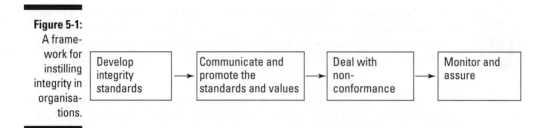

Promoting a culture of integrity and ethical behaviour requires time, resources and commitment, as well as continued scrutinising and supervising by leaders at all levels of the organisation. This is as true for raising a family as it is for running a business. No matter what institution you're involved with, if you fail to promote integrity as a core value, ultimately the organisation will fail.

Acting consistently

Consistency and credibility go hand in hand and reflect both your personal integrity and the integrity of your organisation. For example, you must unwaveringly:

✔ Deliver on your promises each and every time.

✔ Communicate the same values and assurances in your materials (both printed and online), the words you speak and the actions you take.

✔ Focus on your goals and don't give up until you achieve them.

✔ Behave with trustworthiness and honesty.

If you don't act consistently, you can count on customers, colleague, friends and family discounting you as someone they can rely on. If you say you're going to do something, do it. If you want to gain someone's respect, follow through on your promises. If you want to be seen as a person of integrity, consistently demonstrate honesty, reliability and credibility.

In spite of the amount of hype today about branding in the context of businesses and products, I still encourage my clients to think of themselves as brands. A *brand* is a promise, a long-term relationship based on trust, respect and consistency. Building your personal brand takes time and patience, plus dedication and persistence. Being consistent in fulfilling your promise, living up to your values, defining your personality and confirming your character adds to your credibility.

People buy brands based on how the brand makes them feel. If you want people to buy your personal brand, you've got to appeal to their feelings (see Chapter 13). Credibility and consistency are integral to touching on feelings while developing and selling a brand.

Build credibility with your clients through consistent communication. Use email newsletters, blogs, LinkedIn, Facebook, Twitter and other online communication portals to efficiently and consistently communicate with your audience. Send out emails – remembering to keep them short, sweet and succinct – on a regular basis and keep your website up-to-date, in order to position yourself as a credible expert in your field. Track how people respond in order to identify worthwhile efforts and continually hone your approach.

No matter how small the step you take towards reaching your goal, when you behave consistently you're perceived as credible. You become known as the kind of person who takes action to achieving his goals, making the ensuing steps that much easier because you're behaving consistently.

Tell other people about your goals in order to magnify the pull of the principles of consistency and credibility. Studies show that, when you set a goal for yourself and take even a small action, you create commitment within yourself to follow through on achieving what you set out to do. In order to build on that commitment and motivate yourself to continue in your quest, you behave in ways that show you to be consistent in reaching your goal. In short, you create a personal desire to be – and for others to see you as – consistent with what you already did. In Chapter 11, I address the need for consistency when persuading people.

When you're persuading people or influencing their behaviour, gain their commitment by starting off small. By getting people to adhere to your request, you contribute to their new view of themselves. Chances are that the next time you ask them for something, they'll act in a manner consistent with their previous behaviour, even if your request is a big one.

People want to back up their previous commitments or stated beliefs with behaviours that are consistent with what they did or said before. Capitalise on this human instinct by reminding people of what they've said or done in the past. You can also remind people that when they behave in a reliable and predictable way they build trusting relationships.

Keeping an open mind

You never know where a new and improved idea could come from, so keep your mind open. An open mind enhances your integrity by showing that you're receptive to points of view you haven't previously considered, opinions you haven't pondered and beliefs you may have disregarded or overlooked.

In order to ensure your mind is open and ready for new ideas, ask questions, listen and, above all, don't judge. People want you to hear them not evaluate them. While you must critique – and even reject – some ideas and proposals from time to time, don't press the eject button when you first hear about them. (See Chapter 13 for more on letting go of judgmental attitudes.)

While keeping your mind open to feedback and criticism can be a painful process, particularly if you don't like what you hear, you can also see the process as enlightening. Choose to let yourself understand the impact of your behaviour and then do something positive about it. See the 'Soliciting and receiving feedback' section for more.

Aristotle said that an educated mind can entertain a thought without having to accept it. Keeping your mind open to others' ideas can teach you something new or change your perspective on what you previously thought. Freeing yourself of judgment, preconceived notions and personal expectations enables you to view each situation in the clearest, most unbiased way possible and can help you avoid unnecessary conflict.

The following are some techniques that can build your open-mindedness:

- **Apply the rules of brainstorming to your other interactions.** As a result, you specifically:
  - Encourage all ideas.
  - Don't evaluate or criticise ideas when someone first suggests them. Avoid discussing and judging ideas until every possibility has been put forward.
  - Let yourself be as out there in your thinking as you can. Often, the wackiest ideas end up being the most effective.
  - Aim for quantity not quality. You can always weed later.
  - Encourage everyone to come up with new combinations of and improvements on old ideas.
- **Validate differing viewpoints by accepting that disagreement doesn't mean somebody has to be wrong.** When you rid yourself of the notion that people who feel and think differently to you are wrong, you open your mind both analytically and emotionally, even if your viewpoint remains the same.

✔ **Rid yourself of any anger you may feel, and refuse to accuse or belittle other people.** Acting in a disrespectful manner is the fastest route to closing minds. Remind yourself of how you feel when someone puts you down, and resolve not to inflict this feeling on others.

✔ **Research and ask questions about points of view that are different from yours.** If you're against the ownership of guns, for example, seek the opinions of those who are in favour in order to gain insight into their reasoning. Open-mindedness occurs when you let go of the idea that people who feel differently from you are misinformed or less intelligent.

✔ **Listen to what the other person is saying.** While you may be shocked by what you hear, or doubt or be suspicious of what is said, rid your mind of negative chatter. Also, by taking time to listen to someone, he may reciprocate the favour. In Chapter 7 you can find more about listening with an open mind.

✔ **If you're uncomfortable with the differences, seek to find similarities.** When you fixate on the opposite, you fail to see the likeness. Let go of old assumptions, no matter how comfortable and natural they feel, and embrace a new way of viewing people, places and things.

✔ **Remain open to the ideas and reasoning of people whose viewpoint is different from yours.** While you may struggle to see their point of view, if you let go of judgment and see things from their perspective you may find new and exciting ways of approaching challenges.

✔ **Contribute like a collaborator.** Don't hold back from offering your ideas. Just like you're not supposed to judge others' ideas, don't judge your own.

✔ **Step out of your comfort zone in every way you can, as long as the ways are legal.** Sample food you thought you'd never touch, travel to somewhere you never found interesting, try a hobby or sport that never caught your interest. Whether you end up loving or loathing the activity, your opinion after you try it is now based on personal experience rather than close-minded conjecture.

✔ **If someone's beliefs or moral codes are contrary to yours, let this difference be okay.** Being open-minded means that you're willing to accept other people's way of thinking and that your way is not the only way. Rather than defending your own point based on a belief that you're right and they're wrong, simply take yourself out of the situation.

✔ **Look for little points of connection.** Even though someone's world view is totally different from or even conflicts with yours, this individual can still offer at least an idea or two that you can agree with. Look for those connections and build from there.

Demonstrating a willingness to compromise

When you're establishing your credibility and reflecting your integrity, make sure you show you're willing to compromise. Consider these bits of information:

- ✔ Top leaders establish their credibility in many ways, including by listening to others and incorporating their viewpoints into a shared solution.

- ✔ Research shows that managers can only persuade employees and clients to change their attitudes, opinions and behaviours when they demonstrate that they themselves are willing to change theirs.

- ✔ According to the Anglo-Irish statesman Edmund Burke (1729–1797), 'Every human benefit and enjoyment, every virtue and every prudent act is founded on compromise and barter.'

Because being willing to compromise is a powerful attribute, the best persuaders often come to the process prepared with some well-thought-out compromises at the ready. As part of your homework prior to an important discussion or negotiation, clearly identify the specific things you're willing to be flexible about, as well as what you can let go of completely.

Think of persuasion as a process rather than as an event. Avoid making your case with an up-front hard-sell approach based on dogged determination, rational thinking or a bubbly presentation. All you're doing is giving the other person a clear target to shoot at with both barrels blazing. Taking this approach makes others resist compromise, because they see any concession they may have been prepared to make as a form of surrendering to your line of attack.

People only open up to persuasion when they believe that you accept and appreciate their needs and concerns. If you act like it's your way or the highway, you're going to set yourself up for a big bump. See Chapter 2 for more on seeing things from other people's points of view.

Make sure you listen to other people's viewpoints and include them in your approach. Forget about presenting an award-winning argument, and simply act with sensitivity instead as you seek a shared solution while integrating others' inputs.

Being successful requires being open-minded and willing to integrate compromises. When people see that you're keen to understand their perspectives and construct changes that include their needs and concerns, they react positively.

Sharing credit

Helping other people gain recognition and progress their careers builds rapport (see Chapter 10) and can lead to outstanding results. When you credit a friend or family member for a job well done, you raise their self-esteem as well as enhancing your relationship with them.

When you highlight other people's efforts, they see you in a positive light. They are likely to repay the favour whenever and however they can. Giving others credit whenever possible shows that you're generous, thoughtful and considerate of their needs and feelings – all qualities of a credible person.

If you fail to share credit, people tend not to trust you. You may soon find yourself operating in a vacuum as people seek other departments to work in or other people to work with.

There are plenty of ways you can share credit by using simple yet effective phrases. Phrases like 'You did a really good job of boosting morale while we struggled to get the project in on time,' 'You make things work smoothly and I appreciate your attention to detail,' or 'The way you handled that complaint made me proud to have you on my team' will keep individuals motivated and happy to work with you. You don't have to do some elaborate presentation or deliver a speech to give someone credit. A quick positive phrase in front of an audience (even a small audience of one or two others) can do wonders in making people feel good about themselves and their efforts.

I like what the American college football coach Paul William 'Bear' Bryant (1913–1983) said, 'If anything goes bad, I did it. If anything goes semi-good, then we did it. If anything goes real good, then you did it.'

Following through on promises

Watch golfers and tennis players on the green or court. If they fail to follow through on their swings, the ball goes flying off in unintended directions.

Following through on your promises is one way of establishing your credibility and displaying your honesty. If you say you're going to do something, do it. Your integrity, credibility and ability to influence others depend on your trustworthiness (see the section 'Trusting others – and being trustworthy' above).

Promises are often easier to make than keep, and an unfulfilled promise leads to disappointment and loss of credibility. Following through, on the other hand, brands you as a person whom others can trust to keep your word.

If you struggle to follow through on your promises, discover ways of making the process easier for you.

Carefully consider your promises before you make them. In general, you want to under-promise and over-deliver.

Whatever you promise, make sure that both you and the person you're promising are satisfied with what's on offer and that your promise is explicit and clear. Double-check your understanding and the other person's, just to make sure you're in agreement. Making promises is about serving another person, not impressing them.

If circumstances arise that prevent you from doing what you said you'd do or if you've over-promised, get back to the other person as soon as possible and ask for a reprieve. Modify what you promised so it's more in line with what you're able to do.

If you, for example, promise someone a promotion, the chance to re-design a project or an exclusive interview and find that you can't follow through, your credibility is at stake. You must make some changes – and quickly.

The following strategies can help you come up with a solution:

- ✔ **Be speedy.** If you must cancel the interview or put a project on hold, tell the other person as soon as possible to avoid prolonging disappointment.

- ✔ **Cut your losses.** Fretting, worrying and getting yourself into a state doesn't do you or anyone else any good. Be upfront and move on. And next time, follow through – or just don't promise.

- ✔ **Apologise.** Letting people know that your failure to follow through may have messed things up for them shows that you're willing to face up to your own actions – or inactions – and take the brunt of their disgruntlement.

    Whatever you do, don't put the blame on someone else, or you'll look even less credible than you do already.

- ✔ **Speak up.** Don't pretend that you never made your promise. Be transparent and act with integrity. Better to admit that you didn't follow through than pretend nothing's wrong.

- ✔ **Re-negotiate.** If there's any chance of your being able to follow through on your promise in an altered form or within a different timeframe, go for it. And then follow through on your promise.

- ✔ **Be prepared to be humble.** When you revise promises, you may need to eat a bit of humble pie and demonstrate your humility, and that's okay. It's certainly better than not following through at all and completely trashing your credibility.

Focusing on Feedback

According to Mark Twain, 'Supposing is good, but finding out is better.' Asking for feedback shows that you're keen to perform at your best. The more feedback you can solicit from your clients, colleagues friends and family, the better positioned you are to serve others' needs, address their concerns and implement their suggestions.

The purpose of feedback – whether you're asking for it or giving it – is to help people discover what's going well and where there's room for improvement. If you could read people's minds, you wouldn't have to ask for feedback.

Feedback is a normal function of life, especially working life. Yet it's not uncommon for people to feel reticent about providing feedback, especially if performances are waning, attitudes are disturbing or things aren't getting done. On the other side, receiving feedback can also be uncomfortable. Ask for and be open to receiving feedback anyway. The more you know, the better able you are to maintain the status quo or make necessary changes. Feedback allows you to better perform, making you more credible.

A well designed approach to feedback elicits *constructive* criticism from others. One-to-one sessions, employee surveys, 360-degree feedback forms – the means of getting feedback go on and on. Because this chapter is about helping you gain credibility, I focus on how you can solicit feedback that helps you and others work more efficiently and productively.

Providing feedback

Feedback is a process not a judgment. Unfortunately, many people leave feedback sessions with tears in their eyes, grinding teeth or flaring nostrils.

You want to look, sound and feel credible when you're the person providing the feedback. Take the following simple and practical steps to construct and give effective feedback:

- ✔ **Establish a supportive environment.** Feedback is meant to be beneficial. Going into a hostile environment and knowing that your performance is about to be commented on doesn't make for a warm and welcoming atmosphere. When you provide feedback you want to assure the other person that you're on his side and that your comments are directed toward performance not personality. Rather than sitting behind a desk or another piece of furniture that acts as a block between you and the other person, sit at a 45-degree angle to one another to create a comfortable rather than confrontational seating arrangement. For more about seating positions, refer to my book *Body Language For Dummies* (Wiley).

✔ **Be clear about the reason for the feedback.** Give yourself a starting point that is founded on specific information, focused on the issues and based on observations. Be sure you understand the reasons why you're giving the feedback, so the person receiving it can benefit from your comments and observations. Feedback is not about praising or criticising, which are personal judgments based on opinions or feelings and tend to be general and vague. Instead, the purpose of feedback is to provide information about a job well done or to give information about issues that need improving.

✔ **Determine the best time to deliver the feedback.** If something has happened that requires an immediate response, don't wait. You're better off giving feedback there and then so your mind is fresh with your observation and the person receiving the feedback can also easily recall the behaviour or incident. On other occasions, delaying the process is more appropriate. For example, you may need to see additional evidence of behaviour or gain further information. If something happens that you're not happy about, you may need to take some time to cool down. Either way, give feedback in a timely manner.

If either you or the receiver is tired or distracted, wait until you're both more receptive to the process.

✔ **Plan what you're going to say.** Have your points clear in your mind and speak directly to the other person in private. Stick with the specifics and avoid going off the point. Use notes to help you stay on track. Be direct and straightforward without beating around the bush. Avoid giving mixed messages like, 'Roz, you worked hard on this project, but . . .' When you say 'but', 'however' and 'although' in the middle of a sentence, you create contradictions or mixed messages. The real part of the message you want to convey lies behind the 'but', and the other person won't believe what came before.

✔ **Focus on behaviour not the person.** Rather than a character assassination, discuss specific behaviours and their effects. Whether you're offering positive or negative feedback, the purpose is to be constructive not destructive. Refrain from inferring what someone meant by what they said and did. Keep your language free of judgments (see Chapters 13 and 15).

✔ **Listen actively.** Pay attention to how the person receiving the feedback is responding. If he gets defensive, refrain from debating or discussing differences. Flip to Chapter 7 for more pointers on how to be a good listener.

✔ **Use an appropriate tone of voice.** If you're giving negative feedback, put concern into your voice to indicate a sense of care and sincerity. If you sound angry, frustrated or sarcastic, your efforts to provide constructive feedback come off sounding like criticism. In positive feedback situations, express appreciation – including the specifics – to add a dose of sincerity to your message. Turn to Chapter 15 for more information about using your voice effectively.

✔ **Make an action plan.** Decide what's going to happen next, and set time-scales and guidelines. If the feedback session was focussed on negative behaviour, before the other person leaves the meeting, have him write down clear, specific and measurable goals for improving his behaviour. Assure him that you are there to support him in his efforts, and put a date in the diary for another meeting to see how he's getting on. If the feedback session was positive, make a plan for further actions that can build on what's already going well.

✔ **Say thank you.** Express gratitude after the recipient hears what you have to say and gives you his time and attention.

When you have the opportunity to give someone feedback, you're entrusted with making sure the experience is positive. This is your chance to demonstrate your integrity and your credibility. Make the most of the opportunity, seek to serve the person you're speaking with, and be prepared for outstanding results.

Only offer feedback when you've been asked for it. If you go barrelling in offering your point of view without being invited, don't be surprised if you're met with a stony stare and a curt reply. Equally so, if you've asked for feedback, prepare how you're going to respond. If you ever want honest feedback again, make sure your feelings don't lead your responses.

Soliciting and receiving feedback

Some people want to bury their heads in the sand and avoid knowing how their behaviour is affecting or influencing others. Others seek out feedback in order to solidify their performance or find ways of improving. Without knowing what you're doing well or where you can improve, you stand little chance of being able to persuade and influence people when the time comes.

Soliciting feedback has a number of benefits for your performance. It can:

✔ **Enable personal growth.** Knowing how your behaviour affects others allows you to choose how you want to perform.

✔ **Allow you to gain insight.** You may not always be aware of the effect of your actions. By seeking feedback you gain an understanding of the consequences of your behaviour.

✔ **Create an open environment for communication.** People feel comfortable knowing they can provide constructive solicited information, and perform more productively than when they're in a closed, non-transparent environment.

✔ **Aid in preparing for the future.** Knowing what's expected of you helps you make a plan for how you're going to proceed.

Great leaders seek feedback. Taking on board others' views is the most fundamental way of improving performance. If you want to receive feedback and there's no system in place, you can request that your manager or the human resources department at work establishes one. For example, you could ask for yearly, six-month or quarterly appraisals. By seeking a system to provide performance feedback, you're demonstrating that you're serious about your career.

Several specific actions you can take include:

✔ Develop and publish feedback guidelines through the organisation. This lets people know the 'rules of the game'. In addition, the guidelines indicate that feedback is a two-way process, establish standards for talks about performance, and make it clear that everyone is responsible for the success or failure of the process.

✔ You can run or organise training sessions so people can practise giving and receiving feedback. The sessions should be skills based with a trainer or skilled manager explaining the guidelines and modelling an effective feedback conversation. Everyone present must have the opportunity to practise giving, receiving and observing feedback.

✔ Encourage people to practise giving and receiving feedback. Once the guidelines are clear, reinforce the process of giving clear, specific and constructive feedback.

✔ If you are a manager, serve as a role model. Offer feedback and ask for it. This shows that you are walking your talk and encouraging the process.

If you struggle to gain buy-in for a formal feedback system, ask your manager or a trusted colleague to provide feedback on your performance. Put guidelines in place so that the session is productive and not a case of praising or criticising someone or their efforts. In the previous section you can find tips for providing feedback effectively.

Away from the office, you can also establish feedback sessions, albeit on a more informal basis. For example, in your own family you could set up a feedback system for letting your partner and children know how their behaviour affects the rest of the family. When they do something positive, tell them how their behaviour benefitted the family. When their behaviour is causing a negative impact, tell them and set up a system for change. For younger children, this may take the form of a star chart, where good behaviour is rewarded and bad behaviour is punished. For older children, rewards and penalties – such as staying up late or being grounded – may be part of your feedback process.

Whatever system you use, make sure you address the behaviour and not the personality. As one friend says to her children, 'I may not always like the way you behave, but I will always love you.'

Once you've asked for a feedback session, make it easy for the person offering the feedback by listening respectfully. (See Chapter 7 for tips on listening.) Providing feedback is not a natural behaviour – people are more prone to criticise, praise or ignore what's going on – and most people lack the skills to provide effect feedback. And most people aren't good at receiving feedback. In addition to not listening well, they get defensive, offer excuses, blame others or attack the messenger. Do this at your peril. If you ask for feedback and come back with guns blazing, people are going to shy away from offering their observations in the future.

Below are some simple ground rules for receiving both negative and positive feedback:

- ✔ **Solicit feedback in clear and specific areas.** Rather than asking, 'How am I doing?' be precise by asking, 'How do you think I managed the discussion with Peter? What did I do well and where could I have done better?'

- ✔ **Aim to understand the feedback by asking clarifying questions and paraphrasing major points.** When you listen actively, you let the giver know you're interested and are trying to understand what he's saying. See Chapter 7 for tips on listening actively.

- ✔ **Help the giver be effective.** If the feedback is too general, ask for specific examples of what he meant. If the giver gets angry, let him vent. Don't argue or debate the points. Stay calm and wait for him to control himself.

- ✔ **Avoid making the session difficult for the giver.** You asked for the feedback so act respectfully. Avoid getting defensive, angry or feeling devastated. Don't ask for explanations, argue, deny, blame or rationalise. Even if the feedback is positive and you come back with something like, 'Oh, anyone could have done what I did,' you're in danger of turning off the feedback valve.

- ✔ **Show appreciation for the other person's willingness and effort.** A simple 'Thank you' or 'I appreciate the effort and time you took to tell me' sends a clear message that you appreciate the feedback, whether you agree or not. By showing gratitude, you invite the giver to provide feedback in the future.

✓ **Think of feedback as a gift.** The giver has to care enough about you to provide feedback. If you send out negative signals about his observations, he won't want to give you them again.

✓ **In response to the key points in the feedback, tell the giver what you intend to do as a result of what's been communicated.** A simple 'Thanks, I'll think about what you've said' or 'That makes sense. In the future I'll . . .' or even, 'Thanks for that. I'm going to check out your observations with others' lets the giver know you've listened and are going to act in some way on what he's observed.

✓ **Remember that feedback is not a universal truth.** The feedback is based on a person's perceptions of another person's actions. Keeping this point in mind helps defuse any potential defensiveness. If you doubt what the giver has said, check with others to determine whether there's a behaviour pattern going on. If two or more people agree with what's been observed, there may be a pattern in place that you need to do something about.

Chapter 6

Exhibiting and Exercising Your Expertise

. . . .

In This Chapter

▶ Cultivating your capabilities

▶ Proving your proficiency

▶ Putting your know-how to work

▶ Advising others

. . . .

*B*ecoming an expert in your field takes time, focus and determination. Whether you're a brain surgeon who's put in 12 or more years of formal training, a chief executive officer (CEO) of a global corporation who's worked your way up from the shop floor, a superb cook, or a techie who in the past five years discovered the secrets of search engine optimisation, becoming an expert doesn't happen in the blink of an eye.

No matter what your job or role in life, if you want to get ahead at work and enjoy others perceiving you as a persuasive and influential person, you've got to be – and have others see you as – an expert at what you do.

Experts influence decisions. Experts can persuade others to believe what they say and then follow their leads. Experts exert power. People who know their subject inside out, have proven themselves many times over and back up their claims with examples of success can rightly be classified as experts in their fields.

In this chapter I show you ways of becoming an expert and how you can demonstrate your expertise so that people defer to your decisions and respect you for the knowledge and guidance you provide.

Developing Your Expertise

While writing this book, I looked over my notes from interviews with experts in various disciplines including accountants, chefs, theatre directors, property developers, Human Resources professionals, lawyers, voice coaches and website designers. I also did detailed scientific research into what constitutes an expert. Some common themes appear:

- ✔ **Research has found no correlation between IQ, academic success and expert performance.** In fields from music and medicine, painting and parenting to building and blogging, daily practice is the primary part of what leads to expertise.

- ✔ **Experts are curious about their specialism and know that they don't know everything.** They're constantly searching for new approaches, new answers and new ways of expanding their knowledge.

- ✔ **Experts are made, not born.** Devoted teachers and determined parents notwithstanding, without intensive practice even the highest potential performers won't develop into experts. Becoming an expert, no matter what the discipline, is a long, hard slog and contains no short cuts.

Knowledge, experience, time and effort are more likely to turn you into an expert than big bonuses, major promotions and grand titles. You can find countless experts within organisations – both at work and at home – who aren't recognised with financial rewards, impressive labels or elevated positions.

Without a thorough knowledge of your subject and the practical skills to apply your knowledge, you're little more than a rank amateur. No doubt about it, experts know their stuff and put in the time to enhance their understanding. For example, if you want to become an expert persuader and influencer, read this book and practice the recommendations. If you're willing to put in the time and effort, eventually you can become an authority in the field.

Experts have significant experience working with their knowledge and are able to apply what they know in practical and creative ways. You can tell real experts from fakes by the way they solve problems without relying on someone else's solution. They can also identify and anticipate problems that no one else has spotted.

Jim is a freelance writer, a 1960s peacenik and a professor of anthropology at a university in California. The last person you would expect to don a military uniform and ride in a tank, he was recently invited to speak at a conference on anthropology and counter-insurgency, having become familiar with the latter area only after serving with the US military's Human Terrain Team (HTT) programme in the Middle East. In the hopes of understanding local cultures in Iraq and Afghanistan, the army recruited anthropologists to work along-side tactical commanders in the field. Because of Jim's expertise in Middle Eastern beliefs and customs, he was able to educate western troops on tribal traditions and ways of life. As a result of Jim's expertise, and others like him, the military has had substantial success in winning the hearts and minds of people in regions that were once some of the most violent strongholds in Iraq.

Identifying your know-know

Acquiring knowledge is a life-long process. You must put in the time to become an expert if you want to persuade people that you are.

From anthropology to zoology you can find experts in most domains, even in the study of expertise. Professional certifications and documented qualifications such as CPAs, MDs and MBAs indicate that someone is a specialist, but doesn't confirm that she's an expert. Some people proclaim themselves to be experts in their fields – including blogging, social networking and tweeting – but until you're acknowledged by others in the same area as having expertise, you remain at best a specialist and at worst a trumped up fraud.

By definition, expertise is focussed and specific in nature. Because of the time it takes to become expert in a chosen field, I'm amazed when someone claims to be expert in numerous areas. While you can be well-versed, experienced or highly skilled in more than one area, if you don't have more knowledge and experience than others in the same field, I struggle to define you as an expert.

People who study experts – including how someone becomes expert and the general principles underlying expertise – explore expertise on a number of levels. They investigate how the brain's machinery bolsters expert performance, the social and cultural level of expertise – including defining expert knowledge plus how this knowledge is communicated and interpreted – how experts are defined by society, and how you can impart knowledge in such a way as to turn novices into experts. In addition, experts on expertise seek to understand the role of experts and expertise within the legal system.

In his paper *The Role of Deliberate Practice in the Acquisition of Expert Performance*, K. Anders Ericsson says if you want to develop your expertise, deliberately practise, monitor your progress, evaluate your success and figure out how to do it better. A child finding out how to walk is a good example of building expertise. She puts one foot in front of the other, falls down, gets up and gives it another go until eventually she moves from crawling, to tottering to walking.

Some types of expertise

Social scientists Harry Collins and Robert Evans classified different types of expertise, including *no expertise, interactional expertise* and *contributory expertise*. The easiest way to illustrate the differences is to imagine a researcher investigating a topic for the first time. Whether the topic is about music or medicine, most researchers begin their enquiries coming from a position of *no expertise* in the field. As the researcher continues investigating the topic, she interacts with the musician or the doctor, increasing her knowledge and asking more pertinent questions about how music or medicine works. With time, the researcher may even be able to answer questions about the topic herself, even though she can't practice either discipline. Collins and Evans describe this level of expertise as *interactional expertise*. At this level, the only thing the researcher can't do that the doctor or musician can is practice the disciplines. While the researcher has *interactional expertise* – she can talk about the topic – the musician and the doctor have the additional expertise of *contributory expertise*. They can practise what they preach.

Building up your background

If you want to become expert in your chosen field, make gaining knowledge and developing the requisite skills part of your day-to-day activities. If you want to become an expert cake-baker, read all you can about baking cakes, talk to other cake bakers, make a different type of cake every day, attend cake-baking courses, join on-line discussion groups about cake-baking. By gathering as much knowledge and experience as you can, you eventually become an expert.

There's no quick and easy path to becoming an expert, but if you add the following tips to your daily activities you can become one in time:

- ✔ **Continuous discovery:** Experts make life-long acquiring of knowledge part of their daily diet. Constantly be on the lookout for thoughts and ideas both within and from outside your area of specialism that can expand your level of knowledge. Be curious and open to new possibilities.

- ✔ **Networking:** Build strong connections with others in your field. Seek mentors and make yourself available to others with less knowledge than you. Promote yourself to people who can benefit from your skills. Offer to speak at clubs and events. You won't gain experience if you don't get out and practise.

✔ **Practising:** Practise what you preach by reflecting your knowledge and experience every chance you get. Apply your knowledge in creative ways or solve problems that have no pre-existing solutions you can find. Identify challenges that no one's spotted yet.

✔ **Stretching yourself:** Volunteer to do something you've not done before such as leading a project or extend yourself in a slightly different direction (such as a successful copywriter taking on the management of an entire marketing campaign). Pushing yourself beyond your comfort zone increases your capabilities and builds your expertise.

✔ **Presentation skills:** No matter how good you are in your field, if you can't communicate your knowledge your expertise remains hidden. Learn to communicate with clarity, confidence and conviction. You can attend presentation skills courses or join groups that offer you the opportunity to practice speaking in public.

✔ **Sharing:** Let people know what you do and share your knowledge. The more you share information, the more you're seen as the go-to person in the field. Write blogs, articles or even tweet about your subject. Make contact with local media and offer to write a column for the paper or speak on radio. Clubs and organisations are always looking for speakers to talk about their specialist subjects.

In addition to having a wealth of knowledge, you have to know how and where to find further information to enhance and substantiate what you already know. Places where you can find further information in your chosen field include:

✔ The Internet

✔ Trade journals and industry publications

✔ Libraries

✔ Colleges and universities

✔ Online forums

✔ Seminars and workshops

✔ Colleagues

✔ Experts

✔ Students studying the subject

Sharing Your Successes

Experts are able to communicate their knowledge. There's little point in having expertise if you're neither willing nor able to communicate what you know. All too often potential experts fixate on intellectual property rights or 'proprietary information'. By refusing to share useful information with others, they often lock themselves off from the bigger conversation. Being afraid that someone's going to steal your valuable information and insights makes you become inconsequential in the area where you want to be known as expert.

If you can only crack a particular problem because you've held onto the secrets of solving it, you become nothing more than the problem's slave. Passing on to others the secrets of your success frees you up to develop your expertise further.

Janice was a buyer of women's fashion for a well-known department store. She left her job when she had children to devote her time to raising her family. When her children were grown, she applied her skills, experience and knowledge of fashion and started an image consultancy that she wanted to turn into the go-to consultancy for people in the arts and media. Janice's husband works in television, which gave her access to a number of potential clients. In the early days of her business, Janice did quite well but as she gained more clients she was unable to serve them all herself. Rather than bringing on board other experts to help manage her client base or training others, which would have enabled her to expand her business and enhance her reputation, Janice held onto the contacts herself. She didn't want to share them with others for fear that they would take her business from her. While Janice continues to provide image consultancy, she's not expanded her client base nor become the acknowledged authority she had dreamed of being.

Connecting with others

Make an effort to get out and socialise with professionals interested in topics that interest you. Surrounding yourself with other specialists encourages you to exchange ideas and approaches to problems, which over time adds to your expertise. By enlarging your professional and social network, you're likely to find people who need what you offer – and who can contribute to your knowledge bank as well.

Get out and network. Participate in online forums. Attend industry events. Go to as many networking events as you can and then weed out the ones that don't suit you and your needs. If someone you know knows someone you want to meet, ask for an introduction. Build strong relationships with others in your field. Seek out mentors and make yourself available to people who are less experienced than you. Promote yourself to people who need what you know. The more you get yourself known, the more people think of you when a problem arises that you can potentially solve.

Bolstering your reputation

As an expert, you must be skilled and knowledgeable – as well as capable of addressing your subject with confidence and conviction. Based on your expertise, others must believe that you've the wisdom and experience for them to accept your point of view. As an expert you've the power to persuade and influence the beliefs and behaviours of others.

Knowledge is the information, comprehension and skills you gain through formal education or life experience. For example, you can have scientific, practical or social knowledge or an extensive knowledge of the political system. Wisdom is the ability to apply your experience and knowledge by making sensible decisions and offering thoughtful advice. You can gain knowledge though reading and being instructed by others who have knowledge in your chosen field. You achieve wisdom through experience. As my daughter says, 'Knowledge is the retention of facts. Wisdom is knowing what to do with them.' For more thoughts about wisdom, see the sidebar 'The many faces of wisdom' later in this chapter.

In order to build your reputation as an expert in your chosen field, do any and all the following:

- ✔ **Gain knowledge continually.** If you aren't already hungry to find out new things, become hungry. Extend your knowledge and understanding by looking out for ideas and points of view both within and outside your field of interest. (See the earlier 'Developing Your Expertise' section.)

- ✔ **Pay attention to those who disagree or diverge from your point of view.** By challenging or contrasting with your understanding and beliefs, these people can enhance and refine your knowledge, making you a wiser and 'more expert' expert.

- ✔ **Promote an image of expertise.** Without making a meal of it, let your subordinates, colleagues and superiors know where you were educated, what you gained from relevant work experience and how you achieved noteworthy successes. If you're not proud of what you've accomplished, don't expect anyone else to be. (See the later 'Promoting your proficiency' section for specific recommendations.)

- ✔ **Maintain your credibility.** While it takes time to build your reputation as an expert, you can quickly lose it with a slip of the tongue or a few ill-advised choices. If you don't know what you're talking about, don't talk about it. And if a project looks like a loser, stay away.

Saving face

If you've ever been in a situation where you were asked a question that you hadn't anticipated and you don't know the answer, you recognise that sinking feeling in the pit of your stomach. Rather than trying to blag your way through troubled waters, be upfront and admit that you don't know. Follow up quickly by saying that you'll get the information as soon as possible.

If you're not comfortable with that approach, you can give the following a go:

'I don't know, but . . .' and then follow up with something you do know about in that area. For example, 'I don't know who specifically came up with that information but I do know that the whole research and development team has been looking into finding solutions to this problem.'

'I don't know but I know where I can start looking for the answer.' Knowing where to source the information at least assures your listener that you're on the case.

'I don't know. Can you tell me what's important about that?' Asking the other person to clarify their question may lead you to an answer.

You can admit that you don't know something, as long as you make an effort to come up with the information as quickly as possible.

✔ **Act with certainty and confidence in a crisis.** When calamity strikes, others look for someone to take charge and cope with the situation (see the 'Showing Others the Way' section, later in this chapter). People associate firmness, conviction and determination with expert knowledge. Even if you're not sure of the best way forward, you risk losing your ability to influence if you express doubt or act confused. If you really don't know what to do, speak with authority and ask who knows the best way to proceed. By taking charge, even if only to find someone who can handle the problem, you come across as confident and in control.

✔ **Stay informed.** Experts are expected to be knowledgeable in areas both within and outside of their sphere of influence. Keep up-to-date with what's happening within your team, your organisation and the world at large.

✔ **Acknowledge concerns.** Part of being expert is about recognising and responding to concerns and uncertainties within your small sphere of influence – your family, an organisation you belong to, your team or work colleagues, department or those who report to you. Listening to what people say and addressing any problems up-front enhances your ability to persuade them later on. Doing so also gives you examples of your expertise in action, which you can share with others outside your immediate circle. For more about the power of listening while persuading, refer to Chapter 7.

✔ **Enhance others' self-esteem.** As an expert, you naturally know more about your subject than other people do. Flaunting your expertise at the expense of others makes you appear arrogant. Aim to share your knowledge, rather than guard it only to dole out little bits. Encourage others to investigate other sources as well. Remember, you were once a novice too.

Promoting your proficiency

Research shows that people defer to experts. So if you want to persuade someone to go along with your proposal, prove yourself to be proficient in your chosen field. Gain the necessary knowledge, share it with anyone who's interested and keep discovering more. The more you know about your subject, the more expert you become.

Being proficient confers high levels of expertise and achievement as well as being extremely skilled in your chosen field as a result of talent, practise and familiarity. Proficiency is defined on BusinessDictionary.com as 'mastery of specific behaviour or skill demonstrated by consistently superior performance, measured against established or popular standards'.

Never assume that your expertise is self-evident. If you don't let people know you're good at what you do, you can't expect them to figure it out for themselves. Time's short, and people want quick answers. Plenty of other people are happy to blow their own trumpets, so, like it or not, you've got to promote yourself if you want to be recognised as an expert in your field.

Become known as an expert in your chosen area by blogging, tweeting and writing articles for publication. Create webinars, videos and audio files that afford you opportunities to establish yourself as an expert. Get quoted in the media. Hire a PR agent if you have to. Accept invitations to speak at symposiums and conferences. Write a book and get it published. Get yourself out there and network like mad.

The quickest and easiest way to convince people of your expertise is to inform them. If you really are an expert, you don't have to invent any stories or browbeat people into believing you. You just have to make your expertise known.

Doctors, lawyers, dentists and cosmetologists hang their diplomas on the wall where their clients can see them. Companies and professional service organisations display their awards at reception so visitors and clients can easily spot them.

If you're a manager who wants to prove yourself to clients and colleagues, you face a more limited choice of means of informing them about your expertise.

While you may think twice about tattooing your qualifications on your forehead, you can tell people about your accomplishments in a variety of ways.

> ✔ The first time people do business together, they often get together socially before getting down to business. By gathering for drinks or dinner the night before a meeting, you can establish rapport (see Chapter 2), build your profile as an expert in your field and defuse any potential arguments. If you don't have time for drinks or dinner, grab a coffee or water with a client before sitting down to talk business.

✔ The more you can find points of common interest and reasons for liking one another, the more easily you can establish yourself as an expert in your field. See Chapter 2.

✔ If you don't have time for dinner with a prospective client, you still usually have a few minutes before you sit down at the conference table for a little casual conversation in advance of getting down to business. Make the most of these moments. Slip in a mention about your relevant background and experience. Disclosing this personal information from the beginning establishes your expertise early in the game.

✔ A bit of small talk can build friendly rapport. While you can compliment someone on their office, a piece of artwork or a photo of the family pet, keep your remarks non-invasive and avoid getting too personal. You want to appear friendly and interested, not like a stalker or snoop.

Russell is a partner in a global accountancy firm. An acknowledged specialist in corporate tax, he is also humble about his expertise. Russell knows that in order to gain credibility and to demonstrate his know-how when meeting potential clients, he has to let them know about his accomplishments. He has refined his ability to tell brief, effective stories about himself, including an anecdote about how he successfully addressed a complicated tax matter and how he unravelled a complex financial problem. Russell carefully incorporates his stories into the regular flow of normal conversation so as to be seen as an expert and not a braggart. These stories earn him respect, demonstrate his expertise and more often than not gain him new clients.

Activating your expertise

The sheer volume of experts out there who state opinions on subjects ranging from abandonment to zymosis is astounding. Because research can be interpreted in different ways, experts frequently disagree in their opinions. Having an opinion that you're willing to share based on knowledge and experience isn't enough.

In addition to putting in the hours to know your subject, you must present your opinion convincingly, reassuring your listener that you know what you're talking about. You have to stake your claim, stand for something specific and present your case articulately. You must show that you're confident in your opinion by the way you behave.

Showcase your expertise while talking with prospective clients or speaking in front of an audience:

✔ **Assume an open position.** Whether standing or sitting, keep your arms and hands relaxed at your sides in a neutral position.

Unclench your hands and release your fingers. Sometimes doing that quietly and quickly under the table or while you're walking up the presentation podium helps steady your nerves.

✔ **Claim your space.** Remind yourself that you've earned the right to speak on your subject and then occupy the available space in a poised manner. Sitting or standing with your weight evenly distributed on both legs makes you look and feel strong and confident. Imagine your shoulder blades meeting at the base of your neck and melting down your back while your head stays still and upright.

✔ **Move with purpose.** Fidgeting and shuffling makes you appear nervous and unsure. When you want to stress an important point, use your hands and arms. While you may feel overly dramatic at first, your audience perceives you as passionate.

✔ **Look at your listener.** Connect and engage with your audience by looking at them while you speak. You look like an expert and feel like one, too. Avoid staring as that makes your listener uncomfortable and makes you appear robotic. Looking at your listener 65–75 per cent of the time while you're speaking is enough to engage with them comfortably. Remember to blink. Some people's blinking slows down a lot during important conversations and presentations, which can be unsettling for listeners and may dry out your eyes too!

✔ **Breathe from your belly.** Shallow breathing from your chest indicates that you're anxious and makes you sound nervous; it also diminishes the amount of oxygen you bring into your body and brain. When you're exhibiting your expertise, you want to sound like you know what you're talking about. To speak with power and conviction, you need to propel your words on a strong, steady stream of air that originates deep in the bottom of your torso.

For more details on how your voice and body language can influence your listener, refer to Chapters 13 and 14.

Experts understand the issues they're addressing, and the most convincing experts influence opinion by presenting their evidence with clarity and confidence.

Whether through shyness or an overabundance of vanity, if you struggle to speak compellingly on your own behalf, get someone else to do it for you. Experts often ask someone to acknowledge their accomplishments for them, avoiding the pitfall of the individuals themselves coming across as ineffective or arrogant self-promoters. For example, if you've been invited to speak at an event, ask the organiser to invite someone to introduce you and make sure that she has a copy of your resume to refer to while she does so.

Even if you've the knowledge and experience to confirm your expertise, if you come across as boastful or conceited, you're going to turn off your listeners. No matter how credible your credentials, they won't serve you if your style screams stuck-up and self-satisfied. Make your body language open and inviting. Looking straight ahead, as if you were looking through everything and everyone in front or around you, causes you to appear unapproachable. Make eye contact and offer a warm, welcoming smile. A little bit of humbleness goes a long way in building rapport. Give credit to the people and circumstances in your life that have supported you in getting to where you are today. See Chapter 2 for more about building rapport.

I recently attended a networking event at which an online marketing expert was the guest speaker. I was looking forward to hearing what she had to say because I had been seeking someone to take over this part of my business and had heard that she's good at what she does. Unwisely, she made several unpleasant comments about her competition and spoke of her own successes in overtly boastful and unsubstantiated terms that led me to doubt her sincerity and trustworthiness. After the event, I made further enquiries about the speaker and found out that some of her claims about her achievements were unfounded, leading me to reject any possibility of recommending or working with her.

Showing Others the Way

People look to experts for answers. Having wisdom about your area of expertise, you're expected to provide clear direction, sound guidance and satisfying solutions. When you do that, you show others that they can trust you and eventually be persuaded by you. For more about trust and influence, see Chapter 10.

Making sound judgments

When asked the secret of his success, American department-store owner and retail merchandising pioneer Marshall Field responded, 'I have tried to make all my acts and commercial moves the result of definite consideration and sound judgment. There were never any great ventures or risks. I practiced honest, slow-growing business methods, and tried to back them with energy and good system.' People who apply sound judgment to their actions have a canny ability to weigh up conditions and situations and come to sensible conclusions. Experts make sound judgments. Whether you're an officer in the military, a product developer or a political leader, as an expert in your field you're counted on to set an example that communicates the purpose and direction of and the reason for a specific course of action.

The many faces of wisdom

Since the time of the ancient Greeks, philosophers and academics have struggled to define wisdom and explain where it comes from.

Some say wisdom is about making the best use of knowledge, whereas others say wisdom is about knowing why things exist as they do. Still others define wisdom as a profound understanding of people, places and things resulting in consistent behaviour that produces optimal results with the least amount of time and energy expended. Some believe that wisdom comes from experience, others posit that it comes from pure reason, while others maintain it comes from intuition or spirituality.

The following notable definitions of wisdom may help you shape your own definition of this powerful yet elusive virtue:

- Early western cultures have long associated wisdom with virtue, courage and moderation. The four cardinal virtues of Christianity include wisdom – typically referred to as *prudence* – along with justice, fortitude and temperance. In *The Republic,* Plato identifies these four virtues with the various classes within a city and assigns prudence to the rulers. St Augustine, in his discussion of the morals of the church, defines prudence as love that distinguishes what hinders the church and what helps it.

- In his *Dialogues,* Plato describes wisdom as love and knowledge about the Good – the right relations within all existence – and having the courage to act on that knowledge. In his *Symposium,* he distinguishes between philosophers and sages through the concept of love. As he describes it, *philosophers*, the Greek term for lover of wisdom, don't have the wisdom they seek. The sage, already in possession of wisdom, neither loves nor searches for wisdom, because he already has it.

- The Inuits, a tribe of culturally similar people native to the Arctic regions of Canada, Greenland, Russia and the United States, believe that a wise person is one who sees what needs doing and does it without being told to.

- Philosophers, including Jean-Jacques Rousseau, Henry Thoreau and Ivan Illich define wisdom as being based on the holistic principle of the interconnectedness of life, whereby individuals discover their identity, meaning, and purpose through connections to community, the natural world and values such as compassion and peace.

- Confucius says you can gain wisdom through reflection, imitation and experience and that you only offer it when someone else requests it. He also says that the love of learning is analogous to wisdom.

- The Taoists describe wisdom as knowing what to say and when to say it.

- Buddha says that a wise person knows how to behave, speak and think. He goes on to purport that a wise person does what is unpleasant if the action produces a positive result and doesn't do what is pleasant if the outcome is bad. His further thoughts on the subject of wisdom include the belief that a wise person carefully discriminates between right and wrong, is non-violent and harbours neither fear nor hatred.

- The Friends of Wisdom, a group of academics formed from 21 countries in 2006, believe that wisdom is the capacity to recognise what matters in life, including knowledge, understanding and technical expertise. They actively encourage schools and universities to seek and promote wisdom to create a better world.

Making sound judgments requires having sound information. The more quality data you can garner, the better able you are to come up with sensible solutions. In addition to acquiring sound data, people who make sound judgments are able to interpret the information and determine how best to proceed.

Figure 6-1 shows the three-step process that leads to making any sound judgment, specifically:

- ✔ **Gathering facts and analysis.** Begin by putting together the facts and analyse them as your starting point.

- ✔ **Gaining insights and judgments.** These can be gained from trusted confidants (see Chapter 4) and others whose opinions you value and respect.

- ✔ **Considering and choosing your options.** Having looked at the facts and analysed them, and taking on board insights and judgments from individuals whose opinions you regard highly, you make the final choice on how best to proceed.

The process of making a sound judgment is like a tripod: if one of the legs collapses, the structure is compromised and a bad outcome is likely.

The ability to make sound judgments – those that are based on logic, impartiality. discernable facts and deductive reasoning – is an acquired skill that takes time and experience. While you may weigh the evidence without bias and consider it carefully before making a decision, not everyone is going to agree with or validate your choice.

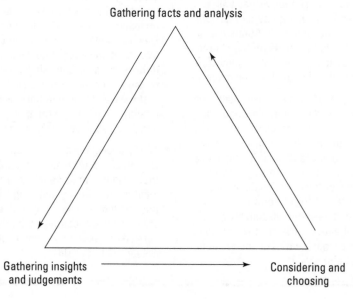

Gathering facts and analysis

Figure 6-1:
The three
activities
that lead
to a sound
judgment.

Gathering insights
and judgements

Considering and
choosing

Being an expert and a maker of sound judgments requires coming to the table well prepared. The best experts take deliberate, thoughtful and incremental steps and consider all options before making decisions, rather than leaping straight into the fray. Take the time to gather information that is precise, meets your intention and provides the most valuable insight. Analyse your facts, assess the situation and consider the long-term consequences of your decision before making a judgment. Do that and people will have no doubt about who's the expert in the room.

As Abraham Lincoln said, 'If I had eight hours to chop down a tree, I'd spend six sharpening my axe.' Lincoln was a man of the country, and was familiar with felling trees. He knew that in order to do a good job, he had to take the time to prepare. On the other hand, people often expect experts to come up with quick answers and sometimes they can. An expert chef, for example, can tell you what temperature is best for cooking a soufflé or an expert horse-person can advise you on the best saddle for your requirements. A champion tennis player makes quick choices the moment a match starts. All these decisions are based on years of experience and practice and are made in a jiffy.

While experts can make correct quick decisions based on gut instinct, the most reliable judgments are ultimately based on dependable facts and deductive reasoning, as long as you don't get caught up in analysis paralysis.

Gut instinct is another expression for intuition and implies that you've beliefs that you can't justify with facts. The word 'intuition' comes from the Latin word 'intueri', which can be translated to mean 'to look inside' or 'to contemplate'. When experts are under pressure, they frequently identify similar situations they've experienced in the past and make an intuitive decision based on gut instinct. When someone is unable to make a decision because they're over-analysing a situation while they seek the optimal solution and fear making a mistake, they're said to be in a state of *analysis paralysis*.

Making a wrong decision is part of life. Making a bad decision is a failure of judgment. A wrong decision is a mistake or your best guess when you've no way of knowing. For example, you go to a new restaurant and the food isn't good. A bad decision is like an unforced error. In spite of the facts being laid out on a plate in front of you, you make the wrong call, such as driving a car when you're drunk.

Acting in a flash

Sometimes an expert has to make a decision quickly when she doesn't have all the information at hand. At those times she must rely on past experience and gut instinct to guide her choices. In his 2005 book, *Blink: The Power of Thinking Without Thinking*, Malcolm Gladwell describes how experts can make spontaneous decisions that can be better than well-thought-out ones, citing the example of a firefighter who answered a routine call. When his men's efforts to extinguish the fire failed, the lieutenant realised that something was wrong and ordered his team out of the building. Moments later, the space where they had been standing collapsed. The fire had been under the floor, not in the room itself. When asked how he knew, the fireman couldn't immediately explain. Had he stopped to analyse the situation, he and his men would have been killed. Instead, he relied on his instinct – based on years of experience – to tell him what to do.

Katie is in her first management position, in charge of a team of five. Recently, tension and disagreement among the co-workers having to do with lack of clarity around roles and responsibilities disrupted and delayed the project they're working on. Seeking to understand the situation, Katie spoke with all involved parties, clarified the facts and everyone's perceptions and perspectives. After considering all the information, she held a group discussion and presented a viable solution that all agreed to. She assigned each member precise responsibilities, and instituted a system of task lists with due dates to make sure that the team worked effectively. Remaining calm, discussing the issues openly and coming up with a positive solution that everyone agreed with and adhered to got the project back on track. Katie's supervisor was impressed with the way she handled the situation and is recommending her for another position with more responsibility and increased remuneration.

Highlighting your winning strategies

If you want to be seen as an expert worthy of the ability to persuade and influence others, let people know how you achieved what you achieved. Sharing your strategy of how you got from point A to point B provides useful information for others to follow and contextualises your success.

When you decide that you want to be an expert in your field, you must formulate a plan and put it into practice. Becoming an expert doesn't happen by chance. It requires thought and action. The simplest strategy for achieving success consists of three parts:

> ✔ **Where you are now:** This part involves understanding as much about yourself as possible. Knowing how you think, behave and how you compare with others in your field gives you a reference point to work from. Be realistic, detached and critical when considering the causes and effects of your behaviour.

✔ **Where you want to be:** Set your goals and determine your means of achieving them. Decide where you want to be in five or ten years and what you're prepared to do to achieve that vision. Figure out where you're going to focus your efforts and find out what others in your field are doing to achieve their expertise.

✔ **What you need to achieve your goals:** Ask yourself what changes in your thinking or behaviour you may have to make in order to become an expert. Figure out the best way of implementing those changes and do it.

Showcasing your successes is tricky, so be careful. If you're anything like me, you've received conflicting messages throughout your life about showing off your successes. On the one hand, you're told not to hide your light under a bushel and, on the other hand, you're told not to brag.

If you're to become a successful persuader and influencer, you have to convince people that you've got the skills, wisdom and experience to guide them to goals that are in their best interest. They don't know this information unless you make it your business to make it known. So let your customers, suppliers, employees and anyone who's interested know your winning strategies and success stories if you want them to believe in your expertise and buy into your vision.

✔ **Make sure that people in your organisation know what you bring to the job.** Your background, formal education, training and personal experience all contribute to your expertise. Without playing the Big I-Am, let people know about your accomplishments. Display your diplomas, licences, awards and any other evidence of your achievements in prominent places in your office or workspace. You've worked hard to get where you are and deserve to get the credit.

✔ **Include references to your education or experience in your conversations.** Subtle mentions of your education and experience such as 'What I discovered on my MBA course is . . .' or 'During my time as CTO at . . . , we confronted a similar situation . . .' add credibility to your perceived position of authority and expertise. Be careful with this approach, however, as getting caught up in your own PR is all too easy and you may inadvertently sound smug or pretentious.

✔ **Share stories that highlight your successes and the strategies you put into action to achieve them.** In addition to seeing you as an expert who not only knows your subject and has attained success in your field, people want to know how you got to where you are now.

Everyone is looking for the right answer. The more you can help people achieve their goals by sharing your winning strategies, the more they acknowledge you as the expert.

Building a winning strategy

In his research into winning strategies, John Sterling, a partner and co-founder of Smock Sterling, strategic management consultants, offers the following advice for implementing a winning strategy:

✔ **Ensure that you've got the talent for the job in place.** The best of plans is likely to implode if you don't have the right people to implement it.

✔ **Think about how your potential competitors may react.** Consider all the ways in which the competition can respond to your strategy and brainstorm what you can do in response. In addition, be on top of what your rivals have got up their sleeves.

✔ **Involve managers from across the organisation in the early stages of strategy development.** People who help create a plan buy into it and feel responsible for its success. Although not everyone may agree with what's decided, they can voice their differences and the whole team can explore the pros and cons of the proposal.

✔ **Communicate persistently and consistently.** Many strategies fail because of a lack of buy-in or understanding or poor communication. Keep people up to date with what's going on. Whether the news is good or bad, people need to know what's happening in order to feel part of the process.

✔ **Plan and budget.** If you want to ensure that procedures are in line with the strategy and that they're implemented appropriately, put together an action plan and a budget – and review them regularly.

✔ **Supervise and hold people accountable.** Keep your eyes and ears open. Know how the plan's coming on, what's happening with the competition, how customers are responding and how you're doing financially. Find out what's working and what's not. Hold people accountable, otherwise your monitoring is meaningless.

✔ **Take symbolic actions.** As a means of motivating your team and reinforcing their efforts, symbolic actions are hard to beat. Company picnics, end of week drinks, a congratulatory note or bouquet of flowers and prizes for excellent performance are all good for building team spirit and boosting morale. Tell oft-repeated, relevant and inspiring stories. Hold ceremonies like celebrations when targets are met or birthday and anniversary parties. Place meaning on environments by placing inspirational quotes or pictures on the walls or flowers in reception. Lead from the top and let your workers know that you care about them. Be creative.

✔ **Make sure that your technology supports your strategy.** Business can't survive without information technology. You must have the right technology to execute strategies – and you can't implement new technology without a strategy behind it.

Put the time into building your winning strategies. Sometimes strategies fail because they're poorly conceived and badly executed. Start by defining the challenge and communicating it clearly to everyone who's involved. Make certain that everyone agrees with and commits to executing the plan. Follow through to ensure that your plan is carried out. Track and measure your goals, identify where they're not being met and take corrective action.

Part II

Developing Your Persuasive and Influencing Skills

The 5th Wave   By Rich Tennant

PERSUASION TECHNIQUES

Law of Reciprocity
Law of Contrasts
Law of Scarcity
Law of Free Beer

"Let's look at some of the laws of persuasion."

In this part . . .

To be persuasive, you need to develop some solid, basic skills. In this part I show you how to listen actively to your target audience so that you can really get to grips with what they care about. I give you the inside track on grabbing and keeping the attention of your audience, and tell you how to tailor your approach to cope with the different ways different people make decisions. You also get to find out how to put yourself across convincingly, no matter what the person listening to you is like.

Chapter 7

Listening Actively

● ●

In this chapter

▶ Showing others that you value them

▶ Going beyond hearing

▶ Perceiving feelings

▶ Responding respectfully

● ●

*Y*ou may think that listening and hearing are the same thing. They're not. *Hearing* is a physiological process, in which your ears process sound waves. *Listening* is a psychological process in which you interpret what you hear and respond in a way that demonstrates your understanding. Hearing happens. Listening is a skill that you develop.

Active listening – paying attention to what the other person is saying as well as how they're speaking – takes communication to another, deeper level. You understand not only the information the speaker is telling you, you gain insight into their thoughts and feelings about what they're communicating. As the Greek moralist and biographer Plutarch (46–120 AD) said, 'Know how to listen, and you will profit even from those who talk badly.'

In this chapter you gain insights into how you can be fully present with other people, letting go of your agenda to focus on theirs. You discover how to recognise feelings and how to respond in ways that make the other person feel valued and appreciated.

While most of the examples and anecdotes in this chapter are work-related, listening skills can make a world of difference with your friends and family as well as with your colleagues and clients.

Whether at work or in your private life, when people feel that you value and appreciate them, they're more open to your influence than if you ignore, speak over them or reject them outright. When you make others feel good about themselves, they're ready to trust you – and when trust is in place, the ability to persuade is close at hand.

Showing Others That You Value Them

The Chinese symbol for listening at a deep and meaningful level (see Figure 7-1) consists of characters that represent several other words, including 'ear', 'you', 'eyes', 'undivided attention' and 'heart'. You can't get much clearer than those elements if you want a simple recipe for making someone feel valued!

Ear   You

                        Eyes

Figure 7-1:   Undivided
Chinese      Attention
symbol for
active
listening.

                        Heart

I have yet to meet anyone who doesn't want someone to pay attention to him. Most people struggle to make themselves heard. Focus your eyes, ears and heart on someone, give his your undivided attention, and watch your ability to persuade or influence increase exponentially.

You know how good it feels when people listen to you, giving you their full attention, focusing on you and putting their own agenda on the back burner while you speak. Or perhaps not. Active listening is a rare commodity. Most people are blessed with two eyes, two ears and one mouth. Unfortunately, most use them in reverse order. If you want to win someone over to your side, consider Winston Churchill's remark: 'Courage is what it takes to stand up and speak; courage is also what it takes to sit down and listen.'

Giving people your full attention shows that you're interested in and care about them as people. Let people know that you value them and watch their self-esteem rise. Make them feel good about themselves and their motivation and morale sky rockets.

Increasing others' engagement

Getting others to engage with you is your pathway to success. In order for others to engage with you, you must show that you care about them by listening to them. Whether you're someone's parent, friend, child or boss, people only care about what you want as long as they know that you care about them.

At work, motivated employees are engaged employees, and engaged employees produce positive results. HR professionals in a recent survey from the Institute of Employment Studies (www.employment-studies.co.uk) define engagement as:

- ✔ Believing in the organisation
- ✔ Wanting to work to make things better
- ✔ Understanding the business context and 'bigger picture'
- ✔ Respecting and helping colleagues
- ✔ Being willing to 'go the extra mile'
- ✔ Keeping up-to-date with developments in the field

While engagement and commitment to an organisation are similar, the concepts differ in certain ways. Most noticeably, engagement is a two-way street. An organisation must first engage the employee, who then decides how much engagement he wants to offer in return. See the sidebar 'Who's engaged?' for more key trends in employee engagement.

If you want to get the best out of your team, praise their efforts. Tell an employee you value him and his work and watch his performance continue to improve. People who feel appreciated perform better than those who don't.

Valuing and involving your staff is the most effective way to gain their engagement. When employees take part in decision-making, feel free to voice their ideas and recognise that their contributions are appreciated, have opportunities to develop their jobs and feel that the organisation cares about their health and well-being, they engage. Responsibility for cultivating engagement resides with managers at all levels throughout the organisation.

Offering empathy

Empathy is a vital component in making someone feel valued. As I discuss in Chapter 3, empathy is the ability to listen with your head and your heart.

Deepak Chopra refers to this way of taking in information as *detached involvement*, in which you allow others to be exactly as they are. When you listen, you don't impose your idea of how things should be. You don't force your solutions onto other people's problems. Instead, you stand back, allowing them to find their own ways through their mazes of uncertainty, until they find ways that work best for them.

Who's engaged?

Research from the Institute of Employment Studies highlights notable trends in employee engagement:

✔ The youngsters and the oldies are often the most engaged age groups, with workers in their thirties, forties and fifties showing dips in engagement.

✔ Ethnic minorities demonstrate a significantly higher engagement level than their white colleagues.

✔ Managers and employees who connect directly with clients or customers demonstrate relatively high engagement. Engagement tends to drop among back-room support employees.

✔ Professionals have the lowest level of employee engagement, committing to their professions rather than to their employers.

✔ As length of service increases, engagement levels decline – until the employee hits 20 or more years of services, at which point engagement levels tend to increase again.

✔ Employees who are injured, have accidents at work or are bullied on the job (particularly if a boss is involved), demonstrate low engagement.

✔ Employees who have development plans in place or access to development opportunities are more highly engaged than those who don't.

✔ Organisations that understand engagement levels and drivers of different employee groups fare better at engaging their staff than those that approach engagement on a 'one size fits all' basis.

While this research was carried out in the United Kingdom, its findings can be applied globally and reflect the conclusions of other organisations, including Dale Carnegie Training.

When Brittany was called into her boss's office, she had no idea that her boss had taken a fancy to her and was about to suggest that they take their relationship beyond the professional. Brittany was horrified, as she valued her job, was on an upward career trajectory and didn't want to jeopardise her chances of promotion. That evening, when she told her flatmate, Camilla, what had happened, Camilla cut in, 'Oh, I know exactly how you feel. When my boss came on to me, it took me months to recover. I don't know whether I've recovered yet. I was completely devastated.' Feeling hurt that Camilla had interjected with her own story, Brittany brought the conversation to a close by saying, 'You don't have a clue how I feel. You weren't even listening to me.' While Camilla was trying to demonstrate she understood by relating Brittany's experience to her own, she ended up showing that she was thinking about herself. A more empathetic response may have been for Camilla to stay out of the equation and keep the focus on Brittany, saying something like, 'You must feel devastated.' This response illustrates that Camilla understands Brittany's situation and feelings, while remaining detached and 100 per cent focused on her friend.

Although empathy and sympathy are both acts of feeling, and many people use the words interchangeably, the two are different. When you demonstrate empathy, you seek to understand what someone is feeling. You aim to feel with the person. By contrast, when you demonstrate sympathy, you may feel for the person and what they're experiencing – but you don't understand what they're feeling. Empathy is about feeling *with* someone. Sympathy is about feeling *for* someone.

When you listen with empathy, you pick up on the other person's feelings, recognising how the situation is for that person without getting emotionally involved. This approach shows that you value the individual and can put aside your own emotions, feelings and agendas, thus allowing the other person room to express himself.

Listen with empathy often enough, and the other person is going to like you. See Chapter 10 to discover the power of liking in the process of persuading.

Paying attention to other points of view first

In order to understand someone's point of view, you have to listen to them first. But wait, you may be saying, what about someone understanding me? Well, your needs must sometimes come second. While curiosity may have killed the cat, satisfaction brought it back.

In his classic *The Seven Habits of Highly Effective People*, Stephen Covey encourages readers to seek to understand before seeking to be understood. In other words, listen to the other person first and then observe how he listens to you.

If you don't try to force your thoughts onto others, they're much more likely to be ready, willing and able to listen to you when your turn to talk arrives.

Brushing Up Your Listening Skills

Listening takes practice. While you may have been taught listening skills at school, most of my teachers focused on reading, writing and arithmetic. That said, listening is a skill that you can hone. It requires practice, concentration, perseverance and a real desire to know another person.

Sincerely, my dear

In order to effectively empathise with another person, you must be sincere. When you're sincere, you're genuine, true and honest in all your thoughts, actions and words. Being sincere and authentic, particularly in how you praise another person, can yield major results and encourage the other person to go the extra mile for you.

You can't fake sincerity – and you're probably best off avoiding attempts at sincerity if you truly don't feel what you're doing or saying. People pick up on insincerity at varying speeds, but most people can eventually spot a fake. And if they do, heaven help you. After you're found out to be a phony, you lose your chance to persuade anyone to accept your point of view.

If you struggle to be sincere in praising the efforts of others, reflect on your own beliefs and perceptions. You may find that you're basing your responses on personal fears and expectations, social conditioning or the examples and opinions of other people. Develop your self-awareness by asking yourself the following questions:

✔ Are my reactions based on how I think and feel or am I giving in to social conditioning and expectations?

✔ Am I allowing others to be who they are with their unique viewpoints or do I want them to comply with mine?

✔ Am I reacting to what is currently happening or am I responding to past experiences?

As a friend of mine told me many years ago, if you can't find anything to praise about another person, reflect on them for five minutes. If you still can't find something to praise, think on them for another five minutes. Eventually, you can find something positive that opens your heart and mind to who they are and the challenges they face.

Preparing yourself

If active listening is a skill you want to develop or improve, take the time to get your body and mind ready to elicit and absorb information. The following preparations demonstrate that you're 100 per cent committed to listening:

✔ **Open your eyes.** Dull, glazed eyes indicate that you're bored or indifferent. Try for an open, relaxed, yet alert facial expression. Practise your listening expression by observing yourself in a mirror until you can assume it without visual assistance.

✔ **Sit up (or stand) with alertness.** People can feel that you don't care about them or what they're saying if you slouch while they're speaking. They can feel uncomfortable if you fidget with your fingers or wiggle your feet. Instead, orient your body in the direction of the other person and remain relatively still. Use gestures only to encourage the other person to talk.

For more about the power of body language, turn to Chapter 13 or read my book *Body Language For Dummies* (Wiley).

✔ **Leave your own issues at the door.** When working to understand someone else, let the discourse be all about the other person. Place your
thoughts and beliefs to one side so that you're unencumbered and open
to what he has to say. Have a look at Chapter 3 to find out more about
being receptive to other people's points of view. You can also pick up a
copy of *Coaching with NLP For Dummies* by Kate Burton (Wiley), which
covers this topic in detail.

✔ **Act like you're interested.** By looking and sounding as if you're interested in what the other person is saying, you start to actually feel
interested. Actors developing a character, often act 'as if' to help them
become that person. Children play the 'as if' game all the time, pretending to be doctors, nurses, or cowboys.

Because your feelings impact on your behaviour and your behaviour impacts
on your beliefs, when you act 'as if' you become whatever you tell yourself
you are. Studies on beliefs and behaviour show that what you believe and
expect determine how you behave. International studies consistently show
the correlation of attitudes, beliefs and expectations on behaviour.

✔ **Be patient.** When seeking to understand other people's points of view,
give them time to express their thoughts and opinions. When people
feel you're rushing them, they aren't comfortable sharing their thoughts
with you. See the next section 'Allowing others to speak' for specifics.

✔ **Be present.** When you're listening to someone else, you need to exist
in the here and now. The later section 'Being present with the speaker'
offers more ideas for how to be completely present with another person.

Allowing others to speak

Often people think that giving advice, trying to solve problems and telling
someone what to do is the way to show support, trust and encouragement.
They're wrong. People just want you to give them the chance to speak while
you sit back and listen.

After you invite someone to speak, don't interrupt. Whatever you do, if you
want to listen to someone else, do not interrupt.

Many people struggle to remain quiet while someone else is speaking. Maybe
you want to jump in and make a bad situation better, or perhaps you want to
defend yourself and remove any possibility of responsibility. Whatever your
motivation, your own agenda can easily take over a conversation. Resist the
urge to tell your own stories, fix problems or quickly assure the other person
that things could be worse (and so telling them to buck up and get on with
the job).

Taking away other people's thoughts, overriding their points with your own and interjecting when they didn't invite you to do so are all sure-fire ways to make others feel undervalued and resist your efforts to persuade or influence them later. When you contradict or add judgements to the mix, you're essentially invalidating their rights to their opinions and beliefs. They end up walking away from you feeling disempowered.

Next time you're listening to someone, consciously relax your jaw and close your mouth. Let your top lip gently rest on your lower lip. Keep both lips in this position until the other person has finished speaking. Then, and only then, allow your lips to part. If you act 'as if' you're interested in hearing what someone has to say – keeping your mouth shut and your mind open – you just might find that you actually pay attention. If the other person struggles to stop speaking and you've heard enough, pick up on a point they made and direct the conversation down the path you want to take. Saying something like, 'In regards to your point about . . .' or 'Based on what you're saying . . .' makes the speaker feel that you've listened and reflected on what he's said.

You may feel tempted to finish the other person's sentences, but if someone has ever done that to you, you know how off-putting the practice is. Jumping in on thoughts sabotages others at a personal level, possibly making them doubt themselves and definitely damaging any trust you may have established.

You clearly can't listen if you're speaking. Wait for the other person to stop what he's saying before you open your mouth. If you interject your thoughts and usurp his story, he's not going to be keen to listen to you.

Co-workers Damian and Jason were discussing their careers over lunch one day. Damian wanted to brainstorm possible paths he could take to further his opportunities, but Jason consistently interrupted and gave reasons why a particular approach wouldn't work, what had happened to him when he tried the route Damian was considering or how Damian was wrong in his thinking. Although they continued working together, Damian lost trust in Jason as a result of the way he'd treated him and sought out other people to collaborate with when new projects came along.

Savouring silence

Sometimes when people are struggling to express themselves, they become silent. Their feelings may be running high and they want to control them, or they may need time to formulate their ideas into coherent thoughts. When the person speaking goes silent, you can be sure that she's reflecting or feeling something, not that she's stopped thinking.

Silence can be uncomfortable but inevitable. Get used to it. Being at ease with silence is vital to active listening. By not interjecting your voice into someone else's stillness, you give the speaker time to think about what he wants to say. If appropriate, reassure him by saying 'take your time' and remain relaxed and ready to listen to what he has to say. Waiting patiently helps others feel that their opinions matter to you and that they can continue feeling calm and confident in your presence.

Sometimes silence can go on for an unusually long time. If that happens, you may interject with questions such as, 'What were you thinking about just then?' or 'What is it that's making you hesitate?' Spoken gently, these questions are affirming ways to encourage speakers to continue talking and sharing information with you without putting them off. If a silence shifts into more emotional territory – crying, rage, or anxiety – stay calm, keep quiet and give the other person enough space to express himself. Arguing with him or trying to calm him down doesn't do you or him any good and can intensify the reaction. If someone cries, offering a tissue is a kind gesture that shows you care.

Turning down your internal noise

You simply cannot listen to someone else when the chatterboxes in your head are chattering away. The internal noise – which I also call the 'uninvited neighbour in your head' – distracts you and interferes with your ability to receive messages. The temptation for your mind to wander is huge. Succumb to that temptation at your peril.

When someone is speaking and your thoughts, senses and feelings divert your attention from him, absorbing his message is pretty difficult. While you pay attention to your own interests, you lose the gist of what the other person is saying. He then feels relegated to the side lines, which isn't a cool place to hang out. Even worse, he may feel downright insulted and close down the conversation entirely.

Research shows that the average rate of speech in western countries is 120–150 words per minute, while the average rate of thinking is 600–800 words per minute. Because you truly can think faster than you can speak, your mind can easily go walkabout when someone's speaking to you.

Finishing other people's sentences because you anticipate what's coming next indicates that you're paying more attention to your thoughts than to theirs. If you're more interested in your point of view than theirs, don't expect them to be interested in yours. Before you jump in, be sure that you take time to also focus on *how* the other person is delivering his message, as well as what she's saying.

When you filter what you hear, you only take in part of what the other person is saying and usually latch onto the words that personally resonate for you. You can easily miss the larger picture that illustrates the speaker's point or key details. Whatever you're doing, you're not actively listening. For more on filtering information, refer to *Coaching with NLP For Dummies*.

If your boss or a colleague is speaking to you, seeking your full attention, and you're thinking something along the lines of, 'OMG. That person's so hot!' or 'What an idiot. I can't believe anyone still thinks that way' or 'If someone doesn't turn down the heat in this room, I'm going to fall asleep in the middle of this meeting', the other people in the room are going to pick up on the fact that what you're hearing in your head has little to do with what they're saying. They're likely to assume that you're more interested in yourself than in them.

Peter was facing redundancy. At the age of 45 and with a young family, he was anxious and troubled. He didn't want to worry his wife, so he didn't discuss his fears and concerns with her. Instead, he sought support and solace from his close friends. Walter, a friend from school days, did not empathise with Peter and instead began to stress out about how awful redundancy must be and how he wouldn't know what to do if that happened to him. Paying attention to the internal noise in his own head, including questions like, 'What would I do if this happened to me?' and 'I don't know how I'd face my wife and children if I were in Peter's place', Walter worked himself up into such a state considering his own concerns that Peter ended up comforting him and reassuring this friend that he, himself, would be fine and not to worry. Peter felt even more isolated and apprehensive as a result of this encounter and avoided Walter for months after.

Shutting down the loudspeakers in your mind and keeping the arena open to receive messages from others requires practice. You can't get a six-pack without doing crunches and neither can you become a top-notch listener without opening your mind and practising. In order to focus your attention on what another person is saying – and thus eliminate time for your mind to engage in internal chitchat – pay attention to the following three aspects of the other person simultaneously:

- ✔ Listen for the facts in what the other person is saying. Identify the relevant details and accurate information. Notice, too, any inaccurate information and emotional hyperbole.

- ✔ Observe the other person's movements and expressions to gain additional insights into how he really feels about what she's saying.

- ✔ Tune into the person's voice, noting the tone, volume, rate and rhythm of his speech. If you notice that the movements and tone are out of synch with what the other person's saying, pay particular attention to how the message is being delivered. Non-verbal behaviour, including gestures, expressions and tone of voice reveal the other person's attitudes and feelings. For more about non-verbal behaviour, turn to Chapters 13 and 14.

You have to care enough to want to listen. If you struggle to care about another person's feelings or situation, think about how his perceptions can impact on you and what you want to have happen. The more you know about someone, the more information you have to refer to when you want to persuade or influence them. See Chapter 5 for more on appreciating where others are coming from.

Being present with the speaker

No matter what's going on outside – honking horns, celebrities passing by, blizzards – stay with the other person. People appreciate that you care enough about them to ignore obvious distractions.

The key to being present with another person is focus, focus, focus. Tune into the speaker as he is right here, right now. Don't respond to him as he may have been before or who you think he may be. Just spend this moment with him as he is in the present.

To be present with someone requires that you connect with them, ridding yourself of external or internal noise. If you're genuine in your desire to listen for understanding, take the person as he is, without allowing your prejudices, biases or preconceptions to cloud your outlook.

Look at the other person with whom you're engaging. The eyes are the window to the soul. When you look at someone, you're able to pick up information he might not otherwise reveal. For example, people who avoid looking at you may be withholding information. Someone who fidgets while she's speaking may feel uncomfortable. And someone who looks dreamily into your eyes may harbour romantic feelings for you.

As a result of building repairs, Beth's monthly session with her coach, Sue, needed to shift from Beth's office to Sue's club. Beth and Sue hoped to find a quiet place to talk, but when they arrived at the club, the meeting area was full and noisy. After they managed to find two chairs, Sue pulled her chair closer to Beth than he would under normal circumstances, in order to help shut out the room's many distractions. When he told Beth what he was doing, Beth felt that Sue respected their business relationship and that her coach was doing everything possible to focus her attention on her.

In certain cultures avoiding eye contact is a sign of deference while looking someone in the eye is considered intrusive and disrespectful. When doing business with people from cultures different to your own, do your homework and find out where the eyes have it. For more information about eye contact, see my book *Body Language For Dummies*.

Gaining Additional Information while Listening

While your words and movements when listening may seem minor, how you express yourself verbally and physically can have a significant impact on how a conversation evolves. In the following sections, I outline some of my favourite techniques to keep someone talking and – in the process – reveal important information that you can use later to persuade and influence.

Although most people avoid speaking directly about their feelings, they offer lots of clues that indicate what's really going on in their hearts and minds. Listen for tone of voice, word choice, rate and rhythm of speech if you want to understand their feelings. Watch for body movements, expressions and posture. Whether they're mumbling, grunting, slouching or standing ram-rod straight barking out instructions, people are sending out signals as to how they're feeling. For example:

- ✔ If someone's body is upright, four-square and solid, she's sending out messages that she's in control.
- ✔ If someone's shoulders are hunched up, she's telling you she's in protective mode.

Of course, you've to dig deeper than just gestures and expressions to get a complete picture of what's going on inside, but you can still get an idea with a few bits of data.

Reflecting back

When you reflect back what you hear another person say, you confirm your understanding of his message including his thoughts and beliefs as well as his feelings and emotions. Sometimes a person just needs to be heard and acknowledged. At other times they need to hear the flaws in their reasoning without being criticised. In addition, reflecting back what another person says helps to identify areas where you agree and disagree, bringing issues into the open where they stand a better chance of being resolved than if they were allowed to burble below the surface.

I am not, repeat, *not*, encouraging you to adopt someone else's style at the expense of your authentic self. I am, however, encouraging you to listen to and observe the way others communicate and then reflect back their patterns in yours.

When you reflect back someone's feelings via words, behaviours and other means, you're

- ✔ Showing that you're paying attention
- ✔ Encouraging the other person to continue to speak
- ✔ Conveying a warm attitude
- ✔ Demonstrating respect for the other person
- ✔ Increasing your understanding of the situation and where the other person is coming from.
- ✔ Building rapport to utilise for future influence

Echoing speech patterns

If you sound like a squire from the home counties and your boss sounds like a market trader from London's East End, you may want to consider the way you speak.

Echoing back words, phrases and speech patterns verbatim sounds parrot-like and insulting. Don't waste time and energy trying to copy the other person exactly. Instead, paraphrase or use expressions such as, 'What I understand you're saying is . . .' or 'So, in other words . . .' to clarify your understanding and make the other person feel that you're listening.

When you pick up on speech patterns, words and expressions, you gain insight into the other person's way of thinking, behaving and feeling. When you understand those three factors and reflect them back, you're better able to gain the other person's approval. For more about how feelings impact on listening and reflecting, see Chapter 3.

When Jan met Don, the head of human resources for a global technology company, she paid particular attention to the language he used when speaking. She heard him frequently use words such as *passionate*, *respect*, *engage*, *value* and *appreciate*. She noticed that when he spoke about learning and development, his eyes sparkled and he sat forward in his chair, using his hands to convey his strength of feeling. By paying attention to his language and noticing his gestures and expressions, Jan was able to reflect his language and behavioural choices in hers, creating rapid rapport. Soon, Jan and Don were exploring ways in which her company could support him in his quest to provide quality coaching for the senior members of the organisation. Later that day, when she sent him an email thanking him for his time, she referred to specific conversation points and feelings that he acknowledged during the interview. Jan is now a preferred supplier to the company, focusing on communication and listening skills. By demonstrating her own ability to listen for feelings and attitudes as well as data and facts, Jan convinced Don that she was the person to coach the company.

Mirroring non-verbal behaviours

Matching people's moods by reflecting back their non-verbal behaviours – such as posture, gestures and expressions – establishes rapport, which encourages positive results.

I'm not suggesting that you mimic other people's behaviour and try to duplicate exact movements and expressions. They're likely to identify you as a sham or an out-of-work actor who lacks subtlety. Instead, I recommend that you respond in an appropriate manner in order to demonstrate respect, establish rapport and produce results. For more about establishing rapport, see Chapter 13.

Gestures, posture, expressions and vocal factors reveal what's going on inside. By responding to these signals in respectful ways, you're more able to connect with people and influence them than if you go barging into their territory without heeding the signs.

Interjecting intelligently

Sometimes, interjecting is appropriate, even necessary, during a listening session. Encouraging others to continue talking – by asking questions or paraphrasing what you're hearing – builds rapport. Other people feel that you're paying attention to them.

However, if you're going to intervene while someone else is speaking, apply your intelligence before opening your mouth:

- ✔ Never attempt to impose your thoughts or judgements on the other person's.

- ✔ Before you interject, identify the benefit of your intervention. Saying something along the lines of, 'I'm struggling to understand what you mean and I really want to. Could you rephrase that last part?' shows the speaker that you value him and what he's saying. If the person is going on and on, interject with, 'So, let me summarise your points to confirm that I understand what you mean.'

- ✔ If you're looking to score points, stop right now. If you want to improve your understanding, further the discussion and demonstrate your care and concern, then intervene.

Because you think faster than you speak (see 'Turning down your internal noise'), your first instinct may be to interrupt. For safety's sake, stay away. Studies show that interrupting someone while she's speaking diverts and distracts her attention. In addition, interrupting negatively impacts on relationships, shuts down communication and reduces your ability to discover anything. If you interrupt without taking care, be prepared for the person speaking to feel less spontaneous and more antagonistic toward you. The person may not open up to your persuasive influence in the future.

Showing support to elicit further information

As I note in Chapter 2, when you connect with people on an emotional level, you're more likely to persuade and influence them than if you dismiss their opinions and reject their feelings. During the listening process, you must use words, actions and empathy (see the earlier section 'Offering empathy') to show you care and bring out additional information that can be helpful later on.

While you're listening to someone speak, demonstrate interest by leaning towards the other person, keeping your eyes on him and nodding to encourage more talking. Say brief and supportive phrases such as 'I see' or 'tell me more', which gently lull the other person into providing further information. Sympathetic non-verbal sounds like 'mmm', 'hmm,' and 'uh huh' also indicate that you're interested in what they're saying and encourage further conversation. Touching the other person on the lower arm can be supportive and reassuring. You can also touch someone on the back, shoulder or upper arm as long as the touch is appropriate and does not violate their personal space. Unless you're shaking hands, avoid touching someone on his hand as that may be open to misinterpretation. Also, before you touch people, ask if you may. Some individuals don't like to be touched and in certain cultures touching is considered to be invasive.

Next time you're listening to another person and want to show support without saying a word, assume this posture:

✔ Sit or stand with your legs and arms uncrossed.

✔ Face the speaker and tilt your head towards him.

✔ Let your face take on an open expression.

✔ Nod as the other person speaks.

Each of these simple yet supportive behaviours encourages the other person to keep talking and revealing information.

Some people are tactile and like to touch and be touched. Others don't. While touch can go a long way in persuading people to follow you, touching others in inappropriate ways without their permission is invasive and disrespectful. If in doubt, don't touch.

Asking sensitive and sensible questions

While I encourage you not to interrupt when someone else is speaking (see the earlier section 'Interjecting intelligently'), I also encourage you to ask questions to elicit information. Asking questions effectively demonstrates that you're listening and that you're interested in the other person and his issues. Use the following tips to formulate effective questions:

- ✔ **Focus on open questions.** *Open questions* encourage people to speak further and more deeply. Open questions give people the opportunity to explore their feelings, thoughts and opinions. An example of an open question is, 'What would you like to do about that?' while a closed question would be, 'Have you thought about doing . . . ?'

- ✔ **Think about your reasons for asking any questions.** Do you want to further your understanding of the other person – or do you want to impose your opinions under the guise of questioning?

- ✔ **Double-check that your questions aren't leading the other person into your way of thinking.** Avoid phrases such as, 'Don't you think it would be better if . . . ' or 'Don't you think you should . . . ', which clearly try to manipulate responses to suit your agenda. Leading questions do not create trust, which is a crucial part in building relationships. See Chapter 5 for more about trust and persuasion.

- ✔ Instead, use phrases like 'What may be the benefits of . . . ?' or 'What other choices do you have . . . ?', which encourage open and thoughtful dialogue while providing you with greater insights into their way of thinking.

When you ask effective questions that encourage and elicit information, you show that you understand the issues that someone is facing. And, as a result of appropriate questioning, you gain additional data that can influence your approach when you want to later persuade that person to adopt your way of thinking or acting.

When you disagree

If you disagree with what the other person is saying, resist the urge to jump in with your opinions. Instead, be patient and hear the other person out. Encourage him to reveal more about his views by asking a question beginning with, 'I'm just curious about your reasons for . . . ' Use non-confrontational language that makes you sound inquisitive rather than intrusive and keeps the other person from becoming defensive.

Prefacing a question with the words, 'I'm just curious . . . ' opens the pathway for clear communication and allows you freedom when you're addressing sensitive topics. This phrase demonstrates your interest, shows respect for the other person's point of view and avoids criticism. Phrasing your questions in this manner is an elegant way of softening hard questions and offers you an easy way out if the other person should turn defensive. For example, if the other person challenges you or accuses you of being negative, you can sincerely respond that you really are curious and interested in understanding what he means. See the earlier side bar 'Sincerely my dear' about the value of speaking with sincerity.

When conversation seems blocked

When people are reluctant to express their feelings – or don't even understand their feelings – you may feel puzzled when you're listening. If you feel blocked or confused, continue to practise good listening behaviours and reflect back what you hear (see the earlier section 'Reflecting back'), even though doing so doesn't make sense at the moment. Over time, this approach allows the other person to gain self-understanding and opens the door for you to understand, too.

The following conversation between Tyler and her supervisor Ed show how sensitive questioning can encourage another person to share more about what's going wrong – even if the other person isn't initially clear about the source of the problem.

> **Ed:** Hey, Tyler. How's it going?
>
> **Tyler:** Not so great. I'm just feeling a bit rotten today. But the weather's pretty lousy, so that's probably why.
>
> **Ed:** Oh, you're feeling low today?
>
> **Tyler:** Yeah, I've been feeling pretty stymied and frustrated.
>
> **Ed:** [paraphrasing the feelings Tyler described] So, you feel as though you've hit a wall, is that it?
>
> **Tyler:** Well, I put in for a loan a few days ago and found out my application's been refused.
>
> **Ed:** That's disappointing.
>
> **Tyler:** Yeah. I was really looking forward to getting that loan so I could get on the property ladder.
>
> **Ed:** So, you're looking to buy a property?
>
> **Tyler:** Yes. But I can't afford to buy a house on my own.
>
> **Ed:** So, what other options do you have?
>
> **Tyler:** I could ask my brother if he wanted to go in with me.
>
> **Ed:** How do you feel about that?
>
> **Tyler:** I'm not all that keen as I don't like his girlfriend much and he'd probably want her to come in on the deal with us.
>
> **Ed:** What else could you do?

By continuing to ask open questions, not only did Ed help Tyler figure out the source of her frustration, he helped her think about ways of dealing with it.

Often people are unaware of their own feelings. Or they're ashamed of or feel guilty about them and struggle to face up to their own emotions. For example, an employee asking his line manager, 'What do you want me to do about this mess?' knows in reality what's expected. He's not asking for instructions. Instead, he's expressing his hostility and resentment. A sensitive supervisor spots the feelings buried under the brusque words and addresses the feelings first. A supervisor who's not listening for the feelings beneath the words may offer an answer that the other person doesn't want, like 'Sort yourself out and fix it!', exacerbating the real problem, which is the employee's hostility.

If someone is concealing emotions, as often happens at work and in personal relationships, ask yourself two questions:

- ✔ In view of the situation, does what the individual is saying make sense?
- ✔ Does the individual's manner of speaking fit his statement?

If the answer to one of these questions or both is a resounding 'no', carefully dig deeper until you get to what's really going on.

When you ask sensible and sensitive questions, you show other people that you care about them and what they have to say. By repeating and refining what other people say, you demonstrate that you understand their feelings and aren't judging them. Keep questioning and repeating, and eventually you get the real facts – not a doctored version meant to please you. When you've uncovered the real facts and emotions, turn to Chapter 12 to see what to do next.

Chapter 8

Gaining and Maintaining Your Audience's Interest

*W*hen was the last time someone mesmerised you to the point that you couldn't take your eyes off her? What did she do that persuaded you to sit up and pay attention? How did she get you on board and keep you there? In other words, how did she grab your attention and hold it?

Engaging with your listeners so they're open to what you say is vital if you're going to persuade them to your way of thinking. Whether you want to gain and keep the attention of one or a hundred people, if you don't connect from the beginning and increase their interest throughout, you're going to have a hard time influencing them.

Fortunately, the ability to gain and keep someone's attention involves simple strategies that you can apply to a variety of situations. Like all new skills, you have to practise if you want to hone your abilities.

In this chapter I share some ideas and concepts that equip you with an arsenal of techniques and tools to draw on when you want to persuade your audience – whether it's one person, a small group of individuals or a cast of thousands – to move from where they are to where you want them to be. The result? You capture their attention, increase its intensity it and win them over to your idea or suggestion.

Getting Others to Notice You

Getting noticed has always been a challenge, and the twenty-first century hasn't made the process any easier. With the shortage of time and a never-ending cascade of ideas and choices bombarding people daily, gaining and keeping someone's attention is an on-going struggle.

The moment people see or hear you, they're noticing you. They're deciding whether they want to bother with you or not. To get yourself noticed, what you say and how you say it must be remarkable – so different, shocking or fresh that people are unable to ignore it.

Auditioning like a diva

According to theatre lore, when Barbra Streisand was still an unknown actress she walked into an audition visibly chewing a large wad of chewing gum. As she took her place on stage, she continued chomping, then stopped and with an embarrassed and coquettish smile, removed the gum from her mouth, stuck it under the stool on which she was sitting, and began singing again. After the auditions were over and all the performers had left the theatre, the show's director walked onto the stage and looked underneath the stool, only to find nothing there. By having faked chewing gum and making a meal out of getting rid of it, Streisand managed to stand out from the crowd. While the story may or may not be true, getting noticed and sustaining interest is a cunning strategy.

While offensiveness can capture people's attention, offending their core values and beliefs (see Chapter 2) negatively impacts on your ability to influence their thinking and behaviour. Avoid bigotry, chauvinism and narrow-mindedness at all costs. What you think is funny may hurt someone else. Making uncouth remarks about someone's sexual, religious or political preferences can make you appear aggressive and unpleasant, while commenting adversely on someone's appearance can make you come across as rude and insulting. As for profanity and titillating imagery, leave it out unless you're prepared to be shown the door.

Garnering a first glance

First impressions count, and you have between four and six seconds to get yourself noticed. Without a doubt, you're competing with factors such as time constraints, fatigue, boredom and external noise – like ringing phones, crying babies and loud music – in your efforts to capture your listener's attention.

Grabbing attention online and offline

With the plethora of online competitors vying for attention, how you come across determines whether you're noticed or not. In a recent study of open rates, 51 per cent of the 4 million participants who were sent a data-driven email deleted the message within two seconds of opening it.

To capture and sustain attention, you need to have a great opening line that piques, pushes and prods your reader to open your email and read on. The same is true for websites. Research into motivation reveals that humans share three basic characteristics: curiosity, controversy and scarcity. Mix those with focusing on the three core goals that most people have – either making or saving time, money and energy – and you're onto a winner.

Here are some examples of headlines that cater to people's basic instincts and make them want to read on:

How to make £1,500 a week without leaving your home.

How to save thousands on your utility bills.

How to make him/her fall in love with you again.

How to lose those unsightly, unwanted pounds fast.

How to get published in 30 days or less.

Whether you're writing copy or delivering a spoken message face-to-face or over the phone, the principle of appealing to people's fundamental characteristics and core goals remains the same.

Identifying what matters to your audience

Everyone has more commitments and less time to focus on any one thing than they'd like. That's why your message must be clear, compelling and concise. However you're conveying your message – in writing or via audio recording, video or speaking directly to a live audience – adopt the following principles:

- ✔ **Turn the complex into simple key points.** Start by thinking about the big picture. Consider what is important about your message, the benefits, who it affects and how. What do you want your audience to do as a result of what you've communicated?

- ✔ **Appeal to your audience's emotions, needs and desires.** Back up your message with compelling evidence such as a single scintillating factoid or anecdotes that capture the emotional seriousness of the subject. While the evidence you choose to support your points will change depending on your audience, having all forms at the ready means you're prepared for anything that comes your way. In addition, make your message memorable by including rhythm, contrast, metaphors and other rhetorical devices to make your message stick.

✔ **Stick to the point.** Messages that ramble on with little focus confuse your audience, leaving them wondering what you want from them.

Whether advertisers are persuading you to shop at certain stores, purchase particular products or travel to distant lands, they're capturing your attention by appealing to your interests, fantasies or values – and often a combination of the three. Check out these examples:

✔ An offer of 50 per cent off sounds good when money's in short supply. Here the advertiser is making a direct appeal to the buyers' interests by proposing to save them money. (See the side bar 'Grabbing attention online and offline' above for more about appealing to human interests.)

✔ An image of beautiful people drinking pina coladas on a sandy beach, and the suggestion of jasmine wafting on a balmy breeze is a pretty persuasive way to appeal to your fantasies and tempt you to a holiday when you're shivering under a mountain of blankets or scraping ice off your car.

✔ A good-looking doctor suggesting you take your cough syrup is more likely to influence your choices than a grumpy old man shoving the bottle at you. Even when you know the doctor in an ad is an actor, the advertisers still gain your attention by combining good looks and authority while tapping into your health needs. Here you've got fantasies – the good-looking doctor – as well as interests and values – your health – working in combination. For more about attractiveness and authority as persuasive tools, see Chapter 10.

To gain your listeners' attention, find out what matters to them. Do your homework to understand their issues and concerns so when the time comes to gain their attention, you can demonstrate that you're already familiar with what's important to them. Whether your homework takes the form of market research, asking people who personally know your listeners, or asking your listeners directly, the more you know about the people you're planning to persuade – the more you know about their interests and issues – the more persuasive you're able to be. However you gather your information, make sure you're behaving in an appropriate, ethical manner. For more about ethical behaviour turn to Chapter 5.

Building up your energy and enthusiasm

You want to speak with enough confidence to demonstrate that you know what you're talking about, without appearing arrogant. Practise some of the techniques below to build up your energy and enthusiasm:

✔ **Smile.** Whether you're speaking to a large audience, a small gathering or just one person, before you say a word, smile. According to numerous studies, smiling suggests trustworthiness, cooperation, lifts moods and provides bursts of insight. Use your smiles selectively, as smiling at upsetting things can make you appear uncaring.

✔ **Take care of yourself.** Look after your body by eating the right foods, getting enough rest and exercising on a regular basis. Take time to socialise with friends and reflect on what's important to you. Like any instrument, your body and mind perform better when you look after them. Refer to Chapter 2 for more about self-reflection.

✔ **Plunge in.** Long before Nike coined the slogan 'Just do it', Dale Carnegie said 'Inaction breeds doubt and fear. Action creates confidence and courage. Fear evaporates when we take action.' Commit to what you're doing and watch your energy and enthusiasm rise.

The average attention span of the typical listener is six to eight minutes at a time. If you question how much time this is, hold your breath and see how long it takes before you're gasping for air. Six to eight minutes can feel like an eternity. In order to hold your listeners' attention you must engage them in the process. Some techniques you can use to keep your audience with you include:

✔ **Ask questions.** Direct and rhetorical questions turn a monologue into a conversation as your listener becomes actively involved.

✔ **Use props.** Relevant props that are visible and colourful help your listener remember what you're talking about.

✔ **Add drama.** Bring what you're saying to life by putting your voice and body into the process. Don't be afraid to act out part of your speech, using your body as a prop and including dialogue, accents and vocal variety.

✔ **Tell a story.** Facts tell, stories sell. Tell stories from your personal experience to develop your point. Include case studies and examples to make your material come alive.

✔ **Pause.** If you pause you show confidence and your audience become curious about what's coming next.

Using hooks

When you want to persuade your audience to listen to what you have to say, get yourself a hook. A *hook* is anything that gains attention and encapsulates in a nutshell the concept of what you're saying. You don't have to buy, make or give a hook away. Great hooks just require a little care and preparation. Use any and all of the following to quickly capture your listeners' hearts and minds:

✔ **Anecdotes.** People still pay attention to compelling, well-told stories. Tell a short personal story that connects you to your listeners and the issues at hand. Some people like to start their stories with the end, while others like to start at the very beginning. Whichever approach you take, make sure your story is relevant to your subject.

✔ **Humour.** Smiling makes people feel good, and laughter binds people together. Start off with a humorous spin on your topic, making sure your wittiness is appropriate to your message. I'm not suggesting that you try to be a stand-up comic, rather I encourage you to share a funny story about yourself or something that happened to reveal your charm. If you do tell a joke and it falls flat, don't push harder. Drop it and move on.

✔ **Statements that create doubt or disbelief.** What you say doesn't have to be true as long as you pique your listeners' curiosity. A statement such as 'What you're about to hear will change your life forever' may not be factually true but it may make your audience sit up in hope.

✔ **Outstanding facts or statistics.** Cite accurate information that's interesting, relevant and not common knowledge.

✔ **Opinions.** Say something contrary to public opinion – such as, 'I see nothing wrong with sweatshop labour practices' – and watch the feathers fly. Your listeners are likely to stay engaged just to see what happens next.

✔ **Current events.** Whether they skim the headlines while waiting for their lattés, catch a bit of the news while driving home from work, or follow sports and current affairs rigorously, most people have some knowledge of something that's been happening in the world.

✔ **Quotes.** They don't have to be from famous people, just appropriate and timely.

✔ **Theatrics.** As a former actor, I'm prone to add a bit of show business into my openings in order to gain the listeners' attention. After you stumble over your opening lines or begin addressing your remarks to the wrong audience, your listeners will want to see what's coming next. Give it a go as a new approach. Practise first to make sure your choices work.

Whatever type of hook you choose, make it relevant to your message. For example, a story about an abused child will grab the attention of your audience if you're fundraising for a children's charity.

Taking an interest in others

For most people, life is a case of 'It's all about me'. But guess what? No matter how charming and intelligent you are, no matter how creative your solutions or how logical your conclusions, if you don't take into consideration the needs and wants of the people you want to influence, or if your product or idea isn't relevant to them, you can't expect to persuade them to adopt your way of seeing things.

Except for people who have something to hide, most people like it when others take an interest in them, because it makes them feel special. And if you make someone feel special, she's much more likely to like you. See Chapter 10 for more on how liking and being liked are part of the persuasion process.

You can capture people's attention by knowing what matters to them and showing that you care. Show your interest in others by exploring any of the following, either by directly asking or doing a bit of research first:

- ✔ **Where they're from.** Every town, city and country has unique characteristics that influence people's thinking and behaviour. Showing you're interested in others' backgrounds shows you're interested in them as people.

- ✔ **What matters to them.** If you don't already know, ask them what their concerns and issues are – and then respond with useful, relevant information. For example, are they concerned about the environment, taxes or government decisions? Do health and safety issues matter to them? Do they have children, pets, second homes? Touch on these pertinent topics and you tap into other people's beliefs, values and concerns. And when you do that, you're well on your way to capturing their attention.

- ✔ **What interests them.** Golf, tennis, mountain climbing? Family, travel, fast cars? The more you know about your listeners, the better position you're in to persuade them to pay attention.

- ✔ **What they fear or are concerned about.** What drives them and keeps them going? By knowing possible answers to their questions and solutions to their problems, you have a blueprint for influencing their decisions.

If you've experienced the phenomenon of someone showing interest in you, you probably enjoyed it. Perhaps someone touched on something that truly matters to you in the course of conversation. Or maybe you discovered that two of you share an experience or passion. These small connections make you more receptive to the other person. The energy flows between the two of you rather than in just one direction. You're more likely to persuade – or be persuaded.

If you're speaking to an audience of more than one or a few, the challenge of discovering everyone's interests, needs and concerns may seem overwhelming. You may even find that some of the people's interests are in conflict. That said, you can always count on people having interests around well-being, including financial, physical, spiritual or family. Turn to Chapter 2 for more on human concerns and motivations.

Demonstrating interest in another person helps you gain her attention, giving you a place to begin influencing her thoughts and behaviour. You need to follow up the initial interest by building trust and respect (see Chapter 5) if you want to become a long-term successful persuader and influencer.

Using names

Addressing people by their names commands their attention. Remembering people as individuals and recalling something personal about them only furthers your connection. I find the best way to remember someone's name is to repeat the name as soon as I've heard it and refer to the person by name during the conversation. For example, 'It's a pleasure to meet you, James' and, later in the conversation, saying something like, 'So tell me, James, how did you discover you and Ben both had a passion for extreme sports?' You can find lots of tips for remembering names in *Improving Your Memory For Dummies* by John B Arden (Wiley).

Utilising key words

When you want to capture someone's attention, choose your words carefully. Because of time constraints and information overload, people are selective in what they hear. While you're speaking, everyone else has additional dialogues running through their heads. Did I pay before leaving the car park? Should I sell my shares in this business? What time is my daughter's school play?

In order to bring your listeners' attention back to you, find and use key words that spark their interest. *Key words* are clear, powerful words that appeal to your listeners' emotions, curiosity and concerns. When you listen carefully to what people say, you can pick out the words that are key for them. For example, if someone talks about connection, passion, beliefs and values you know that those are buzz words you can incorporate into your presentation. When you incorporate key words early on (and, indeed, throughout your presentation) you stand a better chance of persuading your listeners than if your phrasing is haphazard. For example:

- ✔ **Statement without key words:** 'Today I'm here to talk to you about how to make a good presentation.'

- ✔ **Statement strategically packed with key words:** 'If you want to connect with your audience, engage with their beliefs and values, and are passionate about convincing them to follow your lead, you've come to the right place.'

Some key words become apparent only after you spend time with your audience, so make an effort to listen for them. While many people may think they're good listeners, the truth is that most people fail to take interest in and make use of what others are telling them. (Chapter 7 explains how to go beyond hearing into the realm of truly listening.) So pay attention to what your audience say and try to pick out their key words.

Connecting visually

Eye contact is a vital element in both capturing and maintaining your listeners' interest.

Unless avoiding eye contact is part of your theatrical attention-grabbing opening (see the 'Using hooks' section earlier in this chapter), keep your head out of your papers and look at your audience before saying a word. And if looking anywhere other than at your audience is part of your ploy to gain their attention, let them know sooner rather than later why you're behaving that way.

When I encourage you to establish and maintain eye contact, I'm not talking about playing the staring game and making others feel uncomfortable. Blink at a normal rate and shift your focus occasionally.

- ✔ **In a group setting,** spend about three seconds with each audience member, connecting visually and maintaining engagement. Scan the room as if you were talking to a group of interested friends rather than an amorphous gathering of indifferent individuals. While some extol the virtues of letting your eyes wander around the table or down one row and back up the next, I encourage you to take in the whole group before you begin speaking and then direct your comments to individuals in different parts of the room, working from one corner to the next in an M, W or X pattern. The important point is to make sure that you connect with all areas.

- ✔ **In one-to-one settings,** look at the person you're speaking to 45 to 65 per cent of the time. When you're listening, increase your visual connection, looking at the speaker 60 to 85 per cent of the time.

Only when you get to the 'big ask' – 'When will you answer my question/sign this contract/pick up your room?' – should you look your listener straight in the eye and not blink or back off until you've won your point.

When you look someone in the eye as you're speaking to her, you come across as credible. And credible people carry authority. Refer to Chapters 5 and 11 for more information about the impact of authority and credibility on persuading and influencing.

Some cultures consider sustained eye contact disrespectful. Do your cultural research to avoid causing offence.

Maintaining and Escalating Their Attention

Having garnered your audience's attention and established your willingness to listen with all the techniques I cover in the preceding section, you now want to keep them engaged.

Actors, public speakers and people in sales know the importance of maintaining audience interest. Having gained your listeners' attention, you must aim to lift your listeners' interest for as long as possible and prevent it from collapsing, all the while competing with distractions (see the later section 'Dealing with distractions').

Speaking the same language

Capturing and maintaining your listeners' attention requires that you pay attention to them. Observe how they communicate – what kinds of words and phrases they employ – and reflect back what you notice. This approach is similar to my advice in Chapter 7 where I suggest that you reflect back the words and gestures you observe.

Speaking the same language as your listeners improves your persuasive powers. I don't mean you have to speak French to the French and Russian to the Russians in order to get them to understand you. (Of course, being able to speak the language of your clients and colleagues is helpful when doing business in a global world, and I encourage you to learn as many languages as you can.)

When you speak the same language as your audience, you reflect back what you hear and repeat similar words and phrases (see the earlier 'Utilising key words' section) and you further tailor your presentation to your listeners' styles and preferences. For example,

✔ **If you're speaking to a group of people who are fact or logic driven,** present your case in a logical, factual style. Base your remarks on reason to draw a conclusion. Because the basis of logical thinking is sequential thought, give structure to your presentation by arranging important ideas, facts and conclusions in a chain-like progression.

✔ **If your listeners' style is casual,** loosen your verbal reins and reflect other people's words and phrasing in yours. For example, casual speech is usually associated with people who you are close to and trust, and is the language used between friends, family and people who are similar to you. Casual language sounds friendly and tends to use contractions and simplified grammar. In presentations, you would tend to rely less on graphs, charts and hard data and more on anecdotal evidence.

You can pick up loads of information about various learning styles and information-gathering preferences in *Neuro-Linguistic Programming For Dummies* by Romilla Ready and Kate Burton (Wiley) as well as in *Business NLP For Dummies* by Lynne Cooper (Wiley). In addition, you can flip to Chapter 9 now to pick up tips for recognising how your listener prefers to make decisions.

Throughout this book I encourage you to match and pace your listeners in order to influence them. You can find further information and details about this process in both *Business NLP For Dummies* as well as in *Neuro-Linguistic Programming For Dummies*.

Painting word pictures

Creating emotional word pictures is one of the most powerful ways of maintaining your listeners' attention. Great orators like Martin Luther King Jr, Abraham Lincoln, Winston Churchill, John F Kennedy, Socrates and numerous religious prophets understood how to link words and emotions to open hearts and minds.

Emotional *word pictures* are phrases or brief stories that create long-lasting, emotionally resonate images in listeners' minds. They clarify what you are saying and evoke a feeling at the same time, appealing to both the left (analytical) and right (emotional) sides of the brain.

Word pictures are so powerful because they tap into people's values, beliefs, hopes and dreams. They ignite passion and enhance the vision. As I describe in Chapter 3, when you connect at an emotional level, your chances of persuading and influencing others' choices increase.

Follow these suggestions to create successful and emotional word pictures:

- **Make your picture relevant to the time and circumstances.** For example, 'The current economic climate has me feeling like I'm on a runaway coach with no seatbelts or driver at the wheel.'

- **Take into account your audience's interests, passions or hobbies.** If you're describing to your golfing buddy how you envision a smooth leadership transition, you could say, 'It's like hitting a 200-metre drive straight down the fairway with a slow back swing and a full follow-through.'

- **Rely on sources that are proven successes.** You don't need to reinvent the wheel here, just keep an eye open for interesting things that share similarities with points you want to make. Pay attention to recent events, historical happenings, familiar objects and natural phenomena.

- **Go for brevity.** Try to paint your picture in two or three sentences.

- **Rehearse your word pictures before putting them into practice.** Share your ideas with a co-worker or friend before using them on the intended audience. See how they respond and ask for feedback.

- **Be selective and limit the number of images you use.** While tried-and-tested word pictures such as 'snug as a bug in a rug', 'dancing for joy' and 'walking with a spring in her step' are evocative, they're not original. See what range of images you can come up with. If you're using word pictures in a five-minute presentation, limit them to no more than three and stick with a theme. Any more and you begin to sound forced and too clever for your own good. When you add too many different word pictures, your audience becomes confused as to what point you're trying to make.

Repeating yourself effectively

Make your information relevant to your listeners and repeat your message to persuade them to continue to pay attention to you. Clear, confident delivery and pertinent information ensure your listeners don't drift off on an inner journey from lack of interest. See the 'Addressing lapses in attention' and 'Dealing with distractions' sections later in this chapter for more on effective repetition.

Grab your listeners' attention by telling them what you're going to tell them. Then tell them. And finally tell them what you just said. This way, when people do drift off, you're able to regain their attention without them feeling they've lost all of what you said.

Maintain your listeners' attention amid the repetition by varying your tone of voice (see Chapter 14), injecting unexpected words and phrases and throwing a view visuals into the mix.

Your movements, gestures and expressions count as visuals, so consider what you can do physically to attract attention and keep the audience's focus on you and what you're suggesting. See Chapter 13 for more on powerfully persuasive gestures.

Going with the Flow: Your Listeners' Attention Curve

I'm willing to bet, and I'm not a betting woman, that at some point during a presentation, conversation or interview you were distracted by something that had nothing to do with the discussion at hand. Don't worry. It happens to everyone.

When no one's paying attention, no one's communicating. And when no one's communicating, you can enjoy positive outcomes.

Hopefully, you were paying attention at some point during the interaction and were able get back on board, picking up where you left off without too much difficulty or disruption. (Of course, if you weren't interested in the first place, you'll continue to struggle to pay attention.)

Recognising the signs that concentration is faltering is the first step to responding. Signs of lost attention include:

- Dull expressions and glassy-eyed stares
- Little or no steady eye contact
- Talking
- Tapping the desk with a pen or jiggling a foot with impatience
- Obvious attempts to change the subject
- Silence and yawning
- Focussing on fingernails
- Doodling
- Using technology, for example when emailing, texting and making phone calls

The following sections examine those moments that occur during almost all interactions when someone's interest or attention flags a bit. By anticipating interruptions and preparing for breaks in concentration, you can re-engage your listener with appropriate responses.

Picturing peaks and troughs

A useful tool for dealing with people's propensity to drift is to think of attention as following a pattern – in this case, the *attention curve*. While this model is now well-established and accepted, it appears to have originated in the 1940s with the Dutch chess master and psychologist, Adriaan de Groot, who based his theory on the thought processes of chess players. It was originally referred to as the *memory model*.

As Figure 8-1 shows, the ideal attention curve rises sharply at the beginning and continues on a gentle upward trajectory until the end of your presentation. While this experience sounds nice, don't count on it happening in the real world.

Figure 8-1 also shows the more typical attention curve, in which attention rises and falls in waves periodically.

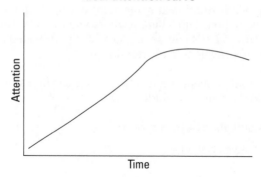

Ideal attention curve

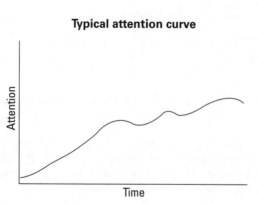

Figure 8-1:
Visualising the ebb and flow of attention helps you stay focused on the outcome.

Typical attention curve

Peaks and troughs are a natural part of conversation. People are always losing the plot and needing to be brought back on board. The problem is people never want to admit that they need you to repeat what you said. Looking stupid, impolite or just plain uninterested does not fit most people's pictures of themselves. In Chapter 5 you can find out about how to reflect your integrity.

As long as you gain your listeners' attention at the beginning and grab it again at the end, you have more of a chance of persuading them than if you start off on the back foot and finish up drifting off.

Putting the curve to good use

By visualising where you are in the conversation, staying on track becomes a simple matter of making the most of a particular moment along the attention curve. Rather like a surfboarder riding the big barrel, you can ride the curve and pay attention to the peaks and troughs. Even if you encounter a wipe-out-threatening wave, you can still land on your feet.

Program a template of an attention curve onto the hard disk of your mind. Take this template with you to all your meetings – any type, any place, any time. This way you've got a visual representation of the peaks and troughs of the conversation. By visualising an imaginary curve with ups and downs, you can evaluate the lapses and be prepared for their eventual appearance.

When a trough appears, figure out what's happening. Are you droning, mumbling or speaking jargonese? Or did your listener not understand your point? Because you can't sit in your listener's head, you've got to be alert to the tell-tale signs of flagging attention and respond quickly when concentration wanes. Some tell-tale signs you may encounter include:

- Rotating the head from side to side as if the listener has cramp in her neck
- Narrowed eyes with her head turned away from you
- Eyes glazed over
- Shuffling feet, rubbing the ears, eyes or nose while turning slightly away from you
- Picking at her clothes and removing link only she can see, or looking around the room
- Clenched fists with tightened facial muscles

Addressing lapses in attention

Too often, people fail to notice when someone's attention lapses. When you're initiating a conversation or presentation, you are responsible for paying attention to your listener, picking up on the signals and responding appropriately.

Engage with your listener from the beginning in order to ensure she can catch up with you after any attention lapses.

You must get your point across on the first attempt. What happens after your first attempt influences what happens next. If someone rejects an idea up front, you're going to struggle to change her mind later, even when she knows she's wrong. Often pride steers this mind set because no one wants to be perceived as indecisive or incapable of making the right choice in the first place.

Never pitch your idea to someone whose attention is not focused on you. If you're competing for attention from the beginning, wait until the person's eyes, ears and body are pointed in your direction. You may have to pause for several seconds until the other person realises what's happening. Waiting for someone's full attention can be uncomfortable, so breathe deeply to calm yourself and hang in there. If you can't gain the other person's complete attention, ask to defer the meeting until a more convenient time for her. Chapter 14 has some really good breathing exercises for steadying your nerves.

If people are interested in what you're showing or telling them, they'll look towards you or the object. If they're not interested, they'll look away. In that case there are several things you can do. Stop speaking until they look back at you, address the person by name, or change your vocal volume. If you're meeting with a group of your peers or you're the boss, it's fair to ask them to turn off their electronic devices – BlackBerrys and the rest – until the meeting is over. If you're having a one-to-one meeting and the other person starts surfing the net or texting while you're speaking or presenting, stop talking until she's finished.

Dealing with distractions

Distractions abound. Because you can't avoid distractions entirely, your best approach is to address them head-on, minimising potential distractions and correcting actual ones – as I explore further in the following sections.

Minimising potential distractions

Sometimes the very space where you're meeting lends itself to distractions – a window that lets in too much sun or frames a busy view, a listener positioned towards an open doorway where people continually cross, and chairs that are placed in such a way the audience struggles to see you all make gaining and maintaining your listeners' attention a challenge. If you can adjust these distractions in advance, do. Move chairs and close blinds. As I say in the preceding section, ask your listeners to turn off their electronic devices during your presentation. You're asked to turn them off when you go to the theatre and the cinema. There's no reason why you shouldn't ask your listeners to do so when you're presenting.

Remedying visual distractions

When you notice something that shifts attention away from you as presenter, deal with it immediately. (And by extension, help other presenters by assisting them as appropriate.) Visual distractions rarely resolve themselves. In fact, they often gain more attention when left unattended.

Whether you see a coffee stain on someone's jacket or some loo paper stuck to a shoe, acknowledging the elephant in the room is usually enough to satisfy everyone's curiosity and get the conversation back on track.

If you sense that something about you – your clothing, your hair or spinach on your teeth – is causing a distraction, ask your audience by saying something like, 'I notice you seem to be having difficulty concentrating on what I'm saying. Is there something I should know about?' This way you acknowledge what's going on and can do something about it.

If the distraction involves another person, inform her discretely. If appropriate, help the other person resolve the situation as quickly as possible.

Recognising disagreement

Lapses in attention may occur when someone in the audience disagrees with what the presenter is saying. Pay attention to your audience's movements and expressions. If your words are causing a negative reaction, engage the listener – or perhaps several listeners – in dialogue about the issue. Address your listeners' concerns head-on and without confrontation. For example, you could say, 'What do you think about what I've just said?' or 'There may be some of you who don't agree with what I've just said. Speak up so we can hear all points of view.' By offering your audience the chance to express their views you're showing that you're open to other opinions and are willing to take them into consideration.

Behaviours that indicate annoyance include tightened lips, flared nostrils, clenched hands, drumming fingers and jiggling feet. If anyone in your audience demonstrates these, stop and change tack. For more information about reading body language, treat yourself to a copy of my book *Body Language For Dummies* (Wiley).

Identify possible areas of disagreement and confusion and prepare responses *before* your presentation. Audiences appreciate speakers who deal with reservations openly and honestly. Planning ahead and responding straight away leaves you in a better position to regain their attention and interest. See Chapter 4 for more about dealing with doubts.

If you fail to gain your listeners' attention – or fail to regain it after it flags – you may find yourself being shown the door. Or the conversation may just end and nothing happens. Either way, your hard work is pretty much for nought. If this happens, regroup, reassess and take another shot. Sometimes it takes more than one approach to land a deal or gain approval. Turn to Chapter 1 for tips on working together to achieve goals.

Curbing constant interruptions

When you're speaking with someone and are interrupted over and over again, you can quickly become annoyed, while the other person becomes distracted. You can both forget where you are in the conversation or decide to cut an important discussion short.

Today's office environments are more pressurised than ever. People have more responsibilities and fewer support systems. Modern offices often feature open floor plans with few doors and walls. Most people's phones and mobile devices never stop ringing throughout the working day.

You must redress interruptions if you want to gain someone's attention and keep it:

- ✔ If someone interrupts your meeting by walking in, you can assess the problem and evaluate its possible impact on your listener's concentration. If the person has been invited to join the meeting, carry on. If it's a matter of someone dropping off some papers for the person you're speaking to, stop until she leaves. If your listener seems distracted by the interruption, ask if she'd like you to come back another time.

- ✔ When phone or email interrupts your conversation, observe how the other person reacts physically and vocally. (Find out more about the effect of body language and voice when conveying messages in Chapters 13 and 14.) If the person you're talking to seems distracted, ask whether she'd like you to leave and come back later. That way you're showing respect and demonstrating that you're paying attention. Turn to Chapter 7 for tips on responding to non-verbal behaviours.

Unless the other person asks to curtail your meeting, go back to where you were before the interruption and quickly summarise what you were saying.

When you summarise, make your points clear and concise. You don't need to take your listeners through the details of what you were saying, just the highlights. If you're in a group setting and one person is taken out for a few minutes by an email or conversation, bring them back into the discussion quickly by saying, for example, 'Nicole was just saying that . . .' That way you quickly summarise and remind everyone where they are.

You may fear that you sound like a repetitive parrot. Rest assured, you don't. People remember only a small portion of what they hear, so recapping your points helps to cement them in your listeners' minds. Plus you're helping others regain their attention and return to the discussion. As I remind attendees of my public speaking programmes, 'summarise to crystallise'.

Regaining attention after a lapse

Distractions and attention lapses are predictable, inevitable and often beyond your control. The key is how effectively you deal with the lapse and how quickly you can bounce back and reclaim attention.

Whatever the source of the interruption or lapse in interest, *stop* and acknowledge what's going on. Ignoring interruptions magnifies them, as anyone who's sat through a keynote speech in which the speaker ignores the beeping pager in the auditorium knows all too well.

In order to acknowledge a distraction or attention lapse effectively and move on quickly:

- ✔ **Remain positive.** When a lapse in attention occurs, stop what you're doing, maintain eye contact and acknowledge the distraction. Respond with respect and a positive outlook. If you adopt a punitive attitude, all you achieve is mutiny.

- ✔ **Revisit your last high point.** Visualise your attention curve and return to the last relevant peak point. Quickly summarise that last positive moment to rein your listeners back in. When your listeners are on an emotional high they're inclined to pay attention to what you're saying.

- ✔ **Block off distractions quickly.** If someone's phone rings during a meeting you're leading and the person insists on taking the call, ask her to leave the room and hold your thought until she returns.

- ✔ **Memorise where you left off.** Make a note for yourself or highlight your place in your outline or presentation. You're in charge of keeping tabs on the conversation, not your listener.

✔ **Make the most of down time.** While someone is away dealing with a phone call or must-answer email, open up the room to questions and observations from anyone who remains. Ask them for feedback so far and engage them in a discussion. By using the time constructively and positively – rather than treating the disruption as problematic – you maintain control of the situation and keep your listeners on track.

✔ **Recap fast and move on.** When a person returns after dealing with a distraction or interruption, cover what she missed, ask whether your recap makes sense and continue with the flow from where you left off.

✔ **Get comfortable with repetition.** Don't worry about repeating information – it's a good way to re-enforce your message. Most people absorb only 40 per cent of what they hear, so repetition is vital in making sure your message is retained.

Avoid repeating just for the sake of repeating, which only serves as a break in the flow of your persuasive story. People can easily lose interest. You know when you're repeating for the sake of repeating when you're not prepared and you keep covering the same territory, adding nothing new to the conversation. While some journalists repeat themselves with great success – for example, 'I've asked you 14 times to answer my question and I'm asking you again' – if you keep going over the same issue without contributing an insight or a point for discussion, you risk having your credibility questioned. See Chapter 5 for tips on establishing your credibility.

Their attention and interest reinstated, your audience can enjoy, understand and positively engage with you. And you're well on the way to persuading them!

Maintaining the emotional high

As I say in Chapter 3, people make decisions based on emotions. People respond more positively when they're emotionally engaged than they do when they couldn't care less. Appealing to people's emotions is more effective than appealing to logic, and goes a long way to convincing your listener to accept your proposal.

Emotional highs are those moments when you successfully transport your audience to a hyper-receptive level. They're excited and willing to commit to your idea. Look for the following signs to tell whether someone's on an emotional high and ready to commit to your proposal:

✔ **Eye contact.** The eyes are wide and bright, the pupils are enlarged and the person is looking directly at you.

✔ **Nodding head.** When the other person nods her head up and down she's indicating she concurs with what you're saying.

✔ **Smiling.** A smile shows that she's ready to reach agreement.

✔ **Leaning forward.** This position signals that the person's ready to get up and go with your proposal.

✔ **Vocal variety.** The person speaks more quickly and the voice tends to be higher than usual.

✔ **Muscle control.** When the muscles are firm but mobile, they're conveying positive energy.

Once you've got your listener's attention and have achieved that emotional high, strike while the iron's hot. Pull out your pen and get her to sign on the dotted line. If you don't have a contract with you, shake hands to seal the deal and get the paperwork in the post poste haste! In Chapter 9 you can find different approaches to take depending on your listeners' preferred decision-making styles.

Chapter 9

Gearing Your Approach to Different Decision-Making Styles

S imply put: people are different, particularly in the ways in which they make decisions.

Some people have strong aversions to risk, while others can't get enough. You meet individuals who are suspicious of any data that doesn't match their pictures of the world, whereas others just rely on their instincts. Some base their decisions on what worked in the past, whereas others focus on facts and analysis, afraid to make independent decisions.

If you apply a one-size-fits-all approach as you attempt to influence others, you're in for a rough ride and, most likely, failure. Instead, you can craft an approach tailored to how the person you want to persuade makes his decisions.

In this chapter I describe the subtle differences between five familiar decision-making styles. I show you how to identify and persuade each type, including specific buzzwords you can use to appeal to each style, as well as the best types of information and presentation formats that win over your listeners.

Knowing Who's Who and What's What

Knowing how to interpret and respond to the words, actions and attitudes of people who make decisions that impact on your life leads to secure and effective relationships. Whether you're influencing your boss, a colleague or members of your family, knowing how to convert your suggestions into compelling cases can turn your proposals into winning propositions.

For their 2004 book, *The 5 Paths to Persuasion*, which explores how leaders make decisions, executive consultants Gary Williams and Robert Miller interviewed nearly 1,700 executives across a wide range of industries. They identified five predictable types of decision-making processes: charismatics, sceptics, thinkers, followers or controllers. Persuasion works best when adapted to fit one of the five. Their findings show that to be a successful persuader you need to:

- **Customise your proposals.** Organise your information in the way that appeals to your listener. You must direct your arguments to your decision-makers' preferred styles, otherwise you don't stand a chance of persuading them to accept your proposals.

- **Become adept at interpreting behaviour.** People only make major decisions after collecting and processing information in their preferred style. As a persuader, you must carefully observe the person you want to persuade in order to know which style you're dealing with.

- **Assemble a full toolkit to draw from.** In order to influence the different types of decision-makers, you need to know what tools to use, as well as when and in what order.

Williams and Miller stress that their research is based on how people make decisions and is not influenced by personality types. Furthermore, while most people's decision-making styles change according to circumstances, when making difficult choices involving complicated issues and significant consequences, people revert to type. In other words, when the pressure's on, you use what worked in the past.

Williams and Miller also note that while some of the names for decision-making types may sound negative, they're simply descriptive terms to explain the main way each group of people makes decisions. No style is better than another. All can produce both good and bad decisions.

Also, like human beings themselves, the five different types can sometimes be tricky to decipher because every person contains elements of all five styles. That being said, Williams and Miller offer a starting point for considering different styles and strengthening your persuasive skills.

As you read through the following sections, consider which style you may belong to. Look for characteristics that resonate and sit naturally with you. While this approach isn't an exact science, it can give you insights into how you go about making decisions.

Convincing the Charismatics

Charismatic decision-makers are identified as *charismatic* because they encompass certain charismatic qualities – such as passion for bold, innovative thinking, out-of-the-box approaches and a deep-seated desire for knowledge. Big picture thinkers, risk-seeking and responsible, a *charismatic decision-maker* needs to see what you're talking about as well as hear what you say. At work, canned Power point slide shows bore them to distraction so come to a meeting with a few prepared charts that can be modified in your head and redrawn on a whiteboard. Away from the office, be prepared to sketch out your ideas on a piece of paper. Although they're initially enthusiastic about a new idea or proposal, they require a balanced set of information before making their final decision.

Charismatics often have short attention spans and thrive on interaction. Start with the most critical information first. Be prepared for them to get up and walk around while you're talking. When they do, stay seated. Charismatics rely on you to refrain from joining in their excitement and count on you to stay grounded. They like to think out loud and get things moving. In addition, they like to bat ideas around and scribble down their thoughts, leaving it up to others to fill in the details later.

You know when you're interacting with a charismatic decision-maker because the person's face lights up with exuberance and enthusiasm when you present your big idea. You feel like you can comfortably introduce bold, even revolutionary thinking. The person may actually jiggle on the edge of his chair with excitement.

While charismatics typically embrace your idea when you first propose it, getting a final decision can be tough. Charismatics have likely experienced past mistakes in which their impulsiveness led to sorrow. Without having enough facts to support their emotions in the early stages of the process, they made previous decisions too quickly, often leading to unfortunate outcomes.

As a result, just when you believe you've persuaded them to commit to your plan, follow your lead or do as you suggest, and you're ready to crack open the champagne, they up and vanish. They may not take your phone calls or respond to your emails. They may delay making the decision to proceed in spite of their initial enthusiasm. To prevent this from happening, begin your persuasion process by giving charismatics the most critical information up front and make sure that you provide enough facts to support whatever information you give. Make sure that you back up your proposals with supporting data and a balanced set of information (see the following section 'Offering balanced information').

If you want to persuade a charismatic, be patient. While they loathe wasting time gaining consensus and can't be bothered with introspection, they avoid acting rashly and can take a long time making their decisions, frequently turning to trusted advisors to help them come to conclusions. While they may appear independent, and believe that they are, they're usually not. Charismatics rely on strong number two people to help them see the forest for the trees. These devil's advocates help keep the charismatics grounded and weigh in with their opinions, helping to think through the details the charismatics undoubtedly overlook or simply can't be bothered with. A charismatic can draw from a stable of trusted advisors – from business partners to life partners. The point is, charismatics seek advice from people they trust. When you're putting your arguments together, consider who they turn to for advice and support. Factor these important advisors into your overall approach.

David is always on the lookout for new and exciting investment ventures. When Stewart approached him with the chance to invest in his film distributorship, David leapt at the opportunity. He had always been fascinated by the film world and, although he was already a multi-millionaire, he saw this as another opportunity to make more money and have fun in the process. Stewart advised David that to gain an equity stake in the company he would have to invest £500,000 with an initial investment of £100,000. David agreed without hesitation and promised the funds would be transferred into the company account by the end of the week. When David got home that night and told his wife, Tina, what he had decided to do, she came in with probing questions including challenging him about his knowledge of the film industry, the people he was dealing with, anticipated returns on investment and other details David, in his excitement for the opportunity, had failed to ask. By triggering doubts in David's mind, Tina got him to think more carefully about his plan and put an end to the deal.

The following sections explore the key strategies for effectively influencing charismatic individuals.

Offering balanced information

Charismatic decision-makers must have supporting data in order to make their decisions. They do want facts to support their emotions and lose their initial enthusiasm quickly if you don't have the details at hand. However, if you hit a charismatic decision-maker with tons of exhaustive facts and number-crunching exercises in the early stages of your persuasion process, you can say goodbye to your proposal.

In spite of seeming exuberant and enthusiastic at first, charismatics are methodical when making decisions and only take educated risks, relying on research and market studies to support their instincts. Having made mistakes in the past, they try to control their initial burst of excitement and douse themselves in reality. With this in mind:

- **Don't bog down charismatics with minutiae, particularly in the early stages of the process.** You quickly temper a charismatic's keenness if you muddy his thinking with too much data and detail.

- **Always know your back-up plans and strategies.** Although charismatics may seem uninterested in the finer details, they want to know that you've a well-developed plan in the background, ready to support any and every recommendation you're making. Because they've been burned in the past, they wait to act until they feel secure that you've crossed every *t* and dotted each *i*.

- **Plan for supporting visuals.** While charismatics can easily absorb a lot of information and can move from the big picture to the details without batting an eye, have visuals on hand to back up your proposal. A lot of verbal or written information often overwhelms and causes this type of decision-maker to lose enthusiasm. See the later section 'Providing visual aids to strengthen your position' in this chapter.

Acknowledging and discussing risks

Risk averse? Not the charismatics. 'Bring it on!' can be their slogan. However, don't take that to mean that you can be rash and reckless when persuading a charismatic. They fight their urge to make on-the-spot decisions and usually have a wing-man close by to hold them back from plunging head first into unknown waters.

Give your charismatic listener supportive data to sustain their interest or they're likely to lose enthusiasm quickly. Be upfront when persuading charismatic decision-makers, telling them the bottom line, including the risks. Keep your arguments simple and straightforward – and explain upfront how you plan to minimise any risks and what measures you're prepared to take. By being truthful and direct, you're more likely to gain their acceptance than if you make the mistake of joining in with their initial excitement.

When you're persuading charismatics, slightly undersell the parts of your proposal that are likely to arouse their curiosity. For example, if a client has a dilemma he believes you can solve, avoid getting caught up in his enthusiasm by pointing out potential obstacles and gathering as much information as you can before committing to a deal. Frequently, and without necessarily being aware of what they're doing, charismatics try to pass a problem onto someone else in order to get rid of it. Simply acknowledge the points they're interested in. You don't need to hype something they're basically on-board with. Then lay out the inherent risks. This reality check makes you come across as honest and as someone who can be trusted.

Don't attempt to conceal any latent threats or dangers. A charismatic is going to discover them later – when you're not around to address any concerns that pop up. Despite their initial enthusiasm for an idea, charismatics are thorough and rely on others – especially those who understand the full implications of a proposal – before making a decision. While charismatics appear to be independent thinkers, they defer to experts – such as a chief financial officer, head of IT or a lawyer – who understand the implications of their choices before making their final decisions. Follow through rigorously, making sure that you do all the work that's requested and turn it over to the charismatics' key lieutenants, or else you may sabotage yourself. When the charismatics' trusted advisors are satisfied and you've followed through on your end of the bargain, all will be plain sailing. If you fail to follow through, you can expect to be seen as untrustworthy, ill-prepared and a questionable character.

Television on demand

Thomas is the chief executive officer (CEO) of a digital television company supplying sports and entertainment programmes on demand to hotels across Europe and the United States. The stiff competition and strict government regulations within those markets has meant that he's not been able to establish his company as he'd originally envisioned. Specifically, he wants to relocate the business to Hong Kong, where he can have easier access to the Middle East, as well as Asian, Pacific and African markets.

Cecilia, the chairperson of Thomas's company, has embraced bold, out-of-the-box ideas in the past – sometimes to her and the company's detriment. While she seems excited at first about Thomas's idea, he knows that he needs to go the extra mile to persuade her and the Board that his idea is viable.

When Thomas made his presentation to the Board, he was prepared. He started off by addressing the current problems with the company's position and his recommendations for solving them. He pointed out how this move would increase the company's competitiveness by serving new markets. He took into account the potential impact of the move, specifically the cost of relocating staff and working in unfamiliar territory. In addition, he prepared a detailed risk assessment of what may happen if his idea failed and the steps they may take to minimise those risks (see the following section 'Acknowledging and discussion risks'). Finally, he pointed out how his idea would impact on the bottom line and handed out a detailed schedule, including milestone dates, for carrying out his idea.

By addressing the problems and presenting recommendations for solving them at the beginning of his presentation, offering a detailed risk assessment plus ways of minimising threats and concluding with a report that highlighted supporting data from research and case studies of similar moves, Thomas presented a persuasive argument that, after considered deliberation, the Board passed.

Providing visual aids to strengthen your position

When you're making your persuasive pitch to a charismatic, make sure that you've got plenty of pictures, images, diagrams and charts at hand. Because charismatics tend to see the world in visual terms, drawings and objects help clarify their thinking. For more information about learning styles and sense preferences, have a look at *Neuro-linguistic Programming For Dummies* by Romilla Ready and Kate Burton (Wiley) and *Business NLP For Dummies* by Lynne Cooper (Wiley), which deal with this topic in detail.

In addition to visual aids, fill your speech with visual metaphors. Compare abstract ideas and concepts to concrete objects. Use words such as 'What I see here is . . . ', 'Focussing on this point . . . ', 'Imagine that . . . ' and 'The big picture we're looking at is like . . . ' in your speech and writing.

Kiera scheduled a meeting with her boss, Nicky, to discuss ideas for a restructuring programme that Kiera believed would save her department more than £50,000 annually. Kiera prepared several visual aids for the meeting – for her own reference as well as for Nicky, who was visually orientated. Before the meeting, Kiera reviewed her visuals and thought about how she could modify and redraw them on the spot if necessary, based on Nicky's reaction to the information. Kiera began the actual presentation by drawing a diagram showing the current financial state of her department. She then presented another chart, outlining her proposal for the new structure and how it addressed current problems. When she saw that Nicky was captured by what she was seeing, the two of them stood at the flip chart, coloured pens in hand, drawing further charts and diagrams together.

Visually orientated charismatics pay careful attention to how they look and are usually smartly turned out. They expect others to dress in a similar fashion. If you want to impress a charismatic, make sure that you're well groomed, and that you add an elegant accessory – a good-quality watch, beautiful piece of jewellery, stylish tie or a smart handbag or briefcase. You don't need to compliment the charismatic on his notably attractive clothing items or office decor as charismatics habitually present themselves well.

Tying arguments to bottom-line results

When you're persuading a charismatic, always link your arguments to the bottom line, be it a financial result, an emotional connection or a desired relationship. Charismatics are results-driven and keen competitors, whether they're working in business, at home or building a relationship with a potential partner.

Even if they don't ask straight away, charismatics want results-orientated information. If you fail to provide it, they become frustrated and annoyed, particularly when they want to explore your proposal in more detail after the initial discussion. Don't waste their time with extraneous niceties or chitchat that may be interesting to some but hold no fascination for charismatics.

When you're persuading charismatic decision-makers, include any (or all) of the following written and spoken words in your proposal in order to capture their interest:

- **Nouns:** *results, actions*
- **Verbs:** *show, watch, look, focus*
- **Adjectives:** *proven, bright, easy, clear*

Swaying the Sceptics

With their strong personalities and what some consider to be antisocial behaviour, *sceptics* tend to have a highly suspicious nature and look for reasons to distrust people and their recommendations. When they do act, their decisions are based on their belief in your credibility. In order to establish your credibility, you can gain endorsement from someone the sceptic trusts, but ultimately you have to earn it through your own behaviour.

Others often describe sceptics as demanding, disruptive and disagreeable; they can also be rebellious. They can be tough – but not impossible – to persuade. They like to take charge and have a combative style. They look for reasons *not* to agree to your proposals; reasons *not* to do business or make agreements with you. Above all, with their suspicious nature, they question everything and accept nothing at face value.

While sceptics are straightforward, make decisions quickly and hop on board with ground-breaking ideas (as long as they trust you), they can also be unruly in meetings by taking phone calls or engaging in side conversations. They may just get up and leave if your argument seems full of holes or unsubstantiated.

Sceptics leave you in no doubt about where you stand. When you first meet sceptics, they always find rationales to be suspicious of you. They look for reasons to distrust you and only if they fail to find them do they begin to perceive you as credible. They don't ever give the benefit of the doubt to someone who's unproven but once you've stood up to their scrutiny and have gained their trust, you're on a winner. They're quick to tell you what's on their minds and don't hesitate to lock horns any chance they get. When they attack with volleys of questions, you're likely to feel as though they're attacking you personally (although that's not really the case). See the following section 'Allowing them their clout', for more about sceptics' questioning.

When you go to persuade a sceptic, be prepared – be very prepared. They can demand a lot of your time and energy, questioning every bit of data you place in front of them, especially those facts that challenge the way they view their world. Ultimately, most sceptics are willing to alter their positions – if you're patient with them, answer all their questions, back up your responses with credible sources and then allow them to draw their own conclusions. Although they can seem challenging, the key is to keep calm and carry on. The following sections cover the best ways of persuading sceptics.

Establishing credibility through similarities

Credibility scores high on a sceptic's list of important attributes, so fill your arsenal with as much credibility as you can.

The intimidation game

Many years ago Maria and I were invited to pitch to a multi-national aeronautics conglomerate to design and deliver a cross-cultural communication programme. Maria had recently met Simon, the head of HR, at an industry conference and seemed to have established a good working relationship with him. At the time, she was president of the hosting organisation, which impressed Simon. He expressed interest in finding out more about what her company could provide.

Although I hadn't attended the conference, Maria vouched that I would be an excellent trainer to run a session on presenting to a multinational audience. Based on his experience of seeing Maria at work and her recommendation of my credentials, Simon invited us to present our proposal at the company's French headquarters. He seemed keen to do business with us, and we were excited. However, we were in for a shock.

From the moment we met, Simon clearly distrusted me. He asked why I hadn't attended the

conference if I was such an expert on cross-cultural communication. He quizzed me relentlessly on my educational background and the other clients I had run the programme for. During my presentation, he consistently interrupted and challenged my approach and ruthlessly disputed my research findings. Aggressive, antagonistic and argumentative, Simon seemed to revel in attacking not only my work, but my integrity as well, completely throwing me off guard. Whenever Simon asked me to explain my methodology, he then argued with my approach. No matter what I said, Simon resisted.

Finally, Maria joined the conversation, at which point Simon backed off me and gave her his attention. He clearly found Maria more credible and trustworthy than he did me. However, because their relationship was still in its early stages, Maria was unable to persuade him that I was the person to run the programme with her, and we didn't get the job.

Sceptics trust people who are similar to them. If you didn't go to the same university, work for the same companies or belong to the same clubs, you need to find another way of proving that you're similar if you're to have any success in persuading them to accept your point of view. For more about the power of establishing similarity, turn to Chapter 10.

While a colleague can vouch for you, ultimately a sceptic only trusts you after you prove that you're credible. If the sceptic has no prior experience of you, prepare yourself for lengthy and aggressive questioning to establish that you're reliable and trustworthy. Earning credibility with a sceptic takes time and for a sceptic to believe in you, you have to stand your ground without getting defensive. If you're able to do that, the sceptic will give you his stamp of approval.

Gaining endorsement from trusted sources

If you haven't already proven your credibility with a sceptic, solicit the endorsement of someone he trusts. Sceptics are more prepared to listen to you if someone they believe in has bought into your proposal. In fact, you may want to ask the trusted person to co-present your proposal with you, transferring their credibility onto you.

However, while this endorsement approach may work for a while, ultimately you have to prove yourself to a sceptic if you're to gain their trust and confidence.

Whether prior to your meeting or during it, gaining the support of someone the sceptic knows and counts on for honest assessments allows you the freedom of having an open discussion of the issues on their level, while the sceptic continues to maintain his superior position. You can get buy in from someone the sceptic already trusts by floating your thoughts by this person before having the discussion with the sceptic. You can also suggest that this person presents any information that may be controversial, as he's already established his credibility with the sceptic. That way your ideas are heard without you being in the firing line.

Allowing them their clout

Persuading sceptics is a risky business. They're like attack dogs and have no compunction about challenging your integrity or your data. Put on your kid gloves, your steel-plated vest and handle sceptics with care.

When you're persuading them to see your point of view and they go on the attack, don't fight fire with fire, no matter how tempted you may be. Aggressive counterattacks only lead to more aggression.

Don't try to examine a sceptic's reasons for behaving the way he does. That's just the way things are. Rather than withering under a sceptic's challenge or putting him on the defensive, accept that sceptics rarely trust anything that doesn't fit into their worldview. They may want to move forward with a good idea – they just need to be certain that the person offering the idea is credible and can be trusted.

Avoid going on the defensive. While sceptics' accusations and criticisms may sting, you're not the only one to feel the pain of their assaults. They're critical and suspicious of everything and everyone. Stay cool, calm and collected as a sceptic flexes his muscles. Stand firm in your ideas and keep your emotions in check as you respond rationally and patiently to the sceptic's concerns. In addition, make sure that when you present data to back up your proposal, it comes from a reliable source and not hearsay.

To persuade sceptics, you must establish trust by allowing them to safeguard their reputation and protect their ego. Whatever you do, don't confront them as you may cause offense, which may just heighten their negative feelings toward you. Whatever criticisms or accusations they fling your way, depersonalise them. Their attacks have nothing to do with you personally – they're suspicious of everyone and everything until they're given clear reasons not to be. Even when they're coming at you with a full frontal attack, remain cool as a cucumber, biting your tongue, breathing deeply from your core or counting inwardly to ten if necessary. (See Chapter 14 for breathing exercises to calm you down.)

Tread lightly around a sceptic's ego by acknowledging the sceptic or someone they respect. For example, when you present supporting information, preface your remarks with a comment like 'You're probably already aware that . . . ' or 'As you know, Apple succeeded by taking a similar approach to . . . '. Be sure that any example you share shows how the company's reputation was enhanced or tainted as a result of the decision made. Away from the office, this approach works equally well. For example, comments like 'Undoubtedly you know how valuable your contribution was when . . . ' or 'When your son shared his experiences of . . . ' provide supporting evidence to your observations.

Sceptics want to be seen as knowing everything. They don't like being helped, and they *really* don't like being contradicted. That said, they're not infallible, and you may need to correct inaccurate information that they hold to be true. While you risk offending them if you correct their thinking, they won't respect you if you acquiesce or back down. A tricky situation, indeed, so proceed with caution. Never accuse them of being wrong or not knowing what they're talking about and do everything you can to avoid judgemental language. Instead, present your case in a neutral, dispassionate way, allowing sceptics to draw their own conclusions and maintain face while you prove your credibility.

When Paul accused his wife, Anne, of grossly overspending on decorating and refurbishing their house and being personally accountable for spiralling costs, Anne remained calm. She asked if Paul was testing her, because she thought that when they had discussed the project several months earlier, Paul had told Anne to spend what she needed to make the house more to their liking. Anne then asked Paul if the situation had changed. Paul re-established the trust he had originally placed in Anne because Anne allowed him to save face.

Sceptics have a little bit of rebelliousness under their stern exteriors. They like to buck the trend and always like taking credit for new or innovative ideas. Whatever you propose, always tie it back into points they've made in the past or accomplishments you know that they're proud of.

Grounding concrete facts in the real world

Sceptics are uncomfortable with abstracts. Like meat and potato people, they like hard facts and concrete reasoning. If something can go wrong, they want to know about it from the start and they insist upon verification of all your information sources.

The more reputable sources you can provide, the better. Be prepared to refer them to the successes of people they admire and put them in touch with other experts.

Craig was in charge of a major restructuring programme that required relocating 500 employees. As he presented his case to Don, his managing director, he included specifics, consisting of how he planned to close the premises in Loughborough and how the company may benefit. Craig suggested subleasing the space, including parking and recreational areas. He also made suggestions for how the building could be used, seeing it as an ideal site to turn into serviced office space, which was much in demand in that area. He provided data of how other companies had taken a similar approach, adding in examples of companies that had failed as well as those that had succeeded. Because Craig approached the situation with concrete examples of what was possible and had data to back up his proposal, he was able to persuade Don to act on his suggestion.

Appeal to the sceptics by including the following words when you speak with or write to them:

- **Nouns:** *power, action, trust*
- **Verbs:** *feel, grasp, look, focus, demand, disrupt*
- **Adjectives:** *suspect, agreeable*

Appealing to the Thinkers

Logical and intellectually astute, *thinkers* can be difficult to understand and tough to persuade. They tend to make decisions primarily from their heads, not their hearts. They explore every nook and cranny of your proposal before making a decision. Picky is a word you can use to describe thinkers because they take apart problems and work their way back through a course of logic-based solutions.

When you're persuading a thinker, pretend you're speaking to an academic. (You may very well be doing just that.) Appeal to their brain power. Present them with intellectual arguments and clever lines of reasoning.

'Bring on the data!' may as well be their cry to arms. Thinkers are ravenous readers and choosy with their words, and don't talk a great deal. If you really want to please and impress them, come armed with a plethora of measurable arguments.

Thinkers are turned on by anticipating change and winning the chase. They get a real buzz from out-thinking and out-manoeuvring the competition. If they think that a bargain's to be had – a relatively risk-free prospect of saving time or money – they side-step their usual decision-making process in the interests of time and money. (Thinkers share this bargain-mindedness with followers; see the following section.)

Thinkers like being in control and don't care about being innovative. They keep their emotions under wraps and play their cards close to the chest, giving nothing away as they meticulously process arguments and ideas. Most of all, thinkers don't like risk.

Thinkers like to be included in the decision-making process, so after presenting your recommendation, ask for their help in filling in any possible blanks. Provide them with all the relevant information, as much as you can muster, and then sit back and wait while the thinker processes your proposal. This waiting period can be a matter of minutes, hours or days. Be patient. Thinkers need time to thoroughly analyse a problem as they explore all the potential pros and cons of every possible solution. Encourage them to solicit the help of others, as thinkers like to work through things with trusted advisors to make sure that they've not missed anything.

Telling your story sequentially

When you're persuading a thinker, present your proposal by starting at the very beginning – a very good place to start – and finishing up at the end. Do everything you can to maintain a logical, sequential order.

Think of the process like feeding them a meal; begin with the appetiser and finish up with dessert. Jumping into the main course – for example, presenting your solution before introducing your proposition – is no way to persuade a thinker.

To persuade a thinker, allow them to confirm that every step in the process is free of error. As my lawyer brother says, 'Never assume facts that haven't been placed in evidence.' Thinkers like to be in control, so don't try to hide any information that would jeopardise that need.

- ✔ If you know of a hole in your proposition, a flaw in your thinking, an aspect that's open to interpretation or a point of contention, address the problem on the spot and encourage the thinker to get involved in analysing the situation before moving onto your next item.

- ✔ If you've made any assumptions based on inklings and intuition, admit it upfront. Thinkers are quick to spot your sixth sense at work.

- ✔ If a thinker doubts your judgement or reasoning on a point you're making and you're not able to defend it satisfactorily, stop and explain yourself. Your entire proposal can become suspect when thinkers disagree with you on an important bit of information.

If you've any concerns about the viability of what you're proposing, tell the thinker at the beginning of your conversation. Being risk-averse, thinkers need to know the possible downsides upfront. They need to explore and understand all the perils inherent in your proposition and may come at you with a battery of questions. Unlike the sceptics, these questions aren't personal and are only intended to challenge your process or data.

Explain your processes and data sources from the very beginning to gain a thinker's attention. If you have to limit the amount of information you offer the thinker to one piece, make that your methodology. They want to know most of all *how* you got from point A to point Z. You do this by defining the problem, highlighting the pros and cons of different options and explaining how they can minimise risk by choosing what you believe is the optimum solution.

Begin your presentation by presenting a slideshow of the project's history to provide thinkers with a framework for your proposal. Away from the office, begin your conversation by giving the thinker background information about the subject you want to discuss and offer them a few options of how to address the situation. Then discuss the pros and cons of each option including the risks involved. Be prepared for thinkers to ask a barrage of questions. They need to understand a situation from all angles before committing to a solution. You can even play devil's advocate to help the thinkers look at every perspective.

Like elephants, thinkers never forget. Bad experiences remain at the forefront of a thinker's mind, so whatever recommendation you make, be sure – beyond a doubt – that your option is the best option. (Of course, always be certain of your recommendations whenever you're persuading someone – but make a special effort when you're dealing with thinkers.)

Providing abundant data

Thinkers hunger for comparative data and aren't satisfied until they consume as much as is available. Burn the midnight oil and do your homework. Fill your proposal with mountains of information, including market research, customer surveys, case studies, cost–benefit analyses and any other substantiating evidence you can muster. The more the merrier. Thinkers thrive on data and do their upmost to understand all perspectives on the subject at hand.

Rather than flood a thinker with options, shape your argument. Highlight the benefits and drawbacks of each option you offer. Supply thinkers with pertinent examples, drawing your data from different situations. Balance the data you provide with examples of wins and losses to avoid seeming prejudiced and deliberately trying to steer the final decision. See the following section 'Letting them draw their own conclusions' for more on the importance of putting a thinker in the driver's seat of the decision-making process.

Because of their need for as many facts and figures as you can provide, you may need to take more time persuading thinkers than you do other types. My advice? Be patient. Let them gorge themselves on facts and figures. Then give them time to digest the information and consider all the ramifications, no matter how long the process takes. The good news is, because thinkers are generally people of their word, when they tell you they'll have an answer by next Thursday morning, they do. Agree to a time frame and let them get on with it. You don't need to micro-manage as long as the thinkers feel engaged with the process. You can bring them on board by openly discussing your worries and concerns about the weaknesses in your proposal and your approach. Thinkers like honesty and being up front with them increases your credibility.

No matter how much information you provide, the chances are a thinker's going to ask for more. You'd be hard-pressed to over-anticipate a thinker's desire for data, but don't let this desire for information worry you. When presenting your proposal, you don't have to have all your arguments firmly in place. Thinkers like to be part of the process and want to help tweak and tune your thinking. That said, once they give you their input, they expect you to come up with the goods.

Present your data in big chunks over two meetings – or more, if needed. This way, the thinker can absorb and make sense of the information. After your first meeting, take on board the thinker's input and incorporate it into your to do list for gathering more data or backing up your arguments in preparation for your follow-up meeting. Let the thinker add his input in order to make him feel he has ownership of the methodology.

Thinkers abhor surprises. After adjusting your proposal based on the thinker's amendments and modifications, point out anything new and different from your first presentation, such as revised data.

Letting them draw their own conclusions

Thinkers like to, well, think, and because they don't like being helped, you have to grant them the right to draw their own conclusions. Steering their responses jeopardises your credibility in their eyes, so keep your thoughts to yourself and give them plenty of time and space to reflect on what they hear and to figure out things for themselves.

Because thinkers like to play their cards close to the chest and often appear inconsistent in their views, you may struggle to detect how they feel about any of your suggestions. Thinkers are a tough lot, concealing their intentions until they're ready to render their decision. Simply remain silent as they digest your information and draw their own conclusions.

Always focus on open communication and involve the thinker as much as possible when you're seeking solutions. Besides engaging them, this approach makes them feel that they own the process, which ultimately helps you by getting their buy-in. Always be candid with thinkers and gain their input about your method. Thinkers like being part of the process and want to know that their input has been acted on. After you first present the process you're using to come up with a solution, schedule another discussion, perhaps a week later, to show the thinker how you're getting on. Holding regular meetings and keeping them in the loop helps the thinker become familiar and comfortable with your approach.

If you're working with a thinker on a major decision, keep him informed of the process you're using to arrive at your solution. Before a meeting, send him a report so he has a chance to review it and, during the meeting, talk him through the details. The bigger the decision, the more you must keep the thinker involved along the way.

Words and phrases that appeal to thinkers include:

- **Nouns:** *quality, numbers, data, plan, competition, proof*
- **Verbs:** *think, makes sense, plan*
- **Adjectives:** *academic, intelligent, expert*

Urging the Followers

Followers are highly conscientious decision-makers. They tend to make decisions in the same ways they did in the past, based on how other, respected people came to their conclusions.

In some ways, followers seem contradictory:

- They fear making mistakes (so don't expect them to be early adopters of a proposal). They're turned on by known brands and bargains appeal to them because both represent less of a gamble.
- They're good at grasping others' points of view, and despite their cautious nature, they can be surprisingly spontaneous.

Identifying followers can be difficult because they share characteristics with charismatics, thinkers and sceptics (see the preceding sections for more on each of these decision-making types) – and they don't see themselves as followers. If you get into a discussion with them about their cautious nature, they'll flatly deny it. Followers are likely to prefer describing themselves as creative thinkers, innovative pioneers, rebels and mavericks – about as far away from their actual decision-making type as possible. The reason for that is simple. Followers don't want to be thought of as followers because of the negative connotation to the word 'follow'. They associate following with weakness and would rather be perceived as leaders, which connotes strength. What some followers tend to forget is that too many cooks spoil the stew and that followers are frequently dynamic and highly effective.

If you struggle to identify the type of person you're dealing with, look at their past decisions rather than what they say about themselves. Actions speak louder than words.

Still can't identify a person's decision-making type? You can safely assume that the person is a follower unless you find evidence to the contrary. Regardless of a person's preferred decision-making style, you can't go wrong by taking the persuasive approach of supplying lots of proof that your solution has a proven track record because everyone likes knowing that.

While you may not think of people in leadership roles as followers, you can find them, particularly within large, traditional corporations. In fact, research shows that 36 per cent of executives are followers and that only 6 per cent of sales presentations are targeted to their decision-making style. See the sidebar 'A follower in the front office' for an example from my own consulting experience.

Helping them understand through successes – their own and others'

Because followers are adept at seeing things from other people's perspective, they like examples of success, especially case studies. By offering them examples of where others succeeded – and purposely leaving out the failures unless they ask for them – followers can often see themselves succeeding in similar ways.

Unless you've got a solid track record of success, don't take the path of persuading a follower based on your own recommendation. Instead:

- **Refer to past decisions they themselves made that support your position.** Remind a follower of how a similar approach that he took in the past worked. You can say something along the lines of, 'This is the way you've always approached this kind of problem. The only difference now is . . . ', 'This reminds me of when you . . . " or 'Remember when you were faced with a similar situation and you . . . '. Followers need to feel comfortable knowing that what you're suggesting has succeeded in the past.

- **Share winning stories of other successful leaders.** Prove that people they trust and respect did well by pursuing a certain strategy, and most followers go down the same route.

- **Draw from examples *outside* of the follower's profession.** Followers are likely to become even more excited about the prospect of following these types of winning strategies because they get to rely on proven ideas while seeing themselves as being the first to pioneer the 'new' strategy within their own industry.

Unlike sceptics, whom I describe earlier in this chapter, followers are not intrinsically suspicious. When they're struggling to understand a point, they gladly turn to you for help. You can comfortably challenge a follower and chances are they'll yield as long as you've got back-up data they respect.

ANECDOTE

A follower in the front office

I've been providing training and coaching pro-grammes for a law firm for close to ten years, working closely with both the firm's director of HR and head of learning and development (L&D). When these contacts were leaving the firm, they introduced me to Patrick, the new head of L&D. Before our initial meeting, my original contacts described Patrick as some-one who likes to take charge and make quick decisions. They assured me that he was open to new ideas, was upfront and liked to take risks.

Thinking I was meeting a 'big picture' person, I assumed I'd be working to persuade a charis-matic (see the earlier section 'Convincing the Charismatics'). In order to renew our contract, I planned to share ideas for new programmes I had in mind for the firm.

During the meeting, Patrick's energetic and pow-erful personality was in full flow. He told me about himself, where he had worked before and what he had done, including designing and delivering interventions for an internationally renowned con-sulting firm. After he finished, he asked about my background. He seemed particularly impressed that I'd written *Body Language For Dummies* (Wiley), pointing to a copy on his bookshelf. In fact, from that moment he seemed quite interested in my ideas and working with me.

During the meeting, Patrick told me about prob-lems he was facing and asked how I thought I may be able to help him. He kept asking me to come up with innovative solutions and out-of-the-box ideas, further convincing me I was dealing with a charismatic.

However, every time I presented a creative idea, he rejected it out of hand, without considering its viability. I had to hold myself in check not to show my frustration with his lack of curios-ity about my proposals and his incessant need to know whether I had run similar programmes with other clients now or in the past. In spite of his acting in certain ways like a charismatic – seemingly powerful, big picture, seeking new horizons – I began to doubt my original assess-ment. No brainstorming, no working together to find new possibilities, no give-and-take occurred.

Instead, Patrick related our discussion to pro-grammes he'd run in the past. At first I thought he was trying to one-up me, but when he told me that one of the firm's partners had chal-lenged his approach and asked me to sug-gest how he ought to respond, the light bulb switched on. I realised that I was dealing with a person who needs guidance and confirmation. He was looking to me to provide answers based on my past successes in the firm.

After our meeting, I sent Patrick case studies of similar programmes I'd run for other firms and offered to provide him with detailed accounts of the examples, with the understanding that he sign a non-disclosure agreement. He told me that would not be necessary and that he would renew my company's contract. What turned the tide? Remembering that followers like the tried and true, I'm convinced that the fact that I am a published author of a best-selling book, that I have a good reputation in the firm and that I was willing to provide successful case studies provided enough proof to persuade Patrick that I was a safe bet.

Minimising risk

Followers are keen to hold onto their hats and keep their jobs. While they want to be associated with solutions that are ground-breaking, original and even revolutionary, they desire answers that are reliable, proven and safe.

Don't expect a follower to adopt blue-sky thinking or out-of-the-box ideas. Unless you present a follower with information they can't ignore, they're most comfortable maintaining the status quo.

If you want a follower to accept a bold, new strategy, show how someone else has succeeded by following the same plan.

When you present your ideas, give the follower options to choose from – three's a good number; neither too many nor too few – and link each option to fully fleshed-out case studies. As you undoubtedly have one option that you think is best, link most frequently to your strongest case study. Even if your listener cottons onto one of your other suggestions (perhaps because he sees a chance for a bargain), you can be prepared to point out that your comprehensive analysis of the data shows that, on a risk-adjusted basis, your preferred option is the most cost-efficient. Presenting your proposal as part of your comprehensive analysis is sure to persuade a follower that you've worked through all permutations of possibilities and identified a winning strategy.

Thrifty followers

If, in spite of all the proof you provide, you're still having trouble persuading a follower to go for your proposal, remember that followers love bargains. More than any other decision-making style, followers have the strongest desire for a good deal. If you want them to try something new – something they usually find risky – lower your price. If a follower thinks that he's getting a bargain, he may get to the point where he thinks that he can't afford *not* to take a risk.

Additionally, followers like to haggle. They like a bit of a tease and can be impulsive. Get yourself into a negotiating mood by thinking of yourselves as two people at the souk, each trying to wrangle a better price. The follower should enjoy the lively interchange, and if you put a time-sensitive element into your proposal, the follower is likely to say 'Okay'.

Keeping it simple

Although followers like to be seen by clients, colleagues and anyone else who's looking as innovative – even though they're not – they really don't like being taken out of their comfort zone. Hit them with too much novelty, and you can kiss goodbye to your chances of persuading them.

Persuading followers is an easy prospect, as long as you give them what they need and nothing more. While followers like you to present them with profuse amounts of evidence that something is proven, avoid the temptation of thinking you need to include further amounts of information unless this information is relevant and explains how your proposed solution has worked in the past. Don't waste your time giving them too much information. They're likely to feel overwhelmed by too much information that they didn't really ask for.

Bottom line: keep your proposal simple, substantiated and straightforward.

Reframe your ideas with new references that affect your specific followers. Relate your proposal to something that's worked in the past that they're familiar with. Use phrases such as, 'Remember when you . . . ' or 'When we took this approach with . . . ' or 'You may recall from past experiences that . . . '. Each of these phrases puts your new suggestions into context for them.

John's an old-fashioned kind of guy who owns a successful property business, but he struggles to understand why the marketing and advertising campaigns that have worked well in the past aren't working so well now. Several years ago, his marketing director Louise suggested that they take a new approach to working with their customers. Rather than sending out costly four-colour printed brochures, Louise suggested undertaking more Internet activity. John baulked at the proposal, leading to a bit of tension in the office. Words and phrases such as *innovative*, *new*, *better* and *leading edge* threatened his perceptions, and he resisted her proposal. Louise was only able to persuade John to take a new approach by showing him how similar her suggestion was to what he was already doing, adding that making use of the Internet simply meant that what they were doing could be done with more ease and less cost.

Incorporate the following words and phrases into your speech and writing in order to persuade followers:

- ✔ **Nouns:** *expertise, experience, good deal, cost saving*

- ✔ **Verbs:** *innovate, expedite*

- ✔ **Adjectives:** *swift, bright, just like before, similar, previous, proven, what works, as in the past*

Winning Over the Controllers

Love them or loathe them, *controllers* provoke strong reactions: on the one hand, they're demanding and frustrating to work with; on the other hand, they elicit fierce loyalty because of their candid way of communicating and their unswerving commitment to standards. When business is in turmoil, however, controllers are the ones you want at the helm because no one's better at getting the job done on time and within budget.

Logical, emotionally contained and detail-orientated, controllers are objective observers. They tend to have strong personalities and can come across as domineering. Whatever they do – whether sales, marketing, strategising or surfing the net – they're the best. At least, that's what they tell you.

Controllers see things only from their own perspective, unlike followers (see the preceding section) who can easily see things from another person's point of view. Snap judgements come easily to controllers and they're known for their cutting and scathing remarks. Loners by choice and tending to be rather egotistical, controllers make unilateral decisions with the possibility of leaving you standing there feeling rather redundant. Oh, sure, they may talk to you about a decision, but they seldom genuinely care about what you say.

Keep two main points in mind when persuading controllers:

- **Fear drives their decisions.** Controllers are always on the lookout for whatever can go wrong. They're never going to sit back on their laurels with smiles of contentment on their faces.

- **They need a lot – and I mean copious amounts – of time to make up their minds.** Persuading controllers is not so much persuading them, as letting them persuade themselves.

The following sections cover the essentials of influencing controllers.

Overcoming internal fears

In spite of their bravado, controllers are inundated with fears and anxieties that they keep safely tucked away. They live in a state of constant tension between their private terrors and timidities, which they deny (even to themselves), and the persona they present to the world.

Because of their fears, they struggle to let go of even the smallest points. They question you about price, fearing that if they don't, you'll perceive them as weak negotiators. They demand that you come in ahead of schedule, dreading that their staff may see them as too soft. As well as doubting themselves, controllers doubt other people and can even appear somewhat paranoid when interpreting other people's motives.

Like wounded animals, controllers may attack with aggressive comments and questions, and you may want to take their fury personally and react defensively. Don't. Instead:

- ✔ **Remain calm, composed and comforting.** I'm not saying this approach is the easiest way of dealing with a controller, I'm just saying it's the best way. In Chapter 7 you can pick up tips for letting go of your own feelings in order to remain present with the other person.

- ✔ **Patiently reassure them that you've worked through all possible permutations of the problem at hand.** Minimise any fears or anxieties they may have about your proposals by providing them with all the information they need; then back off and wait for them to respond.

In order to persuade controllers, you need to help them overcome their fears – without pointing them out. If you were to say something along the lines of, 'What are you so worried about?' most controllers would eat you for breakfast. Instead, patiently respond to their demands – they're bound to have many – while remaining calm and reassuring. Meeting their aggression with your own simply fans the flames and heightens their fears.

Flooding with pure facts and analytics

You can spot controllers by the excessive amount of attention they pay to convoluted processes and procedures. They're likely to thrive on having you chase down further facts and figures as the mood strikes them. When you go to persuade a controller, make sure that you've got your data in place and that you absolutely, unconditionally and without a doubt know what you're talking about. Controllers only credit experts (Chapter 6 covers how to demonstrate your expertise).

Controllers are frequently afraid of making decisions, especially when situations involve lots of unknowns. Prepare for these individuals to become more aggressive and demanding, insisting that you provide them with more and more detailed information. Avoid becoming frustrated as that only adds fuel to their fire. Even when they've got you huffing, puffing and sweating buckets as you source obscure materials that they probably won't even look at, keep dancing to their tune.

Knowing what they want and when they want it, controllers leave nothing to chance and focus on the tiniest details in all proposals.

Making your arguments structured, linear and credible

Controllers look for accuracy and facts presented in a structured and linear way. No jumping in at the middle or presenting your conclusions at the beginning if you want to persuade them. Controllers are persuaded by proposals that are strict and strong. They like discipline, authority and a command-and-conquer approach supported by highly analysed data. Present controllers with information that's ambiguous and open to interpretation, and watch their faces flush in fury. Give them unadulterated facts and clear analytics, and they're smiling. Submit proposals that seem preordained and destined to win, and they sign them off willingly.

You can't really persuade controllers to do anything because they always need to be in control. They draw their own conclusions, reach their own decisions and make up their own minds in their own sweet time. All you can do is give them all the information they need and keep your fingers crossed that they convince themselves to go with your proposal.

Controllers like to own the proposal, regardless of who suggested it. Let them think that your idea is theirs by tying your suggestion back to something they said or did in the past.

Because controllers need to be involved in all aspects of the decision-making process, they can slow things down. They can go beyond their remit or change the rules after negotiations begin. When they pull these punches, stand your ground. Be patient with them – as well as firm. 'That's not what we agreed but if you want to add extras we're prepared to do that at an additional cost' shows that you're both willing to work with the controller as well as resolute in your position.

Thomas is the CEO of a telecoms company that I've had a positive and productive working relationship with for many years. He recently hired a new HR director, Nicola, who is a classic controller. During our yearly contract renewal meeting, Thomas agreed our terms without hesitation, at which point Nicola slammed on the breaks. She questioned company policy on every minor point from accounting procedures to timings and content of delivery. Because Thomas had already approved the proposal, I was thrown off base and had to quickly regain control. I reminded myself about controllers operating out of fear and their need to hold onto even the smallest of points. All Nicola really needed to do was choose one of the three options we had agreed with Thomas. It was pretty much a no-brainer, but Nicola needed to have her voice heard. She suggested that we combine options, which would have made the contract more complicated and expensive than necessary. Patiently, I agreed that we could do as she suggested, but that doing so would add to the costs and that going with one of the three options on the table would be both time and cost effective. By giving her a choice, Nicola had the opportunity to have her say while sticking to Thomas's agreement.

 Avoid aggressively pushing any decision when working with controllers. If you force their hands before they're ready to make up their mind, they see you as the problem and happily put the blame on you for anything that may go wrong. To avoid this from happening, you have to be absolutely clear from the beginning about what is – and isn't – negotiable and hold to your bottom line. Get everything in writing, and if you can, work through the controller's trusted advisors. Like all other decision-making types described in this chapter, controllers have their lieutenants who are invaluable resources of useful information and helpful suggestions.

Working through others

Working directly with controllers can be tricky. They may try to avoid dealing with you, waiting to make up their minds and avoid taking responsibility in case something goes wrong.

If you're able to work with someone a controller trusts rather than the controller himself, go for it. Sometimes you can get lucky and the controller tells you not to deal with him directly, but instead to work with his colleagues – second-in-commands, trusted advisors, lieutenants, call them what you will – who reports back to him. If that doesn't happen, suggest it yourself. You can also recommend that you work with the controller in pairs, thus avoiding one-on-one meetings where the controller may feel sanctioned power to do and say whatever he wants, including having an abusive go at you. Having another person present keeps the controller in check. Whatever you do, be diplomatic when dealing with a controller to prevent him from feeling cornered or that he's being kept in the dark.

Meetings with controllers can be fraught. Because of their need to be right and their demand for perfection, they can be ruthless in casting blame, especially if something doesn't fit their vision.

Seek allies when working with controllers. Because of the controller's need to be in charge, he may unwittingly sabotage your every effort. When you can, work with a partner. Two people together can often keep the lid on a controller's tendency to bully and act abusively.

If you do choose to work with a partner, make sure that you frame the meeting as a discussion and put the controller in charge. You don't want to look as though you're setting up a situation of two against one. You can perhaps say that you and your colleague were batting around ideas and wanted the controller's input. That way the controller feels valued and knows that nothing is going on behind his back.

Several years ago Maggie invited me to speak at a conference her boss was organising. I had worked with Maggie a lot and trusted her unconditionally. She warned me that her boss, David, was a tough cookie who needed to be in charge at all times. At the conference, David was a nightmare. Every time I began to speak, he interrupted, taking over the points I was making. Not only that, he twisted my remarks to suit his agenda, which didn't match what I was presenting. I found his behaviour both incredibly frustrating and quite ironic because he'd paid a lot of money to set up the conference and was sabotaging its success. During the first break, I spoke with Maggie. She told me not to worry and went off to have a word with him, suggesting that he let me present my material and then during the break-out sessions he would coach people. While this solution wasn't ideal, it was better than what had been happening. I also noticed that, during the workshops, Maggie and her team put the people who weren't really interested in hearing what I had to say in one group, suggesting that David may want to coach them, which he later did. Throughout the day, I noticed how Maggie and her team seemed to know just how to handle David by guiding him in his behaviour without his being aware.

My notebook is heaving with information about persuading and working with controllers. (Perhaps *Controlling Controllers For Dummies* should be my next book?) In the meantime, keep the following strategies in mind:

- Controllers need a lot of time to make up their minds. Be prepared for long silences as they draw their conclusions.

- Encourage controllers to make up their minds by giving them deadlines that are imposed by external factors – something out of their control – like new government regulations or a competitor's upcoming launch date.

- In meetings, controllers tend to be self-absorbed, focusing on their own thoughts. Because of that I suggest you schedule as few meetings as possible with controllers, working instead through their lieutenants who can do your persuading for you. If that's not possible, make sure that your meetings are highly structured and that you present your information in a linear way with the implication that your proposal is both unbeatable and unstoppable, thus matching the controllers' tendency to be clear, precise and straightforward.

Incorporate the following words into your speech and writing in order to persuade controllers:

- ✔ **Nouns:** power, details, facts
- ✔ **Verbs:** handle, grab, just do it, make them pay
- ✔ **Adjectives:** reasonable, logical, physically

Persuading the masses

As I say in the beginning of this chapter, people are different with different decision-making styles. This makes persuading a group composed of various types of decision-makers an interesting challenge. Knowledge of the five different styles outlined in this chapter provides valuable clues on how to approach a mixed group.

When persuading a mixed group, begin your presentation with a quick summary of how your presentation is going to progress. As long as your overview makes logical sense, you can grab the attention of the thinkers because they respond favourably to rational thinking. When you've got the thinkers hooked, you can turn your attention to the other styles while the thinkers work through your arguments. As long as you continue to speak in a logical manner, the thinkers will stick with you. As for the controllers, you can't do much with them because they dance to their own tune and are all but impossible to sway in a group setting. Don't despair. As you hook the other styles, you may find some of the controllers get behind you, too.

The three styles you need to concentrate on are the sceptics, charismatics and followers because more people fit into these categories than into the others. Make the sceptics and followers comfortable by establishing your credibility and proving that you know your stuff. More than most,

these two styles rely on your personal integrity and track record to convince them that your proposal merits their attention. (For more about integrity and persuasion, turn to Chapter 5). When you've got the followers and sceptics settled down, get into your ideas quickly to avoid losing the attention of the charismatics.

Having given your brief overview and established your credibility with examples of what you've done, provide bullet points of how you're going to proceed to satisfy the charismatics. When the time comes for you to burrow into those points – in a coherent , meticulous way – the charismatics, thinkers, sceptics and followers will be with you. Who knows, by this point you may have the controllers interested, too.

You may notice that this formula is like the approach: Tell them what you're going to tell them; tell them; tell them what you told them. The reason this approach works for a mixed group is that you hook the charismatics with your big idea. The thinkers join in because of your logical methodology and the followers come on board because others are. You may struggle with intransigent sceptics and controllers. The good news is that once you establish your credibility, you can persuade the sceptics and most people aren't controllers. As for those who are, turn to people they trust and work through them.

For an outstanding example of how to persuade a group of people, watch the classic film *12 Angry Men* , in which juror number 8 – through incessant and logical probing, and by questioning the credibility of some of the witnesses – convinces his fellow jurors, all of whom have different decision-making styles, to change their votes.

Part III
Picking the Right Approach

The 5th Wave   By Rich Tennant

SEMINAR
PERSUASION AND
INFLUENCE

TICKETS

"I couldn't convince anyone to buy a ticket."

In this part . . .

This part, gets to the bottom of how to persuade and influence others according to their needs and desires. Here you find out what makes people make the decisions they do, and discover how to modify the way you persuade accordingly. I let you in on the secrets of getting others to do what you want them to do through developing solid, trusting relationships, and I offer some tips on how you can influence people to follow your suggestions through setting your own examples.

Chapter 10

Getting Things Done with the Help of Others

*I*f you've ever observed master persuaders at work, you may feel both impressed and frustrated. You watch in awe as, with a steady stream of charisma, eloquence and ease, they engage people they want to win over, making them eager to carry out any request put forward.

If you find that your charisma quotient is modest or that your verbal skills are lacking, don't despair. Persuasive techniques are based on scientific principles that you can understand and apply to your everyday interactions. When you put the principles I spotlight in this chapter into practice, others comply with your wishes almost automatically. Why? Because with global technology driving the pace, time is compressed and people barely have a moment to think. In addition, they're swamped with more information than they can absorb. They don't have time to consider their decisions and there's too much to consider anyway. As long as the choice makes sense to them, they do what you ask.

In this chapter I describe six simple, clear and intuitive principles based on the work of Dr Robert Cialdini, as well as significant theories and experiments in social psychology, the psychology of persuasion and the science of compliance. The research shows that people can be persuaded by appealing to a deeply rooted and limited set of basic needs and desires. If you apply these principles of persuasion, both you and the person or organisation you want to influence benefit.

Although I separate the principles and how to apply them into six sections for the sake of clarity, their impact increases when you combine them. For example, while you're establishing your authority during an informal conversation (see 'Exposing your expertise' below), you can also gain useful information about the people you want to influence. Knowing more about the other person's background, particularly his likes and dislikes, helps you uncover common ground (see 'Finding similarities') and areas where you can offer sincere praise (see 'Complimenting others'), further enhancing your persuasive powers.

As I reinforce throughout this book, however you practise the principles in this chapter, do so ethically. Not only is tricking and trapping others into doing what you want them to do morally wrong, the approach is reckless and risky. See Chapters 1 and 5 on the ethics of persuasion.

Highlighting Your Likeability

Renowned US lawyer Clarence Darrow summed up a key aspect of persuasion when he said, 'The main work of a trial attorney is to make a jury like his client.' In a court of law or everyday encounters, if people like you, they're much more apt to say yes to you. So, how do you persuade someone to like you?

According to research, three main factors affect your likeability:

- how attractive you are to the other person
- how similar you are to the other person
- how much you offer praise to the other person

If you want your clients, customers and colleagues to like you, you must take the time to build relationships with them (see Chapter 5). Appeal to their values, demonstrate your similarities and emphasise your association with positive points, such as your involvement in your organisation's outstanding corporate social responsibility programmes or your department's track record of superb customer service.

The following sections cover three major techniques for pumping up your likeability.

Accenting your attractiveness

When Sir Winston Churchill was accused of being drunk, he replied, 'And you, madam, are ugly. But in the morning, I shall be sober.' Unkind but true!

Physical attractiveness goes a long way towards getting people to like you, and can increase your power of persuasion. Recall how much attention was paid to Republican vice-presidential candidate Sarah Palin's appearance during the 2008 election. Despite questions about her qualifications, and amid allegations of money inappropriately used on hair, make-up and wardrobe, Palin and her family strived to appear attractive and coordinated throughout the campaign.

People who look attractive are perceived as talented, kind, trustworthy and intelligent. They seem to draw others to them with ease. Physically attractive people with similar qualifications as less attractive individuals are more likely to be hired for the same jobs. And after they get the jobs, they typically earn more money than their less appealing counterparts.

The power of physical attraction is well known in the advertising industry. When a good looking woman promotes a product such as a car, consumers perceive the car as having a better design and as being more valuable than if the woman weren't present. By using attractive people to promote their products, advertisers create an *attractiveness bias* towards their products without the viewer being aware that the bias exists.

If you're not personally blessed with the good looks of Angelina Jolie or Orlando Bloom – and don't want to undergo cosmetic surgery or spend a fortune on beauty products – you can still make the best of what you've got. Increase your chances of persuading people that you're rather nice-looking by utilising any and all of the following strategies:

- ✔ **Dress appropriately for your shape and style.** Spending your entire salary on clothes isn't necessary; just choose well-made items that fit. Most department stores offer free measuring services and reasonable prices for tailoring.

- ✔ **Preen and prune a bit.** Make a daily effort to appear clean, healthy and polished. Get your hair cut or styled on a regular basis. A fresh 'do can make you feel amazingly confident.

- ✔ **Foster familiarity.** You naturally like people you're familiar with and find them more attractive than people you don't know. From an evolutionary standpoint, familiarity is all about safety, so do everything you can to form relationships whereby others feel safe around you. Even though you don't look like Kate Winslet or Johnny Depp, others will like you and be open to your influence.

  Some simple ways of making people feel safe around you include:

  - Actively listening to them (see Chapter 7 for more about this)

  - Accepting them as they are

  - Being honest, reliable and trustworthy

- Demonstrating empathy; see Chapter 3 for more on this

- Behaving respectfully

The *mere exposure effect* is a psychological phenomenon in which people develop preferences for things based solely on their familiarity with them. In studies of interpersonal attraction, this effect is also known as the *familiarity principle;* thus the more frequently a person sees you, the more likeable you can become to them.

✔ **Keep close.** Research indicates that the longer two people are in close proximity, the greater the chance that they end up liking one another and the more likely they are to find one another physically attractive and be open to each other's influence.

Without coming across as a stalker, some of the ways you can make the most of proximity are by:

- Inviting the other person to join you for lunch or drinks after work

- Offering to share a ride home

- Suggesting you sit together if you're working on the same project

- Asking them to go to a concert, film or museum with you and some other friends

✔ **Invest time.** The more time you spend with someone, the higher the probability that you like them and find them physically attractive.

You can commute together or take lunch at the same time. You could suggest working together on a project, or join forces for a sponsored charity event. You could find out the other person's interests or hobbies and suggest that you do them together.

✔ **Play up positive personal qualities.** Research consistently shows that people with positive personality traits – such as empathy, trustworthiness or generosity – are perceived as being more attractive than those who demonstrate few of those virtues.

Characters such as Shakespeare's Bottom, DreamWorks' Shrek and the Beast in *Beauty and the Beast* all have personalities that outshine their physical flaws. Indeed, over time, their various love interests even grow to find their donkey ears, wobbling green flesh and hairy backs endearing.

If you're naturally considerate or thoughtful, share your knowledge and expertise or offer to help when someone's struggling. If you're optimistic about a project when others are sceptical, show them how they stand to benefit. When you're generous with others, they see you in a positive light.

✔ **Share experiences.** A heart-to-heart conversation or a shared experience that makes a positive impact on your life can change how you perceive someone else and how they perceive you.

> Be proactive and seek out opportunities for sharing experiences. Put together a team for a sponsored event. Attend a concert, go to the theatre or visit a museum. Form a book club, put together a film society, attend a sporting event. By demonstrating your interest, you become more interesting to others.

Finding similarities

People tend to like you because you're similar to them. Similarities create bonds and provide a platform for establishing rapport. A shared background, point of view, sense of humour, comparable lifestyles and parallel personality traits are frequently cited as reasons for liking another person.

If you want to persuade someone, search for what you've got in common and make that person your friend. Salespeople are taught to search for similarities to make their clients feel they have something in common, which helps to develop rapport, deepen trust – and make the sale.

The following sections explore some similarities you can identify or enhance in order to get closer to others.

Common values

Discovering that you and a colleague share the same values creates a bond of trustworthiness and compatibility. Even if you don't share background, religion or lifestyle, you can probably still find some common values.

Shared dress sense

Adopting another person's style of dress is the simplest way to create an appearance of similarity. Similar dress can serve as a shortcut to communication. If you look at all like the people you want to influence, they assume you understand them, their values and their beliefs.

Parallel backgrounds and interests

While you may spend a lot of your energy on business-related matters, establishing a life outside of business is healthy – and helpful. You can get to know your clients and colleagues by talking about subjects other than work.

Discovering that someone comes from the same part of the country or enjoys the same pursuits, hobbies or activities as you provides grounds for liking that person. And after you like someone and they like you, persuading and influencing one another becomes easier.

Extend your interests to things that might not normally appeal to you, if they appeal to the people around you. Without meaning to sound sexist, women who are able to discuss football or the best golf club to use for getting out of the rough stand a better chance of engaging with their male colleagues and clients than those who can't differentiate a driver from a putter.

Between Facebook and other social networking tools, people can end up knowing too much about each other. Set the tone for online interactions and be selective in what you reveal about yourself. What you may see as a prank or bit of whimsy, others may view as grounds for dismissal. See *Social Media Marketing For Dummies* by Shiv Singh (Wiley) or *Facebook For Dummies* by Leah Pearlman and Carolyn Abram (Wiley).

Complimenting others

As Abraham Lincoln said, 'Everybody likes a compliment.' Paying compliments creates goodwill and cultivates relationships. Just make sure you go about offering your praises effectively.

Offering powerful praise

Praising others increases their positive feelings for you, and people are more prone to be persuaded by people they like. When you praise others, you're demonstrating that you're paying attention to and appreciating them.

To be successful at using compliments, limit at-work compliments to on-the-job achievements and avoid comments relating to personal appearance. Avoid commenting directly about the person and instead admire something about them. Many people are uncomfortable receiving direct compliments and feel embarrassed if the compliment is too personal. Instead, try complimenting the effect of someone's behaviour and the reasons for its positive impact.

Telling someone what a great guy they are or how much you want to be like him can be irritating and smacks of disingenuousness if not a bit of toadyism. If you tell someone you think he's wonderful, he may doubt your motives, if for no other reason than they know there are things about them that aren't so wonderful. If, however, you compliment something specific like 'I admire the way you handled that situation because you were direct without being offensive,' 'I could tell the tone and content of your presentation matched the audience's mood and expectations by their positive response,' 'I respect your ability to handle difficult conversations, because you treat people with respect while making your point' or 'I really liked the way you stood up for the team, because they've been working hard on this project without getting any recognition,' you're complimenting specific aspects of the person's behaviour that he can accept as valid.

When complimenting someone, follow these simple rules:

- ✔ **Think before you speak.** Make sure it's something true and that would benefit the listener.

- ✔ **Keep to the point.** Keep your remarks brief and avoid gushing.

- ✔ **Don't come on too strong.** Overwhelming the receiver will make him wonder about your motives.

- ✔ **Compliment an achievement not accidental good fortune.** Telling a good-looking person that they're good looking can be tiresome, because the person wonders if that's all people think of him.

- ✔ **Compliment in a timely manner.** Don't be the last to the post when complimenting someone. You may come out sounding like an also ran.

- ✔ **Stop, look and listen.** Gauge the other person's response and move on. If you continue to compliment, you may sound obsessive.

Avoiding flattery

If praise is crudely transparent or done the wrong way, your efforts can backfire and you can be seen as sycophantic rather than sincere. Be especially mindful of:

- ✔ **Obvious agendas:** A statement such as, 'Good job, Charlotte! Now I need you to produce two more units by next week' may be sincere, but it also indicates that the speaker wants something in return for the compliment. A more effective alternative would be 'Good job, Charlotte! I know you're putting a lot of effort into this project and I appreciate it. Now we've been asked to produce two more units by next week. Can I count on you to make that deadline?'

- ✔ **The all-powerful 'but':** The word 'but' ensures that your listener negates your first statement and focuses on the second. If you say something like, 'Ted, your work has really improved, but you need to be more proactive,' which portion of that statement is Ted going to remember?

  I encourage my clients to replace the 'but' word with either 'and' or a full stop. That way both sides of the message can be heard clearly without interference from the negativity 'but' implies.

- ✔ **False praise:** Avoid making a big show when both you and the other person know that the action being praised was actually mediocre. You just want the person to like you and you're trying to get on his good side. Furthermore, the other person is no fool; your compliment is likely to tag you as phoney. Instead, saying something like, 'So far, so good. Now that you understand what the job entails, I know you can increase your efforts to demonstrate what you're really made of.'

People want to believe good things about themselves; they often believe what they hear and like the person who offers the compliment, even when the praise is clearly false. Be aware of your power and only offer sincere and honest praise. Otherwise, your ethics will come into question. For more about ethical behaviour, turn to Chapter 5.

Relying on Reciprocity

Throughout history in all human societies, one of the most potent forces of influence has been based on the principle of *reciprocity*. You give something to me, and I give something similar back to you.

You may not admit that reciprocation plays a role in your interactions – you may even argue that I'm wrong in my assertion – but empirical evidence demonstrates that when you do someone a favour, you expect the other person to pay you back in some manner.

Further research demonstrates that people feel compelled to pay back any favour they receive, no matter what the cost of the original gift or favour – and often in amounts that exceed. So don't be surprised if you get back something even bigger than what you gave in order for the other person to redress the balance.

Paying people back works because it's a short cut for making decisions. You do someone a favour because he once did one for you. You don't have to spend your time or energy thinking about a decision. You help me out on this project and you can call on me in the future. You give me a gift and I return the favour. You scratch my back and I scratch yours.

The following sections explore how you can utilise the dynamics of giving and receiving in your efforts to persuade and influence others.

Giving first to gain advantage

People in both the profit and not-for-profit worlds understand the advantage of being the first to give – in order to get something back.

A well-known marketing technique for giving and getting is the gift-with-purchase, in which shoppers are encouraged to make a purchase in order to receive a free gift. While a regular practice throughout business, this system is particularly prevalent in the cosmetic industry. Purchase a product and receive free samples, umbrellas or tote bags. Would you have bought any of those items if they hadn't been given to you for free? Probably not. The simple fact that you're offered a free gift in exchange for purchase compels you to buy.

Similarly, when you offer your clients free samples of your product or service, you're giving away something with the plan being to receive something of higher value in exchange later – most likely an increase in sales and referrals.

Give your employees a gift voucher – prepaid debit cards and e-vouchers are particularly popular nowadays – and watch your ability to influence behaviour rise. This system of giving works because it combines convenience and choice. You pick the basic options but leave the final selection to your recipient, who feels rewarded with a treat that has concrete monetary value.

Charities understand the advantages of giving and are therefore able to persuade the great majority to put their hands in their pockets. In addition to offering little gifts such as pens, gummed address labels, lapel pins and greeting cards, charitable donations make you feel good about yourself. Also, donating to charity provides you with tax deductions; in these days of economic challenges, every little bit helps.

Of course, the things you give don't have to be physical objects. The positive dynamic that happens when you give a tangible gift also occurs when you reward someone with special recognition, extra help on a challenging project or the opportunity to leave work early on a Friday.

If someone owes you a favour, not only does he want to repay his debt, he wants to do so as soon as possible. Feeling beholden or indebted to another person is uncomfortable, and the sense of obligation is burdensome. After someone feels indebted to you, you can ask for what you want and then sit back and enjoy the spoils.

Stating 'much obliged' is a way of expressing appreciation across the globe and was first recorded in the *Oxford English Dictionary* in 1548. However, the expression translated literally means that the person saying 'much obliged' now owes the other person a favour and is obligated to pay back at some point in the future.

If you only take and don't give back, others are likely to perceive you as selfish and be less inclined to give to you in the future.

When a person gives you something, thank him with a handwritten note and follow up with an offer of your own.

While phone calls and emails are used more and more as a quick way of communicating, they don't quite cut the mustard when it comes to expressing your sincere appreciation. The time it takes to write a short note is worth the effort for the positive impression your letter leaves. While you don't need to write a long missive, you do need to be specific and sincere in your thanks. In addition, send it out promptly. Rather like fresh vegetables, a late letter becomes less attractive the longer it's left. That being said, 'better late than never' applies, because the recipient always appreciates your thanks.

Quickly come up with something you can provide in return. A meal out, a ticket to a sought-after event or a gift you know he'd particularly like are ways of keeping the relationship going.

There may be times when you'd rather not further the relationship, in which case send a brief thank-you note and leave it at that. While you want to be careful not to burn any bridges, there are just some relationships that are more trouble than they're worth. Or simply aren't worth your time and effort at all. Be polite and move on.

Whatever you do, you want to make sure that the gift you give makes the recipient feel comfortable and doesn't offend or embarrass him. Gifts should be given to honour an established relationship, not to court a new one. If someone gives you a gift that's beyond your ability to reciprocate in kind, in addition to writing a thank-you note, return his generosity with something thoughtful and unexpected that you can afford.

Before you select a gift, ask yourself what message the gift, and your reason for giving it, sends about you. The best presents are those that show you cared enough to offer an appropriate and thoughtful gift based on appreciation and respect. You also want to make sure that the gift is a genuine gesture of appreciation and not just an attempt to curry favour.

Refer to the following list when you want to give an appropriate and effective gift:

- ✔ **Make sure your gifts fits with company guidelines.** Some businesses have no-gift policies or a limit on the value of gifts its employees may accept. Check with the company's receptionist or human resources department to spare you and the recipient any awkwardness.

- ✔ **Consider how the gift will be perceived.** You want to be sure that it will speak favourably of you and your organisation and will benefit the recipient.

- ✔ **Pick gifts with personal meaning.** Pay attention to what the recipient talks about and likes. That way you know what kind of gift would be appreciated.

✔ **Don't be skimpy.** While the gift doesn't need to be expensive, it does need to be top quality, because cheaper and lower-quality products send negative messages about the value you place on the relationship.

✔ **Give appropriate gifts at appropriate times.** If you send a potential client a bottle of wine or box of chocolates before the contract's signed, you may look like you're offering a bribe.

✔ **Include a short handwritten note.** Personal notes along with the gift show you've put extra thought into your giving.

✔ **Avoid inappropriate gifts.** A gift that's overly personal, such as lingerie or other articles of clothing, could insult or offend the recipient.

Negotiating and making concessions

Consider this situation: you want someone to agree to your request. You know he probably won't, so you cleverly make your request larger than what you actually want, knowing that he'll turn you down, which he does. You then ask for something smaller – what you really want in the first place – and he agrees.

As long as you're adept at structuring your requests, the other person sees your second, smaller, request as a concession and is inclined to make a concession of his own. In other words, by skilfully structuring your proposals, people are much more likely to yield and agree to your second request.

When making a request, exaggerate your initial proposition enough to encourage a series of smaller reciprocal concessions that lead to your final offer being accepted. For example, if you want to sell a product or service to a potential buyer and he rejects your proposal, you can ask whether he will help you by referring people who might be interested in your offering. If you present your request as a concession following a purchase request the potential buyer just refused, he may be more willing to agree to your appeal than if you had asked for referrals at the beginning of your pitch.

If you make your first request so extreme that it's perceived as unreasonable, the other person is likely to see you as bargaining in bad faith. He may cut off further discussions entirely – or view your future concessions as fake and avoid reciprocating any concessions.

When you're negotiating, you never want to give something away without getting something in return. Use the 'If you . . . then I' formula. For example, you can say, 'If you agree to a series of programmes over the next three years, then I'll review our discount position.' By using this format you make it clear that your concession is contingent on the other person meeting the conditions you've proposed. When you're negotiating, it's good practice to give in order to get.

For more about effective negotiating practices, refer to the second edition of *Negotiating For Dummies* by Michael C Donaldson (Wiley).

Encouraging Follow-through on Commitments

The desire to be true to your word is a central motivator of behaviour. If you make a commitment, you feel pressure from within yourself – as well as from others – to behave consistently with your decision. When you commit, either orally or in writing, to a proposal or goal, you're likely to follow through because the very act of following through conforms to your view of yourself.

People also commit more readily when they personally *own* their decisions. If you try to force your will on someone else in an effort to meet your own agenda, don't be surprised if the other person fails to follow through. The challenge is getting others to do what you want – while making the choices appear to be theirs, as I explore in the following sections.

Playing to the desire for consistency

People want to appear consistent in their behaviour, and by extension, they appreciate consistency in others. People who do what they say they're going to do are highly valued individuals. You can depend on them to follow through on their promises and commitments. They seldom let you down or do surprising things.

But as you know, people aren't absolutely consistent. They say certain things and do others. That's bad enough in life outside the office, but when your career, due dates or pay package depend on the behaviour of others, inconsistency is tough to live with and can produce unfortunate consequences.

By observing how a person behaves, you discover their values, convictions and outlook. Once you have determined what motivates them as well as what holds them back, appeal to those signs. If, for example, you notice that someone's struggling to complete a project he initially seemed excited about or committed to, remind him of the pot of gold waiting at the end of the rainbow.

Ask how you can help, provide your support, and encourage the other person's efforts. If he continues to struggle, ask what might be holding him back. The more information you can garner, the more resources you have to work with.

Getting others to commit

If you want people to make commitments, rather than forcing choices on them, let the commitments be voluntary and defined in their own terms. By coming up with their own solutions and strategies, people are more inclined to commit to action than if you impose your will on them.

Empirical evidence proves that when you actively make a voluntary choice and publically announce or write down your intention, you're more likely to follow through than if you make the same choice without a public proclamation or statement.

Encourage people to write down what they say they're going to do. Whether setting a goal or agreeing a plan of action, writing down commitments is a vital psychological aid that keeps people to their word.

Committing in writing is particularly effective with people who report directly to you. For example, after one of your employees agrees that he's been slow in submitting necessary information, have him write a memo that summarises his plan for responding to the situation in the future, including whatever assistance he may need if he struggles, and send it to you. Writing and sharing the plan increases the odds that he lives up to what he puts down.

Teams that create mission and vision statements and the individuals who live by them understand the power of following through on promises. These statements are based on personal values, giving you something to own and guide your behaviour. By clearly and publically committing to your principles and promises, you put your reputation on the line.

Following the Crowd

As any successful company leader, politician or head of a voluntary organisation can attest, if you create an environment in which enough people buy in to what you're suggesting, the rest of the group will go along too. Life is just easier that way.

Advertisers, television producers and evangelical preachers are well aware of the power of building their audiences and then getting them to buy in to their products – whether it's body lotion, a comedy programme or a chance for redemption.

Following the crowd is easy but has a downside. As the American intellectual and Pulitzer-Prize-winning reporter Walter Lippmann said, 'When we all think alike, no one thinks very much.' Additionally, when you follow the crowd, you may find yourself acting in ways you didn't expect. The following sections explore methods of working with groups effectively and ethically.

Building your own crowd

You don't need to be physically connected to be part of a crowd. Online groups consisting of loosely linked individuals who share a passion or interest in a particular subject are popping up all over the place. Whether you're building a group of like-minded people in person or online, groups provide the opportunity to discover and feed on one another's ideas as well as influence others' beliefs and behaviours.

Groups provide a means of determining what's correct or acceptable – the more a group behaves in a certain way, the more you're influenced to comply. Groups serve as a short cut for determining how to behave, and work best in times of uncertainty. For example, if people are in an ambiguous situation, they tend to follow the example of the majority. In addition, people are inclined to follow the lead of people similar to them. Once you've got a group on your bandwagon, it's easier to persuade others to join, too. The thinking goes something like this, 'If everyone who is anyone is following her lead, why aren't I?' Most people want to be part of a special inner circle – a desire that gives you the power to persuade the masses.

Build your crowd of support bit by bit. If you can persuade even one member of your team to do what you'd like him to do, that person can persuade another. And then another can persuade someone else, until a crowd begins to form. And after you get a crowd behind you, you can persuade the rest of the team to jump on board.

Following the crowd can be a short cut to success – or a pathway to perdition. For the most part, you make fewer mistakes if you follow what others are doing rather than if you follow your own agenda. While mavericks may struggle with this fact, people often act in a similar fashion because they perceive it as the right thing to do. However, before following the crowd, you may want to check the values and beliefs of the people who are influencing your behaviour. As for the people who want to lead the crowd or use group dynamics to persuade others, ethical behaviour is paramount if they're to be seen as working in the best interests of the group and not simply for their own reward.

Group leaders working for the good of the group have a capacity to empathise and care for others, communicate clearly, and are committed to following through. While there are still leaders whose motives are toxic and who abuse the leader–follower relationship, rendering the group into a worse shape than when it started, most people are aware of those tactics and will abandon the leader rather than follow him. All groups need a leader – someone who can get others to follow willingly. For more information about ethical behaviour, refer to Chapters 1 and 5. If you want to know more about the role of empathy, turn to Chapter 3.

Recognising and responding to peer pressure

People who are comfortable following the lead of others are particularly susceptible to peer pressure. They willingly play follow the leader, appreciating that someone else is making the decisions while all they have to do is go with the flow.

According to social psychologist Irving Janis, when members of a group have similar backgrounds, are insulated from outside options and have no defined rules for making judgments, the group can make faulty decisions. Janis called this situation *groupthink*.

If you're uncertain what course of action to take, don't be surprised if you follow the herd. Because others are acting in a similar fashion, the message being conveyed is that the choice is right. Organised religions understand this principle, as do cults.

As any leader knows, persuading your team members when they work together in a unified way is easier than coercing the unconvinced. Individuals who get along, who are loyal and who work in a united way are the foundation of a cohesive team. Additional characteristics of a cohesive team include:

- ✔ Well-defined roles and adherence to an agreed code of conduct
- ✔ Shared goals and responsibilities
- ✔ A positive team identity and pride in team membership
- ✔ Positive working relationships, built on respect and trust
- ✔ An attitude of empathy and care towards team members
- ✔ Little conflict that is handled, when it does occur, using constructive problem-solving techniques
- ✔ Group members who cooperate with each other
- ✔ Honest, open communication
- ✔ Public recognition and credit for good work, freely given

Asserting Your Authority

Most people have a deep-seated sense of duty to authority – whether they admit it or not – and don't want to defy an authority figure's wishes. If you don't believe me, look at the research.

No matter how rebellious you may think you are, studies consistently demonstrate people's willingness to go well beyond their normal behaviour on the command of the person in charge. Without obeying the people in power, anarchy can reign. Envision your office if no one was in authority: madness and mayhem, perhaps – or everyone taking a siesta.

Making the most of titles and positions

From the moment you're born, you're trained to believe that obeying proper authority is the right thing to do and disobeying is wrong. Authority figures from your youth taught you to do as you're told by the people in charge. These influential people include family members, nuns, priests and pastors, teachers, police officers, fire fighters – even school crossing patrols.

In the worlds of law, politics, medicine and the military, authority rules. You're expected to submit to legitimate rule and assume your place in the hierarchy of power.

Consider the following examples:

- ✔ A senior law partner can more easily persuade others in the firm on a course of action than a recently qualified solicitor, who probably would struggle to even get a hearing.

- ✔ A police officer in uniform has more influence in getting people to play by the rules than a passer-by witnessing a crime.

- ✔ Doctors can persuade nurses to act without questioning.

- ✔ In the classroom, a professor carries more weight than a graduate assistant. And while you don't bow when meeting the chancellor of an elite university, you probably stand a little taller in his presence, out of respect for his position.

Doing what an authority figure wants often comes with benefits. Usually, the person in charge knows more than you do, so you can learn from him. Also, those in authority are in charge of handing out both prizes and punishments.

If you currently lack a title or a position of formal authority – and the ensuing power and influence that come with them – all's not lost. You can still make your voice heard and be noticed by others when you follow these suggestions:

✔ Build strong working relationships with the people you want to influence. Pay attention to their strengths, weaknesses and what motivates them. When you're ready to influence their thinking, present your case in a way that addresses their needs.

✔ Help others. If you want your colleagues to listen to you, begin by listening to them. Support your co-workers' good ideas, help them with their work when you can, offer encouragement when they face challenges.

✔ Be an expert in your area. Take courses, read journals, attend training programmes, tweet and blog to become *the* authority in your field. If you make it known that you're up-to-date with the latest information, people will seek your opinion.

✔ Be true to your values and principles. Treat people well, don't gossip or criticise others in public, and make decisions based on the right thing to do. Act like a role model.

Dressing like an authority figure

One of the quickest ways to gain authority is through your clothing. Uniforms denote expertise, entitlement and power. If you're wearing the clothes of your profession – a police officer's blue uniform, a judge's robes – you're seen as the authority in that area. Resisting requests from people in clothes that denote authority can be very difficult.

Someone wearing a well-tailored suit with polished shoes and classic accessories looks influential, while a person in baggy, sweaty shorts rarely does. Unless that person is Rafael Nadal after a well-won tennis match, of course.

Effective wardrobe choices can make you look more authoritative and commanding. For example:

✔ Wear jackets and blouses with shoulder pads to look broader than you really are. Choose shoes with heels or lifts to look taller. Politicians, celebrities and captains of industry know that size denotes authority, and people bow to authority.

At 5 feet 6 inches, the French president, Nicholas Sarkozy, is one of the world's most persuasive and influential men. He is also smart and understands the relationship between size and authority; he wears lifts in his shoes to make himself look taller.

✔ Accent your outfit with smart accessories. A fine watch, a good pen, and high-quality handbags and briefcases give an impression that you're a class act.

✔ Be well groomed. Polished shoes, a good haircut and well-tended nails say that you care enough to look your best.

✔ While vibrant colours liven up the ubiquitous grey, black and navy-blue suits, it's hard to be taken seriously when you're encased in fuchsia, turquoise and orange. That being said, a splash of red and gold sends out a message that you're someone to be taken seriously, because both colours are associated with power. Red symbolises all things intense and passionate, including excitement, energy and strength, while colour experts say that gold encourages communication and represents optimism, enlightenment and the promise of a positive future.

Exposing your expertise

In today's competitive world, you have little chance of making your mark unless you demonstrate your know-how, skills and abilities. People count on the advice of experts as a short cut to helping them make good decisions. Your job is to let them know that you're the expert they want.

In order to stand a chance of influencing another person, establish your own expertise. Yes, this requires a bit of self-promotion:

✔ Display your diplomas and awards, share testimonials and publicise your credentials to help create your expert persona. If you don't have any of these things, go out and get them. Take courses and put up your certificates of completion. Do volunteer work and ask for testimonials in return for your time. Ask your clients to recommend your services on LinkedIn. It's not enough to be expert in your field; you have to show people that you are.

✔ Whoever you're speaking to, tell stories and anecdotes about your experiences relating to your area of expertise. Stories are entertaining and more interesting than a list of your accomplishments. When you tell stories and anecdotes people engage with you and remember what you say. Three different kinds of stories follow that are sure to capture your listeners' attention:

• **Facing a challenge.** In this story you tell how you overcame an obstacle to get where you are. Rather than declaring, 'I'm really good at customer service,' which sounds boastful and unsubstantiated, you could say, 'I gained my skills in customer service working at a burger bar. People would crowd around the counter calling out their orders, and it was a challenge to keep the customer satisfied.' By telling that story your listener has an image in his mind of you being good at customer service.

- **Acting creatively.** This approach turns on the eureka moment, when an idea changes everything. Rather than saying, 'I sell textbooks' which sounds pretty dull, you could say, 'Although I loved school and reading and wanted to sell textbooks, I couldn't figure out how to market textbooks in a way that would interest the customer. Then I had a brainwave: no one has a favourite textbook, but everyone has a favourite teacher. So, I hooked in the customers by working with the teachers.'

- **Making connections.** This is a good way of communicating how you pulled a group together. For example, 'Our digital games company merged with another digital games company and people were duplicating each others' efforts to create a new game for the 18- to 34-year-old male market. I convinced the teams to combine their designs and create a product together. The game they created was the best-selling game for that market during the Christmas period.'

✔ Attend conferences and conventions, which offer great opportunities to get to know others socially before buckling down to business.

✔ Make the most of golf games, tennis matches, dinner and cocktail parties. Think of these activities as chances to find things out about your colleagues, as well as to establish your own expertise.

Although you may not have a lot of time to talk about yourself, you can always establish your authority by referring to your relevant background and expertise. And never forget: failing to establish your expertise early in the game allows someone else to get the attention.

Providing evidence of your expertise isn't bragging. You're demonstrating your authority. You're letting people know who you are and what you've accomplished – the reasons why they can safely be influenced or persuaded by you. Focus on your achievements and the skills, qualities and abilities you have that helped you succeed. In addition, tell some specific stories or anecdotes that bring life to your qualities and skills. For example, rather than saying, 'I got the project in on time and under budget,' you could enhance your story by saying, 'The project was a challenge because I had to juggle an assortment of personalities and ways of working in my team. The good news is, not only did we come in on time, we were under budget. I like managing people and it's one of my core skills, which is why I believe this project can succeed if you follow my suggestions.' You could then add a few details to explain how you managed the different personalities and got everyone working together.

Taking authority and obedience too far

Conforming to authority can be very appealing because you don't have to think. After the person at the helm gives an order, those under his command often stop thinking and start doing as they're told, even if they suspect the person in charge may be wrong, and regardless of the consequences.

Blind obedience to questionable activity can lead to dire consequences. Examples abound within corporations, professional firms, political parties, the medical field and any group or organisation where someone in a position of power and influence lays down the rules. The fall of major organisations such as RBS, Lehman Brothers and Arthur Andersen each shows how persuasive techniques combined with blind obedience to authority can create horrible results.

Blind obedience can be defined as complying with instructions without applying your personal values, morals, reason or logic to the request and potential consequences. A person acts out of ideological compulsion, obeying with neither need nor want of reason. *Deferring to authority* implies that a person understands that certain authority figures (such as judges, the police and doctors) have earned the right to exercise their power and influence. When a person defers to authority he takes into account his values and reason, and chooses to go ahead with the person's request.

Playing Up Exclusivity

Research consistently shows that the less available an item or an opportunity, the more valuable the commodity becomes:

- ✔ Tell your colleague that he has a limited amount of time to finish a project before the contract's cancelled or given to someone else, and watch him spring into action.

- ✔ Inform a client that his favourite product is about to be discontinued, and watch the cheque book come out.

- ✔ Invite your most valued customers to a pre-sale discount shopping day, and watch them flock through your doors.

Limited time, limited offers and once-in-a-lifetime opportunities persuade people that it's a case of now or never.

Seeking uniqueness

When you want to persuade someone to purchase your product or buy in to your ideas, highlight the unique benefits or exclusivity of what you're offering.

The more unique, beneficial and exclusive your proposition, the more inviting it is. The less available a product, service or piece of information, the more valuable it becomes:

- ✔ Red carpets, velvet ropes and tuxedo-clad bouncers at the entrance to a new club tell you that not just any Tom, Dick or Harry is allowed to enter. Potential customers perceive the venue as exclusive, making them long to be inside even more.

- ✔ In spite of the hype, diamonds aren't rare. However, the number of diamonds on the market at any one time is limited. Since the 1960s, a small group of companies has controlled how many diamonds are mined and where they're sold. Making diamonds difficult to purchase increases their desirability. The marketing slogan 'Diamonds are forever' encourages owners to keep their gems rather than sell them to others, which ensures new markets for additional diamonds.

- ✔ By limiting the number of popular handbags such as Hermès' Birkin bag, companies find that customers are willing to wait months for the chance to pay thousands to own one.

The same principles extend to information. For example, if your boss tells you something that's going to become public knowledge next week, you feel more in the know and ahead of the game than others in your department. Your manager, having shared something exclusive with you – something that may possibly benefit your career – can expect to be able to influence your behaviour in return.

Even dry and dull information, as long as it's not broadly available and supports your initiative, can be effective to share with others. When you position the information as exclusive, it becomes more persuasive than data that's widely available. If someone's unimpressed with your information or questions its exclusivity, you can assure them that what you're saying is true. If they still don't believe you, it's their loss.

Only make offers of exclusive information or opportunities to act now or lose out forever when the offer is legitimate. To do otherwise is dishonest and disingenuous, and ultimately backfires. Deceived colleagues will quickly pull away from offers that once captured them, and they will have no compunction regarding treating you as dishonestly as you treated them.

Playing hard to get can convince people that what you're offering has value. If you're the type of leader who's always available, your team may take advantage of you. Make yourself a little less accessible and observe how others treat you. Their respect increases, and they appreciate your input more than before.

Avoiding losses

When making economic decisions large and small, people prefer avoiding loss to acquiring gains. Studies indicate that if you tell people what they'll lose if they don't follow a particular course of action, you're more likely to persuade them than if you tell them what they stand to gain.

Noted behavioural researchers Amos Tversky and Daniel Kahneman were the first to examine and report this notion of *loss aversion*. Among many other findings, their research shows that inexperienced investors prematurely sell stocks that have done well because they don't want to lose any of their gains. In addition, because the investors want to avoid any potential for loss, they hold onto stocks that have lost value because to sell means losing on their investments officially and irretrievably. This uninformed practice often results in further losses.

Other research confirms that people are willing to go to greater lengths to avoid loss than to realise an equivalent gain. If you think you can no longer have something that you once had, you'll want it even more. Simply stated, losing £100 is a lot more painful than the pleasure of gaining £100.

When you want to persuade your team or customers to follow a certain course of action, point out what they'll lose if they don't act on the information you give them. For example, if you want to persuade your colleagues to work with you on a specific assignment, point out what they'll lose in terms of opportunities and experience if they don't go along with you – as well as what they stand to gain if they do.

Chapter 11

Leading by Example: Quietly Creating Big Change

In This Chapter

▶ Shaking up matters

▶ Turning back attacks

▶ Making the most of every opportunity

▶ Allying with others

Mahatma Gandhi said, 'Be the change you want to see in the world.' Now, there was a man who knew how to persuade through example. Rather than ousting the British with guns as the American colonialists had done 150 years earlier, Gandhi took a non-violent, non-cooperative approach to achieve Indian independence and improve Hindu–Muslim relations. Less obvious and deadly than guns, Gandhi's method was:

✔ **Powerful** because India gained its independence in 1947.

✔ **Persuasive** because Gandhi got what he and his fellow Indians wanted.

✔ **Influential** because his approach is recognised as the standard across the globe for others to model.

A simple man and a wise man, Gandhi led by quiet example, patiently creating change through incremental steps, reflecting one of the different approaches that are explored in this chapter.

At some point in your career, you're going to see things differently from 'the norm' and want to confront the beliefs and behaviours in your organisation that seem counterproductive or unethical. At the same time, you may genuinely like your job, the company and the people you work with, and want to continue doing well in your career.

The difficulty is, if you speak up you may cause resentment in others, and if you don't speak up you'll cause resentment within yourself. The question becomes: how can you rock the boat without falling out? The answer is to put your differences to work to create constructive change.

In this chapter I introduce four moderate persuasive approaches – on a spectrum from personal, individual actions through to those that are more public, requiring working with others – all leading to significant change.

Expressing Your Disruptive Self

If you're working in a traditional organisation where the environment is unproductive and the atmosphere is counter to your values, you can quietly persuade the organisation to change. The most inconspicuous way of initiating change is by simply acting in a way that feels personally right and that quietly challenges others' expectations.

Do something differently and people begin to talk about it. As more and more people talk about what you're doing, someone may emulate your behaviour – making an even greater impact on the organisation.

Whether you make a deliberate act of protest or simply demonstrate your own values, expressing your disruptive self can influence the choices others make and persuade organisations to review their procedures. The following sections explore ways to adjust how you dress, behave and decorate your office in order to create change.

Modifying your clothing

What is it about traditional organisations and their dress codes? While I agree that muffin tops and flip flops for women and cargo pants and sleeve-less tee-shirts for men are inappropriate office attire – unless you're working at a beach bar – most boardrooms are filled with ubiquitous tailored suits in black, dark grey and navy blue.

I'm not arguing that well-fitted jackets and conventional haircuts don't send signals of reliability, dependability and a considered approach. Indeed, in organisations such as law firms, banks and the armed forces, these are desirable characteristics. But what happens if the intensity of the culture around dress is so extreme that you observe creativity being silenced and values quashed? You just might surprise yourself by quietly pushing against the norm.

Expressing yourself in a tactfully disruptive manner reinforces your sense of the importance of your convictions. But a thin line exists between expressing your disruptive self and acting like a self-serving idiot. Pay attention not only to how you're feeling while you're being disruptive but also to how others are responding.

While, for the most part, men have an easier time of deciding what to wear than their female colleagues, they still have questions about their attire that need addressing. For example, do they wear a tie or not? Brown shoes or black? Short sleeves or long? Keep in mind that whatever you choose to wear reflects your personal brand values.

While some women wilt under the barrage of disrespectful and patronising behaviour, others make slight alterations to their dress, allowing their femininity to work in their favour. Without meaning to offend anyone, it's fair to say that it's not uncommon in traditional male cultures for an atmosphere of condescension towards women to exist. Capable and qualified women struggle to maintain their feminine identity and hold onto their integrity in testosterone-filled surroundings where gender discrimination is rife. If you're a woman who has experienced disrespectful and patronising behaviour, you can make some slight alterations to your dress that can allow your femininity to work in your favour.

The subject of clothing and accessories with overt political and religious connections continues to raise debate both for students as well as employees. In some cases judges find in favour of those wishing to display their beliefs, while in other instances they have found in favour of those opposed. Because my personal beliefs may be contrary to yours, and were I to suggest you act according to my values you could find yourself facing legal action, I encourage you to be true to your own values, being prepared to face possible consequences.

Adapting your behaviour

Just because everyone comes into the office at the crack of dawn and stays until midnight, it doesn't mean that you have to. First of all, not everyone does. Second, if those hours conflict with your lifestyle, coming in before the sun rises and leaving when the stars are out won't work for you. And if this schedule doesn't work for you, you won't be working for the organisation for long.

When you start acting differently from the norm – when you disrupt others' expectations by quietly demonstrating your values – you can slowly change the atmosphere at work. It takes only one person to notice the difference in your behaviour to get people talking. In time, they may even take the plunge themselves and emulate your actions.

The more people talk about what you're doing and how you're doing it – or the more they reflect your behaviour in their own – the more influence you have on the culture of your organisation.

Creating balance in your life doesn't mean that productivity has to suffer. Adapt your work habits to complete your tasks more productively. For example:

- ✔ Run meetings on schedule and monitor interruptions during your day.

- ✔ Utilise technology (applications for handheld devices, websites, software and so on) to speed up low-level and administrative tasks.

- ✔ Complete your most challenging tasks first thing. Tackle the tough stuff first when your energy's at its highest.

- ✔ Just start. Once you get started you find you get into the flow and time flies.

- ✔ Work at your most productive times. Find out when you're most productive and work to those times.

- ✔ Make out your to-do list at the end of your working day. When you come to work, you won't have to figure out what needs doing.

- ✔ Build in time for exercise. Physical exercise boots productivity and morale.

- ✔ Organise your workspace. Spending time searching for pens and documents under piles of paper is a waste of precious minutes, if not hours.

- ✔ Delegate. You free up your time and empower others to do what they're good at.

- ✔ Learn to say 'no'. There's no reason for you to do everything for everyone. Save your sanity by making wise decisions.

For more tips for increasing productivity, pick up a copy of *Project Management For Dummies* by Nick Graham and Stanley Portny (Wiley), which has a ton of time-management and productivity strategies.

Altering your environment

When you want to influence the thinking of your clients and colleagues, and your organisation's environment doesn't reflect your personal values and interests, you may have to make a few changes in your surroundings. Showing who you are and what matters to you opens the door for conversation, and after you get people conversing, all things are possible.

People are more comfortable when they get to know you and what you value. And when people are comfortable with you, they're more open to your influence. Invite people into your office for one-to-one conversations or casual meetings. That way, your guests can see a bit of the person behind the organisation. As they get to know you, they may like you. As I note in Chapter 10, if people like you, you're more able to persuade them.

Many heterosexual couples display wedding and family photos in their offices as a simple way of connecting with others and reflecting what's important to them. So, if you are half of a gay or lesbian couple, what are you to do? If your relationship is important to your identity, and having a photo of your partner and you together brings you pleasure, put it on show. While some people may be uncomfortable seeing you in a same-sex relationship, by displaying a photo of you and your partner together, you're expressing your authentic self. You are living your values and presenting yourself in a way that invites discussion around what matters to you.

However you reveal your values and beliefs, make sure your behaviour is non-offensive.

When you're about to make an offensive comment or gesture, take a deep breath and count to ten. Vulgarity has no place in the office or anywhere else, as my children remind me. That said, it's not uncommon. A colleague once said that every time he was tempted to call someone a rude word or speak in an offensive or coarse manner, he'd think how he'd feel if someone spoke to his mother, sister or daughter that way.

If you feel you need to offend someone to wake them up, think about ethical behaviour, which you can read about in Chapter 5. If you still need to wake someone up, I find that telling her I'm disappointed in her behaviour usually does the trick. Then there's always the technique of handing out a warning when things get really bad.

Turning the Energy Around

The samurai of feudal Japan developed a method of neutralising an enemy in which the attacker's energy was used against him. This was in direct contrast to the traditional approach of hitting, punching, kicking and striking back in opposition. This new form of self-defence was called *Jujitsu*.

Similar to Jujitsu in combat, you turn the energy of a verbal or personal attack back on your aggressor. The following sections detail what you can do when someone comes at you with objectionable or demeaning words or treats you in an unwarranted way. By redirecting your attacker's energy, you can influence others' responses and turn these aggressive behaviours into opportunities for change.

Redirecting insensitive statements

When you hear someone speak in an insensitive way, what are you going to do? Walk on by like it never happened? Hurl back an equally insensitive statement at the person? How about you respond in a way that can influence future behaviour?

By turning an insensitive statement, action or behaviour back on itself – and making the other person's negative energy work *against* them rather than *for* them – you become a proactive persuader.

The strategies listed below are designed to help you communicate respectfully when someone else is acting like a jerk. While the approaches may not be foolproof, they're better than coming back with an insult which is bound to make conversation and cooperation more difficult. Although insulting or offending the other person may give you a momentary sense of satisfaction, it's unlikely to lead to an agreeable outcome.

- ✔ Don't play along. Act as if you didn't get what the other person was saying. If you're in a one-to-one situation, you could calmly comment, 'Really? That's not my experience.'

- ✔ Use Socratic questioning. Paraphrase neutrally what's been said and follow up with questions.

- ✔ Calmly request they refrain from making insensitive remarks. By letting the offender know how you feel by saying 'I feel (name the emotion) when you (come up with a non-judgemental description of the behaviour) because (describe the tangible effects)' you're informing them and taking responsibility for your feelings, not blaming them.

- ✔ Ask for clarification. Ask follow-up questions to confirm the other person's basis for her remarks. This is not an opportunity for you to make a statement, it's a way of discovering information that will help you understand what the speaker feels, means or believes.

- ✔ Provide information. Tell the other person why you find her comments insensitive. She may be unaware of your feelings.

Neutralising awkward actions

Whether someone's intentionally causing another person pain or suffering by purposefully being rude, hurtful or unkind, or they're simply gauche, inept or socially clumsy, awkward situations are common occurrences in the workplace. Some people just can't help themselves and will make demeaning statements or actions. Others relish a good argument and don't shy away from being verbally aggressive, attacking another person's character or flinging about other abusive comments. The fact that others may feel ill at ease, embarrassed or uncomfortable in these situations doesn't seem to bear much weight when the person behaving awkwardly is in full flow.

When someone makes a comment or behaves in a way that can lead to discomfort – whether intended or not – you can act like a samurai by redirecting her negative force to change the situation.

If you're a manager wanting to promote your valued team members and protect them from being unintentionally ignored, you may have to speak like a samurai. By that I mean protect your valuable team members and their contributions. For example:

✔ Someone may make a constructive comment, a useful suggestion or a wise observation in a meeting, only to have it ignored and then repeated later by someone else to much acclaim. If you see this happening, interject with a supportive remark crediting the colleague with the original comment. For example, you could say something along the lines of, 'Jeremy, that's an important point. I'm glad you picked up on Felicity's concerns. Felicity, did Jeremy correctly summarise your points?'

✔ Rather than attacking the person who interrupted, listen and watch what's going on, constructing your response in such a way that you can disarm rather than harm the interrupter.

Instead of pointing out people's faults and inappropriate behaviours and remarks, or lashing out when you think the situation warrants a quick flip of the whip, you can quietly make a big change by practising self-control and emotional intelligence. Holding your tongue and listening and watching with a keen ear and eye for what's being communicated, then responding in a way that defuses any potential harm rather than fanning the flames, you can initiate small yet meaningful changes in people's beliefs and behaviours. You can identify fundamental issues without coming across as accusatory, as well as relieving potential conflict by addressing the underlying tensions clearly and calmly, without making any accusations or assumptions.

Reacting like a samurai requires self-control and emotional intelligence. While you may want to let rip with the first thought that pops into your head, bite your lip, count to ten and think before speaking. Once your words have left your mouth, there's no getting them back. Listening more than you speak gives you the advantage of learning about the other person, her feelings and her issues, giving you the advantage when it comes to responding. In addition, listen empathically, paying attention to not only what's said, but the way it's said as well. This way you take your own thoughts and emotions out of the frame and can see the situation from the other person's point of view. For more tips about how to practise self-control and emotional intelligence, flip to Chapters 7 and 12.

When you identify underlying issues and want to relieve unconscious tensions and make meaningful changes in your colleagues' attitudes and behaviours by voicing these concerns, avoid making accusations. Doing so only annoys other people and definitely doesn't persuade them to change.

For example, if you're in a situation where you believe your boss isn't paying attention to you when you're speaking, rather than accusing her by saying something like 'You never listen to me,' you could say, 'I feel that I'm not being heard.' This approach removes any need for your boss to respond defensively, because you're taking the responsibility for your feelings. Other samurai-like behaviours include:

- ✔ **Give them the responsibility.** If someone wants some information from you that you don't want to, or can't, tell them, rather than saying 'I can't tell you that,' respond with 'I'm not allowed to say.'

- ✔ **Give her choices.** Rather than telling someone what she 'needs to' or 'must' do, suggest that 'you could' or 'you might'. This allows the other person to save face instead of having to agree to your demand or allegation.

- ✔ **Avoid confrontation.** If someone makes a point that you don't agree with, instead of saying, 'You're wrong!' reply instead with 'I would argue that . . .' or 'The way I see it is . . .'.

- ✔ **Convert an accusation into a query.** Accusations are like rhetorical questions in that they're meant to make a point without the expectation of a reply, except an accuser hopes you come back with a denial or a hardened attitude she can push against. Don't give her that opportunity. Instead, rephrase her accusation as a question. For example, rather than coming back with a comment like 'I don't see the point in continuing with this conversation,' you could respond with 'What is your desired outcome for this conversation.'

✔ Stay positive. Instead of saying 'That's not what I said,' you could reply with 'Let me explain my point again.' This makes you sound more agreeable, with the aim of fostering a productive relationship.

✔ Practise tact. When you speak harshly or in an unkind manner, your listener's going to protect herself by shutting down or lashing back. If the point of your conversation is constructive and you disagree with what's being said, reply with 'I'm not sure I agree with . . .' rather than a quick 'You're wrong' or 'I disagree' or more negative comments. In addition, you could begin your sentence with, 'As I understand . . .' or 'Am I correct in understanding that . . .?' This way, you leave the door open for neutralising potentially awkward situations.

Getting Creative

Some people look for and value new ways of doing things, and take responsibility for the risks and outcomes of these methods. They approach their work in an entrepreneurial manner. Not only are they innovators or the people who set up new ways of doing things, they're the ones who can invigorate and rejuvenate organisations when they spy opportunities for improvement lurking around the corner.

Spotting, creating and capitalising on short- and long-term opportunities for change are the hallmarks of great influencers and persuaders. If you're flexible, adaptable and prepared to make the most of chance circumstances, if you're prepared to be an agent for change rather than a victim of situations, if you're prepared to see opportunities for action in the routine of everyday life, you're well positioned to influence others around you.

Like a boxer bouncing on his toes or a jazz pianist off on a riff, influencers and persuaders must be prepared to respond creatively to the moment when it arises. After you're in the moment, you can take over and direct the flow. As I say in Chapter 13 on emotions and body language, persuasion and influence are a lot like dancing: now you curtsey; now I bow.

Spotting opportunities

Low-hanging fruit are the easily winnable actions, activities or decisions in a negotiation or business. Going for the low-hanging fruit is unlikely to rustle anyone's feathers and rarely requires you to expend a lot of extra effort. For example, if you want to cut down on the amount of paper wastage in your office, encourage employees to single space, use a smaller font, and print on both sides of the paper. Other low-hanging fruit opportunities are:

- Politicians who set a number of easily attainable goals they can accomplish with minimal effort
- A sales person who seeks out the easiest customers to sell to
- Enable your customers to shop with mobile devices. Research shows that approximately 90 per cent of Americans between the ages of 18 to 64 have mobile phones and of these, nearly 50 per cent use their phones to shop.

Go for these opportunities as often and as readily as you can. Over time, you end up filling your basket with bushels of wins that you can use to further your cause when you want to prove your credibility and convince your listener.

Other opportunities – the not-so-easy wins – take a little longer to work through and require proactive approaches. Focus on your long-term strategy in these cases rather than on how you can score fast wins. For example, if the opportunity to influence an organisation's values or business practices is important to you, be patient and persevere when the going gets tough. Realise that you're probably going to take many small (but not always simple) steps in order to reach your goal. It took some time for those issues to become established within the organisation, and it will take some time to change them.

Always keep your senses attuned for new opportunities. As one of my mentors told me early in my career, 'Keep your eyes and ears open – and your mouth shut.' Look and listen first – and wait to speak or act.

Opportunities to persuade people to behave differently can appear unexpectedly. If you know what you want and are quick off the mark, you can influence people's thinking and behaviour.

Capitalising on opportunities

If you gather your small wins, build some interest and keep plugging away at your agenda, you can eventually influence enough people to create a big change.

Publicly arguing with and attacking the keepers of the flame doesn't win you friends and certainly doesn't influence people. What you have to do instead is take advantage of opportunities when they come your way.

If you want to advance your career, being good at your job isn't enough. Others have to see you being good at it. For example, if an opportunity arises to make a presentation about something you've been working on, be the first to volunteer. That way you can reveal your subject knowledge and others can see you as courageous, proactive, bold, credible and daring – because most people appreciate just how terrifying giving a presentation can be.

If you're going to make a presentation, make sure you've done your audience research. Too often, presenters spend all their time developing the content, failing to consider their audience's needs and concerns. See Chapter 8 for getting yourself noticed and Chapter 9 for understanding how your listener makes decisions.

If you're a manager, encourage your team members to present at meetings. They gain experience, recognition and prestige in front of their colleagues and superiors, while you're seen as a leader who demonstrates faith in your people.

While some companies I work with still have a 'command and control' approach towards management – and experience lots of ensuing turf wars – many businesses are going over to the other side, a land where collaboration and power-sharing are the norm. Most organisations find this philosophy leads to less stress and more productivity. When senior executives encourage the line managers below them to delegate responsibility as much as they can, they empower individuals and teams within their departments. When initiative taking is openly praised in front of their managers, people take pride in their work. When calculated risks are encouraged and you're free to challenge the boss, creativity and transparency become the norm.

Too many times, people at the top of the pyramid – or just in charge of a well-established department or division – lose touch with their beliefs and values as they seek fortune and fame. Make sure that you have people around who challenge your approach. Only by seeing all angles and issues can you successfully capitalise on opportunities that come your way.

Building Strategic Alliances

It is often said that an optimist and pessimist make the best partnership, because one sees the profits while the other sees the risks.

If you want something to happen, whether organising the office Christmas party or building a global conglomerate, you must persuade others to work with you. No matter how willing and able you are, you can't do it all on your own.

Your initiative gains clout and has a bigger impact when you have others on board to further your agenda. You and your allies can persuade the people in power to pay attention more quickly and directly when you work as a team rather than each going about her quest as a lone individual.

When you build strategic alliances, you gain:

- A sense of power and legitimacy within the organisation
- Access to additional expertise, resources and contacts
- Assistance getting tasks done more quickly and effectively
- Emotional support
- Advice

Alliances come in all shapes and sizes and aren't limited to formal teams or contracts. What's required is a desire to collaborate, a readiness to think big, and a willingness to build relationships. In addition, for the alliance to work, both parties must gain value.

Below are six points to remember about building alliances:

- Work with someone you know.
- Share your ideas and be willing to join forces.
- Weigh up what each of you has to offer.
- Confirm that there's a win–win for each of you.
- Be sure that you're each ready to commit.
- Verify your agreement.

Promoting change together

Getting people who are on your side to join you is fairly simple. Depending on their constraints, if they're able and the cause sits comfortably with their beliefs and values, persuading them to come on board shouldn't be a problem. For example, there's a free online site for leading social change that provides daily news and information about important social issues and offers people the opportunity to sign petitions for actions they believe in (www.change.org) This website appeals to my beliefs and values, is easy to use, and is an instrument for making a difference. In barely a blink of an eye I signed up and I now regularly sign petitions that address social issues that I feel strongly about, many of which I wouldn't be aware of if it weren't for the information on this site. Because it's easy to use and because it sits comfortably with my beliefs and values, the organisers had no trouble getting me on board.

Strategic alliances are committed relationships that work best when the benefits to both parties and the way they will work is clear and agreed from the outset.

Persuading the opposition to join you requires a more thoughtful approach. You have to open your mind and let go of any preconceived ideas you may have about the other side. Treat people you perceive to be a threat as equals. Even better, treat them as your friends.

Assumptions about competition contradict the law of nature that says that everyone is unique. The same holds true for businesses. It's not possible for two businesses to serve the same client's needs in the same way. Businesses exist for their own specific purposes and missions to serve their customers in their own special ways. That is why businesses don't need to compete in traditional ways. Instead, owners and managers can collaborate in ways that truly serve their own needs and their customers' interests. For example, in the classic movie *Miracle on 34th Street,* Kris Kringle, as Santa Claus at the department store Macy's, sends a customer to Gimbals, a competing department store, because he knows that the customer will find there exactly what she's looking for. Kringle understands that by serving the needs of the customer, he's serving the best interests of Macy's even if it means losing one sale. He's building Macy's reputation as the place to shop because if they don't carry the item, they know who does.

Today's world is one of abundance. Businesses know not just their own products but the products and services offered by others in their industry. By collaborating with others, you can increase your offerings, bringing greater success to everyone. Not every client is going to be the right one for you. There may be a lack of synergy, and interactions may be confusing and unfulfilling. If your business can't serve all of your customer's needs, having alliances with others in your industry can ultimately serve you well.

In my own business, I have developed an extensive network of working relationships with consultants, coaches, trainers, facilitators and marketers in order to learn about their ideal clients. The more I know about what they want to achieve and the approach they take to their work, the better able I am to refer clients and customers to them. While it may appear that we do similar work for similar types of clients, I consistently find that our work is complementary, not competitive, and that by collaborating together, we're all better able to serve our clients.

Lack of trust is what usually gets in the way of collaboration. The best way to get around that is to collaborate only with those individuals and businesses that treat you the way you want to be treated. Start by making a list of qualities that you want your collaborator to demonstrate. Below are some of the qualities you might look for:

- ✔ Open to collaboration
- ✔ Knowledgeable and experienced
- ✔ Ethical
- ✔ Committed
- ✔ Honest

Once you have your criteria in place, seek alliances with people who match your profile, starting with those associates you already know and the products and services they offer. Consider how else you could provide mutual assistance to serve one another's clients. For example, if you're a website designer, you probably know a number of software designers, hardware representatives, installers, networkers, trainers and consultants. Ask them what additional services they provide that your customers may find useful now or in the future. You could get together with your perfect collaborators to offer a free seminar to your customers on the latest technological developments. Your customers, and those of your collaborators, will appreciate your time and the solutions you've provided.

Outside of your existing contacts, you can find potential collaborators by raising your profile. Become involved in industry-related organisations, write for trade publications, speak at forums, and actively pursue collaborative relationships. By seeking mutually advantageous relationships with others within your industry, you can extend your client base and serve your existing customers even better.

People who represent the majority are integral in gaining support for your cause. When you want to challenge the status quo and know that the organisation is committed to upholding it, you have to tread carefully. Befriend those who support the system, seeking guidance from insiders who can advise you how far you can go. While not everyone is your ally, there's no point in turning those who represent the status quo into your enemy. The issue is about procedures and principles, not people. Constantly consider all possibilities. Question your reasons, the circumstances, conditions and issues to determine how you can best build a supportive alliance.

Adding weight to your argument

Support comes in various forms, so look for your support in any and all of the following ways:

- ✔ Offer a claim that states in one sentence why someone should support your proposition.

- ✔ Provide personal experiences from yourself and others.

- ✔ Enlist the help of like-minded co-workers who are similar in temperament to you, thus adding weight to your argument and giving you more clout and support when persuading others.

- ✔ Find people who are sympathetic to your cause and who are in a position to influence the decision-makers.

- ✔ Seek allies in high places to persuade others to adopt your point of view.

- ✔ Befriend people whose point of view is different to yours to challenge your thinking and help you see all sides.

- ✔ Present evidence that can substantiate your position.

- ✔ Refer to others who have succeeded in similar situations.

- ✔ Provide a conclusion that sums up your argument.

When you want to persuade people to adopt a new way of doing anything, seek out the support of people who are part of the status quo. Share your ideas and actively listen to their feedback (see Chapter 7). These individuals will let you know just how hard you can push for change and warn you of potential minefields.

Consider all possible courses of action before seeking a strategic alliance. Ask yourself, 'What are the right conditions, the right issues and the right circumstances for me to consider joining forces with others?'

Strategic alliances can offer a clear benefit to the organisations involved and their clients, and increase sales of defined products and services. To avoid confusion, customers need to know which company is responsible for which product or service. By creating strategic alliances, both the parties gain visibility and strengthen their company's profile. With an alliance, revenues for both companies increase and costs are shared.

Before forming a strategic alliance, consider the questions below:

- ✔ What are the clear benefits for both parties in building a strategic alliance (for example, financial, product or service, relationship)?

- ✔ How will you clearly define your strategic alliance so your customers can understand what it means to them?

- ✔ What can you do to network the individuals throughout your organisations to strengthen the alliance bond?

- ✔ How much strategic alliance business do you plan to deliver and how much can you fulfil?

✔ What plans have you in place for the scope of work to be delivered through the alliance? How will you define and measure the success of your strategic alliance?

✔ How clear and honest is the communication between all the partners in the strategic alliance? How strong are the people who are responsible for the implementation and success of the programme?

✔ How committed are both partners to promoting the image and success of the strategic alliance?

Chapter 12

Appealing to Other People's Drives, Needs and Desires

*Y*ou must tap into what interests, excites or means something to other people if you hope to get them to do what you want. Lighting someone's fire, revving a person's engines and engaging your listeners at the level where they chomp at the bit to do your bidding is fundamental to success whether you're at work, home or at play. Mind you, I'm not saying this prospect is easy. Just fundamental.

The adage 'different strokes for different folks' rings loud and clear when getting people to come on board with you. Although I do share a few reliable categories of motivation in this chapter, everyone is different, and you must do your own homework. Seek to know what drives someone to show up and do his best. Discover what he needs to convince him that your way is the best way. Dig deeper and uncover your audience's innermost desires. Do all that, and you're on the right track to creating friendly persuasion.

Rather than coercing and compelling people to do what you want them to do, targeting their drives, needs and desires produces generally positive results and good feelings for all. In this chapter you discover how to couch your comments in ways that others can understand, appeal to your listeners' ideals, work with people whose point of view is different from yours and build enthusiasm and commitment to compelling goals in difficult times.

Making the Most of Others' Feelings

Emotions play a big part in how people respond to your requests. If you don't strike the right chord with others' values, moods and feelings, you stand little chance of getting them to agree to your agenda. See Chapter 3 for more on emotions.

Advertisers have long known that the more they can find out about what matters to consumers, the more success they have in affecting behaviour (in this case, getting people to buy their products). The same goes for you at work and when interacting with other groups. Knowing what inspires people, what's important to them and what they can't live without serves as a guide when the time comes to influence their beliefs and behaviours. For example, if you're working with a group of young people who are keen to go into politics, provide them with an opportunity to meet government leaders as part of their curriculum, with the stipulation being that they must reach a certain standard of academic achievement in order for this meeting to happen.

Touchy stuff

In addition to hearing and seeing, your sense of touch plays a role in communicating with others. *Haptic communication* is communicating by touch. (*Haptic* refers to the sense of touch and comes from the Greek word meaning 'I fasten onto'.) Research conducted by Joshua M Ackerman (Massachusetts Institute of Technology), Christopher C Nocera (Harvard University) and John A Bargh (Yale University) demonstrates that the sense of touch affects how people view the world. For instance, these researchers found that:

- Interviewers who held heavy clipboards during a meeting with job applicants thought the candidates took their work more seriously than the interviewers who held light clipboards.

- After handling jigsaw-puzzle pieces, subjects were asked to read a passage about an interaction between two people. Those individuals who had been given rough pieces saw the interaction as adversarial, while those who had handled smooth pieces did not.

- During a price negotiation process, people who were seated in hard chairs without cushions were less inclined to compromise than those who were seated in soft, comfortable chairs.

- People who held warm cups of coffee judged others as more caring and generous than individuals who held cold drinks.

This research highlights the deep link between minds and bodies. You develop your understanding of physical characteristics such as roughness, hardness and temperature early in infancy, and this development is critical to how you develop abstract concepts around meaning.

Just think of expressions like 'hard hearts', 'warm smiles', 'weighing in with all the possibilities', 'having a tough time of things' or 'being an old softie'. These expressions and many others reflect the impact of sensations on how people view the world and make decisions.

Observe *how* people move and speak. While the actual words and movements are important, pay equal attention to their tones of voice, their facial expressions and the attitudes behind their actions. These subtle details tell you a lot about how they're really feeling. For example, a simple phrase like 'Thank you for your time' can come off as warm, energetic, dismissive or bored, all depending on your tone of voice and facial expression.

The following sections provide you with tips on how to tap into people's feelings to realise their goals, dreams and desires.

Rising to difficult challenges

Throughout your life, you're going to face difficult challenges. Taking personal risks and persuading others to do so too may be one of the greatest challenges you face. When people see success as unlikely – and failure a surer bet – your job is to come up with the right approach to get them to take the plunge.

Rather than trying to talk someone into doing what you think is the right thing to do, persuade them to rise to the difficult situation by appealing to their personal beliefs and values. See Chapter 2 for identifying others' values.

✔ **Hold candid and honest discussions about the probability of success.** Encourage others to talk candidly about their trepidations. Dig deep to discover their fears and anxieties. Let them unload. Ask them what they're afraid of, what may be holding them back, or what's the worst thing that may happen if they committed to tackling the situation. Enquire about a time when they rose to a difficult challenge, what happened and how they felt afterwards. To paraphrase Franklin D Roosevelt, when they explore their fears, they discover the only thing they have to fear is fear itself and that, rather than fail, they just may succeed.

✔ **Make roles and responsibilities crystal clear.** Many concerns that emerge during discussions are likely to deal with performance and how it may impact on their careers and the organisations. Help people understand what others expect of them and break the challenge down into achievable, step-by-step measures that they can accomplish. Describe what is expected and, together, put a plan in place for how they're going to get there. Communicate constantly to help them stay on track.

✔ **Spread the risk.** Encourage others to discuss where they see potential risks and assure them that they're not alone. Arrange for support systems such as a mentor or additional resources when you can. Encourage them to consider potential difficulties and put plans in place to prevent these difficultues from happening. Let others know they're supported and cared for.

> ✔ **Provide visible and unconditional support regardless of the outcome.**
> Keep encouraging people and reward them for their efforts. Even if they
> don't meet this challenge, if you praise them for their efforts the next
> time a challenge comes up they may be more open and able to rise to it.

The preceding process takes time. You can't just command someone to 'talk
candidly' with you and then expect great results. And the follow-up steps
require thought, care and concern on your part as well.

In emergencies or during a crisis, when the situation you're facing can harm
people or property, and you've no time to spread risk, provide support and
discuss the probability of success, you have to rise to the challenge quickly,
decisively and without hesitation. Whether you're a leader or a follower in
those situations, breathe deeply from your lower abdomen to keep your mind
clear (See Chapter 14 for proper breathing techniques). Stay focussed on the
outcome and not what may get in your way.

Desiring to make a difference

Influencing people with passion, vision and the willingness to put in the time
and effort to realise their dreams is a lot easier than pushing and pulling
along people who are more like rocks than rockets.

If you're lucky enough to work with people who want to make a difference,
my advice is simple: let them. Encourage them, trust them and support them
as they seek to leave their legacy.

People who want to achieve something rare and remarkable, or even cool
and groovy, are assets to any organisation. Appeal to their sense of greatness, offer them chances to make meaningful contributions – and watch in
wonder as they rise to their own challenges. Reach out to their values (see
Chapter 2), celebrate the gifts they bring and give them the opportunity to
shine. As long as you don't ask them to compromise their own standards and
values, you should have little trouble persuading them to fulfil their desires.
When you praise their efforts, encourage their talents and give them the
support they need to contribute to the organisation – be it a family unit or a
global conglomerate – everyone benefits.

When most healthy people have satisfied their need for food, shelter and a
sense of belonging, they seek opportunities to fulfil further goals and aspirations . Whether they want to find a cure for cancer, organise a fabulous party
or eradicate polio, when someone gives them an opportunity to use their
talents and abilities to make a meaningful and lasting contribution and to
achieve something rare and wonderful, they go for it. See Chapter 2 for more
about satisfying needs and self-esteem.

Support, encouragement and trust are fundamental to influencing people who want to make a difference. For these people, the work and the opportunitiy to make a difference is more rewarding than money, prestige and incentives. See the following section on incentives.

Offering encouragement

Encouraging people is one of the greatest gifts you can give them. You're not filling their minds with fantasy. You're inspiring them to be themselves at their very best. For example:

- ✔ If someone thinks he has a winning idea that may be the next Microsoft, Apple or the solution to world hunger, encourage him to go for his goal. No matter if you think his idea is too farfetched. If he thinks he's onto something, give him the chance to find out.

- ✔ If someone has a project to complete that he's struggling with, giving a few cheers from the sidelines may be all he needs to become re-engaged with the task at hand.

Encouragement motivates people to strive for the difficult and to make continuous improvements in their performance. It enhances self-confidence and can make someone feel courageous when they've been feeling downhearted. Encouragement expands people's visions and fosters a 'can do' attitude.

During the course of writing this book, I often thought I wasn't going to finish it. The task seemed too big, and I feared that what I was writing was complete rubbish. I created scenarios in my head in which my editor said, 'Nice try, Elizabeth, but it's just not working.' Katie, who works for me, seemed to know when I was losing hope. She sent me unsolicited emails with messages of encouragement that made me smile. Simple words such as 'you can do this' and 'you're almost there' pulled me out of negative beliefs while her faith and confidence in my abilities recharged my depleted batteries. I returned to the project with a renewed sense of vigour, interest and excitement that carried me through the tough times.

Strange as it may seem, even the most talented, capable and influential people sometimes need words of encouragement. No matter who you are and no matter how capable and talented you may be, I'm willing to venture that you've experienced times filled with self-doubt – times when you would have benefitted from the odd word of encouragement. The world can be dark and lonely at times. By encouraging people who are struggling, you validate their abilities and remind them of their strengths and talents.

Offering encouragement creates bonds between you and the person you're supporting. They feel capable and compelled to respond positively to your support, knowing that you believe in them. They don't want to let you down.

Furthermore, encouragement breeds encouragement. For example, when you encourage one of your team members to do his best, he's likely to encourage others to do theirs. Positive energy leads to more positive energy.

The next time you see someone who needs encouragement, let them know how special they are. Instead of just flattering the person with nice words, respond to something specific he's doing, such as the way he's following through on leads, developing younger members of the team or adding value through his artistic talents. Highlight something about his character that you admire – or a positive difference you see in his performance. For example, saying something like, 'I really appreciate the time and attention you take with our presentations. Even though you have to stick with the corporate template, you manage to make the slides look interesting and exciting.' You can also say, 'I really appreciate and admire the extra effort you put into your work. Your 'stick-to-itiveness' inspires me to apply myself more, too. Thank you.'

When you're influencing other people's behaviour, don't deliberately make them feel anxious ('the result of the project may mean the life or death of this department!') or ashamed ('I expected more from someone with your level of education'). While both approaches can yield temporary gains, scared team members often get frozen in their fears, and shamed people slink away depressed or revolt. State your remarks positively ('I know we can count on you to see this project through on time and on budget') or ('with your education and experience, you possess knowledge and insight that others don't have'). See the section 'Establishing Goals and Expectations' later in this chapter.

Appreciating the relationship between individuals and groups

Many would-be persuaders mistakenly take a limited view of who they're attempting to influence. They seek to understand the ins and outs of one key person and then wonder why their efforts to persuade fall flat.

If you focus only on the one individual you want to move from Point A to Point B, you're forgetting about all the other people who have persuasive powers over your target. People are influenced by a variety of sources. When you want to persuade someone, think about the other people whose needs and opinions influence that one person's behaviour. From friends and family, to clients and colleagues, other people and their circumstances impact on the direction someone takes.

Some people like to think that they're a rock and an island, and in many ways they may be. That being said, the needs and desires of people whose opinion matters to them are still going to influence them.

Pay attention to the people who surround the person you want to influence. These trusted and informed people exist in all groups both at home and at work and influence your target's behaviour. The person you're aiming to persuade seeks their opinions, needs their advice and includes them in meetings. Not only are they channels of information, they also can put pressure on your target when a choice has to be made and they can reinforce the decision once everyone has agreed to it.

ANECDOTE

Influencing her sphere of influence

Sabrina is a graduate student studying for her PhD in engineering at a prestigious university. She recently met Alex, who has started up his own technology company, which he's convinced is going to be the next big thing. Alex quickly realised that Sabrina is a high achiever and hungry to succeed – just the kind of person he's been looking for to join his organisation.

He was keen to get Sabrina to leave her PhD programme and come on board now, but Sabrina's conservative and ambitious family and boyfriend weren't convinced this move was right for her. Her grandparents were concerned about the sustainability of the business, her parents thought about the money they'd paid for her education going down the drain without an impressive degree behind it, and her boyfriend was worried that the business would take too much time away from him.

In order to convince Sabrina, Alex knew he first had to persuade the others whose opinions matter to her. He met with her family, sharing with them details of the business, including how much money venture capitalists had invested and his impressive board of directors. In addition, he pointed out the relevancy of applying her education in a real-life experience. He highlighted the fact that large companies are looking for innovation, and that start-ups are the places to try out new ideas. He continued to appeal to their need for status by suggesting that Sabrina would be so successful at his company that she'd be able to teach at higher-level institutions – or would soon be making so much money that she'd be able to endow a chair at her current university. As for Sabrina's boyfriend, Alex reassured him that he was well aware of the time and effort that goes into start-ups and that he puts offering an equitable balance between work and home life high on his agenda.

By addressing the needs and desires of the people whose opinions matter to Sabrina, Alex was able to persuade them that his suggestion was not completely off the wall.

Knowing Who You're Talking To

One size does *not* fit all when it comes to motivating, persuading and influencing people. What gets me up and going in the morning isn't what persuades my beloved husband to flick back the duvet, bound out of bed and embrace the day. Or, as Paul Simon sang, 'One man's ceiling is another man's floor'.

Some people are rational and orderly in their approach to life. To persuade these people, provide fine details in a structured style. Others prefer to think in terms of big pictures and get charged up when you present your case in terms of future possibilities. To persuade people who seek harmony in their relationships, present points of agreement and accord. The list of different types of people, all of whom have their unique view points and needs, would fill a book on its own. I have chosen to write about these three because they're common types. Of course, you can argue that your family is filled with feisty, argumentative types or that you've yet to find a seeker of harmony at work. The point to remember from this chapter is that the more you understand what drives the people you live, work and engage with, the better able you are to address their needs and desires. The more you can accept and respond positively to what is important to them, the more success you can have in creating constructive, persuasive relationships. (Turn to Chapter 9 to gain further insight into people with different decision-making styles.)

What a piece of work is man

The study of psychology – which literally translates into 'study of the soul' - dates back to the ancient civilisations of Egypt, Greece, China, India and Persia and has continued ever since. One well-known instrument used for exploring and defining personalities is the Enneagram, which identifies psychological motivations and emotions for nine different and distinct personality types. Understanding what motivates people and how their emotions come into play when they interact with others puts you in the driver's seat when you want to influence their behaviours. If you're interested in finding out more about Enneagram types, you can take an online test, work with a practitioner or read any of the numerous books that are published on the subject.

In addition to the Enneagram, you can find the Myers-Briggs Type Indicator (MBTI), a similar tool for understanding personality preferences, which defines 16 different personality types. (You can read more about the MBTI in Chapter 9) Neither of these instruments, or others like them, puts people into boxes and your type doesn't constitute your entire personality. Rather, your type is simply part of your identity – like your sexuality or national origin – leaving plenty of room for individual variation. Personality tools help you understand your own behaviours and thinking processes, as well as those of others and are valuable for figuring out how to motivate staff as well as interacting with family members. If you're interested in understanding human nature, go to Google and type in 'personality types', where 3,580,000 listings pop up. That should be enough to get you started!

Reading other people correctly and pushing the right buttons to influence their behaviour requires insight and finesse. Take the time to listen to what they say, watch how they work and reflect on what it all may mean. See Chapter 7 for more on effective listening.

Make listening to others and observing their behaviour part of your daily routine. It doesn't matter where you are – at home, at the grocery store, on public transportation or in a shareholders meeting – practice your observation skills every time you get the chance. The more you notice about people, the more in tune you become with them and can adapt your persuasive powers to meet their needs and desires. Reflect back words and phrases people use and match their behaviours to gain rapport. As you establish rapport with other people, you're better positioned to influence their thinking and behaviour. For further information about establishing rapport turn to Chapter 13. You can also refer to *Neuro-lingustic Programming For Dummies* by Romilla Ready and Kate Burton (Wiley), which covers rapport in detail.

Listen to the language people use. If people pepper their speech with negative words, they likely want to control others and make them feel inferior. A partial list of negative words to listen out for may include:

Idiot	Loser	Inferior	Wrong
Dumb	Stupid	Never	Bad
Horrible	Queer	Hideous	Feckless
Inane	Insipid	Gormless	Misgivings

On the other hand, people who fill their sentences with positive words tend to have an optimistic outlook and want to make people feel good. Examples of positive words include:

Abundance	Appealing	Clear	Confident
Dynamic	Dependable	Outstanding	Passionate
Sensational	Wonderful	Valued	Smart
Worthy	Bright	Terrific	Splendid

 If someone refers to another person as 'stupid' and you don't agree, don't say, 'No, that person's smart!' Instead, reflect back the other person's language and describe the behaviour you observe. You can say something like, 'I don't understand what you mean by *stupid*. Are you saying that he takes his time to get to the point?' By repeating the other person's language and asking for clarification, you're acknowledging his point of view without agreeing with it. At the same time, you're making him consider his word choice and attitude.

In addition to paying attention to what people say – their actual words – observe the way they speak and move. You can tell how someone's feeling by the tone in their voice plus their posture, gestures and facial expressions. For example, some people speak quickly, with excitement and energy in their voices. You can tell from the high pitch and quick speed that they're keyed up. Depending on the circumstances, this pitch and speed may mean that they're agitated or happily animated. Other people lack variety or expression in their voices and tend to speak in a monotone. This kind of speech indicates that they're emotionally uncommitted to what they're saying. Some people speak in long sentences, wanting to hold the listener's attention for as long as they can, while others rely on basic nouns and verbs to convey their message simply and quickly. For more information about how your body and voice impact on your ability to persuade and influence, turn to Chapters 13 and 14.

By noticing the way people speak, gesture and move, you can identify their energy levels, feelings and reactions to what's going on around them. By honing your radar, you can pick up information about their needs and desires as well as what drives them to do the things they do. When you put all these insights together, you can apply what you've found out when the time comes to influence their attitudes and actions.

Nick speaks in clear, concise sentences. His language is simple and direct. He speaks with certainty and conviction, never leaving you in doubt about what he means. For example, I never hear Nick talk about 'trying' to do something. Instead, he uses expressions like, 'Our aim is to . . .' or 'The goal is . . .'. In addition, Nick's gestures are equally clear in conveying his meaning. Contained and confident, you can understand the feelings behind the facts in Nick's message even if you can't hear his words because his gestures reflect what he's saying. For example, when Nick describes a long-term plan, he tends to widen his arms, and when he talks about short-term goals, he brings his thumb and index finger close together. When Nick communicates, he gestures purposefully and comes across as confident and committed. As a result, his listeners believe that he is. People who have the most success working with Nick communicate in a similar way, matching his style and demonstrating that they're confident and committed, too. (For more about conveying messages through gestures and expressions, turn to Chapter 13 or pick up a copy of *Body Language For Dummies* by Elizabeth Kuhnke [Wiley].)

If you speak quickly and are conversing with someone whose speech pattern is more sluggish, take your foot off the accelerator and slow down to match the other person's speech pattern. Doing so indicates that you're operating at the same speed and makes the other person feel comfortable with you. After speaking at the same speed for a couple of minutes – pacing him until he's at ease – you can increase your rate to one that suits you better. (The same exercise works in reverse.) As long as you build up a respectful relationship with the other person, you can match and pace him until you sense that he's ready to let you lead the conversation. For more about matching, pacing and leading, turn to Chapter 13.

The way people speak and move signals how they think and feel.

Avoid staring at other people to avoid coming across as a stalker or a creep. You can successfully observe by watching and listening to someone for 1–2 minutes with a look of pleasant interest – a slight smile, bright eyes and a tilted head – and then look away. You can take in a lot of information in a few minutes when you're paying attention. (See Chapter 3 for more about eye contact).

People are complicated. Although similarities exist among family members, people within the same team, department, club, organisation or any other group where people gather together to achieve a common goal, you also find important differences and distinctions. The more insight you have into the subtleties of what motivates individual members of a group, the more success you have persuading them. See the earlier section 'Appreciating the relationship between individuals and groups' section for more.

In addition to considering others' beliefs and behaviours, take a closer look at your own. Get to know your style and then identify how it may or may not match the people you want to influence. The more you know about yourself, the better able you are to adapt your approach to get others to respond to your proposals and propositions. For more about understanding yourself and others, see Chapter 2.

During times of strain and stress, applying your persuasive powers is particularly important – as well as highly challenging. As you may have experienced, both at home and at work, people in stressful situations are often the ones most in need of your persuasion and influence. Smoothly functioning, perfectly stable teams and individuals don't typically require extensive effort to develop motivation, enthusiasm and commitment. When you've the opportunity to persuade others during stressful times, grab the chance to make a positive difference. Encourage people to talk about what's happening, listen to what they say and reflect back what you hear. When people feel listened to and have their feelings acknowledged, they're likely to be open to your proposals.

For example, if your partner complains that you don't give him enough of your time and attention, acknowledge his feelings and ask him how he'd like things to be. Allow him all the time he needs to talk through his feelings without interrupting him and refrain from judging or arguing with what he says(see Chapter 7 for tips on how to listen effectively). Once he's finished speaking, you can respond by saying, 'I understand what you're saying about my not giving you enough of my time and attention and appreciate how you feel about that. How would you like things to be and what suggestions do you have for making things better? I'd like to make this work for both of us.' By giving him a chance to express his emotions, demonstrating that you respect his feelings and engaging him in the process of improving the situation, you've opened the door to influencing the outcome and making things better. The following sections cover three common categories of people you're likely to encounter and seek to influence. While many other types abound, I have chosen to concentrate on these three here as I kept coming across them during my research for this book, particularly in the *Harvard Business Review on The Persuasive Leader* (Harvard Business School Press).

If you're serious about wanting to improve your ability to persuade and influence others, make it part of your daily routine to observe the different types of people you come across in your day-to-day life and reflect on how they respond to events and occurrences. The more you notice, the better prepared you become to adapt your style to meet theirs when the time comes to persuade them.

The types identified below are fairly easy to spot from their behaviours. Others are trickier as they can be a complicated blend of different styles. If you come across people you can't immediately pin-point, refer to Chapter 2, where you can find tips for figuring out what drives different types of people.

Swaying the rational and orderly

Some people like a place for everything and everything in its place. They tend to make their decisions based on choices that lead to the best outcome for themselves, as opposed to what may be best for others. Guided by their intellect rather than their experiences or emotions, their behaviour is driven by a need for structure and orderliness and they reason in a clear and consistent manner. They often respond well to facing reality and moving forward to achieve clearly defined goals. In organisations, you frequently find accountants fit into this group, as do lawyers.

Persuading rational and orderly individuals requires a consistent, unswerving message. Rational and orderly people respond particularly well when you:

- Approach your interactions with openness, honesty and candour – particularly if tough challenges lie ahead. See Chapter 5 for more about acting with openness and honesty.

- Set high aspirations for them to strive for. See the 'Establishing Goals and Expectations' section later in this chapter for much more on goal-setting. One of the highest aspirations people can face is honestly confronting and dealing with inescapable critical facts that they, and others, have made about their performance.

✔ Establish a step-by-step approach that takes them from where they are now to where you want them to be. Set guidelines and milestones that they can refer to as they head toward their goal.

✔ Encourage them along the way. See the 'Providing incentives for successful results' section later in this chapter.

Bluntly presenting your interpretation of a tough situation to your listeners or beating them over the head for something you see isn't working is not the most persuasive line of attack, especially when you're facing less-than-happy news. The best thing to do when the state of affairs is grim is to hold up a mirror for your listeners. Help them to see the situation with their own eyes and empower them to respond. See the sidebar 'Seeing themselves clearly' for an example of this process in action.

Seeing themselves clearly

Dillon was hired to take over the leadership of a long-established hotel and ski resort, reinvent the organisation, make it competitive in today's heavily saturated leisure industry and avoid bankruptcy.

Rather than finding fault with previous management, he confronted the situation head on. He first honoured the company's illustrious history and then invited current management to participate in its revival. Gathering together the organisation's leaders, he implemented a rigorous appraisal of their customers, their competition and their performance. At the first management meeting, he wrote on a flip chart comments the managers themselves had made about the company at previous meetings, including the observations that the resort was slow to adapt to current trends and was unsure of what steps to take. He also handed out a summary of customer feedback, which included the good, the bad and the ugly.

When the managers were confronted with what they had said about the organisation themselves, as well as their customers' comments, they had no place to hide. They had to face the truth that was right in front of them.

Working from a new-found point of honesty and openness, Dillon then set ambitious and doable goals based on customer and the group's self appraisal. He knew that bridging the awkward gap between where they were and where they wanted to be required steps that were gradual and achievable. Every aspect of the organisation's procedures was addressed, including reservations, equipment hire, food service, check-out systems and feedback methods.

As his team got into their stride and achieved measurable successes, Dillon made sure to praise their efforts along the way, including presenting them with symbolic rewards, reminding them of how far they had come and how much closer they were to achieving their goals. For more about the value of symbolic awards, turn to Chapter 6.

By taking an honest look at a dire situation, setting clear and achievable targets and taking the necessary steps to reach their goals, Dillon and his team were able to save the resort.

No matter what the make-up of your audience is, all groups benefit from clear communication. When organisations are in transition, as many businesses and other groups frequently are, stakeholders need to know where they're going and how they're going to get there. Quarterly updates, status reports and occasional emails aren't enough to keep the fires burning. You must regularly repeat messages that remind employees of the company's direction, encourage them to keep going and reassure them during uncertain times. With email, Twitter, Facebook, mobile devices and other tools at your disposal, you don't have any excuse for not communicating.

You don't need to go into the gritty detail. TMI – too much information – can overwhelm and confuse employees and other interested parties. Just stick with the basic message – your explanation of what's happening, your expectations and your vision of what their future holds – and your ability to persuade people to follow your course escalates.

While constant and consistent communication may make you sound like a broken record, keep talking. Reassuring all your stakeholders – from investors to customers to staff to the media – benefits the business. When employees get clear messages from the corner office, they feel part of the team. Even more importantly, they feel respected (see Chapter 3). That alone is enough to persuade people to do what you ask of them. If an organisation or an individual think that they're rational and orderly because they have established processes and procedures but they are, in reality, totally chaotic and dysfunctional, point out the facts. Have them look at what they've said about themselves in the past and include feedback from others so that they can reflect on their behaviour and see how they're actually functioning. Then redefine rational, orderly processes to help them achieve their goals. For more on how to achieve this process, refer to the sidebar 'Seeing themselves clearly.'

Persuading big picture visionaries

Look to see who's coming up with innovative ideas and the chances are you're looking at a big picture visionary. These people typically have a clear view of what they want to do and how they want to do it and serve organisations best during times of major transitions. In plays, novels and films, they're the protagonist, the person to whom others look for leadership and advice. At work, they're the ones who look around their organisations and see possibilities where others seen chaos and problems. Examples of big picture visionaries include Steve Jobs, the Google inventors Larry Page and Sergey Brin, Henry Ford, and, some may even say, Julian Assange, founder of Wikileaks.

Big picture visionaries are, the leaders of the pack in that they provide long-term direction and vision. They're clear about what they want to do and adept at getting individuals to buy into their vision. They win people over because they take the time to understand what drives and motivates them. Rather than telling you what to do, visionaries appeal to your values (see Chapter 3) and then work to win you over by tying their vision to yours (see Chapter 4). While they work best working in partnership and create a shared sense of vision and meaning with others, they're not always the most popular nor accepted members of an organisation because they tend not to be mainstream.

Big picture visionaries are the darlings of moviemakers because of their ability to win people over rather than telling them what to do. In *Remember the Titans*, Herman Boone (played by Denzel Washington) is a high school football coach. In one of the film's most moving scenes, he explains why, in the American South during the early 1970s, uniting the black and white players on the football team is about much more than just sport, but rather treating people with respect and acting like men. If you want to listen to the speech go to www.americanrhetoric.com/MovieSpeeches/moviespeech rememberthetitans.html

When you work for visionary leaders, you may irritate them if you offer your vision, especially if it conflicts with theirs. Big picture visionaries see their job as figuring out and conveying the possibilities. They can feel threatened if you try to do the same thing.

Instead, persuade these big picture people to do something you need by reflecting back their picture to them. Let them know that you understand what they're striving for and what you need to achieve it. Pick up on their ideas and build on them. Visionaries make decisions quickly, even impulsively, focusing on ideas rather than details. Match their style and speak in broad, general terms about what can be rather than what is.

Big picture visionaries have little patience with minutiae and complex detail. They're interested in future possibilities and don't like being hampered by barriers or limits. More than wanting to know facts, which can bore them or make them impatient, they're interested in implications and relationships. They're stimulated by possibilities, seeking to create and share new ideas. If you tend to focus more on the here and now, adjust your view. Observe how these big picture people communicate, the way they think and the language they use. The more you can adapt your style to theirs, the more success you have in persuading them to see your point of view. In Chapter 9 I look at matching styles and how you can adapt your style to suit another person's.

When you're persuading big picture visionaries, assure them that you're going to convey their vision to your team or other relevant individuals in inspirational terms rather than presenting their ideas in matter-of-fact, everyday language. Use metaphors, analogies and other forms of symbolic language. If you want your team to increase their efforts, rather than admonishing them to do a better job, say something along the lines of , 'Now is your chance to embrace those opportunities that you've longed for . . . .'

Big picture visionaries respond particularly well when you

- ✔ Provide a thumbnail sketch at the beginning of your remarks, focussing on long-term, future possibilities
- ✔ Offer a reality check without discarding their ideas, helping them to link their visions to what's real and actual
- ✔ Suspend reality when necessary to brainstorm and generate ideas
- ✔ Avoid getting bogged down in facts and details

For more about persuading people who see the big picture, turn to Chapter 9.

Influencing seekers of harmony

People who seek harmony want to feel connected to what they're doing. They're able to empathise and develop rapport easily with others, often seeing and appreciating others' perspectives. Supportive, nurturing and interested in other people, they enjoy cooperating and collaborating, connecting with others and creating a harmonious environment. In addition, harmony seekers need to feel an interdependence with others, in which they're mutually responsible to and share a common set of principles with others. They also seek personal influence and a sense of belonging to something larger than themselves. If you want to get the best from people who seek harmony, show them where they fit into the grand scheme of things. Show them their place and purpose and how their contribution impacts on the bigger picture.

People who seek harmony become alienated when they're unsure of what's expected of them, whether in family situations, within a working group, committee or larger organisation. Rather than performing with a sense of 'you and me together', a feeling of 'them against me' may arise, leading to negative behaviour that adversely affects the other people they're engaged with as well as the overall goals of the project they're working on.

Cathy has the reputation of being a good team player. A reliable employee, she both seeks and creates harmonious relationships at work, shuns conflict and brings value to projects. When Cathy was recently moved to a large, well-established team, her new manager gave her little direction. Everyone on the team seemed to know what was required of them, and Cathy was expected to fit in and find her own way. Because being clear about her role and knowing how she contributes to the big picture is important to Cathy, she started feeling restless and confused. When she asked her manager what his expectations of her were, he told her he expected her to fit in with the group and get on with her job. Try as she did, Cathy couldn't seem to connect with her job or the team. She began feeling apathetic, a condition she'd never experienced at work before, and dreaded going into the office. Eventually, with her tension having risen to a point of despair, Cathy requested a leave of absence. Away from the office, she was able to assess how working in an ambiguous situation was affecting her, her team and the project. She requested a transfer to a different department. As a result of her manager's poor influencing skills, Cathy's sense of purpose suffered, the team felt let down and the project was indefinitely delayed. Not long after the debacle, the manager lost his job.

People who seek harmony long to maintain balance and avoid disruption. They look for the best in people, are fundamentally optimistic about the future, and tend to have a calming and stabilising effect on their co-workers. They're supportive, go with the flow, don't worry about the small stuff and, as a rule, are pretty easy to work with, if you like that type of person.

People who seek harmonious relationships tend to be reserved and focus on people and feelings. They support others and seek honest, open and friendly relationships. They're tolerant and prefer a collaborative approach to establishing and maintaining harmony within a group. They can feel that others take advantage or ask too much of them. People whose styles are different from theirs may see them as people-pleasers who are constantly compromising for the sake of harmony.

When you're influencing people who seek harmony:

- ✔ **Encourage open communication.** Support harmony-seeking people in expressing their views and ideas. Ask for feedback and provide meaningful, clearly defined and realistic goals.

- ✔ **Foster a good work/life balance.** While you can rightly expect someone to give their all on the job, you get the best out of people when you recognise that they have lives outside the workplace. If you want something from them, make sure that you give them something back in return that meets their needs and relates to their values. The more you respect people's issues away from work, the happier and more productive they are at work.

✔ **Provide platforms for personal development.** Whether you offer in-house training, time out for study leave or tuition for external courses, providing such opportunities shows people that you care about them, which leads to their giving you their best.

✔ **Praise generously.** Seekers of harmony respond well to positive feedback. And when they do slip up, point it out and move on. Conscientious people typically take on board feedback from their mistakes quickly.

✔ **Pay attention to tone.** While harmony seekers can deal with tough news and criticism, you need to use a soft, gentle voice when presenting it. Your message may even feel out of synch with your soft, warm voice when you're talking with harmony-seekers. That okay. They're typically conscientious and listening to everything you're saying.

Cultivating an Unbiased View

The most persuasive people I know are able to stand outside of situations and look at them clearly and in an unbiased manner. The best persuaders embrace differences among people and look to find approaches that suit everyone. Turn to Chapter 5 to find out more about compromising and the process of giving-and-taking.

Whatever you do and whoever you are, when you want to persuade or influence another person, leave your biases at the gate. If you want to get someone to agree with your proposal, proposition, or simply your point of view, telling them they're wrong to feel, think or behave the way they do is sure to scupper your plans when you go to persuade them to do something you want them to do.

A bias is a partial perspective – a preferred view – that eliminates other equally valid alternatives. It tends to be a pejorative term and is frequently interchanged with prejudice. A bias is a prejudgment or an assumption lacking substantiating evidence. A person with biased opinions usually holds them against people based on personal characteristics including race, social class, gender, sexual orientation or religion. In addition to other forms of bias, including that found in judgment and decision-making, you often can find media bias, where standards of journalism are disregarded.

If you force your views and values on people you want to influence, you're likely to find yourself at the wrong end of the stick. In all my research for this book, I was unable to find any long-lasting successful examples of people persuading others to follow their lead by coming in with a heavy-handed approach. Oh, sure, you may be able to bludgeon others with your viewpoint and get them grudgingly to do your bidding. But they end up resenting you and don't want to have anything to do with you again.

The following sections help you cultivate a neutral, unbiased attitude, which improves your ability to achieve good results in challenging situations.

Letting go of judgment

Being able to render sound judgement at appropriate moments is essential to being an effective persuader. However, when your judgments are condemnatory, self-righteous or constantly critical of another person's worth, your point of view and ability to see a situation from all sides becomes skewed. People tend to disregard others who speak in judgmental terms because their comments have a ring of negativity about them.

Let go of thoughts and feelings like, 'he's so dumb . . .' and 'that's so stupid . . .' and 'his idea will never work'. Replace them with positive outlooks. Earlier in this chapter, I provide lists of negative and positive words to help you understand the impact of language on your thoughts and behaviours. If you want to understand more about how substituting unhelpful thoughts and feelings with more positive ones, have a look at *Cognitive Behavioural Therapy For Dummies*, by Rhena Branch and Rob Willson (Wiley) as well as *Emotional Healing For Dummies* by David Beales and Helen Whitten (Wiley) both of which cover the topic in detail and provide step-by-step activities.

I'm not suggesting that you become a Pollyanna figure – although positive, optimistic people do bring oomph and energy to their projects and are generally more fun to be around. Simply being neutral – or at least not negative – can be useful when you're interacting with others. By demonstrating no bias for or against a proposition, you allow others to draw their own conclusions without being influenced by yours. See Chapter 7 for tips on remaining neutral when you're listening.

Uncovering shared interests

Persuasive people are passionate people. They pursue and project their passions with enthusiasm, making themselves interesting and inviting to be around. When you're around people like that, you want to follow their suggestions; especially when you find that you share similar interests or feel passionate about the same things. For more about how similarities can help you influence others, see Chapter 11.

Seeking to understand people leads to more positive results than what you get when you judge others. The more you find out about the people you want to persuade, the more chance you have of finding similarities between you.

Discover similar interests by doing any and all of the following:

- **Believe that everyone has passions.** Everyone feels passionate about something. Your job is to find out what the other person's passions are. Sports, food, family and fashion are often fruitful places to start. If you're up to the challenge, find out how they feel about politics or religion.

  If you struggle to find any passion points, keep digging. Eventually, something will surface. But if it doesn't, you may have to give up on that person as a lost cause.

- **Take the attitude that you've something in common.** If you think that you've something in common, you've a much better chance of finding it! Having a positive outlook gets you where you want to be faster than assuming that you share nothing in common.

- **Be diligent in your research.** As long as you've got a computer, or at least access to one, you've little excuse for not being able to find out about the people you want to persuade. Between Google, Facebook, LinkedIn and Twitter, tons of useful information is out there. And if you can't find out more about someone online, ask around.

- **Take note of what you observe.** You can find clues about people's passions by looking around their homes, desks and offices. I'm not suggesting that you snoop, just that you observe. For example, if you notice a picture of a family skiing holiday and you're a skier, you ask where the photo was taken and share a skiing story of your own. You can also find out about people's passions by listening to what they say. (Turn to Chapter 7 for more about active listening skills. Chapter 2 is filled with tips for finding common points of interest.)

Establishing Goals and Expectations

Establishing clear goals and expectations is a powerful tool for persuading people. Compelling goals and expectations build on people's drives, needs and desires – while encouraging worthwhile contributions to the entire organisation or a greater cause.

Imagine working without specific goals in place for a moment. Your daily life would be meaningless, chaotic and, quite frankly, a waste of time. Working in an environment where you've no purpose to your efforts would be enough to make you call in sick on a regular basis.

The following sections offer a quick course on how to set goals that inspire without being too easy and that motivate without being overwhelming.

Thinking SMART

For people in today's working world, SMART is a five-letter word that comes up again and again when talking about goal-setting.

SMART is a handy acronym that highlights five key characteristics of any well-constructed goal. Every SMART goal is Specific, Measurable, Attainable, Relevant and Time-bound.

- ✔ **Specific:** Without a specific goal, you don't know what you're aiming to accomplish. When you're determining your goal, include what you specifically want to accomplish, who you may need to call on for help, by when you want to achieve your goal, your reasons, purpose or benefits for accomplishing your goal and potential requirements and constraints.

- ✔ **Measurable:** Put in place concrete criteria for measuring your progress. When you measure your progress, you're more likely to stay on track, reach your targets and feel a sense of achievement that spurs you on to reach your ultimate goal. To confirm that your goal is measurable, ask questions such as How much? How many? And How do I know when I've met my criteria?

- ✔ **Attainable:** Once you've identified goals that are most important to you, you figure out ways to make them happen. You develop the attitudes, skills and resources to reach them. When you plan your steps wisely and establish a time frame that allows you to carry out your steps, you can achieve your goal.

- ✔ **Realistic:** A realistic goal is one that you're both willing and able to strive for. Only you can determine how high a goal you want to set for yourself. Be sure that whatever goal you establish has enough motivational force to keep you going. If you truly believe you can accomplish your goal, that goal is probably realistic. Measure it against anything similar that you've accomplished in the past. You can also ask yourself what conditions would have to exist in order for you to accomplish this goal.

- ✔ **Timely:** Ground your goal in a time frame. Without a deadline, you've no sense of urgency and you may let your goal drift on and on. With a definite date, you've set your unconscious mind in motion to begin working toward your desired outcome. (T can also stand for **tangible**. When you can experience your goal with one or more of your senses – touch, taste, sight or smell), you've a better chance of making it specific, measurable and therefore attainable.)

Dr Edwin Locke pioneered research on motivation and goal-setting in the late 1960s. His findings proved that employees are motivated by clear goals and appropriate feedback. By putting goals in place, people are motivated to reach them, which, in turn, improves their performance. Several years later, Dr Gary Latham studied the effect of setting goals in the workplace. His findings corresponded exactly with Locke's. In their seminal study, *A Theory of Goal Setting and Task Performance* (1990), they emphasise the need for explicit and challenging goals. While this information is hardly revolutionary today, it does confirm how goal-setting and performance are intrinsically intertwined.

Making your goals clear

The secret to making your goals clear lies in the first two letters of SMART. You must make your goals specific and measurable, or quantifiable.

When you appeal to people's needs and desires and let them know exactly what's expected of them, they're more likely to hop on board than when instructions are vague and ambiguous. When you include a clear-cut time frame for tasks to be completed, you enhance your ability to persuade others to follow your agenda.

Don't waste your time telling someone to 'try hard' or 'do your best'. Give them a specific target to shoot for, such as 'aim to reduce your turnaround time by 40 per cent' or 'cut your costs by a third this next quarter'.

In addition to making your goals specific, make them challenging to achieve. Studies show that, when you present teams and individuals with specific and difficult goals, their performances are measurably better than when the goals are vague and easy.

If you set targets that are easily achieved, they're not exciting. And if people aren't excited about what they're doing, they don't tend to bother doing it. On the other hand, by setting high goals, people feel a great sense of accomplishment after they get there.

Ensuring that your goals are attainable

As I point out in the preceding section, stretching yourself to meet challenging aspirations is important in creating a sense of pride and fulfilment. However, you also need to make sure that the targets you set aren't *too* challenging. Persuading someone to give their all when the person has no chance of crossing the finish line is pointless.

Set targets that strike a balance between challenging and realistic and watch people leap at the chance to attain them. If you set a goal that stands no chance of being met, your team becomes more demotivated than if you set a goal that was too easy to achieve. People have a strong need for achievement and success. Setting challenging and realistic goals is one way of persuading them to go for gold.

Tight deadlines spur people into action, while impossible ones make them throw their tools down in defeat before they even begin. Goals need to be challenging enough to make you strive for them but not so challenging that they're impossible to achieve. Challenging goals also have to be under your control, not dependent on what other people do or random events (such as becoming an astronaut at the age of 60 or winning the lottery). Examples of appropriately challenging goals include:

- ✔ Losing 10 pounds in 5 weeks and keeping them off for minimum of a year. At an average rate of 2 pounds per week, this goal is appropriately challenging. Losing 10 pounds in a week and keeping them off for at least a year is unrealistic.

- ✔ Becoming conversant in a foreign language in six months. If you attend classes regularly and practice daily, you should be able to converse within this time frame. Only giving yourself a week to go from non-speaker to conversant would be an unrealistic challenge.

People often use the words *goals* and *objectives* interchangeably. Without meaning to sound pedantic, goals and objectives are different and designed to complement, not replace, one another. Goals are high level and more general than objectives, which are lower level and specific. An example of a goal is to state how a project reflects a company's mission, while the objectives stipulate in specific terms how the project does that by using clearly defined steps laid out in the SMART approach.

Providing incentives for successful results

You can persuade people to go to great lengths when you place a meaningful reward for them at the finish line. Whether you're presented with a trophy, given a letter of commendation or a public pat on the back with a heartfelt 'Thank you for your contribution', research and real-life scenarios show that recognition and achievement are influencing factors in getting people to produce their best.

For the most part, the more difficult the goal, the greater the reward. You can persuade people to reach for the stars by assuring them that you intend to repay their efforts when they come up with the goods.

Research consistently shows that money is not a prime motivator for most people. Oh, sure, we hear tales of people who don't get out of bed without huge pay packets awaiting them, but for the most part people are influenced to go for goals that offer the chance for achievement and recognition, as well as passion for the work itself. That being said, except for monkeys, no one wants to work for peanuts. Challenging goals require appropriate rewards.

Douglas worked at the Houses of Parliament as an intern, earning £10 per day to cover his lunch and tube fare. During his 12 months there, Douglas gained a reputation as a young man who relished taking on challenging projects and seeing them through to the end. While he had to live at home in the country, commute every day to the city – leaving early and coming home late – and take jobs bartending and working as a waiter during the weekends to earn money, both he and his parents knew that his passion for government and his chance to be recognised for his work were worth the long hours and lack of pay. At the end of his internship, Douglas was rewarded with three outstanding letters of reference, and was one of five interns invited to a private dinner with the Prime Minister and his Cabinet. Douglas was offered a job to work in a paid position in the British Embassy in Washington DC, which he accepted with a sense of achievement and pride.

Gaining commitment

When setting goals, make sure that individuals understand and agree to them. If they don't, everyone ends up frustrated and disappointed.

Avoid frustration and disappointment by getting people to help create their own goals. Involve individuals in setting goals, making decisions and being responsible for the outcome and watch their efforts increase.

The A and R in the SMART acronym stand for *attainable* and *relevant*, but they can also stand for *agreed* and *realistic*. Get someone to agree to a goal they consider realistic and watch them work to their word.

The more difficult goals are to achieve, the more commitment they require. Easy goals are no-brainers and entail little effort. Tough goals demand that you dig deep to find inspiration and enticement.

While it would be unreasonable, pointless and a complete waste of resources to negotiate and gain approval for every goal a company or large organisation sets out, the goals you do persuade individuals to strive for need to be consistent and in harmony with previous expectations.

Strive to show that the goals you're proposing are in the interests of the organisation and are consistent with stated aims. Also, let people know what's happening throughout the organisation so that they can see that the proposed goals are consistent with the organisation's overall strategy. Goals work best when they're written down and signed by all relevant parties. Posting goals in a public spot – like the bulletin board in the break area or the home page on the company intranet site – reminds everyone of what they've agreed to do. At a personal level, write down your goals, sign and date them. Research shows that when you commit to goals in writing, you're more likely to achieve them because the act of writing them down provokes and reminds you to take action.

Providing feedback

You may find it a lot easier to influence a person's behaviour when you provide feedback to let them know how they're doing along the way towards meeting the agreed goals and expectations. Checking-in on an informal and regular basis encourages people to keep going when times are tough and lets them know that you recognise and appreciate their efforts.

In addition to informal feedback, be sure to build informal sessions where you sit down face to face and discuss goal performance. Without providing specific and structured responses to people's efforts, they don't know where they stand. Expectations can be ignored, goals can be missed, and disappointment and resentment inevitably arise. If you want to influence others' long-term performances and persuade them to take the necessary actions to meet their goals, take the time to provide them with feedback to keep them going, especially when times get tough.

When you provide feedback, make sure to focus on the person's performance and not their personality. Making personal remarks about another person is sure to do more harm than good. For example, if you say

> 'You really messed up on that presentation. You were unorganised, lacking in confidence and didn't know what you were talking about'

you probably won't help matters; whereas if you say

> 'You tried to cover a lot of material in a short amount of time. When you lost your place on your second point, you turned away from the audience and looked at your notes and the screen for the rest of your presentation. At the end, when you said, 'Thank you' you were looking at your notes. This behaviour disengaged you from your listeners. If you ever lose your place again, what can you do differently?'

you're much more likely to produce positive results.

Part IV
Putting Persuasion and Influencing Skills into Practice

The 5th Wave   By Rich Tennant

"Nothing like a little story, some metaphor, and a miraculous phenomenon to make a point."

In this part . . .

Time to get physical. In these chapters, I let you in on the power of your body and voice as instruments of persuasion. Here you can discover how to make your movements and gestures speak as persuasively as your voice, and how, when you do speak, you can modulate your voice to maximum influential effect.

Chapter 13

Getting Physical: Putting Body Language to Work

. . . .

In This Chapter

▶ Reading gestures and postures

▶ Responding to signs and signals

▶ Getting in synch, non-verbally

▶ Reinforcing your message

. . . .

*I*f you want to persuade other people, begin by paying attention to them. In addition to hearing what the other person says (see Chapter 7) and tapping in to what she really means, notice her posture, gestures and expressions. Do her feet bounce, fingers drum and toes tap while you're talking with her? Is she leaning back in her chair and staring over your shoulder with a far-away look in her eye as you discuss plans for next week's event?

The three main purposes of body language are to:

- ✔ replace speech
- ✔ reinforce speech
- ✔ display – or betray – a person's mood

Another purpose of body language is to establish *rapport*. People who are in rapport with one another have what the Italians refer to as *simpatico,* which translates roughly into having a shared mental connection or bond. When you establish bonds, the path to persuasion is much smoother. You can demonstrate that bond in several ways, including the way you use your body. (See Chapter 2 where I look at how to mirror and match someone's movements to establish trust, and where you can find out how to use your body to show that you care about someone or what's important to them.)

Gestures, postures and expressions indicate feelings, moods and attitudes. You can identify a person's mood and attitude by the way she bites her lip, swings her legs and holds her hands. Sensing and reflecting back another person's feelings indicates that the two of you are simpatico. And persuading someone whom you're simpatico with is much easier than persuading someone you're opposed to.

In this chapter I show you how to mirror and match another person's movements in order to establish rapport and demonstrate compatibility. You explore the benefits of moving at other peoples' pace before shifting gear into your own and taking them where you want them to go. Finally, you discover how to send powerfully persuasive signals with a raised brow, the flick of your finger or a wave of your hand.

Using Your Body as a Persuasive Instrument

Your body is a tool of influence. Whether you choose to sit straight-backed and tight-lipped or lean forward with a warm smile, your movements, gestures and expressions can win or lose you persuasion points.

Over the past 60-plus years, anthropologists and social psychologists have been reporting on the impact of non-verbal behaviour on communication. Not only does *non-verbal behaviour* include physical gestures, movements and expressions, which are the focus of this chapter, the term also describes vocal characteristics such as pitch, pace and pause. Chapter 14 covers your persuasive voice in detail.

For better or for worse, people project the way they think and feel by the way they arrange and move their body parts. Whether you're chewing on your lip with your hand on your hip, or rubbing your hands together, you're indicating your state of being. A sharp intake of breath, a closed mouth, a blank gaze or a warm smile all show your feelings too.

My book *Body Language For Dummies* (Wiley) offers detailed analysis of the impact of body language on communication in general. In this chapter, however, I focus primarily on how mirroring and matching other people's body signals helps you persuade and influence others.

Getting in synch

Taking the time to read, recognise and respond to other people's body movements demonstrates your desire to show respect, establish rapport and produce results. And isn't that the foundation for ethical persuasion?

You often hear people talk about *rapport,* but do you honestly know what they mean? Allow me to translate. Having rapport is about being on the same wavelength. You feel comfortable and in tune with one another. When you're in rapport with someone, it's a simple step to being able to influence them.

Behaving in a similar fashion shows you appreciate the person's feelings, mood and attitude, and demonstrates your compatibility. By physically displaying like-mindedness, you're on the path to persuasion. In other words, you're more likely to influence others if you're able to pick up and reflect back their gestures, expressions and movements than if your behaviours are contrary to theirs.

When you show respect for another person, you can almost instantly feel the compatibility factor rise. When people feel compatible with you, they're open to your influence. When your body movements and facial expressions are *congruent* with those of your client or colleague, your mind and movements appear well-matched and choreographed to work together in harmony.

In her book *Coaching with NLP For Dummies* (Wiley), Kate Burton describes *congruent* as 'having a sense of peace', when your words, tone of voice and body language are consistent and fit together in harmony.

Think about congruency as dancing with someone whose body fits comfortably with yours, and whose rhythm, movement and timing match yours to a tee. Nice. Now think about dancing with someone who is stiff and rigid. This partner steps on your feet as the other dancers swirl around you. Not congruent and not such a nice experience. The body language you and another person display in the course of a conversation can inspire similar nice or not-so-nice feelings.

When you find yourself feeling comfortable and at ease with someone, take a look at your body language and note the other person's. Chances are you're both sitting, standing or reclining in a similar manner. You almost appear to be looking in a mirror at yourself; of course, you don't have to be the same sex, ethnicity or size in order for this to happen.

Taking in others' body language

From the moment you first see another person, you begin to read to her. You notice what she looks like, what she's wearing and how she's moving. While there's room for interpretation within the rainbow of your observations, what you see can alert you to what you can expect. And after you know what to expect, you quickly figure out how to respond.

For example, how a co-worker stands or sits tells you how open she is to engaging with you:

- ✔ If her eyes are focused on the computer screen and her fingers hovering over the keys in anticipation, your presence is probably an interruption. Right now may not be the best time to jump into a non-essential conversation.

- ✔ However, if she lifts her eyes from the screen and acknowledges your presence with a welcoming smile, you have her attention. Look her in the eye and start talking.

The moment you walk into another person's space, whether at work or at play, take a pause and look at them. Observe people as they are and then match their moods (see the following section, 'Mirroring and matching').

Fine tune your ability to observe another person's physicality with this exercise. You need a partner, someone you trust enough to role play along. Ask your partner to get into a comfortable position.

1. **Ask your partner to think of something.**

   It doesn't matter what. It could be a film, friend, flower, news story, recent experience or another person. Whatever. Call this thought 'A'.

2. **As your partner thinks about his or her chosen subject, notice what's happening physically.**

   What does your partner's body look like? How's his or her posture? What expressions and gestures do you notice? How is your partner breathing? Are any muscles tense?

   As your partner is thinking about 'A', take a mental snapshot. What you're observing is how your partner characterises 'A'. Store this mental snapshot.

3. **Have your partner move around the room and clear his or her mind.**

   For example, ask your partner to name five things he or she can see. This activity helps your partner reorientate, get 'A' out of their head and return to their normal state.

4. **Have your partner think of something different and observe his or her physicality.**

   While this second thought doesn't have to be the opposite of the first thought, it does have to be something completely different. Call this second thought 'B'.

   After your partner thinks about 'B' and you notice his or her physicality and take another mental snapshot, have your partner break this state as you did in Step 3.

5. Ask your partner to get into a comfortable position and think of either 'A' or 'B'. Tell them not to say which they're thinking about.

If your empathetic antenna are working and your earlier snapshots were correct, you can identify which subject your partner is now thinking about simply by reading their physicality including expressions, muscle movements and breathing rates.

By becoming more adept at recognising changes in another person's physicality as you talk about certain topics, you gain clues as to how the other person feels about various subjects.

Don't reciprocate aggressive behaviour; doing so merely results in escalating emotions and less opportunity for you to persuade or influence the person. So if someone greets you with a snarl when you enter her space, don't feel you have to snarl back. Simply nod your head, retreat and return another time. Before you enter that person's space again, check her body language as you approach. If she smiles when she sees you, smile back and enter. If she frowns or ignores you, walk on by. If you really have to speak with her, make an appointment.

Mirroring and matching

In *Neuro-Linguistic Programming (NLP) Workbook For Dummies* (Wiley), Romilla Ready and Kate Burton describe the process of mirroring and matching as being a 'dance of rapport' in which people who are getting on well move in unison, leaning forwards, moving backwards and making similar gestures at the same speed and rhythm.

While the words 'mirroring' and 'matching' are frequently used interchangeably, as I do in this chapter, there is a subtle difference:

✔ When you *mirror* someone, you are the mirror image of them. For example, if you were standing in front of another person who raised her right hand with the palm facing towards you, you would raise your left hand with the palm facing her, creating a mirror image. Mirroring is not mimicking, and should be subtle and respectful so as not to cause offense or embarrassment. It is a way of establishing deep, unconscious rapport and is meant to be used ethically. (For more about ethical behaviour, refer to Chapter 5.)

✔ On the other hand, if you were standing in front of someone who raised her right hand, and you raised your left, you'd be *matching* her. Matching is less obvious and more outside your conscious awareness than mirroring. When you match someone's behaviour, you allow a bit of time to pass between when the other person gestured and you reflected back what you observed – unless, of course, you're dancing together, in which case you reflect the movements in synch to avoid stepping on one another's toes.

Matching and mirroring are ways of tuning in to how someone else is thinking and experiencing the world. Think of the two behaviours as a method of listening with your whole body. Simple mirroring and matching happens naturally when you and someone else are in rapport, making you more susceptible as well as more capable when it comes to persuading and being persuaded.

- ✔ When you're susceptible to persuasion, you're open and receptive to the process.

- ✔ When you're adept and competent at mirroring and matching, you're more capable of persuading than if you lacked the skills.

In addition to matching other people's gestures, expressions and movements, you can also match and mirror their voices, which I look at in greater detail in Chapter 14.

Matching others' actions doesn't mean playing them back exactly, movement by movement. Rather, you reflect *the sense* of what they're communicating, rather like paraphrasing other people's words as opposed to quoting them directly.

If you don't have natural rapport with someone, you can build it through consciously mirroring and matching to build the relationship. Some non-verbal behaviours you can observe and then match and mirror include:

- ✔ **Breathing patterns:** Observe the other person's breathing rate. Is it fast or slow? Noisy or quiet? Notice the other person's neck, shoulders, chest and torso and how these body parts move as the person inhales and exhales. Look for fine movements indicating where they're breathing from, and try to breath from the same place. For example, if someone's taking short, sharp breaths from her upper chest, make your breathing pattern short and sharp as well. If she's breathing slowly from deep within her body, let your breathing go slow and low, too.

    If the person you're observing is a woman, avoid offending her by focusing on movements in her neck and shoulders while she breathes.

- ✔ **Rhythm of movement and energy levels:** Is the other person bouncy or still? Can you describe the other person's energy as high or low?

- ✔ **Body postures, gestures and expressions:** Does the other person look at you as she speaks? How are her movements similar to yours? Does she have any distinctive gestures?

There may be times when you want to avoid mirroring and matching someone's behaviour. For example, if someone's talking to you non-stop and you want to end the conversation, break the rapport by mismatching her behaviour. Break eye contact, turn your body at an angle to her, change your breathing to be in contrast to hers, alter your facial expression – whatever you do, make it different from what the other person's doing. She will soon get the message that it's time to move on to someone else.

You may wonder what you should do if you're with someone who's depressed or in discomfort. Begin by matching your behaviour to meet hers to build rapport, and then mismatch the behaviour by using different patterns or contradictory responses to those that she's exhibiting to redirect, interrupt or end the conversation. Because mirroring can lead to you sharing the other person's experience, avoid mirroring people who are distressed or suffering from severe mental issues.

In the following section I talk about pacing and leading, where you match someone's behaviour, then slowly change yours to lead her to where you want her to be.

Mirroring and matching may be instinctive for you and come effortlessly. For others, it is behaviour you must work on. Whether you find reflecting back the characteristics listed above easy or difficult, the good news is that you can, with practice, become much more adept at mirroring and matching others.

If you want to practise mirroring, begin gradually, in no-risk situations (a casual gathering with friends) or with people you know you'll never see again. Be prepared to get so good at mirroring that the people you reflect end up wanting to be your friend.

Beware the fine line between mimicry and moving in rhythm with someone. People instinctively know if you're making fun of them or being insincere. Try to be subtle. For example, every time the person across the desk fiddles with her papers, you don't have to immediately fiddle with yours. Instead, notice what she's doing and respond in a comparable way – by rubbing your palms together or jiggling your foot in tempo with her actions for example – reflecting her mood rather than her exact movements.

Pacing and leading others

If you want to persuade someone, you must *pace* the other person first. To do this you must listen, listen and listen some more to what she's telling you. You then pick up on her behaviours and vocabulary adapting yours to meet hers. At all times you act in a respectful way to establish genuine rapport.

To see effective pacing in action, observe really good salespeople. Notice how they pace their customers by listening carefully and demonstrating genuine interest. These people are acting with integrity rather than trying to bamboozle the buyer. If you're interested in integrity, turn to Chapter 5.

Pacing, mirroring, matching and leading are all cut from the same cloth and fit neatly together like parts of a puzzle. Once you have noticed someone's behaviour and reflected it back in yours – mirroring and matching – you've begun the process of pacing. Once you're running alongside someone at the same speed – which is a figurative way of describing pacing – leading comes next, whereby you take her to where you want her to be. Later in this section I give you ways of leading someone to go along with you.

In order to pace someone, you need to acknowledge the other person, be patient with her and give her your full attention. You know how good it feels when someone takes time to be with you, just as you are, rather than trying to push or pull you to where she wants you to be. Give the same feeling to someone else.

In order to effectively pace others, first meet them where they are – and then move them to where you want them to be. Imposing your energy levels onto someone whose liveliness is at a different point can lead to a breakdown in communication before it even begins. Specifically:

- ✔ Acknowledge the other person, giving her your full attention. Listen to what she says without judging or anticipating what's coming next. Notice her breathing patterns as well as her posture, movements and expressions, adapting yours to hers. Pay attention to the words she chooses and her vocal quality, reflecting them in your speech pattern.

- ✔ Be patient. Spending just a minute or two at the other person's energy level will make her more amenable to your influence.

- ✔ To lead someone to where you want her to be, you can ask questions, give directions or explain something. You can also alter the way you talk about the subject and see whether she goes along with your point of view. If she doesn't, continue pacing until she's ready to accept the change you're introducing.

- ✔ You can lead through non-verbal means by pacing the other person's breathing, for example, and then adjusting your rate to see whether she follows. If she isn't ready to change, go back to her rate and try again in a few moments.

- ✔ Refrain from making judgements or telling her what is right for her to do. Listen to what she tells you and reflect her words back so she feels understood, respected and acknowledged. Once she trusts you, you should have no problem leading her to where you want to go.

Speaking Effectively with Your Movements and Gestures

Mimes depend totally on gestures, movements and expressions to convey messages. Actors and dancers rely on their bodies to send signals, too. And so do you.

As I say in Chapter 3, people buy on feeling and justify with fact. Furthermore, words convey ideas, data and information, while non-verbal behaviour conveys feelings, moods and emotions. Therefore, getting your body working for you in order to establish emotional connections makes sense.

Whether you're smiling, frowning, slumping or standing upright, your emotions are on show. While being true to your authentic self is core to your success (see Chapter 2), allowing your feelings to leak out of your body may play to your disadvantage.

Jennifer's body language is more than expressive: she really tends to be exuberant and flamboyant, and can sometimes appear out of control. She's had to learn to temper her behaviour to her environment to make people feel safe and comfortable around her. She's intellectually very bright and has had to work hard on containing her emotions, because she often fails to understand the effects of her behaviour.

Studies on the impact of body language on communication rate non-verbal behaviour as more influential than the words you speak. That doesn't mean that you can fling out any old clap-trap as long as your body is moving persuasively. As I say earlier in this chapter, your words and actions must be congruent in order for your message to be believed.

Gestures, expressions and body positions are all powerful tools that can subtract from or add to your message. The following sections explore ways to accentuate the positives and minimise (or even eliminate) the negatives.

Making powerful first impressions

You've heard it before and you'll hear it again: you never have a second chance to make a first impression. Make a good first impression and your chance of influencing the other person increases. Make a bad one and you struggle to gain the other person's trust and confidence.

Research consistently demonstrates the importance of first impressions and the impact they make. Getting off the starting block is very difficult if the first impression you send out is contrary to what the other person is looking for.

First impressions are lasting impressions and set the pace for the rest of the relationship. Men and women in personal and professional relationships consistently report that confidence is the sexiest, most impressive and attractive characteristic a person can convey. Genuine confidence is projected in a combination of outside traits – firm handshake, eye contact, upright posture, warm smile – and a high sense of self-belief and personal value.

If your personal value is at a low ebb, stand in front of a mirror with your head up, shoulders back and a smile, and repeat, 'The values I bring to relationships are . . .' filling in the blank with positive observations about yourself. If you struggle with this exercise at first, speak to yourself as if you were your best friend. If you think you bring something positive to the table, others believe so, too. In addition to treating yourself with respect, treat others with respect. Show interest in them, call them by name. The more respect you demonstrate, the more respect you receive and the more persuasive and influential you become.

Until the end of her life, my mother would remind me to 'Stand up straight, put your shoulders back and hold your head high!' These reminders remain vital to creating a good first impression, whether you're heading out on a first date, going for an interview, speaking at a school assembly or requesting the best table in the hot new restaurant.

Follow the recommendations below when you want the impression you make to be top notch:

- **Establish and maintain eye contact.** When you look someone in the eye, you come across as self-assured and like you mean business. Maintain eye contact 85 per cent of the time during a conversation to appear trustworthy and interested in what the other person's saying. Avoid staring, because that can make you look intimidating and somewhat creepy.

- **Smile.** A warm and friendly smile puts others at their ease and makes you look comfortable and relaxed. When you and the person you want to persuade are at ease and comfortable, you find persuading a lot easier than if you both are feeling tense and uptight.

- **Stand tall.** Place your weight evenly on both feet – hip width apart, one foot slightly ahead of the other – to make you look and feel grounded and confident. Instead of slumping, lift up from your waist and chest, imagining that your shoulder blades are meeting at your spinal cord and melting down your back, and hold your head horizontally to give the impression of someone who's in control.

✔ **Claim your space.** Wherever you are, act like you belong there. If you're feeling nervous or insecure, silently say to yourself, 'I'm glad to be here and people want to hear what I have to say.' Giving yourself encouraging messages makes you feel good about yourself and sends out an upbeat impression.

✔ **Move with purpose.** Fiddling fingers, shuffling feet and darting eyes make you look nervous and ill at ease. Make your gestures and expressions clear and meaningful and when you move, do so with focus and energy.

✔ **Offer a firm handshake.** Whenever you shake someone's hand, put the best of yourself into the gesture. A limp handshake comes across as uncommitted, while a knuckle-cruncher is painful. Meet the other person's hand in an upright position, palm to palm with the webbed skin between your thumb and index finger – known as the thenar space – meeting hers.

✔ **Focus on the other person.** Engage in a bit of small talk resembling a tennis match, with each person contributing to the conversation in turn. If you monopolise the conversation, you come across as self-involved and uninterested in the other person.

✔ **Speak with energy.** Your voice conveys an impression of who you are, so make it good. Monotones are uninspiring, and a voice that can't be heard comes across as uncertain. Although people think faster than they speak, if you stick to about 145 words per minute, loud enough to be heard without blasting your listener's ear drums, you should be able to maintain people's attention. For more about capturing someone's attention turn to Chapter 8, and if you want to know more about speaking persuasively have a look at Chapter 14.

Masking your feelings

'Smile though your heart is breaking,' 'Big girls don't cry,' and 'Put on a happy face' are some of the expressions you may have heard as you were growing up. Acting as if you're brave, confident and courageous when you're fearful, in doubt and terrified is intended to project an image of confidence and control and convince others that when you say 'It's all good,' things really are.

Sometimes you may not want others to know how you're feeling. When someone displays a blank expression, also known as a poker face, she's intending to disguise her emotions so others won't know what really going on inside. For example, if your girlfriend just dumped you, you might want to put on a display of bravado, indicating that you don't care, in order to protect your ego and image. Perhaps you don't want to talk with your friend's sister-in-law at a drinks party, yet do to be polite. Or maybe you're having a bad day but mask your sadness so as not to burden others with your problems. While it's best to tell your friends and family how you're feeling to avoid any confusion or misunderstandings, at work there are times when it's advisable to mask your true feelings.

Frequently, when people are in conflict or negotiating a deal, they conceal their emotions to appear in control and not to give the game away. They might feel emotionally exposed, defenceless or in a weak position if they revealed their true mood, feelings and attitude. For example, if you're persuading your teenage daughter to clean up her room, and are ready to tear your hair – or hers – out in frustration because this is the umpteenth time the two of you have had this conversation, letting her know how angry you are may not be the most persuasive technique, because she's seen you angry before and you've failed to persuade her with your loud voice and flailing hands. Instead, you could conceal your annoyance by playing cool and letting her wonder what's going on inside you. By putting her on the back foot and leaving her in doubt as to what may happen if she doesn't clean up her room, she just might put away her clothes for fear of what could happen if she doesn't.

At work, you may frequently have to mask your true feelings. Being required to toe the company line when you personally don't agree with something is tough. If you let your true feelings show, you may find yourself escorted off the premises. Unless you're in a position to walk away from gainful employment, you're better off masking your feelings.

Masking your feelings is particularly important when extreme or intense emotions – such as anger or physical attraction – arise at work. Although you may see stamping feet and little winks of the eye once in a while, protocol dictates that certain behaviours and attitudes are inappropriate in business. Although you may feel like throwing your pen at your boss, colleague or subordinate – or desire a little cuddle with that cute worker in accounting – I suggest you don't. There's a time and place for everything, and inappropriate behaviour will come back to haunt you.

In addition to anger and intense physical attraction, other emotions you might want to mask at the office include:

- ✔ Cynicism
- ✔ Lack of respect
- ✔ Humour at someone else's expense
- ✔ Sarcasm

One technique you can adopt to mask your true feelings is to pretend you're playing a different role. Actors do this all the time. Like an actor taking on a role, you're portraying a character rather than yourself. You connect with your character's feelings, moods and attitudes, adopting the character's behaviours and mannerisms.

Watch children at play and see how easily they become the person they're pretending to be. Whether they're playing the part of a fairy princess or a brave warrior, children persuade you they are the character by their costumes, mannerisms and behaviours. They throw themselves into the role as if they're the person they're playing – until the game changes, when they drop their facade in the blink of an eye. You can do that, too. For example, when you're with friends at a party, you might kick off your shoes and dance with exuberance. When you get home and check on the children, you might temper your enthusiasm as you put yourself back into the role of the responsible parent. In neither instance are you lying or pretending to be someone you're not, you simply acting according to the scene's requirements or given circumstances.

If you feel your preferred way of acting isn't serving you well, you may want to consider adapting your behaviours to suit the scene. For example, when I moved from the middle of Manhattan to a small English country village, my father suggested that I take things slowly. While I can act slowly, it's not my natural style, and at first I struggled to make friends. When I discovered that my normal way of being was overpowering and I was putting people off rather than pulling them towards me, I knew I had to adapt if I was to make a successful life for myself and my family. By adjusting my behaviour, making it easier for others to be around me, I acted according to the scene's requirements, as an actor would say. I wasn't being a fake or a fraud, I was simply drawing from parts of me I didn't often use. Once I had made it easier for people to be with me, I was able to revert to my natural style, albeit slowly. This is an example of pacing others' behaviour and leading.

You are a complex person made up of many parts, including your:

- ✔ Experiences
- ✔ Emotions
- ✔ Expectations
- ✔ Needs
- ✔ Desires
- ✔ Strengths
- ✔ Weaknesses

By drawing from these different parts you can show sides of yourself other than the one you most often reveal, demonstrating that there's more to you than meets the eye.

In addition to drawing from your own self, you can create a character by referring to someone whose behaviours reflect the way you want to be perceived. For example, if you've been told that your effusive gestures and raucous voice are making you seem out of control, you could observe someone whose style is more contained and adapt your style to match hers. You could also picture yourself behaving in the way you'd like to, and like children at play, adapt your style to suit the scene. Rather than suggesting you become someone you're not, I'm encouraging you to dig deep into your soul and draw from your experiences to find parts of yourself you don't often show, if doing so will help you when it comes to influencing and persuading others. It's easier to persuade others when your style matches theirs. You can read more about how similarity aids in the persuasion process in Chapters 9 and 10.

When you play a different role, continue to be true to yourself, or others are likely to quickly detect you're putting up a false front and may even consider you a fraud, lacking credibility. Without credibility, your chance of persuading and influencing others shrinks. You might ask, 'How can I be true to myself when I'm acting as if I was a different character?' Actors do this all the time by releasing their energy outwards rather than worrying about what others think of what they're doing. Having decided what you want to project of yourself, be completely present with your mind, body and spirit working together as one. Let go of any fear that you're not good enough and that what you're doing isn't right. You are a complex person made up of many parts. What you're showing when you're playing a different role from the way you normally act is just one side of you that you may not often reveal.

Leaking information

The body never lies and is a great barometer to what's going on inside your mind, whether you're admiring a potential lover, negotiating for the best table in a restaurant or closing a major deal. The unconscious blink of your eye, twitch of your mouth or the position of your hands or feet reveals more about your thoughts and feelings than your actual words and can either help or hinder when you're persuading and influencing others.

For example, if you're trying to persuade someone that your idea's a good one, and you notice she's frowning and shaking her head, you can bet she's unconsciously telling you she doesn't agree. This offers you the chance to stop and ask for her feedback on your proposition, giving you further information to use as you continue to negotiate with her. On the other hand, when the stakes are high and you're trembling inside, you may want to conceal your thoughts and feelings so as to come off as calm, cool and collected.

If you're familiar with how someone behaves in a relaxed state and can compare it with how she behaves under pressure, you're in prime position for seeing where the leaks occur and can judge how she's responding to what's going on, regardless of what she says.

People frequently leak when they're under pressure, and I'm talking about more than pure perspiration! Hand-to-face gestures are typical leakage signals. When you hear or see something you don't like, don't be surprised if your hand flicks away from your face, as if warding off the intruder. Of course, this behaviour may seem a bit extreme, so you often see people trying to do something else with their hands instead, such as:

- **Hand to eyes.** The hand moves to cover the eyes and at the last moment changes to rub or pull the corner of the eye. The hand may also rub the forehead or stroke the brow.

- **Hand to mouth.** The hand rises to the face and diverts to wipe the mouth, scratch the face or stroke the chin. This gesture often happens when a person is listening to someone else speak, wants to interject, but knows holding back words is best.

  Be careful not to mistake this gesture for deep thought. When someone is thinking deeply, the hand tends to be lower on the face, holding or stroking the chin without touching the mouth.

- **Hand to throat.** This gesture indicates discomfort or uncertainty. Women disguise it by playing with a necklace, while men pull at their collars or adjust their ties.

- **Hand to ear.** This gesture indicates that you'd like to interrupt the speaker who's going on too long or whose point you want to argue.

- **Hand to nose.** If you've been asked a difficult question and are considering how to reply, don't be surprised if you find your finger rubbing your nose. This gesture also indicates that you may be lying. Of course, it could mean that your nose itches, but if that were the case you'd be using your fingernail and scratching more vigorously. Putting your hand to your nose is a slower gesture and uses the knuckle or fingertip to scratch or pinch the bridge of the nose.

Bottom line: when you're trying to persuade someone, keep your hands away from your face.

There may be times when you want to check your understanding of someone's gestures and expressions. For example, if you're trying to persuade someone to join you for a drink and they break eye contact, you could say, 'From the way you just looked away, should I take that to mean that you'd rather not go out with me?' This shows that you're paying attention to the other person and care enough to want to know the truth.

If you think you may be giving away too much information – or not enough – through your posture, gestures and expressions, ask your partner, friend or co-worker to assess your body language and report back what she observes. The more information you have about the way others perceive you, the better able you are to adapt your style when you want to persuade people whose behaviour is different from yours. This approach is similar to *pacing*, which I explore earlier in this chapter.

You can also observe yourself in mirrors or windows. Be careful when you do this as someone may catch you out and think you're narcissistic and more interested in yourself than in what's going on with them.

When you're under pressure and fear you may be leaking information, breathe deeply from your abdomen. Fill yourself from the bottom up, allowing your ribcage to expand while your upper chest remains still. Breathing in this way will calm you down and keep you from leaking your thoughts and feelings.

Physically reinforcing your message

If you've ever been in a meeting where someone pounded her fist on the table or slapped the side of her head, you know how persuasive non-verbal communication can be.

People take in messages through their senses. Not only can you see your boss leaning over her desk with clenched fists, furrowed brow and gritted lips, and hear the tightness in her throat (I tell you more about persuasively using your voice in Chapter 14), if you're unlucky, you may even smell some sweat. The bottom line is, what she's doing with her body is enough to influence your belief that she's very angry or frustrated.

Reinforcing your message by using selected, specific and clear gestures sends visual as well as aural confirmation of your meaning. For example:

- ✔ Bowing your head shows deep thought
- ✔ Lifting your head towards the heavens implies inspiration
- ✔ Tilting your head to either side shows interest
- ✔ Fixing your glaze on the person you're persuading means business

When you want to influence behaviour or persuade others to accept your point of view, make sure your body supports your words.

Clients often ask me how they should stand, how they should sit, and what they should do with their hands – as if their bodies are made up of unrelated parts that have nothing to do with them as people.

Rather than prescribing specific movements or postures right from the start of our session, I begin by having my client engage in some physical exercises such as shaking out her arms and legs, blowing air out of her mouth like a horse, and releasing tension wherever she finds it. Letting go of tension can be a lot of fun.

I encourage you to spend a few minutes doing whatever you need to do in order to let go of tightness in your body and relax into yourself. I recommend you do this in a safe, private place such as your own home or the back stair-well at the office, of course. I sometimes practise relaxation exercises in the privacy of my car when stopped at a light or in a traffic jam, figuring that if anyone notices me, I'll never see them again! If you're up for it, try these exercises now. First raise and lower your shoulders, roll your head and shoulders, and squeeze and release your facial muscles, fingers and feet. Take a long, deep breath and let it out quickly; take a short, sharp breath and let it out slowly. These are great exercises for relaxing and for connecting with yourself, what you're saying and your listener. They're also good for pumping up your energy to get your message across. When you rely on your body language to convey your meaning, your body needs to be up for the job. If you don't begin from a state of calm, connected control, you're never going to be able to manage the messages your movements send.

The more able you are to manage your movements, the more able you are to persuade and influence other people. For example:

- ✔ **If you want to show someone that you're listening and open to hearing what the person is saying,** tilt your head slightly towards your shoulder. By looking inquisitive you can persuade the other person to keep talking while you can uncover more about her. The other person sees you as interested and open to her influence, so she keeps going.

- ✔ **If you want to show someone that you're neither interested nor in any mood to be persuaded,** turn your head away while she's talking and avoid making eye contact. She'll either stop talking or babble on for a few more minutes until she realises that she's not going to persuade you.

If you hold a handshake limply, slouch and focus your eyes on the floor, you're going to struggle to persuade anyone that you're the person for the job. If you want to persuade someone that you're strong, caring and a capable leader, act like it. Make your gestures fit the part. See that you're sitting or standing in an upright position, look the person in the eye, make your gestures clear and purposeful, adding in a smile for a touch of warmth and likeability. If you want to know what likeability has to do with persuasion, turn to Chapter 10.

Substituting gestures for words

Substituting gestures for words is effective when you're in a situation where it would be inappropriate or unadvisable to speak. If you were in a library and the person across the table from you was chatting on her mobile phone, putting your index finger to your closed lips could be all that's required to tell her to stop talking. Through that simple gesture you've respected the rule of silence while telling her to be quiet.

The more gestures you have at your command, the more effectively and efficiently you're able to communicate. Not only can your gestures and expressions physically reinforce your spoken message, they can convey your message without you having to open your mouth. For example, if you're in a group of people and someone says something you don't agree with, but you don't want to contradict her in front of others, a quizzical glance including a raised eyebrow with a downwardly tilted head and a closed mouth is enough to let her know you're not convinced about what she's saying.

Gestures in prepared speeches and presentations support the message by giving a visual representation of what you're saying, adding an extra element to enhance your point.

The following list contains some useful gestures and their meanings:

- ✔ **Hand to heart.** This gesture demonstrates care, concern and personal relevance.

- ✔ **A raised arm with open palm.** This gesture indicates great possibilities and forward thinking.

- ✔ **A pointed index finger.** Calls attention to someone or something.

- ✔ **Crossed middle and index fingers.** A sign of good luck.

- ✔ **Thumbs up or down and with fingers curled inward.** The first is a sign of 'well done' or 'things are great' while the thumb pointed downwards is a way of expressing lack of acceptance, or failure or rejection.

Further examples of effective gestures can be found in Chapter 18 and in my book *Body Language For Dummies*.

Gestures don't always translate across cultures, and in today's world of international travel and business you need to educate yourself to local customs. What's acceptable in one country may be rude and offensive in another. For further information about this tricky subject refer to *Cross-Cultural Selling For Dummies* by Michael Soon Lee and Ralph R Roberts (Wiley) or the second edition of *Body Language For Dummies,* which has an extensive list of signs, signals, gestures and expressions and where they can and shouldn't be used.

If you want to come across as an effective communicator, try out different gestures before putting them into practice. Whether you're speaking to a potential lover, a friend, your boss or the queen of England, you want to make sure your gestures and expressions are right for the occasion. While you don't want to come across as unrealistic or odd, you do want to look like you're comfortable in your own skin. Before their wedding, the Duke and Duchess of Cambridge practised their gestures and movements to ensure that they presented themselves at their best in front of a world-wide audience, proving that practice makes perfect.

Sometimes, words don't need uttering. The right gesture is enough to send a message:

- ✔ A pat on the back tells you that you've done a good job.

- ✔ Rolling raised eyes indicates what you're hearing is a lot of rubbish.

- ✔ Tapping your finger by the side of your nose indicates that what you're about to say is just between you and the person you're speaking to.

- ✔ Holding your hand in the 'stop' position deflects an oncoming verbal or physical attack.

In these days of political correctness, touching someone may be seen as patronising or invasive. If you're the kind of person who conveys your feelings through touching, let your team know so they don't question your intentions.

Sometimes, you're better off letting gestures do the persuading and leaving your thoughts unvoiced. For example, if you're in a meeting and see that the approach your colleague is taking is annoying the client, you can make a previously agreed gesture to indicate that your colleague should stop speaking. Be sure to keep your movements subtle, or else the client may catch on to what you're up to.

Chapter 14

Perfecting Your Persuasive Voice

*Y*our voice is you. It is your history. It is your present. Your voice reveals your excitement and your anxiety, your pleasures and your pains, your victories and your defeats. Your voice is more than an instrument for relaying facts and data: your voice exposes your attitudes and emotions, too.

Both at work and in your private life, the words and phrases you adopt, the tone and pace at which you communicate, and the way you embrace the powerful pause reflect your beliefs and values as well as your thoughts, attitudes and feelings.

Knowing Your Different Voices

The most effective voices are:

- **Relaxed.** The sound freely resonates throughout your body, free of blockages in your head, nose, throat, upper chest and elsewhere caused by pressures and anxiety.

- **Approachable.** This voice is void of obstacles such as judgments, prejudices and sarcasm that hamper your ability to connect. It sounds warm and inviting and encourages others to listen and respond.

- **Flexible.** It is filled with variety, including differing pitches, rhythms and levels of intensity. This voice engages and entertains your listener, opening the door for others to connect with you and respond in a positive way.

Whether you're speaking out loud or putting your thoughts in writing, your voice is at work. Some of the areas where you may find yourself using your voice include:

- ✔ Face-to-face
- ✔ On the phone – mobile, landline and Skype – one-to-one or in a conference call
- ✔ On a video or audio recording
- ✔ In a letter or email

In order for you to persuade or influence people, you must:

- ✔ **Discover and connect with your true, authentic self.** People can spot fakes and tend to mistrust them. When you embrace your strengths, address your weaknesses and let go of your fears, you can release a voice that is strong and solid. Once you discover and accept yourself for the person you are – your genuine, authentic self – you release your ability to persuade others. As long as you hide or shut off from yourself, you're never going to persuade anyone, no matter how many voice lessons you take.

  Your authentic self exists at your absolute core. Rather than being defined by your job, function or role, your authentic self is the combination of all your skills, talents and wisdom. You're not thinking about what people expect of you, nor do you worry about your past mistakes. When your body, mind and spirit are working together as one and you feel 'in the flow', releasing positive energy while focusing on the here and now, you are connected to your authentic self.

- ✔ **Free your natural voice.** Your vocal qualities are as important as the words you say in getting your point across. A dull, flat, lifeless voice offers the listener little incentive to follow the speaker's lead. Poor articulation makes your message difficult to understand. But like a magnet, a voice that is powered by energy and commitment pulls the listener in.

- ✔ **Connect with your message.** When you engage with what you're saying, your listeners do too. When you're interested in what you're saying and speak with passion, clarity and in terms that your listener can grasp, your audience becomes interested too.

- ✔ **Connect with your listener.** If you don't know who they are, what concerns and pleases them, as well as how they respond to words and sounds, you're going to have a hard time getting a hearing. Offer your listeners statistics, examples and analogies that are relevant to them. Provide them with examples and demonstrations that relate to them. You can make your message real and compelling for your listeners by drawing upon their personal memories and their own life experiences.

✔ **Connect with your environment.** Whether the space is large, open and airy or small, dark and dank, your voice must fill the space. Feel the surface beneath your feet, notice the space around your body, smell the air in your environment and let your senses guide you. A booming voice in a small room turns off your listener just as much as a small, thin voice in a large auditorium is uninspiring. In this chapter, you discover ways of connecting with yourself in order to free your voice. You unleash your voice and make it work for you not against you. You find ways of engaging with your listener through the way you pitch, pace and pause. Finally, you develop your ability to claim your space and speak with purpose.

Building Your Vocal Foundation

The physical act of making a sound begins in your brain. You think about producing a sound, your brain sends messages to your body about how you're going to respond, and your body, in ideal circumstances, becomes filled with dynamic and flexible energy. In worst-case scenarios – such as when you're angry, uninterested or depressed – your body becomes stiff, dull and lifeless.

Sometimes you are mindful of how you want to sound; other times the thinking–speaking process happens in an unconscious flash. Whether you are aware of the messages your brain is sending to your body or not, studies show that the pathway between the brain and the body is comparable to a busy two-way street.

A voice based on a firm foundation sounds powerful and substantial. It bounces off a strong, supporting structure and resonates throughout your body. In this section you discover what it takes to produce a sound that can persuade others to sit up and listen to what you have to say.

Preparing your mind

Speaking persuasively starts with being at peace with yourself. Feeling comfortable and confident with who you are is a cornerstone for creating a persuasive voice. When you are centred and connected with the true you, people pay attention. You radiate an aura that makes others feel confident in your presence, while you express your coherent thoughts and feelings. Your voice and message are congruent – what you say and how you say it are consistent – and your listener understands your meaning without struggling. People know where they stand and are open to your input.

The King's Speech

The 2010 award-winning film The King's Speech is based on the true-life relationship between King George VI and his eccentric speech therapist Lionel Logue. During the course of the film you see Logue make the King, or Bertie (as his family, friends and Logue called him), explore his self-beliefs, many of which are negative and are based on his relationships with his father and with his brother, David (who was briefly Edward VIII). To convince him of his strengths, the King undergoes an unorthodox treatment of speech therapy, including swearing vulgarities at full volume, reading Hamlet's soliloquy 'To be or not to be' with music blaring in his ears through a set of headphones, and rolling around on the floor to loosen his body and free his mind. When Logue provokes the King shortly before the coronation, the King surprises himself with his own eloquence as he argues with Logue for what he perceives as Logue's disrespect. With Logue's continued coaching, the King eventually overcomes his debilitating speech impediment. While not a naturally fluid speaker, the King was able to communicate to his countrymen in a way that inspired and united the nation throughout his reign.

If you're anything like most people, you have a voice (or several voices) in your head that occasionally fills your mind with negative messages. I call my negative voice The Parrot. A friend of mine calls it The Uninvited Guest. Whatever you choose to call it, the point to remember about this negative voice is that it inhibits your ability to communicate effectively, leading you to doubt your abilities and contributions. (You may have heard or read about negative *mental tapes* that cause similar interference.)

Those little voices in your head may tell you that you're not very good, and that some day, everyone's going to find out that you're a sham. The cacophony and negativity can create quite a commotion. If you listen to and believe these negative messages, you can quickly become consumed with worry and self-doubt. As a result, your ability to connect with your listener and activate your persuasive voice are null and void.

In order to feel comfortable and confident with who you are, you must first cage the parrot that's reciting negative messages in your mind. These old messages can originate from anywhere, but some of the most powerful are likely to be things you heard as a child or teenager, such as

- Don't speak out of turn.
- Wait to be asked before you voice your opinion.
- Your contribution doesn't add much to the discussion.
- You're getting pretty big for your boots.

✔ You'll never amount to much.

✔ You made a mess of that.

✔ That's just not good enough.

✔ Can't you get anything right?

✔ Stop complaining!

Because your thoughts affect your body and mindset, think positive thoughts in order to get yourself in the right frame of mind for speaking persuasively. One of my favourite positive thoughts is 'Every day in every way I am getting better and better.' Speak to yourself as if you were your best friend. Tell yourself that you've earned the right to speak and be heard. Recall times when you've spoken persuasively in the past and how people reacted positively to what you had to say. Write down a list of things you do well. When you carry positive thoughts, your voice rings with certainty and clarity. If your thinking is more 'whatever' than 'just do it', your voice sounds flat, uncommitted and bored, and your listeners end up feeling that way too. Move and gesture as if you bring value (see Chapter 13), and experience the sensation of your voice resonating with strength and conviction. As Henry Ford said, 'Whether you think you can or think you can't, you're right.' Tell yourself you can and you can.

For more tips on filling yourself with positive messages, refer to *Cognitive Behavioural Therapy For Dummies* by Rob Willson and Rhena Branch (Wiley) or *Emotional Healing For Dummies* by David Beales and Helen Whitten (Wiley), both of which deal with this topic in detail.

If you find yourself falling prey to restrictive messages, turn on the 'positive speak' tap. For the next 30 days, say something encouraging about yourself first thing in the morning. In addition, every time the negative mental tapes start – or The Parrot starts squawking – replace the unhelpful message with a constructive one. Doing so allows you to acknowledge that your old negative voice is talking to you and that you can release it by playing a new mental tape – a positive one – that empowers you to communicate with confidence and conviction. Here is a positive affirmation you can use: 'I realise that in the past I have viewed myself as (negative message). Now I realise that I am (positive message). I celebrate my skills of . . . and . . . and today I will make every effort to put them to use in a caring, confident and committed way.

Filling your mind with negative messages is unproductive and prevents you from communicating with clarity, confidence and credibility.

While you may not have the natural communication skills of a born diplomat, you can develop greater self-awareness, which can lead you to identify your specific strengths. Turn to Chapter 2 for more information about understanding yourself.

Research shows that visualising yourself performing at your best helps create your desired outcome. Whatever you visualise you can create, so make your pictures positive and compelling. For example, imagine yourself speaking with clarity, confidence and commitment. You're breathing deeply from your lower abdomen, and your chest is still and relaxed. Your eyes are sparkling with excitement, and you're smiling. Hear the strength and freedom in your voice as it resonates throughout the space in which you're speaking. See yourself standing or sitting upright and proud, feeling positive energy surging through your body. Picture your listeners looking at you with their eyes wide with interest and smiles on their faces as they nod in understanding and agreement with what you're saying. Smell the clean, fresh air around you and taste the delicious sensation of success. Recall times when you have communicated well, and recreate the experience by re-enacting what was happening at the time. Draw from the positive examples of others whose skills you admire. Seek role models from both your private life and public figures. Turn to anyone who communicates the way you want to and observe what they do, so that you can incorporate their behaviour into yours.

People have employed visualisation techniques for thousands of years to aid in physical and emotional healing. By conjuring up positive pictures – by yourself or with the help of a coach or other guide – you can change your view of yourself from negative to affirmative. Visualisation stimulates your mind to draw from the area of the brain that controls creativity and emotions. You focus on the specific issue you want to address. As the visual, imaginary experience continues, your blood pressure and heart rate tend to lower. Deep, even breathing throughout the exercises fills your body with new energy and vitality. See *Cognitive Behavioural Therapy For Dummies* for more on visualisation techniques.

Benazir was born and raised in the UK, but her first language is Hindi-Urdu and her Indian parents speak no English. A Cambridge graduate, Benazir worked in an international law firm. Early in her career, she spoke with such hesitancy and quietness that the partners weren't convinced that she was committed enough to the firm for them to promote her, although she showed a strong business case for being promoted. Because Benazir grew up in a family culture in which women are expected to show deference – in particular to men and elders – Benazir's voice was trapped inside her. By tapping into her emotions, practising physical exercises to release her voice and visualising desired outcomes, she caged her fault-finding parrot and discovered her persuasive voice. She's able to release her thoughts and ideas and now speaks with variety, power and conviction.

In addition to freeing your mind of negative beliefs about yourself, let go of prejudices, biases and any sarcastic thoughts you may harbour towards others. While negative remarks about someone else may make your point in the sort term, no one wants to listen to a bigot or wise-guy for any length of time.

Warming up your body

When your body is calm and relaxed, your voice is free to make whatever sounds you want to produce. You're in control of what you say and how you say it. When your body is tense and uptight, you struggle to speak clearly with confidence and commitment. Thoughts get trapped in your mind and words stick in your throat, rendering you rigid and inarticulate.

Think of your body as an instrument for communication that needs to be warmed up before it can work properly. Just as you wouldn't jump into your car, rev the engine and drive off at speed after the car's been sitting out overnight in the cold, you shouldn't begin speaking without warming up your body to make the most of your voice. Research shows that a daily dose of simple warm-ups does wonders for your body and mind, increasing your self-confidence and lowering symptoms associated with mild depression and anxiety.

Pencil time in your schedule to make your exercise programme a priority. I find that ten minutes first thing in the morning and any time during the day when I feel my muscles tightening is enough to free the stiffness and put my body at ease. If you're not used to practising relaxation exercises, you may feel a little silly at first. That's okay and to be expected. Stick with the exercises and discover how good you feel afterwards.

The following exercises are designed to help you release tension from each part of your body. While ideally you practise these exercises lying on your bed or on the floor with a pillow under your head, your knees bent and your feet flat on the floor, you can do the exercises either standing or sitting in a straight-backed chair. If you are uncomfortable practising these exercises where you can be observed, take yourself to a quiet space where you can have a few minutes of uninterrupted time alone.

- ✔ **Neck.** Drop your head forwards with your chin pointing towards your chest. Hold this position for several seconds, feeling the muscles along the back of your neck stretch. Roll your head over towards your left shoulder. Hold this position as your feel the muscles along the right side of your neck stretch. Drop your head back to the centre then roll it to your right shoulder. Again, hold as you feel the muscles along the left side of your neck stretch. Do a series of three complete rolls. Do not drop your head backwards, because you may strain your throat muscles.

- ✔ **Shoulders.** Raise both shoulders up towards your ears, roll them back and down, bring them forwards and up again. Do this three times. Repeat the exercise, this time bringing your shoulders towards the front first, then rolling them backwards.

- ✔ **Face.** Tighten your facial muscles into a strong grimace. Hold for three seconds and then let go. Rest and focus on the relaxing feeling. Repeat the exercise.

✔ **Eyes.** Focus on a point on the ceiling. Without moving your head, slowly roll your eyes to the right as far as they can go, then to the centre, then to the left, then back to the centre. Rub the palms of your hands together until you feel heat. Close your eyes and cover them with your hands. Feel the heat warm your eyes. Hold for a count of 20 as you feel the tension release through the warmth.

✔ **Feet, calves, thighs and buttocks.** Tighten the muscles in each part of your leg from your foot to your buttocks as tightly as you can. Hold for ten seconds or until the muscles start to tremble, then release. Pause for ten seconds, focusing your attention on the relaxed feeling in those muscles as the tension flows out. Repeat the exercise with the other leg.

✔ **Hands and arms.** Do the procedure above twice for your hands and arms.

✔ **Entire body.** Clench your feet and fists. Pull your shoulders up. Tighten your face and jaw. Hold for as long as you can until you feel your body tremble. Release and feel the tension drain away.

✔ **Getting totally relaxed.** Close your eyes and let your attention slowly wander over each part of your body that you've just exercised. If you notice any residual tension in part of your body, make that part tighter and then release. Feel the tension draining out of you. Don't worry if there is still a little left. Keeping your eyes closed, stay in this relaxed state for the rest of the ten-minute session. Think of a peaceful, pleasant place. Imagine floating in a small boat on a quiet lake with a soft breeze gently rocking you back and forth. Alternatively, imagine yourself floating in space, lighter than air, weightless. Notice the peaceful, calm feeling as the tension leaves your body. Slowly open your eyes, breathe deeply from your lower abdomen and notice the environment around you, paying attention to the temperature, sounds, smells and colours. (You can read about proper breathing in the following section.)

A daily dose of exercise releases tension and puts you in the right mindset for speaking persuasively.

Getting your posture right

In order to produce a persuasive voice, your body must be balanced and in alignment. If your muscles are slack and your body is slumped, your chances of speaking effectively are nil.

Figure 14-1 shows a body that is efficiently aligned. To create an aligned and balanced body, imagine a line dropping from the top of your head, falling through your ear, your shoulder, the highest point of your pelvis, just behind your kneecap and just in front of your ankle. When your body is in this position you are well balanced and can move easily.

You can maintain this position when you're seated by keeping the crown of your head in the same alignment to your pelvis. (The crown of your head is at the top, where the head slightly raises before curving downwards. If you were wearing a beanie this is where it would sit.)

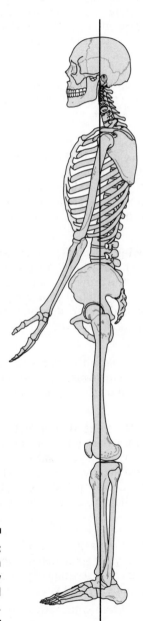

Figure 14-1:
An efficiently aligned body.

To confirm your alignment, stand next to the edge of a door or anything that is horizontally straight and videotape yourself to see the result.

Your shoulders go *out* not back. If you pull them backwards you will experience tension in your neck and back, sending your head forward. Pulling your shoulders back also cramps the chest, inhibiting your ability to breathe correctly. When you pull your shoulders back you end up with aching shoulder muscles and a body badly pulled out of alignment, preventing the free flow of air into and out of your body.

The following exercises are for establishing and improving your posture in order that you can speak in a persuasive tone of voice. The principles apply whether you're standing or sitting.

1. **Make sure your feet are fully on the floor.** From this position you will feel secure and grounded. Imagine every pore on the bottom of your feet connected to the floor. You can pretend that your feet are attached by Velcro to the ground, even if you're wearing shoes with lifts or high heels. From this position you can shift your weight forwards from the ankles (when necessary) without your heels lifting, so that you stay connected to your spot.

2. **Imagine the crown of your head growing upwards.** The crown is the upper back of the skull. It begins at the point where the top of the head begins to curve downward. Envisioning the crown growing upwards lengthens the back of your neck and helps you feel your spine lengthening as well. Do not lift your chin, because doing so shortens the back of your neck, puts tension in your throat and forces you to look down your nose at others.

3. **Keep your knees loose and flexible.** People with bad posture tend to lock their knees, pushing back on them. This causes the buttocks to rise and the lower back to arch, putting strain on the supporting muscles and ligaments.

4. **Balance your weight evenly between the balls of your feet and heels.** When your feet are secure on the floor beneath you, you can change your balance by moving your whole body from your ankles. You can test your balance by rising on your toes: ideally, you can rise by pushing through your feet. Many people try to rise by first shifting forwards, leading with their pelvis or head. If you have to move forwards to rise, your weight has been too far back.

To improve your posture, grab yourself by the nape of your neck and pull your head up with your hand. You should feel your spine begin to lengthen while your upper back begins to stretch. You can also think of yourself as expanding in every direction as you fill the space around you.

Your body has to be balanced and aligned in order to breathe properly. (See the following section for breathing techniques.) Slouched, slumped and crooked bodies make it difficult for the air to pass through your vocal cavity. Bends and crevasses along your physical structure obstruct and inhibit the in-and-out flow of air. If your breath isn't free, your voice stands little chance of being persuasive.

You can enhance your posture by practising Pilates, the Alexander Technique, yoga, martial arts and other disciplines where efficient physical balance is required for ideal performance.

Breathing for inspiration

Zen master and human rights activist Thich Nhat Hanh says that 'Breath is the bridge which connects life to consciousness, which unites your body to your thoughts.'

How often have you heard people speak on a thin breath of air that barely penetrates the room? How compelled have you been to listen? No matter how clever your thinking, if your message isn't conveyed with purpose on a strong stream of well-supported air, you stand little chance of persuading your listener.

Although breathing is a natural reflex that occurs approximately 24,000 times a day and without which you'd die, most people past the age of four have got into bad habits that lead them to gasp for air, heaving from their chests and leaving themselves short of oxygen, unable to speak with confidence and conviction. With no muscles controlling the in-and-out flow of air, the sound comes out in a rush, sentences are short and the noise sounds strangled.

Anne was a vivacious child, full of energy and conversation. From the time she was four years old her grandmother told her to stand up straight, pull her tummy in, put her shoulders back, hold her head high and not talk so much. For years, Anne lived by this advice, which inhibited her ability to speak freely, by restricting the natural flow of air, constricting her posture and feeding her with negative messages about her self-worth. Her voice sounded strained, thin and lacking in personality, and she often suffered from sore throats. When we began working on her voice, we had to realign her posture in order for her to breathe properly. (See the section above on posture.) Once her body was aligned and balanced, she stopped gasping for air through her mouth and allowed her neck and shoulders to relax in order that the air could flow in and out freely. By adjusting her posture and her breathing habits, Anne now has a voice that is strong and flexible, and she can speak at length without discomfort. People can hear what she says and they pay attention because her voice is both powerful and pleasant to listen to.

Speaking is a process that goes in stages:

1. **You inhale air.**
2. **As you exhale, the air passes over your vocal cords in your throat, which then vibrate.**
3. **The vibrations resonate throughout your body, including in your head.**
4. **You shape words through the use of your jaw, lips, tongue and teeth.**

While the process of speaking seems simple, it's also complex, involving many muscles and different parts of your body. People often struggle to speak with full, clear and rich voices because of poor breathing habits that limit the control they have over their body, brain and voice. Poor breathing habits that sap your energy, make you feel edgy and strangle the sound include:

✔ Gasping for air

✔ Not taking enough air into your body

✔ Breathing from your upper chest

By using the muscles in your lower body, including your diaphragm, and keeping your upper body still and tension free you can breathe deeply, filling your body with enough air to produce a sound that is rich and that resonates.

The diaphragm (see Figure 14-2) is a large muscle that sits horizontally across the base of the rib cage, separating the thoracic cavity (the chest cavity) from the abdominal cavity (which houses your stomach, liver, intestines and other organs). The diaphragm connects to the rib cage at the front, along the sides of your lower ribs and also at the back. It resembles an oval-shaped plate turned upside down. When you inhale, air enters your body through the trachea, or windpipe. The diaphragm contracts and flattens as it pulls downwards, making your ribs flare out slightly while pulling the bottom of the lungs downwards to bring in air, decreasing the pressure in the thorax (the chest cavity where your lungs sit). When you exhale, the diaphragm releases, moving upwards to its original relaxed state, increasing the air pressure in the thorax (because there is now less air space), and the air goes out. Diaphragmatic breathing leads to a sense of calm and peace. While the upper chest and lower abdomen stay still during proper diaphragmatic breathing, you may have to be patient in perfecting this breathing technique; it can take some time and practice to move only the diaphragm itself.

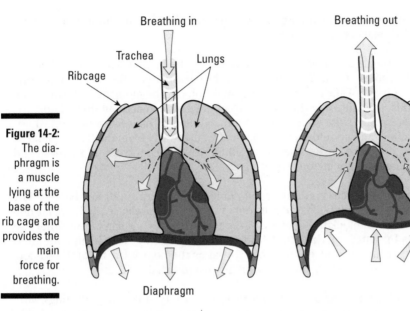

Breathing in

Breathing out

Trachea

Lungs

Ribcage

Figure 14-2:
The dia-
phragm is
a muscle
lying at the
base of the
rib cage and
provides the
main
force for
breathing.

Diaphragm

Many people put so much effort into their breathing that it's a wonder they have any energy left for speaking. If you want to speak with a persuasive voice, practise *passive breathing* in which you open up your mouth and throat as if you were yawning, and let the air fall into you. As you practise this exercise, be sure that your throat stays open, your jaw is relaxed and the back of your tongue lies flat in your mouth:

1. **Imagine a tube going straight down your throat and ending up in a little air sack at the base of your abdomen. While I know that there are no lungs in your abdomen, there is the diaphragmatic muscle – see above – so it feels and looks as though you can put air down there. When I talk about breathing I remind you to 'Breathe into your lower abdominals' even though your lungs sit above your abdomen in your chest cavity.**

2. **Hold your fist right below your navel and exhale, flexing only the lower abdominal muscles while you squeeze out a little puff of air. Pretend that you're a giant turkey baster as you squeeze the air out of the bottom of the rubber bulb.**

3. **Let air enter your body by imagining yourself hollow below your waist. Open your mouth, loosen your jaw and open your throat as if you were yawning, while letting your abdominal muscles relax. Keep your throat open and relaxed so the air can flow in. Picture a fistful of air falling directly into the bottom of your torso.**

4. Squeeze the air out again by a gentle grip of your abdominal muscles. Guess what. You're breathing!

If you struggle to breathe freely, lie down on the floor and bend your knees with the soles of your feet on the floor, hip width apart. Rest your hands on your stomach. Take in the calmness and quiet of the moment. Breathe for 30 seconds, thinking of nothing other than the gentle in-and-out flow of nurturing, supportive air. Note your lower abdomen filling with air like a balloon while your chest and shoulders remain still. Get up slowly from the floor, taking a similar deep breath, and begin speaking. Experience the depth, richness and connected quality in your vocal tones.

Think of the process of *passive breathing* like squeezing a turkey baster. When you squish the bulb flat, air goes out, and when you release the bulb, air flows in. When you block the opening of the turkey baster, air can't flow either way no matter what you do with the bulb. In order for air to flow in and out, there has to be an opening. Picture your throat as the hole at the tip of the baster, and make sure it stays open as you inhale and exhale.

Never fill your lungs beyond your resting capacity. If you fill your lungs with too much air, you constrict your throat, cutting off the resonance and flexibility in your voice. The more air you force into your body, the more your body tightens.

Building a sound foundation

If you've ever seen Elvis Presley perform in person or on video clips, you know what I mean about supporting your voice with your whole body. Hunkering down in a karate-like crouch, dropping his head over his microphone, curling his upper lip and looking out from underneath sultry eyes added power and passion to the King's voice.

Whether he knew what he was doing or not, Elvis created a strong foundation by spreading his legs wide, flexing his knees and pushing his feet into the floor while keeping his upper body relaxed and resonant. By rounding his head downwards, he lengthened the back of his neck, giving space for his voice to vibrate. His loose lips enabled the sound to come out of his mouth freely, and his smouldering eyes added to the mix of forceful energy. I'm not suggesting that when you want to persuade someone you should take up the King's pose, but you may benefit from adapting some of his style into yours to create a rich tone filled with warmth and flexibility.

Your voice is at its most persuasive when it's well supported from your lower body and abdomen and has lots of air to bolster the sound. (See the preceding section for more about supporting from your abdomen.)

Often before you have to speak, whether at a public meeting or laying down the law to your family, you may find yourself feeling tense and tight. Practise the following exercises to connect with your foundation, giving strength and clarity to your words. Because some of the exercises are a bit off-the-wall and you may feel a little self-conscious doing them, I suggest you find yourself a private place where no one can observe you.

1. **Loosen your body. Shake out your hands and feet. Wiggle your hips and shoulders. Roll your head and swing your arms. Circle your elbows, wrists and fingers. Do the same with each leg, knee and foot, then with the toes. Do this for about 30–60 seconds until you feel your body release any pent-up tension.**

2. **Take a balanced position. When standing or sitting, position your head horizontally as if your chin were floating on a gentle lake. Allow your back to rest straight with your shoulder blades melting down your back and your chest open like a book. Tuck your hips under your pelvis. Place your feet hip-width apart. Your spine is now straight and your body is a cavity of open air.**

3. **Relax your jaw. Move your lower jaw up and down. Replicate a chewing movement as if you have a mouth full of toffee. Move your jaw from side to side to unhinge any further tension.**

4. **Release your lips. Blow through them, making a 'motorboat' sound. Feel your lips bounce. Let the spittle splatter.**

5. **Untie your tongue. Stick it out as far as you can. Try to touch your chin and the tip of your nose with the tip of your tongue. Trill it like the Spanish 'rr' sound. Move your tongue back and forth from side to side, like you're licking a giant melting ice cream cone. Flick your tongue in and out of your mouth like a snake. (Be sure to wipe your mouth after this step!)**

When your body is loose and well supported and filled with free-flowing air, your voice is filled with warmth, flexibility and a richness of tone that can persuade even the most recalcitrant listener.

Although I've spent a lot of time advising you to release tension from your body, not all tension is bad. To support your voice, you have to put your body weight behind it. Tension in your lower body is okay, and you need some to produce a solid sound. Just as you tense your muscles when you lift a heavy object, you must put some oomph into your legs and lower abdomen to produce a full and rich sound. Just make sure the tension doesn't get near your throat if you don't want your sound to sound strangled.

Listen to singers like Celine Dion, Christina Aguilera, and Natalie Maines of the Dixie Chicks, who all support from the centre of their bodies. No matter what size you are (Aguilera is just over five feet tall) you can pack a wallop of a sound when you support your body from your abdomen through the tips of your toes, leaving your upper body free to resonate.

Feeling good vibrations

The human body is like an acoustic instrument that needs space in which sound can vibrate. Like any musical instrument, your body must be relaxed and supple for your voice to resonate without restraint.

Think of yourself as a gong. When a gong is struck it vibrates freely, just as your voice is meant to vibrate when you speak. The moment you touch the gong, the vibrations stop and the sound dampens. The same thing happens to your voice when your upper body is tense and tight.

In order to produce a rich and resonate voice you must allow the sound to spin around your body and up into your head.

When sound leaves your body it needs to strike against something specific in order to resonate. You can direct that flow of energy to your throat, nose, lips, jaw or any other part of your face. My preference is to direct the vibration to your teeth. That may sound weird, but the centre of your front teeth is the sweet spot where you can focus the vibrations while the other areas pick up the rest of the resonance.

Relax the tip of your tongue and gently press the sides up against the hard ridges where your teeth meet the roof of your mouth. Supporting from your lower body (see the previous section) say 'zzzzzzz', feeling the sound buzz where your tongue meets your teeth. Keep your jaw relaxed, your throat and upper body loose and remember to tuck your hips under while you support with your lower body. You're aiming to have an equal amount of pressure between your abdominal muscles and against your teeth. Do this exercise again, this time curling your upper lip a bit. By lifting your lip you can feel and hear the buzzing sound more clearly.

Humming is a great way to build resonance into your voice. Any time you get the chance, especially when you're in the shower where the sound is amplified, hum your favourite song. Even a simple rendition of 'Row, Row, Row Your Boat' or 'Happy Birthday' will do. As you hum, notice where you feel vibrations. Experiment with different pitches and volumes. (You can read more about pitch and volume later in this chapter.) Your ultimate aim is to experience vibrations across your face, including above and below your eyes, along your jaw line, across your lips and through your nose, as well as in your throat, upper chest and throughout your body. To achieve rich resonance takes patience and practice, and if you're willing to put in the time and effort you can create a voice that others hunger to hear.

When you practise humming exercises, imagine that your head and chest are echo chambers where the sound can reverberate against your bones and soft tissue. As you hum, let your fingers play over your face, throat and torso to experience the varied vibration points.

Articulating for clear communication

Words are made up of vowels and consonants. No surprise there, then. What may surprise you is that consonants are the mystery ingredient that make your words sound powerful and compel your listener to listen. Consonants give texture to your speaking voice. They grab your listeners' attention, providing clarity, intensity and emphasis.

Vowels, the musical part of the voice, convey feelings and emotion. If you want to add interest to your voice, allow plenty of space in your mouth for vowels to spread and lengthen.

When you accentuate your consonants and lengthen your vowels, you speak more clearly and increase your impact, and people can connect to what you're saying. Sloppy speech makes you sound uninterested and uncommitted to conveying your message. When you articulate clearly, your listeners:

- ✔ Form a positive impression of you, seeing you as educated, knowledgeable and worthy of their trust.

- ✔ Are able to focus on what you're saying rather than being distracted by the way you're expressing yourself.

To articulate clearly you must include your jaw, lips, tongue, teeth, soft palate and facial muscles in order to form the shape of your words. The parts need to be mobile, tension-free and flexible so that the words you speak can be easily understood. If you're used to speaking with a locked jaw or tight lips, the exercises in this section may feel unnatural. Stick with them. The freer your speaking mechanism, the easier it is for you to speak persuasively.

Before practising any vocal exercises, warm up your speaking mechanism first. Make funny faces by vigorously moving your mouth, lips, jaw and teeth, chomping and stretching in all directions. Hum and make weird noises, feeling the reverberations throughout your body. Make a sound like a horse whinnying by blowing 'Brrr' through loosely held lips. Put energy into what you're doing while keeping your jaw, tongue and facial muscles relaxed.

Loosening the jaw

The freer your jaw, the better able you are to articulate and make yourself understood. The following exercises are designed to help loosen the mechanism. Practise each exercise ten times twice a day to increase the mobility in your jaw.

- ✔ Place two fingers on your lower front teeth. Slowly open as wide as is comfortable while pushing down with your fingers.

- ✔ Cup your palm under your chin, open your jaw slowly, gently resisting with your cupped hand.

 ✔ Looking into a mirror, bite your teeth together and look at the position of your two centre teeth on your lower jaw. Open your mouth slowly while watching these two teeth, keeping your lower jaw centred as your jaw moves downwards.

 ✔ Open your jaw slowly, as wide as is comfortable.

 ✔ Open your jaw about two to three centimetres from a clenched bite. Move your lower jaw to the right as far as is comfortable. Bring your lower jaw back to the centre and move it to the left.

Releasing the lips and the tongue

In order to enhance your articulation you must to involve your tongue and lips. Practise the following exercise several times a day to strengthen your tongue and lips to help you communicate clearly:

1. **Keep your chin steady.**

2. **Release and strengthen your tongue and lips by saying the following sequences of repeated sounds in a steady stream. As you say these sounds, use only your lips and tongue.**

 > **Gagagagagagaga**
 >
 > **Kakakakakakaka**
 >
 > **Dadadadadadada**
 >
 > **Tatatatatatata**
 >
 > **Lalalalalalala**
 >
 > **Mamamamamamama**
 >
 > **Papapapapapapa**

One of my favourite articulation exercises for releasing the tongue and lips is, 'The tip of the tongue, the lips and the teeth.' Say these words slowly at first, exaggerating the movement of your tongue and lips as you pronounce the vowels and consonants. Notice how your tongue moves across your lips and teeth and in your mouth, rising and falling, pulling in and out, resembling the movements of a serpent.

Connecting with your consonants

Consonants enable you to speak clearly and powerfully. When you lengthen the consonant on an accented syllable, you make the words stand out. Long consonants are m, n, f, v, s, z, w, r, sh and h.

Say the following sentences, feeling how you can add expression by lengthening the consonant:

The dinner was **mmmmm**arvellous.

Nnnnnever talk to your mother like that again.

His presentation was simply **hhhhh**orrible!

Let's **rrrrr**ock and **rrrrr**oll!

If the consonant is short – b, c, d, g, p and t – you can give the word emphasis by stressing the consonant. Pronounce the consonant sharply to make the word stand out:

Don't do that again!

It was a **t**ragic ending.

Of **c**ourse you may go.

Your **p**ronunciation is **p**erfect!

Reciting tongue twisters

Tongue twisters emphasise consonants and are a challenging way to exercise your jaw, lips and teeth.

Recite the following tongue twisters to increase your clarity and flexibility. In order to say the phrases effectively, you must keep your jaw, kips, tongue and teeth relaxed and mobile. Begin slowly, and as you feel more confident increase your speed:

How much wood would a woodchuck chuck if a woodchuck could chuck wood?

Irish wrist watch

Betty Botter bought some butter, but she said this butter's bitter, so she bought some better butter.

Copper kettle bric-a-brac

Nanny nudged Nicola not knowing that Nicola now needed new knickers

Great Greek grape growers growing great Greek grapes

Knife and fork, bottle and a cork, that's the way you spell New York!

Relishing your vowels

Vowels convey feeling and emotion and can add interest to your words. When you lengthen your vowels, you can increase the impact of what you're saying.

Practise the following sentences to experience the power of an elongated vowel:

> Your speech was fan**ta-a**stic!
>
> I **nee-ee**d a new computer.
>
> That was a **lo-o**ng journey.
>
> He de**ma-a**nds a lot.

Say the following sentences out loud in front of a mirror to help improve your articulation. Notice how your lips purse and retract when you speak and how your tongue moves in your mouth and across your lips. Repeat the sentences, this time saying them slowly, and exaggerate your facial muscles. If you practise these sentences for five minutes a day, your ability to articulate will soon improve.

> I'm going to have to rethink that bid.
>
> Waiting to hear back from the bank is very nerve-wracking and stressful.
>
> Before starting my business, I considered a number of different opportunities.
>
> There's more to learning than just reading, writing and arithmetic.

Paying Attention to Paralanguage

In addition to the words you use to communicate thoughts, data and ideas, you communicate your emotions, feelings and attitudes through the way your voice sounds. The tone in your voice – including pitch and volume as well as the speed at which you speak – expresses unspoken messages, revealing your mood, outlook and mindset. When you add variety to your voice – changing your pitch, altering your volume and including emphasis – people pay attention, anxiously awaiting to hear what's coming next.

A varied voice is an appealing voice, making what you say interesting and effective. Because words just convey content – like dates and hard data – the way you speak conveys how you feel about what you're saying and the response you expect from your listener.

Whether you're writing a message or communicating through the spoken word, the way you deliver your points signals how you feel about what you're saying. Because your goal is to capture your listeners' attention and keep them interested and motivated to do something, the way you deliver your words must create impact. The variety of tools offered in the following sections can make your voice heard in today's information-saturated world.

Turning the volume up and down

If you complain that no one seems to pay attention to you when you speak, you may have to adjust your volume. A weak signal is hard to hear, and all that may be required is a little more sound. If it's hard for people to hear you, they become frustrated and eventually tune you out. On the other hand, if you speak too loudly your listeners may feel assaulted as you invade their private space with your booming voice. The expression 'loud and obnoxious' fits this scenario. Better to save your loud voice for when you really need it, like calling out to a child crossing a busy street.

Ask your friends whether you can tape-record a conversation with them. Listen to how your voice sounds in comparison to theirs. If your voice lacks power, you may be perceived as weak, while a strong voice denotes confidence, conviction and certainty. If you need to increase the volume, go back to the earlier sections in this chapter that address posture, breathing, support and resonance, and practise the exercises. If your voice is habitually louder than that of others, it may be time for you to adjust your level.

When you vary the volume in your voice, you can highlight specific words and phrases. A loud voice startles people into paying attention. It's great for calling out a warning, but beware of speaking loudly for long for fear of turning your listeners off. Better to lower your volume suddenly to regain your listeners' attention, making them wonder what's coming next.

A quiet voice can be very engaging and holds an inverse power. Listen to recordings of Jacqueline Kennedy, Alfred Hitchcock and Marilyn Monroe to hear how these quietly spoken people packed a powerful vocal punch. If you want to include a quiet voice in your speaking pattern, that's fine. A mixture of volume levels makes for an interesting voice. Just be aware that it takes a courageous person to speak at a level where others have to strain to hear.

To create a comfortable volume that your listeners can hear, you must have good breath support and looseness around your shoulders, neck and jaw. (See earlier sections in this chapter for building support and relaxing your body). The following exercises are designed to help you be heard. They should be practised at a time and in a place where you feel uninhibited and are free to make as much noise as you want. The results you get aren't important. What matters is that you give yourself permission to do the exercises without inhibition:

1. Loosen yourself up and get into a playful state. (Observe children at play if you've forgotten what a playful state looks, sounds and feels like.)

2. Jump up in the air and when you land – just as your feet hit the floor – shout out a loud 'Ha!'

Do this several times. If you feel uninhibited enough, do it with someone else. The more fun you have with this exercise, the more striking the results. By letting go of control, you can produce a sizeable volume.

3. Next, shake your whole body energetically. Shake your head, hands, arms, shoulders, hips, legs, knees, feet, waist and bottom. Leave no part still. As you're shaking, let out a long and energetic 'Aaaaaah!' The freer your body, the freer your sound.

As you shake your body, say some simple sentences or a nursery rhyme like:

Mary had a little lamb, it's fleece was white as snow, and everywhere that Mary went, that lamb was sure to go!

Don't try to control the sounds you make. Just let them come out as they want to.

Getting the pace right

Speak too quickly and your listener struggles to keep up. Speak too slowly and your listener starts thinking about other things. Droning on in a mono-tone with a wearisome lack of variation in your speed – as well as in your volume, pitch and emphasis – leads the listener to wonder if you care about what you're saying, while rushing along at a rate of knots makes you sound stressed or out of control. The problem with speaking either too quickly or too slowly is that the pace interferes with communication, leading to your listener straining to grasp your message.

Listening is a two-step process: first you hear and then you translate the words into meaning. If you speak too quickly, garbling your words, phrases and sentences, your listeners don't have time to make sense of what you're saying. They can't keep up with you and soon stop trying. Some of your mes-sage may get through, but most of it won't. If you speak too slowly, leaving gaps between words and drawing out syllables to extremes, your listeners have too much time for processing the information and lose interest in what you're saying.

 Focusing on your enunciation – the way you articulate your words – is a good way to slow down your speech. When you enunciate clearly, you stop slurring your words and omitting syllables when you speak. Your listener can under-stand what you're saying, and you sound like you know what you mean. See the earlier section on articulation for exercises to help you precisely enunci-ate your words.

Speaking quickly is effective if you want to add humour to your content. A quick pace is also effective if you want to share a sense of frenzy or convey panic. On the other hand, if you want to convey a sense of might and power, slow down your speaking. Politicians have delivered some of their most memorable phrases slowly:

> 'Yes, we can.' (Barack Obama)
>
> 'The lady is not for turning.' (Margaret Thatcher)
>
> 'We will never surrender.' (Winston Churchill)
>
> 'Ask not what your country can do for you, ask what you can do for your country.' (John F Kennedy)

If you want to speak with authority and have people pay attention to what you have to say, slow down. Just be sure you don't stall in the process!

Combining different paces, tempos to your speech pattern creates an interesting, compelling and natural-sounding voice.

Placing the pitch

Friedrich Nietzsche, a nineteenth-century German philosopher, said, 'We often refuse to accept an idea merely because the tone of voice in which it has been expressed is unsympathetic to us.'

Persuasive voices are filled with a variety of highs and lows. They go up and down the musical scale easily and naturally. By pitching your voice at different levels you add interest to what you're saying. High sounds project energy and excitement, while lower sounds communicate authority and wisdom. Below are some examples of where to pitch your voice depending on the effect you want to create:

✔ **Head.** When you pitch your voice in your head, you convey excitement and energy. A voice placed in your head is also easy to hear. The head voice when it's not strongly supported by the rest of your body can also sound gentle and caring. If you use only your head voice, you may come across as childish or shrill. Women must be particularly aware of this hazard, because they can be singled out for sounding strident, shrill or childish and weak if their voices remain high in their heads. By adopting deeper tones in their voices, women can gain more variety, interest and impact.

✔ **Chest.** You project authority, maturity and trustworthiness when you speak from your chest. When sound bounces off the sternum – that long, flat bone running down the centre of your chest – your voice sounds mature, confident and purposeful. Your chest voice conveys conviction and determination. Bill Clinton, Winston Churchill, BBC journalist Kate Adie, and Mary Robinson, the ex-President of Ireland, used their chest voices effectively, giving weight to their words.

✔ **Heart.** The voice of the heart conveys feelings and caring. This voice wins hearts and minds alike because of the passion it can convey. You can speak from the heart in warm and caring tones, with joy and excitement, or with loudness and desperation. The voice of the heart is usually soft and low. It connects with your listeners' emotions and draws them into your world. Tony Blair often spoke from his heart, especially when he wanted to win public favour.

✔ **Gut.** When you speak from your gut, you're conveying truths that are fundamental to you. When every part of you is committed to what you're saying, your voice resonates deep within your body. (See the earlier section in this chapter about resonance.) This is the voice that highly influential people use when they convey their deepest-held beliefs. As my friend and voice teacher Judy Apps says, 'It is the quiet voice of intuition, the voice that captures a deeper felt truth . . .'

Your voice is at its most persuasive when you stay within your natural range. As soon as you find yourself struggling with a pitch that's too high or one that's too low, you know you're out of your comfort zone. You can find your perfect pitch by practising these exercises:

✔ Without putting any effort or energy into the process, quietly half sing and half hum a few lines of 'Happy Birthday' or your national anthem. Then say a few sentences at that same pitch.

✔ When someone speaks to you, agree by nodding and saying 'Mmmm' or 'Ummmm', letting the sound resonate in your body, without saying a word out loud. (You can read about resonance earlier in this chapter.) When it's your turn to respond, speak at the same pitch.

Below is a list of exercises to help develop your vocal variety. As in all the exercises I recommend, warm up before exercising and if you feel any strain in your muscles, stop. Begin with the breathing and humming exercises I describe earlier in this chapter.

You may find some or all of these exercises challenging. (I never said getting a perfect pitch was easy!) But if you practise on a regular basis, you can develop a repertoire of persuasive voices.

✔ **Show enthusiasm and excitement by speaking from your head.** Practise by making a whooping sound that starts in the lower part of your body and whizzes its way up on a quick and steady stream of air.

Make the sound louder and louder until it pops out of the top of your head in a single shot.

✔ **Demonstrate authority and conviction by speaking from your chest.** Widen your shoulders and proudly drum your fists against your sternum as you release a Tarzan-like 'Ahhhhhhhhhhh' from an open and free mouth. Be sure not to over-arch your back, because you may strain the supporting muscles and ligaments

✔ **Engage with passion and emotion by speaking from your heart.** Dig deep into your memory and find something that plucks your emotional strings (such as when you cradled your first child, gave your daughter away at her wedding or spoke at a friend's funeral). Connect with the emotions surrounding your memory and talk out loud to yourself or anyone who's willing to listen about what you're feeling. If you hold tightly to your emotional reins, you have to ease up on the bit to do this exercise effectively. Because this particular exercise requires getting in touch with your heart rather than your head, you may find yourself feeling emotional when you speak. Let the emotions out when you practise, so that they don't come flooding out when you speak from your heart in front of an audience.

✔ **Bring out the deep tones of wisdom and authority by speaking from the bottom of your body and soul.** Slow, low, rich and resonant, these sounds embrace every fibre of your being. Stand up straight and relaxed. Hum and bring every part of your body into the sound. Feel your fingers tingle and your lips buzz. Think of yourself as a vibrating chamber in which wisdom and authority reign. Think about what is fundamentally true for you. This could be your deepest purpose, why you're here, and what your life is all about. Let your body settle as you quietly hum. Feel your body vibrate deeply inside your whole self. Speak the words that convey what's true for you.

If your voice is dull, flat and downright boring, you don't stand a chance of connecting and persuading anyone. In these days of non-stop communication, the call on people's time and attention is fierce. Let your voice be monotonous, incoherent and inaudible at your peril. Rather than influencing people with a persuasive voice, you may push them away with the sounds of boredom.

Putting in the pause

Shhhhh. Silence is golden. The space you put between your phrases can be as powerful, if not more so, than the words you speak. Great speakers – including journalists, preachers, teachers and public servants – hold their listeners' attention by creating powerful pauses. They get you to listen to what they're saying by making you wait for what's coming next. Pauses set up suspense. They grab your attention. They underline your points and highlight your content.

Pauses can emphasise powerful emotions. For example, if you were to say 'I'mnotgoing' while rushing your words one into the other, your listener won't get the full impact of what you're saying and may think you're not serious. If you really want to make your point, separate the words with abrupt, clipped silence – 'I'm // not // going!' – to make your point.

Use the powerful pause when you want to give your listeners time to think. When you're about to say something that you really want them to pay attention to, pause slightly before your remark and again afterwards. A pause before the word grabs your listeners' attention, preparing them for the unexpected. A pause after the word allows listeners time to absorb what's been said.

Sir Winston Churchill spoke with power and used the pause effectively. During the dark days of World War II his oratory inspired his countrymen to fight on despite horrendous circumstances. Listen to recordings of him to recognise how powerfully he mastered the pause. 'This is not the end. // It is not even the beginning of the end. // But it is, // perhaps, // the end // of the beginning.' The spaces between the words keep the listener on edge to hear what's coming next.

Comedians make great use of the pregnant pause. Pay attention to how your favourites manipulate silence. They set up their punch lines by taking a brief pause just before hitting you with the joke. Even teenagers know how to make the most of the power pause. Imagine your daughter coming home and telling you, 'Mum and Dad, I'm going to have a baby // sitting job this weekend!' While you, as her parents, may not think it's very funny, your daughter may think she's hilarious. You may even call this a 'pregnant pause'!

If you don't want people to remember what you've said, rush your words together the way you hear a disclaimer being spoken during car and pharmaceutical commercials. Advertisers don't want you to focus on negative aspects of their products, so they sprint over them.

During a negotiation process, it's vital that you practise pausing. Often when people are stressed or anxious they tend to babble on and fill a void with too much talk. Giving away too much information during a negotiation can squelch the deal. Take a tip from Asian negotiators and make your listener wait for your response. One of the greatest lessons I ever got came from a Japanese friend who told me, 'The best way to save face is to keep the lower half of it closed.'

The next time you're in a stressful situation and feel the urge to spill out your thoughts, count silently to three before speaking. The more you practise this, the more powerful and in control you feel and seem.

If you want to compete successfully, you have to become comfortable with silence.

As Mark Twain said, 'The right word may be effective, but no word was ever as effective as a rightly timed pause.'

Speaking from your listener's point of view

No matter how firmly you support your sound, or how clearly you enunciate your words, if you can't experience a situation from your listener's perspective and incorporate his language into yours, no amount of perfect pitching, pacing and pausing will persuade him. Aim to incorporate his language into yours. For example:

- ✔ If someone says words along the lines of 'I can see a bright future ahead' he's indicating that he thinks primarily in a visual way, so think this way yourself, imagining his description and including the same type of language in your response by using words like 'see', 'picture' and 'imagine'.

- ✔ People who use words and phrases like 'I hear what you say' or 'It sounds good to me' indicate that they think in an auditory manner. When you match their words, you start thinking the way they think, creating rapport as you begin 'speaking their language'. Include words such as 'say', 'tell' and 'hear' when you speak. For more about matching behaviour and creating rapport, turn to Chapter 13.

- ✔ When someone speaks in terms like 'I'm getting to grips with the problem' or 'Things are progressing smoothly,' he's letting you know that he experiences the world kinaesthetically, through feelings and touch. When you get a feel for how he expresses himself, use similar words and figures of speech to increase rapport. Appropriate words include 'feel', 'touch' and 'tap'.

If you want to know more about using language to connect with others, have a look at *Neuro-Linguistic Programming For Dummies* by Romilla Ready and Kate Burton (Wiley), which explores in detail different language patterns and how to use them effectively.

The greatest speakers are clear, articulate and passionate about what they're saying. They own their words and the emotions behind their message. Some of my favourite speakers include James Earl Jones, Martin Luther King, John F Kennedy, Barack Obama, Julia Roberts, Sean Connery, Vanessa Redgrave and Winston Churchill. You can hear them speak in recordings and on You Tube. As you listen to them, notice the warmth and conviction in their voices. Their voices resonate with rich vibrations, and they clearly enunciate their words.

Part V
The Part of Tens

The 5th Wave   By Rich Tennant

"They say you can influence people by projecting
a sense of trustworthiness."

In this part . . .

*I*t wouldn't be a *For Dummies* book without a Part of Tens, a whole bunch of top tips to help you get the most from your persuasive skills. Here I lift the lid on the nitty-gritty of how to persuade anyone, anywhere, any time, before moving on to discuss persuading at a distance, whether by phone, electronically or in writing. I finish up by outlining the ten persuasive strategies you just can't do without.

Chapter 15

Ten Sure-Fire Ways to Influence Anyone

*I*n Henrik Ibsen's play *The Master Builder,* the lead character imagines that by wishing for something, it will come true. At the end of the play, he falls to his death. I'm not suggesting that you might die by wishing to become a great influencer! Rather, I'm suggesting that becoming a skilled persuader leads to a much happier outcome than simply wishing, hoping, thinking and praying ever can.

If you've ever watched in awe as someone persuaded another to do something she originally disdained (or at least doubted), this chapter serves up ten secrets from successful persuaders that you can utilise in your own interactions.

Establish Trust

Try to get someone to follow your lead without first establishing trust, and watch your efforts collapse at the starting gate. If someone doesn't trust you, why would she possibly want to follow you? Being perceived as trustworthy requires that you demonstrate your credibility.

'Walking your talk' is one way of building a reputation for being trustworthy and credible. Behaving in a way that reflects your beliefs and values shows you're a person who's true to your word. Walking your talk manifests itself in simple, everyday activities: show up on time, tell the truth and act in other people's interests. Do these consistently, and people see you as someone whom they can trust to do what you say you'll do. See Chapters 1 and 5 for more on trust and credibility.

When my sister Wendy wanted our late grandmother to do something she wasn't convinced was in her best interests, all Wendy had to do was look her in the eye, smile and say, 'Trust me, Memaw!' Sure enough, Memaw would do what Wendy wanted. Memaw and Wendy liked one another, and because Wendy always told Memaw the truth and acted in her best interests, Memaw trusted her. 'Trust me, Memaw!' has become the rallying cry in our family whenever we want our parents or siblings to do something they're not so sure about doing.

Set Out Crystal-Clear Goals

The best persuaders and influencers are confident about what they want. They state their desired outcomes from the start in clear, concise and compelling terms that their listeners can understand and relate to.

Revisit your goals regularly as you travel along your path to persuasion. Whether your goals are quantitative or qualitative, simple or multi-faceted, you'll struggle to achieve them unless you know what they are. See Chapter 1 for more on clarity and Chapter 4 for advice on using compelling language.

Step Into the Other Person's Shoes

Sun Tzu writes in his classic *The Art of War* that the person who knows both the enemy and himself need not fear the result of a hundred battles. The more you know about what matters to other people, the more ammunition you have for persuading them to accept your point of view. Gear your proposal to the other people's needs and concerns, and watch them flock to your fold.

You can find out how to identify what motivates your listener in Chapter 2, and in Chapter 3 you gain tips for figuring out people's attitudes and beliefs. Ask questions and focus on the answers you receive. Listen not only for the words others say but the way they say them too. Someone's non-verbal behaviour – including body language and vocal qualities (see Chapters 13 and 14 – often reveals feelings and attitudes that are as much a part of her perspective as the words she speaks.

Find out as much as you can about what matters to your listeners and let them know that you respect them as individuals as well as respecting their points of view. The more you acknowledge their perspectives, the more willing they are to take on board your suggestions – or even join your proposed plans. Turn to Chapter 12 if you want to figure out who you're talking to.

Behave Congruently

When the words you're saying and the way you're saying them match, you're behaving congruently. Your message and delivery match, and your listener knows what you mean. If your words say one thing and *the way* you say them communicates something different, your listeners are likely to feel bewildered. Consider the pitch, pace and tone of your voice. People generally believe what they observe more than the words they hear, so also pay attention to your non-verbal behaviours such as your posture, movements and gestures.

The way you talk and the way you move your body tell what's going on inside (see Chapters 13 and 14). Make sure you're certain about what you're saying and say it as though you know what you're talking about.

If you're uncertain and unconvincing in the way you present your case, you send out a message of doubt, uncertainty and indecision that your listeners will remember. Speak clearly, concisely and with conviction. Move like you mean it and eliminate ums, ers and ahs from your vocabulary.

Ask for More than You Expect

My son has a quote on his pinboard that says, 'Shoot for the moon. Even if you miss you'll land among the stars.' Or to paraphrase former US Secretary of State Henry Kissinger, your effectiveness at the conference table depends on overstating your demands.

Asking for more than you expect to get gives you some wiggle room, some space for negotiating. For example, when you're selling, you can always come down from your initial offer, but never expect the buyer to suggest that you ask for more. Conversely, if you're buying something, your offer can always go up, but you'd be hard pressed to go down from your original offer. See Chapter 12 for the ins and outs of establishing useful expectations.

Respect Your Relationships

What goes around comes around. How you treat people determines how they respond to you. Treat people with respect and watch them return the favour.

Aim to identify with, understand and respond to other people's feelings, emotions and experiences. Demonstrating empathy (see Chapter 3) goes a long way in building a positive relationship that in turn benefits you.

Build Your Case

As Henry Ford said, 'Before anything else, getting ready is the secret to success.' Knowing what you want, knowing your audience and knowing how to present to your audience in a way that captures their attention and sustains their interest boosts your chances of walking away a winner.

As I detail in Chapter 9, the most successful influencers present themselves as credible characters appealing to their listeners' emotions as well as to their logical minds.

- Start with a strong opener that grabs your listeners' attention and resonates with their values.

- Express each point clearly in a single sentence and assert your claims as statements of fact.

- Avoid overwhelming your listener with too much information. Try limiting yourself to three main messages, each of which needs to be compelling on its own.

- Back up your claims with appropriate supporting material that your listener can believe and accept. Make sure your claims are correct.

- Deliver your message with feeling.

- Conclude your case with a call to action that ties in with your opening. Make your case short, sharp and memorable.

Whatever you say, make sure it's relevant. Be creative. Include stories, analogies and vivid language to help your audience visualise and connect with what you're saying.

Offer Your Most Captivating Reasons

People need reasons for knowing why you want them to do what you want them to do. Although 'Because I said so' may gain their compliance, it's unlikely to gain their hearts and minds.

Let your audience know how your request benefits them. Appeal to their values and tie your reasons into their self-interests and then watch them jump over themselves to comply with your request. Use language that's both accurate and exciting to get your audience visualising your recommendations. Provide your listeners with significant facts and figures if they're into the detail. Tell them captivating stories, including metaphors and analogies if they like to look at the big picture. The more captivating the way you present your case, the more chance you stand of success.

Limit the number of reasons you throw their way. Too much information is overwhelming and results in no decision at all.

Seek Common Ground

When people like you, they're more likely to comply with your requests. The more you have in common with the people you want to persuade, the more likely they'll like you. Turn to Chapter 10 to find out about the power of liking someone.

Effective persuaders seek out similarities between themselves and the people they want to influence. The more you know about your target audience and the more you establish genuine shared aims and chances for camaraderie, the more likely your chances of persuading them. Chapter 2 is filled with tips for finding out about other people.

Own Up to Your Weaknesses

To gain buy-in – to get people to commit to you and your proposals – you've got to gain trust. One of the most effective ways to persuade others that you're trustworthy, honest and credible is to admit your weaknesses.

Before giving all the reasons why someone should agree to your request, present a minor, relatively obvious drawback immediately and then hit them with your most compelling reason for gaining their agreement. Admitting a small weakness builds credibility. And the more credible you are, the more willing others are to follow you.

In Chapter 6 you find out how to admit to your weaknesses without damaging your credibility.

Chapter 16

Ten Ways to Persuade Electronically: Emails and Beyond

*H*ard to believe, but once upon a time business was conducted through phone calls and snail mail, and by investing in lavish gatherings and international flights. Today, an office without electronic communication – especially lots of emails – is like a bank without money. It just doesn't work.

Modern life includes lots of forms of electronic communication. Several recent studies indicate that the number of emails people are writing has levelled off or is decreasing because people are relying on other forms of electronic communication to get things done.

Electronic media are not going away, and mastering them is essential for your success. Writing persuasively is a core competency for anyone who wants to influence others. Although businesses and relationships today utilise various fast-moving technologies, you still need to be able to write persuasively within the limitations and strengths of emails, blogs and for those of you who twitter, tweets!

Without the ability to persuade and influence through the written word, you stand little chance of motivating anyone or convincing people of anything, whether you want to pitch a new product to a client or convince the people in your street to help with your neighbourhood watch scheme. As you work across national borders and continue to reduce your carbon footprint in a world where time is of the essence, your ability to communicate clearly, concisely and persuasively in cyberspace is vital.

While differences exist in how you write an effective email, a blog post, website text or a tweet – good communication is good communication. Many of the tips and techniques I include in this chapter apply to electronic texts in various forms.

Establishing Electronic Rapport

While email and other electronic communications are great ways for transmitting factual information, they're pretty poor at conveying tone and attitude. Readers can interpret direct and blunt language as rude, which can lead to misconstrued messages. Attempts at humour may end up sounding hostile. (And while emoticons have their place, put them in a professional email without first having established rapport at your peril.)

The most persuasive emails are one-to-one and include statements referring to your relationship with your receiver. Phrases such as, 'Thanks for being flexible on . . .' or 'I appreciate your willingness to . . .'demonstrate gratitude and imply that you're willing to reciprocate the favour if the other person should call on you. See Chapter 10 for more about reciprocity and persuasion.

While you wouldn't necessarily comment on emotions or your burgeoning relationship when speaking face-to-face with a person, highlighting specific feelings in emails replaces the non-verbal behaviour that helps establish rapport in face-to-face meetings (see Chapter 13).

Beginning and ending electronic communications with pleasantries goes a long way when you're building a relationship. For example, you could begin an electronic message with:

- ✓ 'Hi Brian. I'm very much looking forward to working with you on this next project.'

- ✓ 'Dear Claire – It was terrific seeing you at Kerry's last week. You made me feel very welcome.'

- ✓ 'Hey Simon, I was thrilled to hear that you completed your project on time. I know how concerned you were about meeting your deadlines.'

- ✓ 'Rachael, I understand from Nicole that we share a passion for running. I'm training for next year's marathon and wonder if you'd like to join me and share my pain!'

If you've already established a relationship with the person, or have communicated with him in the past, you don't have to include a formal greeting like 'Dear'. If you've not met before and the person is senior to you, begin with

'Dear Mr/Ms . . .'. While that may sound a little formal, it's always better to err on the side of formality rather than jumping in with someone's first name when they've not invited you to do so. On the other hand, if you're peers or colleagues of equal stature, it's fine to start off with first names.

To sign off you could use phrases like:

✔ Looking forward to meeting you

✔ Really excited about working with you

✔ Can't wait to meet you again

✔ Thanks again for a fabulous time. Haven't laughed that much in ages!

✔ Hang in there. Remember, there's light at the end of the tunnel.

✔ Warmest regards (or best wishes)

While emails are meant to be quick ways of communicating, a little pleasantry every now and then goes a long way in building relationships.

Pay attention to how people communicate in their emails and reflect their style back in your response. For example, if someone is short and to the point, leaving out greetings and sign offs, you can safely do the same. If, on the other hand, someone starts off with a friendly greeting, respond in a similar way. Mirroring and matching the way someone writes is a quick way of establishing rapport. See Chapter 2 for more.

If you don't know the person you want to persuade, and if it's possible, speak to him on the phone first. In order to help avoid misinterpretation and mistrust, introduce yourself, give the other person a little background information, even send a photograph – anything you can do to establish a relationship before getting into the nuts and bolts of your electronic request.

Knowing What You Want to Say

Before you press the Send button – before you even begin typing – ask yourself what you want to happen as a result of your email or other digital communication.

Whatever your answer, be clear about your purpose. You don't stand a chance of getting others to do what you want them to do if you don't know what you want them to do yourself. Establish for yourself one simple, clear goal for each email.

For example, you may be really stressed due to problems at home and you're struggling to get a project turned in on time. Venting your emotions by telling your boss how tough things are with your family and how pressured you feel isn't going to do you any favours. Rather than going on about your problems, tell him what he needs to know. Perhaps something along the lines of, 'There's been a delay in the project, which I'm dealing with. You'll have the necessary materials by next Thursday. Let me know if you need further information.' You've brought him up-to-date without burdening him with excess information he can't do anything about. As tempting as it may be to dump your emotional overload onto him, keep your message short and to the point and say what you have to say, adding nothing more.

Sometimes you may want to complain, moan or just groan. Unless you stand to benefit from sending such a message, I suggest you write it, read it and then hit Delete.

Be clear about what you want to convey. Avoid blabbering on and on. When you don't know when to stop, it's probably because you're not clear about what you want to communicate. All you do then is waste the reader's time and yours!

If you have several messages you want to send to your reader, each with a different purpose, plan and send multiple messages that address each critical step. Asking your reader in one email to buy your product, attend your course, visit your website, fill out a questionnaire, provide a reference, make a donation, give your son a job – you get the point – confuses the issue and enrages the reader.

If your request is complicated or requires excessive detail, attach a document to the email, also written in clear, concise, persuasive language. Reading a long email is a big ask of a busy client or colleague.

Getting the Subject Line Right

If you write a vaguely worded subject line or leave it out entirely, don't be surprised if your readers hit Delete. If you don't indicate from the very start of your message what you want your readers to do, why would they want to read what you have to say? Make reading your emails easy for them. Grab their attention with a pithy title, making the title personal to the reader.

Appealing to your readers' emotions, curiosity and – dare I say it – vanity, even indicating how they can benefit as a result of what they're about to read, improves your chances of persuading the recipient to open the email and respond positively. Research on email open rates shows that the most effective subject lines are short, straightforward and set out clear expectations. Any more than 45 characters and your reader will cut you off, so load your most important information up front. Make sure your subject line is honest: if your email doesn't follow through on what you promise, your chances of getting your readers to open your emails in the future are limited. Some of my favourite subject titles include: 'Be the light this holiday season', 'The 5 most effective ways to get into Facebook's top news feed', 'POD myths dispelled – get the scoop here!' and 'Three top tips for writing great subject titles'.

Make your subject titles specific. Include dates, important part numbers and relevant invoice numbers to notify your reader of what's in the message.

Focusing on Your Reader

As in all forms of communication, the person you're persuading needs to feel that you have his best interests at heart. Naturally, you want something from him or you wouldn't bother writing. At the same time, your reader wants something from you if he's going to bother reading what you wrote.

Whatever your reasons for writing, make your message about your reader. You want to attract attention, create interest and build desire (see Chapters 3 and 4).

The ultimate goal of your email is to encourage the reader to perform an action. For example, in your email:

- ✔ Clearly let your reader know what he should do and the benefit he will gain as a result of his action.

- ✔ Anticipate questions before your reader even thinks of them, and provide him with answers.

- ✔ Get personal. Use the word 'you' to make your reader feel you're speaking directly to him.

- ✔ Ask a question that's relevant to your reader to get him thinking about how he can respond.

If you know the person you're writing to, use similar language to his (see Chapter 12). If he talks about feelings, and your preference is to engage in thoughts, adapt your style to address his touch points.

Prompting Your Reader to Take Action

Encourage your readers to act by offering incentives or placing a constraint on the time they have to respond.

Whenever you want someone to respond to your request – whether it's signing up to your blog, buying your product or finding out what time he plans to be home for dinner – offer him an incentive and watch him take action. For example, you can offer freebies – like relevant e-books, PDFs, reports or his favourite drink ready and waiting when he gets home. Promotional offers, discounts, money-back guarantees and personal introductions to someone you know he wants to meet are also effective for getting your reader to respond. (If you're offering introductions, confirm with the people you're introducing that it's okay with them, or you may lose a lot of friends, colleagues or clients!) The bottom line is that every incentive you offer must provide value if you want your reader to take action.

Whatever you do, let your reader know what you want. Don't assume he can figure it out for himself. Write your request in its own paragraph at the end of the message so it stands out from the rest of your content. Burying your request will only frustrate your reader and make him wonder what you expect him to do. 'Buy now while stocks last', 'Send your suggestions now' and 'Tell me what time you're coming home' send a clear message of what you want your reader to do.

Putting a time limit on an offer almost always increases response rates. If you make your time limit too long, your call to action may send your request to the bottom of the pile, while a completion period that's too short can stop at the starting gate if your respondents think it's impossible for them to act in time. Make your request for immediate action as easy and convenient as possible if you want to persuade your reader to reply to your request. 'Click here now', 'Only four minutes remaining' and 'Only two items in store' imply a sense of urgency, which increases response rates, as those of you who have purchased in online auctions know! By making your offer unique and placing time limits on your readers' response rates, you will find they react more quickly than if they thought they had all the time in the world. Turn to Chapter 10 to find out more about the power of deadlines and exclusivity.

Getting Your Spelling, Grammar and Spacing Right

Mis-spelt words, poor grammar and massive chunks of unending text make for a poor reading experience. If you can't be bothered to refer to spellcheck, if your grammar's sub-standard and if you don't incorporate enough white space around your words, your reader's going to have a tough time getting through your email.

This isn't a book on grammar and usage – for that you can pick up a copy of *English Grammar For Dummies* by Lesley J Ward and Geraldine Woods (Wiley) – but the following are some essentials to keep in mind:

- ✔ Break your content into chunks so that the reader can scan it easily. Start a new paragraph every time you address a different aspect or sub-topic of your message.

- ✔ Allow for generous margins so your reader's eyes don't have to cross back and forth along the entire length of a page or screen.

- ✔ Choose a straightforward, clear font like Times New Roman, Arial or Cambria. All are easy on the eyes – and available on most devices that people use to read email.

- ✔ Avoid using upper case, which looks like you're shouting at the recipient.

- ✔ Leave out the emoticons and cutesy acronyms unless you know your reader well.

- ✔ Use formatting sparingly. Fancy colours, fonts and characters don't translate to all reading programs and devices. Simple bullets (or even asterisks) can set off your key points. Boldface highlights key words or phrases. Whatever you do, don't overuse these techniques. A page of bulleted items is boring, and boldfacing every other sentence means nothing is really emphasised.

Including Good Links and Attachments

If you've ever been encouraged to 'click here' in an email or on a website only to find that the link doesn't work, you know how annoying a broken or inaccurate link can be. If you include clickable links, make sure they work by testing them.

Just to be safe, include a clickable link as well as a text-only version that readers can paste into their browsers. While this doesn't always work – for example, when a site is no longer active – it's better than not offering your reader the choice.

People often get fed up and delete an email if a link or two is faulty. Like poor grammar and sloppy spelling, links that don't work erode your persuasive powers.

Including links to additional material you want to share with your reader or an online order form to purchase products is fine, even effective, as long as they're easy to access.

As for attachments, if you include one with your email, make sure it's critical or absolutely amazing. Also, avoid attaching large files if you can, particularly large image files or graphic design files (Quark, InDesign, PageMaker and Illustrator). Scale down images and convert graphic-intensive files to lower-resolution PDFs.

Keeping in Touch with Lots of People

Targeted email – in which you segment your email lists by customer interests – is one of the most cost-effective and least time-consuming ways of maintaining communication with your existing customers and encouraging repeat business. Your customers can read your emails in their own time and absorb your message without feeling rushed. Also, if you keep the information succinct and relevant and deliver it on a regular schedule, your recipients may even look forward to your next email correspondence, whether it's a newsletter, blog or special offer.

When sending out emails to a list of people:

- **Keep your message simple.** Don't overburden readers with cumbersome details. If you're selling products or providing services, give your readers details about just one or two relevant items. Include a few links to your website or a way for readers to contact you directly in case they want to know more.

- **Do some research.** While you're not writing a unique message to each recipient, you can still tailor your message to various categories of readers. For example, if you're selling a lot of a particular product to one group of readers, offer another product that fits well with the first one at a discounted price. When already-happy customers see that you're offering related products, they'll be encouraged to buy more.

- **Stay true to your word.** If you tell your readers that they will be the first to know of sales, discounts or new offerings, follow through on your promise. Email your customers in advance *before* any relevant new information goes onto your website or is released in the press. Customers remain loyal to you when you remain loyal to them.

When you're persuading several, many, hundreds or even thousands of people to step up to the plate, include the person's name in your greeting. Doing so makes him feel you know him – whether you do or not – and when you make a personal appeal, people are more likely to respond. If people see that others are receiving the same message, their responsibility for taking action is diffused. They assume someone else will do what you are requesting.

Appealing to Emotions

When you're persuading via email, remember you're still dealing with people who have moods, feelings and emotions. If you fail to consider your readers' various personalities and their communication preferences, as well as how your means of communication may affect them emotionally, you're risking your chances of persuading them (see Chapter 9).

Every spring, Jed offers clients and colleagues a mini-retreat at one of his luxury hotels to experience a day of pampering. The event takes a lot of time to arrange and with his business expanding, Jed no longer had time to devote to the logistics. He gave the project to one of his assistants, who did an outstanding job of designing the email invitations and following up with reminders. When his assistant told Jed that he hadn't received an email from Jacqui, one of Jed's long-standing clients, Jed asked his assistant to send her another reminder. Jacqui responded personally to Jed in a querulous tone alerting him that all was not well. In her email, Jacqui intimated that she missed the personal touch of Jed's invitations from previous years, and felt that the current invitation was more of a blanket advertisement for a sales event rather than an invitation for good day out with like-minded people. Jed didn't want to upset Jacqui, with whom he had a long and profitable relationship. He immediately sent her a personal email, encouraging her to come, telling her how much her presence would be valued and explaining why he himself hadn't made personal contact as he had in the past. Because Jed showed that he respected Jacqui's feelings, they both got what they wanted. Jacqui went to Jed's event feeling listened to and cared for, while Jed got to spend a fun day with one of his favourite people.

Remaining Respectful and Circumspect

If what you write in an email or other electronic communication can potentially lead to problems, don't write it. Commenting on an individual or putting private or privileged information in an email is asking for trouble, as many former heads of industry and masters of the universe can attest to.

Persuasive emails need to show the same kind of respect for the receiver that you show in any written or verbal public conversation. People forward emails, link to online postings and even re-tweet your (seemingly) pithy comments. Privacy does not exist on the Internet.

When writing an email, ask yourself whether you'd want what you've written to be read by others. Stories of emails that have gone viral – have spread through cyberspace faster than a speeding bullet – and have fallen into the wrong hands are legion. If the answer is no, make a phone call or an appointment to meet face-to-face. Once you've sent an email, there's no getting it back. Anticipate how your receivers may react to your message and never use offensive or sexist words. Once you've written your message, read it over to check the tone and the attitude. If you think there's a chance that what you've written may be misinterpreted, it probably will be. Revise what you've written until you've got it right.

Chapter 17

Ten Ways to Persuade over the Phone

In This Chapter

▶ Putting your message into your voice

▶ Imagining the person at the other end of the line

▶ Extending courtesy and respect

Steady yourself. Take a deep breath. Prepare yourself for what you're going to say after you say 'Hello'.

In many ways, persuading someone over the phone is more difficult and daunting than if you were face-to-face in the same space. Even with modern tools like smart phones, Skype and conference calls, the lack of physical presence makes conversations challenging.

If you find persuading over the phone (or other audio-based tool) a nerve-wracking event, this chapter features ten tips for making the experience happier and more productive for you and the person you're communicating with . . . and wanting to influence.

Preparing Yourself

Before you make or take an important call, pause. Be sure you're well prepared. Clear your mind and your physical space of all unnecessary clutter. Breathe deeply and visualise yourself speaking with clarity, confidence and conviction (see Chapter 15 for lots of tips about finding your voice).

If someone calls you at an inconvenient time, let the call go to voicemail. Be sure that the voice on your voicemail is easy to understand and that your message asks the caller to identify herself, leave a contact number and a brief message about the purpose for the call. That way, when you return the call you have all the details to hand.

Have your information and questions clear in your mind before picking up the phone. If possible, jot down some quick notes to remind you of the key topics you must touch upon. In addition to knowing what you're going to say, anticipate how the other person may respond (see Chapter 4). If you're prepared for nasty surprises, you're able to handle whatever comes your way.

Knowing the Purpose and Benefits

Have in the forefront of your mind the purpose and benefits of what you're proposing. Know what you're talking about – *really* know what you're talking about. Chapter 6 gives you lots of ideas for showing that you know your stuff inside and out.

Make your offer simple to understand, and gear what you have to say to your listener's needs and concerns. Play to her emotions – something she feels at the core of her being. See Chapter 3 for more on capitalising on other emotions. After that:

- ✔ Back up your proposition with logic and facts. Be specific. While not all listeners need complete details, every listener needs to know dates, times, places and costs. See Chapter 4 to pick up tips for making your proposition compelling.

- ✔ Demonstrate that you understand the spot that your listener is in by acknowledging what she tells you.

- ✔ Let your listener know the precise results you helped others who were in a similar position attain.

- ✔ At the end of your conversation, ask your listener, 'What questions do you have about what I've just said?' This gives the other person the chance to respond with more than a curt 'no', which tends to happen when you ask, 'Do you have any questions?' Chapter 7 has lots of pointers about asking sensible questions.

Speaking Clearly

Speak clearly, concisely and with conviction. If you can't be understood, no one wants to listen.

Spit out the chewing gum, swallow your coffee, clear your throat and prepare to speak. Speaking when you've got something in your mouth is incredibly annoying and downright rude. The phone amplifies sound, so any chewing, sucking or slurping is going to distract from what you're saying.

Warm up your voice prior to picking up the phone. A few humming and articulation exercises (see Chapter 15) before speaking enhance your ability to be understood. Wiggle your tongue then purse your lips and pull them back in a big smile.

Mirror the person you're speaking with over the phone (see Chapter 10). If she speaks quickly and you tend to be slow and deliberate in your speech, pick up the pace. If you're a fast talker and she's more considered in her tone, slow down. Matching someone's vocal inflections indicates that you're in synch with her, making the other person more receptive to what you have to say.

Checking Your Attitude

Check your attitude, body language and mood *before* you pick up the phone. If your attitude is anything less than upbeat and positive, don't call or answer when the phone rings. See Chapters 1 and 2 for more on getting to know your attitudes and boosting your mood.

If you find that your attitude needs a quick tune-up, picture yourself being self-confident and powerful. Imagine your voice sounding assured and energetic. Visualise yourself as the CEO of a multi-billion-pound corporation wanting only the best for the other person you're speaking with.

Whatever happens during the call, be flexible. If you're not calling at a good time for the other person to speak, schedule another time and show you're willing to accommodate her needs.

Think of the person on the other end of the call as a customer (because that's exactly what she is). You're there to serve the other person. Treat people at the end of the line as if they're special, which they are. Make this call all about them.

Smiling and Having Fun

Smile before you dial or pick up the phone. Smiling lifts your energy and enhances your vocal tone, injecting your words with passion, excitement and enthusiasm.

Keep a small mirror close by your phone so you can see yourself when you're speaking. Put a twinkle in your eye, and say to yourself, 'I'm a success, and she's lucky to know me!' Positive affirmations transfer to others. If you feel good about yourself, so will the person you're speaking with.

Standing up and walking around when you speak increases your ability to breathe deeply and put your body into your message. When you stand and move around, you gesture more, increasing your vocal inflection and bringing life and energy to your message.

Working with a headset or Bluetooth device can free your hands and loosen your neck, which enables you to incorporate better posture and more gestures. Speaker phones can have a similar effect, but the microphones on most speaker phones are touchy, so use a hands-free device when possible.

Energise yourself, and you energise your listener.

Treating the Other Person with Respect

Treat someone with respect and watch the rapport level rise. Care about the person you're talking to and show that you're interested in her and what she needs. Chapter 5 is filled with tips for demonstrating respect for others.

Whether you're the person making the call or the one receiving it, identify yourself up front. Speaking to someone when you're not sure who the person is, where she's from or what she wants is incredibly annoying. If you're calling someone who doesn't know who you are or the purpose of your call, give the person a reason to talk to you by identifying yourself and the name of your company.

Acknowledge that the other person's time is valuable by asking at the start of your conversation whether now is a convenient time for the two of you to talk. When you ask this question, you sound courteous and respectful of that person's space and schedule. If someone's in a rush, the person doesn't have time to speak to you and is likely to find your intrusion annoying.

Sometimes it's just not convenient for someone to speak on the phone with you, even if she wants to. If an unexpected interruption crops up, you can hear it in the person's voice. Her tone may become clipped and she may try to cut you short, or you may hear her vocal pitch drop and she may sound distracted as she interjects with 'um's and 'er's. The tone changes. You need to respond to the changes you hear. Acknowledge any interruption and ask whether the person needs to do something about it. By demonstrating empathy and treating the person with respect, you're making yourself sound like a champ rather than a chump.

If the other person tells you it's not a good time to talk, reschedule the call for another specific time. If she sounds really distracted, offer to email some alternative times to give her a choice. That way she has time to think, rather than you putting her on the spot when she's already distracted.

Tuning Your Antennae

Even if you're on Skype or taking part in a video conference, getting a full sense of the other person's state without being physically present with her is challenging. Listen for the feelings behind her words in order to gain a deeper understanding of the person you're speaking with. In Chapter 10 I examine the importance of tuning in not only to *what* other people are saying but also *how* they're saying it.

Listen for feelings, attitudes and emotions as well as the other person's stated needs and concerns. By paying attention to the messages being sent through pace, pitch, tone and rhythm, as well as the words she's speaking, you're able to gear your message and the way you present your proposition to the other person's ability to receive it.

 If you're speaking on a webcam or Skype, make sure you look at the camera and not at your screen. If you look at the screen, you lose eye contact with the person at the other end. If you must see yourself, make your own image small and put it in the corner of your screen. Keep the person you're speaking with in full view.

Eliminating Distractions

If you're worried about being overheard, if a jackhammer is drilling outside your office window, if a full-blown argument is taking place at the workstation next to yours, get rid of the noise. Go to another room and shut yourself off where you can concentrate.

You don't need to go into a long-winded explanation of the distraction you're dealing with. Keep it simple and emotion free. If the disruption is going to take more than a moment to sort out, apologise and offer to call the other person right back. Trying to muffle the sound by putting your hand over the mouthpiece doesn't sound very professional.

When you're persuading someone to do what you want her to do, you need to direct your energy and efforts to the task at hand. Clearing your surroundings of all distractions focuses your mind. Whether your distractions are visual such as 'to-do lists' piled high on your desk, audible such as music blaring in the background, or kinaesthetic like off-putting smells or your need to go to the loo, deal with them so you can concentrate on the purpose of the call.

When you're on a webcam, put down your pen and avoid using your keyboard unless you're writing notes based on what's being said. The other person can see everything you do in front of the camera, including gestures, movements and expressions. Focus on the conversation. See Chapter 7 for more on effective listening strategies.

No matter how good you may be at multitasking, don't even think about it when you're having an important phone call. Don't drive, don't check email and don't file your nails. Just focus on the conversation like your job depends on it, which it just may.

Asking Questions

Asking questions puts you in the driver's seat. Questions give a direction for the call, and the answers you receive tell you which route to take. By asking questions and responding to what you hear, you can create a dialogue.

Courteous and respectful behaviour sets a positive tone for the conversation and creates a trusting environment. Getting to know the person you're speaking with builds rapport and demonstrates that you care about her. With this in mind, ask permission to ask questions or probe. Questions like 'What are the current top issues that your industry is currently facing?' get the ball rolling.

Dig deep to uncover your listener's needs, drivers and concerns. Pay attention to what she tells you and respond appropriately. When you listen with a clear and unbiased mind to what someone says (see Chapter 7), the other person feels you care about her as an individual, increasing your chances of connecting and being able to persuade the other person to consider your proposition.

Finally, recognise that you win some and you lose some. The good news is that you always have a chance for another try. Whatever the consequences, don't get emotionally involved. Act with a positive intention, be clear about your goals and remind yourself that business is business and some days are better than others.

Speaking to Several People at Once

Conference calls are a normal part of office life and often involve a number of people across the globe. Different time zones, different languages and different concerns make conference calls particularly challenging. Clear speaking and clear thinking plus respectful behaviour are paramount. You can find tips about these issues earlier in this chapter.

To run a successful conference, set clear guidelines from the start. Send all the participants an email including detailed guidelines and logistical information such as:

✔ The teleconference number and pass code

✔ The date, time and time zone

✔ Information on technical support in case of difficulties

✔ Reminders to be in a quiet space with no distractions

✔ An agenda

If you are leading the call, take time at the beginning to remind participants of the important points of teleconference etiquette that you listed in your email. For example, if they need to speak with someone who's not on the call, tell them to push the mute button and to release it when they want to re-join the conference call.

Before people speak they should state their names. Everyone should keep their statements brief and to the point. Because some people need time to process what they've heard before responding, it's okay to have silent gaps. If someone on the call is aggressively talkative, graciously acknowledge her for her input and ask others for theirs. At the end of the call, summarise what's been said, confirm expectations and thank the participants for their contributions.

You have good phone conferences only when you prepare carefully and include conscientious stage management.

Chapter 18

Ten Essential Instruments for Your Persuasion Toolkit

*Y*our moment has arrived, your chance is here, your opportunity to influence someone's thinking and persuade him to follow your suggestions is upon you.

Don't sweat. This book gives you a bevy of persuasive tools that you use individually or combine to create killer proposals, negotiate compromises and wrap up satisfying deals. So roll up your sleeves, open up your persuasion toolkit and pull out any and all of the essential influencing strategies I highlight in this chapter. With a little practice, your target audience will be trotting alongside you, heading for a happy conclusion.

Rapport

More than 2,000 years ago, Aristotle noted that logic alone is not enough to persuade others to do what you want them to do. Before anything else, he said, you must establish a common set of shared values. While you don't have to like each other, you do have to trust one another, and you must demonstrate your understanding of the other person's reality. Aristotle was essentially laying the groundwork for the oh-so-modern concept of *rapport*. Flip to Chapter 2 for more on rapport.

Rapport rarely just happens; it requires effort on your part. You must take a genuine interest in what's important to the other person. Begin by seeking to understand the person first – before adding on your agenda.

✔ **Listen to key words and phrases – the way people speak.** Subtly build these into your language pattern. Listen to other people for what they're not saying as well as for the words they speak. (See Chapter 14.)

✔ **Pay attention to how other people like to take in information.** Do they like loads of detail or do they prefer to take in the big picture? When you speak with them, provide information in the same way (Chapter 12).

✔ **Connect with the other person by demonstrating your trust.** Respect others for who they are, no matter how different they are from you (Chapters 1 and 5). Take time to invest in your relationship, both in building it to begin with and nurturing it as it develops.

✔ **Move in similar patterns.** Try breathing in unison with the other person, and see what happens (Chapter 13).

✔ **Allow your intuition to take over.** When you're in tune with other people, your radar picks up on what's working and what's not. Be flexible in your thoughts and behaviour toward the person you want to persuade. Turn to Chapter 9 to discover how you can adapt your approach when your natural style doesn't seem to fit the bill. You can also read about intuition in Chapter 13.

Not only is rapport about your needs, it's also about the other person's concerns. You're travelling on a two-lane highway to success.

One-to-One Engagement

Whenever you want someone to do something for you, make the entire experience as personal as possible. Use a two-part approach in order to engage others on a personal level (see Chapter 2 for more):

✔ **Put your personality into what you're saying.** That way other people know who you are and why what you're asking is important to you.

✔ **Let other people know what your message means to them.** Whether you're speaking to an audience of one or one thousand, give others a stake in the game.

For your message to make others sit up and take notice, whatever you say needs to resonate with your listeners at an emotional level and have personal meaning for each individual. Let them know the direct impact your proposal has on them. Sprinkle your message with specific references to your listener's goals and aspirations. Regardless of your message, instil in your listener the understanding that they're accountable for their actions in response to your message.

Empathy

Be curious about what it's like to be the other person. Accept him as he is, rather than trying to force him into being someone who's easier for you to understand. Being sensitive and responsive to other people, knowing what a situation looks like from their point of view, demonstrates care and concern. When people feel you care about them, they're more likely to do as you ask than if they feel you're only out for yourself.

Do they like to speak on the phone, or do they prefer to communicate via email? Do they make decisions quickly, or do they prefer to ponder their responses before committing. Do they favour casual conversations, or would they rather have a formal meeting? The more you know about the people you want to convince, the way it feels to be them, the better prepared you are to persuade them.

In order to be a great persuader, you must open yourself to seeing the world from someone else's point of view. Build empathy with others by:

- ✔ **Experiencing vicariously other people's thoughts, feelings and attitudes.** This effort in turn enables you to develop relationships built on respect, trust and understanding.

- ✔ **Leaving your own thoughts and feelings out of the conversation.** When you allow someone to speak without imposing your issues onto the discussion, you demonstrate that you care about and are interested in what's important to him.

- ✔ **Listening deeply.** Focus on understanding the person from all sides, emotionally as well as intellectually. The more you display your desire to connect with someone, the more that person's going to open up to you.

When you build empathy in your relationships, the other person feels understood, affirmed, validated and appreciated. You demonstrate that you feel *with* them and that you really care about what's going on for them. Turn to Chapter 3 for more on empathy.

You're not trying to fix anything for other people. You're just understanding where they are and accepting them for who they are, with no judgment getting in the way of your relationships.

Integrity

Integrity is more than a thing – it's a way of acting, a way of going through life. Behaving with integrity means you're consistent and certain in all you say and do. You're telling others that they can count on you to act in a dependable manner.

Behave with integrity, and people trust you. Demonstrate honesty, truthfulness and reliability, and others feel safe and secure around you. Show that you're the kind of person who backs his words with actions, and people follow your lead.

People draw security from certainty and predictability, so fill your words and actions with integrity. (Chapter 5 offers lots of advice on how to speak and act with integrity.) When you consistently live in this manner, people trust that you consider any request before making it. They feel confident that whatever you ask of them, you're prepared to do yourself.

Fine-Tuned Senses

The world's great persuaders pay attention to their target audience in every way they can. Hone your own observation skills in order to gain insights into others as well as adapt your behaviour to match theirs.

Persuasive people put *all* their senses to work to help figure out the state someone's in before beginning their persuasive pitch (see Chapter 3 to discover more about identifying someone's attitudes and beliefs). To begin activating your senses:

- ✔ **Listen to what people say as well as to what they don't say.** Try to pick up on the other person's tone of voice, the volume at which he speaks and all those little non-verbal expressions (grunts, groans and sighs of contentment) that he uses to articulate his moods and emotions.

- ✔ **Listen with your eyes as well as your ears.** Pay attention to how people's body language and gestures match their moods and attitude – and how they seem out of synch. Look for the colour in a person's face. Is the other person white with fright or pink with embarrassment? And

watch for beads of perspiration as well as dry lips for telling how apprehensive someone's feeling. If you notice red blotches on someone's neck
or upper chest, they're sending silent messages that their emotions are
running high, and if they're pulling at their collar, they're feeling pretty
uncomfortable. When someone's smiling at you while giving you bad
news, they may be thinking that from their point of view the news is
pretty good. (See Chapter 13 for more.)

✔ **Note word choices and phraseology that others repeat or emphasise.**
Picking up on verbal ticks in conversation, or repeated phrases in writing, helps you understand the other person's point of view and state of
mind (Chapter 14).

Flexibility

It is counterproductive to expect people to accept you for who you are no
matter what. The great persuaders know themselves well, but they also know
they may have to adapt their style to match where others are coming from
(see Chapters 2 and 5).

By putting your intuition into practice, you can figure out how someone
views a situation and how your proposal may possibly affect him. Then you
can add flexibility to your approach to match his style (see Chapter 13).
Every time you aim to convince people, you need to address their issues and
concerns. Instead of relying on simple, straightforward facts and figures that
appeal to a rational mind, you may encounter complex emotions that require
more empathy than rationality (see Chapter 2).

You may think someone's being unreasonable, but if you want to persuade
him, you still must adapt your style to cater to his.

Savvy persuaders understand the importance of self-esteem and use it to
energise their persuasive processes. Forcing people to go along with your
ideas rather than adjusting your style to appeal to others rarely gets you
want you want over the long run. Sure, you can use authority to make things
happen for a while, but if you consistently rely on it, prepare to see morale
plummet.

Instead, focus on the outcome you want to achieve and determine the best
approach for reaching your goal. While some people respond well to the
stick, others are more motivated by a carrot (see Chapter 1). In addition, do
everything possible to remove any barriers that may prevent others from
hearing your message. Barriers to listening include:

- ✔ **Environmental distractions.** While all environments have their distractions, choose an area that is free of high levels of activity, loud noises and uncomfortable temperatures, and ask your listeners to turn off their mobile phones.

- ✔ **Lack of sensitivity.** Check yourself for any personal prejudices, judgements or biases you may be conveying. If you inadvertently insult or offend your listeners, they're sure to turn you off.

- ✔ **Poor preparation.** If you can't be bothered to prepare what you want to say, you can't expect others to listen. Speak clearly, concisely and with credibility to capture your listener's attention.

- ✔ **Lack of eye contact.** Look at the person you're speaking to. When you establish and maintain eye contact, it opens up the communication channels.

- ✔ **Irrelevant content.** If your message has no meaning for your listeners, there's little reason why they will listen to what you say.

Turn to Chapter 7 for more about the power of listening.

Different people think differently and have different ways of processing information. When you alter your own style to make it more similar to the other person's, you significantly increase your chances of influencing him. For instance, some people are willing to let the numbers speak for themselves, and figure that as long as the numbers support their case, that's enough to bring people on board. The problem with that approach is that most people remember images and stories better than facts and figures. Include charts, graphs, pictures and other visual illustrations to help the information come alive. Incorporate stories and anecdotes that make your points relevant to your listener. In Chapter 4 I show you how vivid language can help you present your message in a compelling way.

Clear Outcomes and Goals

Focusing on the outcome you want to achieve and having a specific goal in mind gives you – and the people you're persuading – a point of reference to aim for.

Whatever your goal:

- ✔ **Show how your listener benefits.** Analyse your audience in advance of making your proposal, so you know what matters to them and can then appeal to their values, needs and concerns (see Chapter 3).

✔ **Make sure the goal, activities and timeline are specific and measurable.** Clear, measurable objectives allow you to check back and make sure you achieve what you set out to do. Give lots of detail as to exactly what you want your listeners to do (see Chapter 12).

By knowing what you want and knowing what matters to your audience, you're able to craft propositions that satisfy you and appeal deeply to your listeners' emotions (because people buy on emotion and justify with fact).

Dynamic and Adaptable Body and Voice

When you're persuading or negotiating, your body's movements and the sound of your voice can make or break a deal. Posture, gestures and expressions, plus the pitch, pace and volume of a your voice reflect your mood, feelings and attitude. Being aware of the meanings behind movements and sound – yours as well as others' – puts you in the driver's seat when it comes to negotiating with and persuading other people.

When you're observing others' body language, always read signals in clusters – just as one sentence doesn't tell the whole story, one gesture doesn't tell the whole tale. Because body language is tied to thoughts and not words, you can sometimes get mixed messages. When in doubt, listen to what the body's saying, not the words you hear.

In addition to observing someone's body language, listen for how he speaks. Does the tone come from the centre of his chest – deep, rich and full – or is it somewhere high in his head, and breathy and hard to hear? A committed voice resonates and conveys strength of character. A weak voice indicates that the speaker's unsure about what he's saying. When you're persuading someone to your point of view, speak with authority and move with purpose.

Listen with your eyes and see with your ears.

The body language signs and signals listed below are guidelines based on the European and American cultures and can help you figure out the messages you're sending and the ones you're receiving:

✔ **Hand on cheek.** This gesture shows evaluation and sincere interest. It demonstrates that the person likes what he's hearing and is taking it all in. Relax and encourage him to speak by asking for him to comment.

✔ **Chin stroking.** This is a common gesture when someone's making up his mind. If he leans back and crosses his arms, chances are he's responding negatively. Get agreement on points and clarify where there's disagreement. If he leans forward, keep quiet and let him speak.

✔ **Sitting forward.** This position demonstrates excitement and agreement. If this movement immediately follows chin stroking, the message is positive and you can begin using 'we' to indicate that you're both in agreement.

✔ **Tilted head.** A tilted head shows that the person's taking in what's being said. People who tilt their heads when they're listening are good listeners, because the body language is sending the brain the message that it's time to pay attention.

✔ **Dilated pupils.** This is one sign a person can't control. When people are interested in something, their pupils dilate up to four times their normal size, showing that they're excited and engrossed.

✔ **Contracted pupils.** These are a sure sign that a person's unconvinced. If you're negotiating with someone and notice that his pupils are contracted – and it's not a bright, sunny day – ask how he feels about what's being discussed.

Chapter 13 is full of further examples for how to read and use body language, and you can find even more detailed information in my book *Body Language For Dummies* (Wiley).

Non-verbal behaviour communicates what someone's thinking and not saying.

Speak clearly, concisely, and in a way the listener can understand. Use words that mean something to your listener and that he can remember. Flip to Chapter 14 for more information about speaking persuasively.

Credibility

If you demonstrate from the start that you're credible by the way you look, sound and behave, your listener is more inclined to do as you ask than if everything about you is suspect.

Pay attention to your personal appearance and attire. Knowing who you're speaking to helps dictate how you present yourself. Whether you're wearing the corporate attire of a city banker or the black-on-black ensemble of Steve Jobs, everything about you must reflect your professionalism. Chapter 5 covers credibility for stem to stern.

Show that you know your stuff. Have all the information you need at hand to display confidence in yourself and your argument. Having researched your audience and gathered your data, and having the appropriate experience, expertise and engagement with your subject makes you a credible candidate for being a top-notch persuader. See Chapter 6 for many more ideas and insights.

Creative Win–Win Solutions

Collaborating to find a solution whereby both parties come out feeling they benefit from their choice is the ideal, so aim for win–win as often as possible.

Win–win solutions can take many forms, and the specifics depend on your unique situation. However, these solutions generally:

- ✔ **Take into account everyone's interests.** People feel that their needs, desires, fears and concerns are acknowledged, respected and sensitively dealt with.

- ✔ **Integrate everyone's interests.** You may come up with a solution in which everyone gets all of what they want – or in which everyone at least gets a portion.

- ✔ **Allow for everyone to claim some gain.** When everyone involved feels they've won something, they are much more willing to be persuaded by you in the future.

- ✔ **Are creative.** By thinking outside of the box, you expand your list of potential solutions.

- ✔ **Take time.** When you're patient, you can stand back, consider the pros and cons of every possibility, and come up with the right deal that benefits both parties.

- ✔ **Are clear.** Confirm that everyone involved understands your desired results, specific guidelines, resources, accountability procedures and consequences, to avoid any ambiguity.

- ✔ **Make good sense.** Only agree to a solution in which both parties benefit.

By identifying all the interests that will be affected by your proposal, you enhance your chances of coming out a winner.

Index

• *M* •

Notes

Notes

Notes

FOR DUMMIES®

Making Everything Easier! ™

UK editions

BUSINESS

Bookkeeping
978-0-470-97626-5

Leadership
978-0-470-97211-3

Project Management
978-0-470-71119-4

REFERENCE

British Politics
978-0-470-68637-9

DIY
978-0-470-97450-6

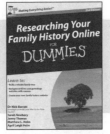

Researching Your Family History Online
978-0-470-74535-9

HOBBIES

Growing Your Own Fruit & Veg
978-0-470-69960-7

Allotment Gardening
978-0-470-68641-6

Electronics
978-0-470-68178-7

Asperger's Syndrome For Dummies
978-0-470-66087-4

Boosting Self-Esteem For Dummies
978-0-470-74193-1

British Sign Language
For Dummies
978-0-470-69477-0

Coaching with NLP For Dummies
978-0-470-97226-7

Cricket For Dummies
978-0-470-03454-5

Diabetes For Dummies, 3rd Edition
978-0-470-97711-8

English Grammar For Dummies
978-0-470-05752-0

Flirting For Dummies
978-0-470-74259-4

Football For Dummies
978-0-470-68837-3

IBS For Dummies
978-0-470-51737-6

Improving Your Relationship
For Dummies
978-0-470-68472-6

Lean Six Sigma For Dummies
978-0-470-75626-3

Life Coaching For Dummies,
2nd Edition
978-0-470-66554-1

Management For Dummies,
2nd Edition
978-0-470-97769-9

Nutrition For Dummies, 2nd Edition
978-0-470-97276-2

30093 (p1)

FOR DUMMIES®

The easy way to get more done and have more fun

LANGUAGES

978-0-470-68815-1
UK Edition

978-1-118-00464-7

978-0-470-90101-4

MUSIC

978-0-470-97799-6
UK Edition

978-0-470-66603-6
Lay-flat, UK Edition

978-0-470-66372-1
UK Edition

SCIENCE & MATHS

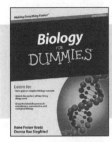

978-0-470-59875-7

978-0-470-55964-2

978-0-470-55174-5

Art For Dummies
978-0-7645-5104-8

Bass Guitar For Dummies, 2nd
Edition
978-0-470-53961-3

Criminology For Dummies
978-0-470-39696-4

Currency Trading For Dummies
978-0-470-12763-6

Drawing For Dummies, 2nd Edition
978-0-470-61842-4

Forensics For Dummies
978-0-7645-5580-0

Guitar For Dummies, 2nd Edition
978-0-7645-9904-0

Index Investing For Dummies
978-0-470-29406-2

Knitting For Dummies, 2nd Edition
978-0-470-28747-7

Music Theory For Dummies
978-0-7645-7838-0

Piano For Dummies, 2nd Edition
978-0-470-49644-2

Physics For Dummies, 2nd Edition
978-0-470-90324-7

Schizophrenia For Dummies
978-0-470-25927-6

Sex For Dummies, 3rd Edition
978-0-470-04523-7

Sherlock Holmes For Dummies
978-0-470-48444-9

Solar Power Your Home
For Dummies, 2nd Edition
978-0-470-59678-4

The Koran For Dummies
978-0-7645-5581-7

30093 (p3)

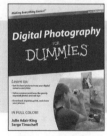
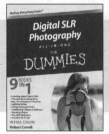